Bringing Medical Devices to Market

CHARLENE CHO, EDITOR

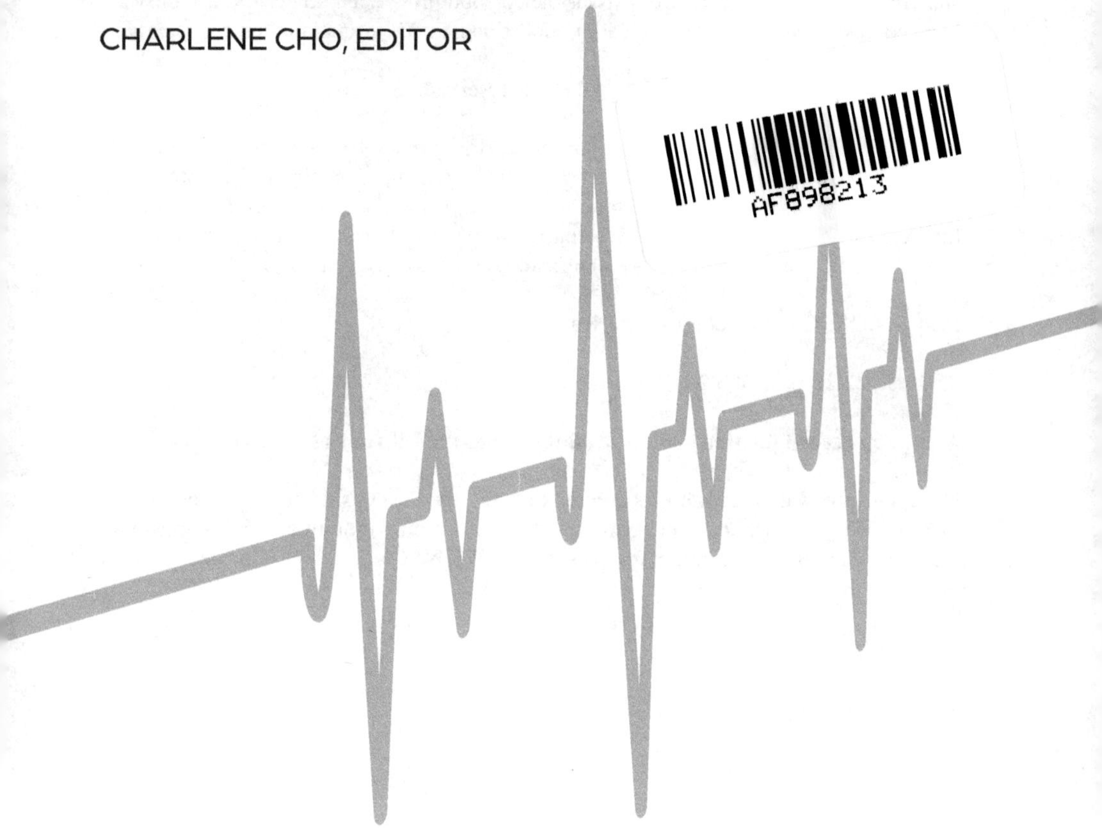

AMERICAN BAR ASSOCIATION
Health Law Section

Cover design by Sara Wadford/ABA Design

Printed in the United States of America.

25 24 23 22 21 5 4 3 2 1

A catalog record for this book is available from the Library of Congress.

Contents

CHAPTER 2
FDA Regulation of Digital Health Care Products 15

Jeffrey N. Gibbs and Allyson B. Mullen

CHAPTER 3
Data, Clinical Trials, and Good Clinical Practices 47

Gerard Prud'homme, Kristin Zielinski Duggan, Megana Sankaran

CHAPTER 4
Intellectual Property Protections for Medical Devices 113

Ed Buthusiem, Jeffrey Klenk, and Eric Carlson

CHAPTER 5
Business Arrangements and Contractual Agreements 139

David Hatch and Robert Miller

About the Editor

Charlene Cho

Charlene Cho, PhD, JD, is senior counsel for Medical Devices at Johnson & Johnson. Her experience as an attorney includes time in public service as well as the private sector. Prior to joining Johnson & Johnson, Dr. Cho was senior counsel at the Office of the Inspector General at the Department of Health and Human Services (HHS-OIG), where she advised on various matters related to statutory interpretation and administrative law. Dr. Cho's experience as a government attorney also includes time at the U.S. Food and Drug Administration (FDA) as Regulatory Counsel, advising on regulatory, compliance, and quality matters at the Center for Biologics Evaluation and Research (CBER) and at the Center for Devices and Radiological Health (CDRH). Dr. Cho also has spent time in private practice. At Hyman, Phelps & McNamara, P.C., she advised large, small, and startup companies regulated by the FDA about the regulatory framework for biologics and medical devices, promotional activities, and FDA submissions, including those in response to Form FDA 483s and Warning Letters. At Sidley Austin, LLP, she counseled clients about enforcement risks, regulatory strategy, and patent litigation, as well as due diligence in connection with transactions in the life sciences. Dr. Cho is a member of the District of Columbia Bar, Maryland State Bar, and the Patent Bar. She received her JD from Vanderbilt University, her PhD in the biological sciences from the University of Chicago, and her BA from Smith College.

About the Authors

Edward J. Buthusiem

Edward J. Buthusiem is a director in the health analytics practice of Berkeley Research Group, LLC. Mr. Buthusiem advises executive management and general counsels on a variety of strategic business and operational issues. He is an expert in food and drug law, mergers and acquisitions, technology licensing transactions, and innovation. Mr. Buthusiem leverages his experience as a former senior executive of two major divisions of two multibillion-dollar global life sciences companies, where he was responsible for all aspects of transactional and legal support, compliance, trade operations, and environmental health and safety. He has counseled and coordinated responses to foreign and domestic congressional and government investigations, including in the areas of Foreign Corrupt Practices Act, bribery and corruption, antitrust and competition, clinical trials, Food and Drug Administration promotional and manufacturing, and Office of Foreign Assets Control matters. He has also managed intellectual property and commercial litigation; legal, regulatory, and trade compliance; and domestic and international arbitrations and has provided expert support and testimony on related matters.

Mr. Buthusiem has designed, developed, implemented, and monitored compliance programs and processes to comply with legal obligations (including FCPA and anti-kickback laws), as well as with government-imposed consent decrees. He has also developed and implemented legal department operational efficiencies in contracting, resource allocation, and technology.

Eric Carlson

Eric Carlson is a director at Burford Capital, with responsibility for assessing and underwriting legal risk, particularly in the intellectual property space. Mr. Carlson is focused on working with law firms, corporations, and IP holders to assess legal claims and leverage litigation finance.

Prior to joining Burford, Mr. Carlson was a patent litigator at Katten Muchin and Jones Day. His work included matters relating to a wide range of technologies, such as computer software, computer hardware, semiconductors, smartphones, and medical devices. He also represented clients in copyright, trademark, contract dispute, and other complex litigation matters.

Mr. Carlson has a JD from the University of Illinois College of Law and has a BS in computer science from the University of Illinois College of Engineering.

Olivia Cusimano (assisted with Chapter 6)

Olivia Cusimano is a corporate associate at Wilson Sonsini Goodrich & Rosati. Ms. Cusimano advises a wide range of clients in the tech space, including biotech and emerging medical device companies in capital markets, M&A, and financing transactions. She has written on FDA's regulation of medical products as well as cannabis. Ms. Cusimano attended law school at the University of Chicago Law School and holds a BA in English and legal studies at the University of California, Berkeley.

Terrence (Terry) J. Dee

Terrence (Terry) J. Dee focuses his practice on product liability and product-related class actions, antitrust, and other complex litigation. He has tried cases in federal and state courts throughout the country, including Illinois, Ohio, Washington, D.C., Maryland, Arizona, and Missouri, and has handled numerous commercial arbitrations. Mr. Dee has served as lead counsel in joint defense groups in federal multidistrict litigation and multiparty litigation, crafting the national strategy and coordinating the joint defense of those cases. Mr. Dee also provides premarketing advice to McDermott clients developing products in the health, medical device, and pharmaceutical industry to assess and manage potential risk areas.

Kristin Zielinski Duggan

With a background in biology and economics, Kristin Zielinski Duggan provides strategic advice to companies on scientific and U.S. Food and Drug Administration (FDA) regulatory challenges, while always keeping business needs in mind. For over 20 years, she has been counseling cutting-edge companies regarding the development and regulation of medical devices and combination products. Ms. Duggan's practice covers products in many therapeutic areas, including software products, cardiovascular products, orthopedic and gynecologic implants, plastic and reconstructive surgery devices, radiology devices, gastroenterology devices, wound care products, dental implants, endoscopes and minimally invasive surgical solutions, and in vitro diagnostics.

Ms. Duggan has a wealth of experience with the entire FDA regulatory process and agency interactions, from devising regulatory strategy for innovative products to pre-submission meetings; to assisting with preclinical and clinical programs and IDEs; to preparing regulatory submissions (510(k)s), de novo petitions, and premarket approvals (PMAs); to appeals of agency decisions.

Ms. Duggan previously served as vice president for Strategic Consulting at a Washington, D.C.-based scientific consulting firm. Throughout her career, she has published and presented on various FDA regulatory issues. She is also an adjunct professor at Georgetown University.

Allison Fulton

Allison Fulton is a partner in our Washington, D.C., office. She is the leader of the Life Sciences and FDA Team. Allison advises life sciences companies, including pharmaceutical, medical device, dietary supplement, food, and cosmetic companies in matters relating to the development, manufacture, and marketing of products regulated by the U.S. Food and Drug Administration (FDA).

Ms. Fulton's areas of focus include assisting U.S. and international companies with complying to premarket and postmarket FDA requirements, including marketing authorization, clinical trials, compliance with GxP, product promotion and labeling, and recalls and other product safety issues. She regularly advises companies on preparing for FDA inspections, responding to FDA Form 483s and Warning Letters, remediating GMP and data integrity issues, and handling adverse events and medical device reports (MDRs). Allison also provides regulatory advice during acquisitions of life science companies, and counsels clients on a variety of life science transactions, including supply agreements, quality agreements, and product licenses.

Prior to attending law school, Allison was a software engineer, specializing in software validation. She earned her law degree from the University of Texas School of Law, where she was the managing editor of the *Texas Intellectual Property Law Journal.* She received a BS degree in industrial engineering from Northwestern University.

Paul Gadiock

Paul Gadiock is Of Counsel in the San Francisco office of Wilson Sonsini Goodrich & Rosati, where his practice primarily focuses on representing medical device companies, small and large alike, in efficiently navigating local and national regulatory requirements. He brings unique firsthand experience with the development and application of regulatory programs to counsel clients at all stages of the medical product life cycle.

Mr. Gadiock provides premarket and postmarket regulatory solutions for medical product clients. Previously, he served on the senior leadership team at the Center for Devices and Radiological Health of the U.S. Food and Drug Administration (FDA). In this role, he advised key agency officials on issues related to the application of policies, programs, regulations, and legislation and was instrumental in appropriately encompassing or excluding devices from the scope of medical product regulation. Paul also minimized legal risk in Government Accountability Office (GAO) and Office of Inspector General (OIG) investigations, major national programs such as unique device identification (UDI), and medical device cybersecurity, as well as specific matters involving petitions and appeals to the FDA. In addition, he conducted numerous presentations and trained staff on how to streamline complex processes to reduce costs. Before his directorship role at the FDA, Paul served as a business development executive at a national diagnostic biotechnology company, advising international directors on how the company could comply efficiently, leading to cost-effective development of products that could be marketed in multiple countries with different regulatory requirements.

Jeffrey N. Gibbs, Esq.

Jeffrey N. Gibbs is a director in the Washington, D.C., law firm of Hyman, Phelps & McNamara, P.C. Before entering private practice, he was an associate chief counsel for enforcement at the Food and Drug Administration. He previously served as general counsel and then as chairman of FDLI's board of directors.

Mr. Gibbs assists medical device companies with a variety of regulatory issues, including product jurisdictional questions, FDA product approval, pre-submissions, regulatory strategy, clinical studies, promotional and marketing programs, and product appeals. He received FDLI's Distinguished Service and Leadership Award in 2013, LMG Life Sciences FDA Medical Device Attorney of the Year Award in 2013, and was inducted to LMG Life Sciences Hall of Fame in 2018. Mr. Gibbs was co-editor of Thomson Reuters 2013, 2015, and 2018 editions of "European Lawyer Reference: Commercialisation of Health Care, Jurisdictional." He is co-editor and co-author of FDLI's 2021 publication, "Diagnostics at a Crossroads: Navigating IVD Regulation in a Changing Environment." Mr. Gibbs previously served on the Human Subjects Review Board of

George Mason University, and has taught medical device law at the University of Maryland and George Washington University. He has published numerous articles regarding FDA regulation of devices. Mr. Gibbs graduated from Princeton University and New York University School of Law.

Beth Halpern

Beth Halpern helps health care clients achieve coverage and reimbursement for innovative technologies. She advises pharmaceutical and device manufacturers, health care providers, and trade associations about Medicare and other payers' policies and develops strategies to improve access to care. Ms. Halpern helps clients advocate before administrative agencies and Congress, and she advises about Medicare law for clients involved in litigation. She frequently speaks at conferences on coverage, coding, and payment and testifies before advisory committees to the Centers for Medicare and Medicaid Services. During secondments to a large biotechnology company, Ms. Halpern also served as in-house counsel, advising on government affairs and promotional compliance matters.

David Hatch

David Hatch is managing partner of the Los Angeles Office of Hooper, Lundy & Bookman, P.C., and a member of the Hooper, Lundy & Bookman, P.C.'s Business Department. Hooper, Lundy & Bookman, P.C. is a nationally recognized health care law boutique with offices in Boston, Washington, D.C., Denver, San Francisco, Los Angeles, and San Diego. His practice involves assisting health care clients with a broad range of business, transactional, and regulatory issues. Mr. Hatch has significant experience representing major national technology companies, as well as startups, in navigating complex health care regulatory issues and establishing or expanding health care operations. He also frequently assists nonprofit and tax-exempt health care providers with their unique legal issues. Mr. Hatch's broad experience includes representing clients in connection with practice integration, asset purchases, mergers and acquisitions, health care joint ventures, and health care fraud and abuse compliance. He advises clients regarding federal and state anti-kickback laws, self-referral laws, pharmacy laws, restrictions on the delivery of drugs and medical devices, regulation of ambulatory surgery centers, and the corporate practice of medicine doctrine.

Mr. Hatch's clients include physicians and physician groups, for-profit and nonprofit hospitals, diagnostic centers, ambulatory surgery centers, durable medical equipment companies, mental health providers, pharmaceutical companies, medical device and prosthetic distributors, application developers and technology companies, and other health care providers. Mr. Hatch completed his undergraduate studies at the University of Michigan and is an honors law graduate of the University of Texas.

Jeffrey Klenk

Jeffrey Klenk is an economic expert who focuses his practice on the application of economic theory to analyzing a diverse set of issues. Much of Mr. Klenk's work revolves around the analysis of alleged anticompetitive conduct and the valuation of intellectual property, but he has also been retained to offer economic insight into such issues as the economic effects of tariffs, the effect on interstate commerce of certificate of need laws, and the economic incentives underlying civil forfeiture. Mr. Klenk also has extensive experience addressing economic issues related to class certification, particularly with respect to alleged antitrust violations and alleged product defects.

Jennifer E. Michael

Jennifer Michael is a member at Bass, Berry & Sims, PLC. She draws on her experience as the former chief of the Industry Guidance Branch at the U.S. Department of Health and Human Services (HHS), Office of Counsel to the Inspector General (OCIG) to help health care providers and life science companies avoid potential fraud and abuse landmines and defend them in fraud and abuse investigations. Jennifer helps her clients structure their arrangements to comply with the federal Anti-Kickback Statute, the federal Civil Monetary Penalty law, and other state and federal fraud and abuse laws and navigate government investigations under the federal False Claims Act. She leads internal investigations for health care companies to identify and quantify potential overpayments from federal health care programs; advises on fraud and abuse risks relating to existing and proposed arrangements in connection with pending and proposed transactions; and designs, implements, and evaluates compliance programs.

Ms. Michael represents clients before the Office of Inspector General on advisory opinion requests, corporate integrity agreement (CIA) negotiations and CIA implementation, and voluntary self-disclosures. During her tenure at OCIG, Jennifer led the Industry Guidance Branch in issuing dozens of advisory opinions; the first-ever rescission of an advisory opinion; and Special Fraud Alerts, policy statements, and other guidance documents. She interpreted federal fraud and abuse statutes for the industry and supervised agency rulemaking and the issuance of waivers of fraud and abuse laws for specified arrangements involving alternative payment models being tested by the Center for Medicare & Medicaid Innovation. She also provided technical assistance to congressional committees and other parts of the executive branch, including the U.S. Department of Justice and the Centers for Medicare & Medicaid Services. Ms. Michael spoke regularly on behalf of the Office of Counsel to the Inspector General at industry conferences.

Prior to attending law school, she worked four years as a certified public accountant for a Big Four accounting firm. Jennifer is a member of the District of Columbia Bar. She received her JD from the University of Virginia School of Law, and her BBA from James Madison University.

Robert F. Miller

Mr. Miller advises a wide variety of health care companies on corporate and regulatory issues. Recognized for his creative problem solving and unusually broad-based experience in both business and health law, Mr. Miller advocates for clients from Hawaii to Maine, including health systems, hospitals, technology companies, physician groups, management organizations, and investors in health care businesses.

Mr. Miller draws on his keen insight into transactions within the heavily regulated health care industry to counsel large, sophisticated organizations grappling with multifaceted problems that can't be resolved with off-the-shelf solutions. He understands his clients' business needs and enthusiastically assists them in devising ways to meet goals within multiple frameworks. Mr. Miller consults with clients who are motivated to improve both health care delivery and their bottom lines; he walks them through potential growth strategies, innovative approaches to value-based care, and advanced data-use technology, all with a focus on achieving their individual objectives.

Health care provider clients depend on Mr. Miller to counsel them on business entity structure and formation, technology transactions, capital generation through private offerings and syndications, and other general corporate concerns. He also advises provider clients on fraud and abuse issues in the context of both transactions and regulatory compliance, including internal investigations, analyses of reporting requirements, and related disclosures to governmental agencies. Mr. Miller routinely directs companies on contractual matters, including the development of agreements regarding software licensing, distribution, nondisclosure, professional services, and consulting.

Anisa Mohanty

Anisa Mohanty advises life sciences companies on U.S. Food and Drug Administration (FDA) premarket strategy and postmarket compliance issues, from advertising and promotion to disclosure and periodic reporting. Her experience encompasses such matters as premarket pathways, good laboratory practice and good clinical practice and good manufacturing practice (cGMP) and quality system requirements. Ms. Mohanty offers guidance to her clients on the regulatory requirements and industry standards for the development, creation, and review of advertising and promotional materials for drugs and medical devices. She also supports investors and companies on scoping and developing appropriate due diligence strategies for transactions and investments involving FDA-regulated drugs, medical devices, and other products. Her tenure as a regulatory counsel at the FDA provides valuable perspective for clients in the life sciences industry. Ms. Mohanty received her BA in biology and political science from the University of North Carolina and her JD from the University of Richmond School of Law.

Allyson B. Mullen

Ms. Mullen is a director in the Washington, D.C., law firm of Hyman, Phelps & McNamara, P.C. Before entering private practice, she was in-house counsel at Waters Corporation, an IVD company. In this role, she conducted a range of legal and regulatory functions.

Ms. Mullen assists medical device and in vitro diagnostic (IVD) manufacturers with a wide range of premarket and postmarket regulatory topics, including developing regulatory strategy, preparing regulatory submissions, drafting regulatory policies and procedures, reviewing advertising and promotional materials, and addressing enforcement matters.

In the premarket area, Ms. Mullen develops regulatory strategy, including obtaining breakthrough device designation and preparing pre-submissions to obtain FDA feedback. She also assists clients in understanding FDA's pre-submission feedback in an effort to prepare for and represent clients at pre-submission meetings with FDA. She also assists with preparing premarket submissions, including IDEs, 510(k)s, de novos, and PMAs. As part of this process, she assists clients in responding to FDA additional information requests during premarket review with a view toward fully understanding and addressing FDA concerns at the earliest possible time. She also represents clients on medical device appeals within FDA, including those relating to deficiencies raised in premarket responses from FDA (e.g., NSE letters, de novo denials).

In the postmarket area, she advises clients on regulatory compliance matters, including complaint handling, MDRs, field actions, promotional review, and QSR compliance. Ms. Mullen also helps clients with contract matters and regulatory due diligence.

Ms. Mullen graduated from Worcester Polytechnic Institute and New England School of Law.

Vernessa Pollard

Ms. Pollard is chair of McDermott Will & Emery's FDA practice. She provides strategic business and regulatory advice to FDA-regulated companies on complex issues related to the development, manufacture, marketing, postmarket safety, and compliance for FDA-regulated products, including drugs, medical devices, and digital health technology. Ms. Pollard counsels companies on product development and premarket strategy, good manufacturing practice/quality system requirements, advertising/promotion, adverse event reporting, FDA warning letters, FDA inspections, recalls, import detentions, corporate compliance programs, and regulatory due diligence in mergers and acquisitions. She is a former associate chief counsel for enforcement in FDA's Office of Chief Counsel and has been recognized in numerous law and life sciences publications, including Chambers USA 2014 to 2020, Healthcare: Pharmaceutical/Medical Products Regulatory (DC) and LMG Life Sciences, Regulatory Attorney of the Year: FDA Medical Devices, 2018. Ms. Pollard received her BA in communications from Howard University and her JD from Temple University School of Law.

Gerard J. Prud'homme

Mr. Prud'homme works closely with medical device companies to get their products approved by the FDA. He has more than 25 years of experience helping companies with FDA regulatory strategy and medical device submissions, including investigational device exemptions (IDEs), premarket approvals (PMAs), 510(k)s, and de novo applications. He is one of the few FDA lawyers in the country who is also a biostatistician with expansive experience in clinical studies. Mr. Prud'homme has worked on more than 100 PMAs and many more IDEs.

With 30+ years of experience in clinical trials, he routinely helps clients design and analyze all types of medical device clinical studies, from first-in-human to feasibility, pilot, pivotal, and post-approval studies. He is widely recognized for his experience in this area, having worked on hundreds of clinical trials. Mr. Prud'homme often lectures new FDA employees on IDEs and PMAs.

Understanding the critical nature of FDA panel meetings to clients, Mr. Prud'homme works hand-in-glove with medical device and pharmaceutical companies, together with their expert clinicians and statisticians in preparing for advisory committee meetings. He brings a wealth of knowledge and experience to clients preparing for panel meetings and is nationally well regarded for his capabilities and depth of experience, and has worked on more than 50 panel meetings.

Mr. Prud'homme has authored a number of articles and book chapters on topics relating to regulation of medical devices, as well as scientific articles relating to medical devices, drugs, and clinical studies.

James Ravitz

Jamie Ravitz is a partner in the Washington, D.C., office of Wilson Sonsini Goodrich & Rosati, where he is a member of the firm's U.S. Food and Drug Administration (FDA), health care, and consumer products compliance practice.

Mr. Ravitz regularly works with manufacturers and distributors of products that are extensively regulated by the FDA, such as medical devices (including digital applications), drugs, biologics, food, cannabis, dietary supplements, and cosmetic products. He has worked with clients at all points in the product life cycle, from providing strategic regulatory approval direction at the product concept stage through post-marketing issues, including product marketing, labeling, advertising, and recalls and crisis matters.

A substantial part of Mr. Ravitz's practice includes counseling manufacturers and providers on health care compliance matters, including broad-based fraud and abuse laws, the Anti-Kickback Statute, the False Claims Act, the Sunshine Act, patient privacy statutes, and product reimbursement. He has worked with clients on numerous internal investigations and responses to Office of Inspector General (OIG) and U.S. Department of Justice (DOJ) subpoenas and has assisted in the defense of qui tam whistleblower suits alleging violations of the False Claims Act.

Megana V. Sankaran

As a director of regulatory sciences, Ms. Sankaran advises clients on medical device matters, with a particular focus on the premarket clearance and approval of new devices and statistical considerations.

Ms. Sankaran has experience in the design and statistical aspects of clinical trials. She has also advised clients about the presentation of clinical data for FDA submissions and the design of clinical studies, and on premarket submissions.

Prior to joining Hogan Lovells, Ms. Sankaran was a clinical research coordinator at Millennium Clinical Trials and oversaw the daily operations of several pharmaceutical clinical trials. At the George Washington University, she completed her master of public health in epidemiology, which she now adapts to her work in the forms of the creative design of clinical studies and problem solving for her clients. Ms. Sankaran is also pursuing a law degree part-time.

Eva Yin (assisted with Chapter 7)

Eva Yin, PhD, MPH, Esq., is an associate in Wilson Sonsini Goodrich & Rosati's FDA Regulatory, Healthcare, and Consumer Products Practice. Her practice includes conducting FDA and health care regulatory due diligence for corporate transactions; providing legal counsel to manufacturers regarding FDA approval/clearance for various products, including medical devices, mobile apps, diagnostics, biologics, and drugs; FDA compliance; regulation of promotional materials and labeling; manufacturer compliance under federal and state health care laws, for example, the federal Anti-Kickback Statute, False Claims Act, Sunshine Act, state licensing laws, corporate practice of medicine, and fee splitting laws; reviewing contracts and compliance policies for manufacturers; and providing legal analysis and risk assessment of business models and fee arrangements involving patients, health care professionals, or hospitals/clinics under federal and state health care laws and regulations.

Introduction

The United States remains the largest medical device market in the world and is expected to grow to $208 billion by 2023.[1] The World Health Organization (WHO) estimates the total number of medical devices to be about two million globally, spanning approximately 7,000 general categories,[2] including cardiology; orthopedics; neurology; anesthesia; respiratory disease; urology; nephrology; ear, nose, and throat (ENT); ophthalmology; diabetes; wound care; in-vitro diagnostics (IVDs); dental instruments; diagnostic imaging; surgical equipment; patient monitoring; and hospital supplies.

Over the last decade, powerful inputs have spurred innovation and growth in the medical device industry. Advances in artificial intelligence (AI)/machine learning (ML), surgical robotics, additive manufacturing (e.g., 3D printing), and telemedicine have generated excitement about the promise and potential of medical devices to diagnose and treat disease. Additionally, longer life expectancies, higher standards of living, and an increasing prevalence of infectious and chronic diseases continue to drive global demand for improved medical devices.

For those seeking to bring medical devices to market, the heaviest burdens and largest source of risks are legal in nature. For example, what intellectual property issues must one consider while proof of concept efforts are underway? Once a prototype is validated and verified, what regulatory barriers must be overcome before the finished medical device can be sold legally in the U.S. market? While promoting the medical device, what are the rules of engagement with health care practitioners, health care entities, and federal agencies to ensure compliance with the various health care laws? Will Medicare cover the cost of the medical device? What types of contracts with third parties should be in place before selling a medical device? During? After? And what, if any, steps can one take to mitigate product liability risks?

---

1. See https://www.selectusa.gov/medical-technology-industry-united-states.
2. See https://www.who.int/health-topics/medical-devices#tab=tab_1.

While by no means exhaustive, this book attempts to answer these questions, and more. Each chapter describes the general concepts that frame a given subject area and addresses some of the basic administrative, regulatory, and compliance concerns that arise in the context of bringing a medical device to market. To facilitate readers' further review of topics, all the chapters include references, which are current as of the date of publication. Please keep in mind, however, that laws, regulations, and policies are not static and may change over time, depending on various factors.

The authors of these chapters are some of the most well-respected professionals in their fields, and their expertise derives from their experiences in public service advising government leadership, in private practice counseling clients, or, in some cases, both. I am confident that the knowledge that infuses these chapters will not only provide valuable insight to readers who seek to learn about the legal matters that animate the medical device industry but also serve as an excellent resource for our experienced colleagues.

Charlene Cho, PhD, JD
August 2021

CHAPTER 1

FDA Premarket Requirements

Vernessa T. Pollard and Anisa Mohanty[1]

I. Overview of Device Regulation

A. Definitions

The U.S. Food and Drug Administration (FDA) regulates the development, manufacture, labeling, marketing, and distribution of medical devices in the United States. The agency's mandate is to ensure that medical products distributed domestically are safe and effective for their intended uses. A product's intended use informs both its regulatory status and the specific legal and technical requirements that govern its development and distribution.

The Federal Food, Drug, and Cosmetic Act (FDCA) defines a "medical device" as an instrument or apparatus (including accessories or components) that is "intended for use in the diagnosis, treatment, cure, or prevention of a disease or condition" or "intended to affect the structure or function of the body."[2] FDA distinguishes a "finished device"—any device or accessory to any device that is suitable for use or capable of functioning, whether or not it is packaged, labeled, or sterilized—from its accessories, components, or parts.

An accessory is a "finished device that is intended to support, supplement, and/or augment the performance of one or more parent devices."[3] Accessories may include items such as monitors, handsets, special

1. The authors would like to thank and acknowledge Gugan Kaur for her input and assistance with this chapter.

2. 21 U.S.C. § 321(h).

3. *See Medical Device Accessories—Describing Accessories and Classification Pathways*, FDA (Dec. 20, 2017), https://www.fda.gov/media/90647/download.

surgical kits, or tools that are either developed for use with a specific finished device or may be used with a variety of devices. FDA may regulate an accessory as a stand-alone device or as a part of the finished device with which it is intended to work.

A "component," is "any raw material, substance, piece, part, software, firmware, labeling, or assembly which is intended to be included as part of the finished, packaged, and labeled device," that is, intended to be used by the manufacturer to make or manufacture the medical device and is typically integrated into the device.[4] Components differ from accessories in that most components are integrated into the finished device and are not capable of functioning on their own. Examples of components include screws, circuit boards, and foam mountings or insulation. FDA exempts most components from many of the medical device requirements that apply to finished devices or accessories. Rather than directly regulating component suppliers, whose products are often made to order or are industry-agnostic, the agency requires finished device manufacturers to ensure that the components they source or purchase comply with the manufacturer's specifications and applicable quality standards. As a result, FDA's regulations exempt components from most medical device requirements, including establishment registration and device listing[5] and current Good Manufacturing Practice (cGMP) requirements under the Quality System Regulation (QSR).[6] Further, finished device manufacturers may also determine that manufacturers of a component that is "critical" to the safety and effectiveness of the finished product take special precautions to ensure its safety, including heightened qualification, selection, and quality control processes. If the component manufacturer is a "critical supplier" for finished device manufacturers, there is a greater likelihood that the component manufacturer may be subject to FDA inspections[7] or more heightened quality requirements by downstream finished device manufacturers. As such, a "critical supplier" may be subject to stringent requirements under quality agreements and/or FDA scrutiny during inspections.

Note, however, that manufacturers of accessories or components that are packaged or labeled for commercial distribution for health-related

4. 21 C.F.R. § 820.3(c).

5. *See id.* pt. 807 (establishment registration and device listing for manufacturers and initial importers of devices).

6. *See id.* pt. 820 (quality system regulation).

7. *See id.* pt. 820.50.

purposes to an end user are required to register and list and pay an establishment registration fee.[8]

B. Intended Use

FDA determines the regulatory status of a product (e.g., whether it is a component, accessory, or finished device) based on its "intended use." The intended use of a product refers to the "objective intent of the persons legally responsible for the labeling of devices."

> Intent is determined by such persons' expressions or may be shown by the circumstances surrounding the distribution of the article. This objective intent may, for example, be shown by labeling claims, advertising matter, or oral or written statements by such persons or their representatives. It may be shown by the circumstances that the article is, with the knowledge of such persons or their representatives, offered and used for a purpose for which it is neither labeled nor advertised. The intended uses of an article may change after it has been introduced into interstate commerce by its manufacturer . . . if a manufacturer knows, or has knowledge of facts that would give him notice that a device introduced into interstate commerce by him is to be used for conditions, purposes, or uses other than the ones for which he offers it, he is required to provide adequate labeling for such a device which accords with such other uses to which the article is to be put.[9]

II. Classes of Medical Devices

FDA classifies medical devices into one of three classes—Class I, Class II, or Class III—depending on the degree of risk associated with each medical device and the extent of control needed to ensure safety and

8. *See* 21 C.F.R. § 807.20(a)(6).

9. 21 C.F.R. § 801.4. On September 23, 2020, FDA issued a proposed rule that would revise the definition of "intended use" by amending its "intended use" regulations for drugs and medical devices at 21 C.F.R. §§ 201.128 and 801.4. FDA intends to clarify that how health care providers (HCPs) prescribe or use a product cannot be the *sole* basis for determining intended use, that is, FDA would not hold a manufacturer responsible for a downstream use of the product solely because the manufacturer is aware that HCPs use or prescribe the product for unapproved uses or in a manner the manufacturer did not specifically intend. This proposed rule is a nod to the fact FDA does not regulate the practice of medicine and the fact that HCPs frequently use medical products off-label in their professional judgment.

effectiveness. Class I devices represent the lowest risk, and Class III devices represent the highest risk.

A. Class I

Class I devices are those that have a low risk to the patient or user. FDA will classify a medical device as Class I if it determines there is sufficient information to support the classification and that general controls are sufficient to "provide a reasonable assurance of the device's safety and effectiveness."[10] General controls are the baseline requirements of the FDCA and apply to all medical devices—unless specifically exempt—and include the provisions of the FDCA related to adulteration, misbranding, device registration and listing, premarket notification, banned devices, notification, repair, replacement, refund, records and reports, restricted devices, and cGMP. However, some Class I devices are specifically exempt from certain of these requirements, such as the QSR.

Devices that are intended for use in supporting or sustaining life, that are of importance in preventing impairment of human life, or that present a potential unreasonable risk of illness or injury are not eligible for classification as Class I.

B. Class II

Class II devices are those that have a moderate-to-high risk to the patient or user. The majority of medical devices licensed in the United States are Class II devices. These devices must comply with general controls, and most require premarket review by FDA through the premarket notification (510(k)) process. In addition, many Class II devices must comply with other special controls, including certain performance standards or adherence to certain technical criteria. Special controls may include performance standards, postmarket surveillance, patient registries, special labeling requirements, premarket data requirements, or other guidelines.

C. Class III

Class III devices are typically those that are used to sustain or support life, are implanted, or present potential unreasonable risk of illness or injury. Class III devices require a premarket approval (PMA) application approval.

---

10. 21 C.F.R. § 860.3(c)(1).

III. Premarket Submissions

A. 510(k) Clearance

Unless a Class II device is exempt from premarket review, the manufacturer must submit to the FDA a premarket notification submission demonstrating that the device is "substantially equivalent" in intended use and technology to a "predicate device" that is either:

- A device that has grandfather marketing status because it was legally marketed prior to May 28, 1976, the date upon which the Medical Device Amendments of 1976 were enacted, or
- A device that has previously been cleared through the 510(k) process.

If the FDA agrees that the device is substantially equivalent to a predicate device, it will grant clearance to commercially market the device in the United States. The FDA has a statutory 90-day period to respond to a 510(k) submission, or a guidance-based 30-day period for "special" 510(k) submissions, which have a more restrictive scope and generally involve more specific or very limited changes to a legally marketed device. As a practical matter, clearance often takes longer. The FDA may require further information, including clinical data, to make a determination regarding substantial equivalence. If the FDA determines that the device, or its intended use, is not "substantially equivalent," the FDA may deny the request for clearance.

The abbreviated 510(k) is available when the manufacturer can demonstrate that the new device meets FDA-identified performance criteria to demonstrate that the device is as safe and effective as a legally marketed device. Specifically, the manufacturer could demonstrate conformance to an objective performance criteria established in FDA guidance, FDA-recognized consensus standards, or special controls in lieu of providing data from direct comparison testing between the manufacturer's device and the legally marketed device. The use of performance criteria is only appropriate when FDA has determined that (1) the new device has indications for use and technological characteristics that do not raise different questions of safety and effectiveness than the identified predicate, (2) the performance criteria align with the performance of one or more legally marketed devices of the same type as the new device, and (3) the new device meets the performance criteria. FDA plans to maintain a list of device types appropriate for the abbreviated 510(k) program, which would include guidance documents that identify the performance criteria for each device type.

After a device receives FDA 510(k) clearance, any modification that could significantly affect its safety or effectiveness, or that would constitute a major change in its intended use, requires a new 510(k) clearance or could require a PMA approval. The FDA requires each manufacturer to make the determination of whether a modification requires a new 510(k) notification or PMA in the first instance, but the FDA can review any such decision. If the FDA disagrees with a manufacturer's decision not to seek a new 510(k) clearance or PMA approval for a particular change, the FDA may retroactively require the manufacturer to seek 510(k) clearance or PMA approval. The FDA also can require the manufacturer to cease U.S. marketing or recall the modified device until 510(k) clearance or PMA approval is obtained.

510(k) submissions are subject to user fees under the Medical Device User Fee Amendments (MDUFA). The standard fee for Fiscal Year 2021 (through September 30, 2021) for a 510(k) submission is $12,432 and the small business fee is $3,108.[11] Annual establishment registration fee is $5,236.[12]

B. De Novo

For products that would otherwise be automatically classified as Class III because the technology employed is sufficiently novel or there is no available predicate device enabling it to be classified as a Class I or Class II device, the de novo 510(k) classification process may be available. The manufacturer would have to be able to describe why the device is low-to-moderate risk and would more appropriately be classified as Class I or II than Class III to be eligible for this regulatory pathway.

Like 510(k) submissions, de novo requests are subject to user fees under MDUFA. The standard fee for Fiscal Year 2021 (through September 30, 2021) for a De Novo Classification Request is $109,697 and the

11. *Medical Device User Fee Amendments (MDUFA)*, FDA, *available at* https://www.fda.gov/industry/fda-user-fee-programs/medical-device-user-fee-amendments-mdufa.

12. *Id.* In order to qualify for a reduced fee for a submission, a company must be qualified and certified as a "small business" through the Center for Devices and Radiological Health's Small Business Program. A small business is defined "as business, including its affiliates, whose gross receipts and sales are less than $100 million for the most recent tax year. A business can submit a Small Business Certification Request if they meet this definition. *See Reduced Medical Device User Fees: Small Business Determination (SBD) Program*, FDA, *available at* https://www.fda.gov/medical-devices/premarket-submissions/reduced-medical-device-user-fees-small-business-determination-sbd-program.

small business fee is $27,424.[13,14] Annual establishment registration fee is same as for the 510(k) submission.[15]

C. Premarket Approval (PMA) Application

If the de novo process is not available for a product, the FDA may classify the device, or the particular use of the device, into Class III, and the device sponsor must then fulfill more rigorous PMA requirements. A PMA application, which is intended to demonstrate that a device is safe and effective, must be supported by extensive data, including data from preclinical studies and human clinical trials. The FDA, by statute and regulation, has 180 days to review a PMA application, though the review more often occurs over a significantly longer period of time, and can take up to several years.

Before approving a PMA, the FDA typically will inspect the facility or facilities where the product is manufactured. The FDA will not approve an application unless it determines that the manufacturing processes and facilities are in full compliance with cGMP requirements and are adequate to ensure consistent production of the product within required specifications.

In approving a PMA application or clearing a 510(k) submission, the FDA may also require some form of postmarket surveillance when necessary to protect the public health or to provide additional safety and effectiveness data for the device. In such cases, the manufacturer might be required to follow certain patient groups for a number of years and make periodic reports to the FDA on the clinical status of those patients.

Like 510(k) submissions and de novo requests, PMAs are subject to user fees under MDUFA. The standard fee for Fiscal Year 2021 (through September 30, 2021) for a De Novo Classification Request is $365,657 and the small business fee is $91,414.[16,17] The annual fee for periodic reporting on a Class III device for PMAs is $12,798 and the small business fee is $3,200. Annual establishment registration fee is same as for the 510(k) submission. [18]

13. *MDUFA*, *supra* note 11.
14. *Id.*
15. *Id.*
16. *MDUFA*, *supra* note 11.
17. *Id.*
18. *Id.*

D. Humanitarian Device Exemption

The Humanitarian Device Exemption (HDE) pathway, established under the Safe Medical Devices Act of 1990 and amended under the 21st Century Cures Act, is available for products intended for diseases or conditions that affect small (i.e., rare) populations. A device intended to benefit patients in the treatment or diagnosis of a condition that affects or is manifested in not more than 8,000 individuals in the United States per year is a humanitarian use device (HUD).

FDA may grant an HDE if the device:

- Will not expose patients to an unreasonable or significant risk of illness or injury, and the probable benefit to health from use of the device outweighs the risk of injury or illness from its use while taking into account the probable risks and benefits of currently available devices or alternative forms of treatment
- The device would not be available to a person with the disease or condition in question without the HDE, and no comparable device (other than a device approved under an HDE or investigational device exemption) is available to treat or diagnose the disease or condition

The HDE marketing application is exempt from the effectiveness requirements of sections 514 and 515 of the FDCA[19] and must be labeled accordingly. An HUD is also subject to certain profit and use restrictions.[20] Specifically, a manufacturer may only sell an HUD for profit after receiving HDE approval if the device is intended for treatment or diagnosis of a disease or condition that either (1) occurs in pediatric patients or a pediatric population and is labeled as such, or (2) occurs in adults and not pediatric patients or occurs in pediatric patients in such numbers that the development of the device for such patients is impossible, highly impracticable, or unsafe. HDE devices that may be sold for profit are also limited to an annual distribution number, which is calculated by taking the number of devices reasonably necessary to treat or diagnose an individual per year and multiplying it by 8,000.

E. Expedited Pathways: Breakthrough Device Program

The FDA's Breakthrough Device Program has grown out of and replaced the earlier Expedited Access Pathway program. Devices subject to the 510(k) process, PMAs, or de novo designation requests are eligible to

---

19. 21 U.S.C. §§ 360d, 360e.
20. *See id.* § 360j(m).

participate in the Breakthrough Device Program if (1) "the device provides for more effective treatment or diagnosis of life-threatening or irreversibly debilitating human disease or conditions" and (2) it meets at least one of the following: (i) represents a breakthrough technology, (ii) no approved or cleared alternatives exist, (iii) that offer significant advantages over existing approved or cleared alternatives, or (iv) device availability is in the best interest of patients.[21] A company can request breakthrough designation for a device at any time before submitting the marketing submission to FDA.

This Breakthrough Designation status confers a number of benefits on the development path of medical devices. These benefits include:

- A dedicated FDA team, including senior management engagement, to facilitate development of the device
- A defined process for resolving disputes that may arise between the sponsor and the FDA
- A commitment to interactive and timely communication between the FDA and the sponsor
- Increased flexibility in clinical study design
- Options for data collection in the postmarket setting, in place of a full clinical study prior to approval
- Priority review status, meaning that a sponsor's submissions will be placed at the top of the relevant review queue and receive additional FDA resources as needed
- Expedited review and potential deferral of manufacturing and quality systems compliance audits
- Advance disclosure to the sponsor of the topics of any consultation between the FDA and external experts or an advisory committee
- An opportunity for the sponsor to recommend external experts for such consultations
- Assignment of the FDA staff to address questions by institutional review committees concerning investigational use of the medical device
- Any additional steps the FDA deems appropriate to expedite the development and review of the medical device

21. 21 U.S.C. § 360e-3.

IV. Evidence

A manufacturer must have "valid scientific evidence" for the safety and effectiveness of its device,[22] which means that there is

> evidence from well-controlled investigations, partially controlled studies, studies and objective trials without matched controls, well-documented case histories conducted by qualified experts, and reports of significant human experience with a marketed device, from which it can fairly and responsibly be concluded by qualified experts that there is reasonable assurance of the safety and effectiveness of a device under its conditions of use. The evidence required may vary according to the characteristics of the device, its conditions of use, the existence and adequacy of warnings and other restrictions, and the extent of experience with its use. Isolated case reports, random experience, reports lacking sufficient details to permit scientific evaluation, and unsubstantiated opinions are not regarded as valid scientific evidence to show safety or effectiveness.[23]

There is a reasonable assurance of *safety* when the manufacturer can demonstrate, through valid scientific evidence, that the probable benefits to health from use of the device for its intended uses and conditions of use, when accompanied by adequate directions and warnings against unsafe use, outweigh any probable risks. Additionally, the valid scientific evidence must adequately demonstrate the absence of unreasonable risk of injury or illness associated with the use of the device when used for its intended use.[24] There is a reasonable assurance of *effectiveness* when the manufacturer can demonstrate that in a significant portion of the target population, the use of the device for its intended uses and conditions of use, when accompanied by adequate directions for use and warnings against unsafe use, will provide clinically significant results.[25]

A. Preclinical Testing

Preclinical testing may include investigations using laboratory animals, nonclinical investigations, analytical studies (for in vitro diagnostic devices), and other bench testing. Any such preclinical testing is

---

22. 21 C.F.R. § 860.7(c)(1).
23. *Id.* § 860.7(c)(2).
24. *Id.* § 860.7(d)(1).
25. *Id.* § 860.7(e)(1).

subject to FDA's good laboratory practice (GLP) regulations,[26] which are designed to ensure that data collected are valid and accurately reflect the responses of the test system. The GLP regulations are also designed to generate quality data and to improve the data integrity of studies used to support regulatory decisions about product safety.

B. Early Feasibility Studies

An early feasibility study (EFS) is a limited clinical investigation of a device early in development. An EFS may be used to evaluate the device design concept with respect to initial clinical safety and device functionality in a small number of subjects (generally fewer than ten initial subjects) when this information cannot practically be provided through additional nonclinical assessments, or appropriate nonclinical tests are unavailable. Information obtained from an early feasibility study may guide device modifications.

FDA recognizes that early clinical experience obtained from an EFS can provide insights into device safety and proof-of-concept, human factors and patient characteristics that may impact performance, and operator technique refinements and other device modifications.

C. Pivotal Trials and Clinical Studies

All clinical trials must be conducted under the supervision of one or more qualified investigators in accordance with FDA's good clinical practice (GCP) regulations. They must be conducted under protocols detailing the objectives of the trial, investigational procedures, subject selection and exclusion criteria, and the safety and effectiveness criteria to be evaluated. Each protocol must be submitted to the FDA as part of the investigational device exemption (IDE), and progress reports detailing the results of the clinical trials must be submitted at least annually. In addition, timely safety reports must be submitted to the FDA and the investigators for serious and unexpected adverse events. An institutional review board (IRB) responsible for the research conducted at each institution participating in the clinical trial must review and approve each protocol before a clinical trial commences at that institution and must also approve the information regarding the trial and the consent form that must be provided to each trial subject or his or her legal representative, monitor the study until completed, and otherwise comply with IRB regulations.

Medical devices typically rely on one or a few pivotal studies rather than the Phase I, II, and III clinical trial structure to which drugs and

26. *Id.* pt. 58.

biologics are subject. Clinical trials are subject to extensive monitoring, recordkeeping, and reporting requirements.

V. FDA Engagement during Product Development

During the development of a new medical device, sponsors are given opportunities to meet with the FDA at certain points. These points may be prior to the submission of an IDE and prior to the PMA submission. Manufacturers may also request meetings at other times. Collectively, these are known as Q-Submissions (Q-Sub) and include Pre-Submission (Pre-Sub) Requests, Submission Issue Requests, Study Risk Determination Requests, Informational Meeting Requests, PMA Day 100 Meetings, Agreement Meeting and Determination Meeting Requests, Designation Requests for a Breakthrough Device, Qualification of Medical Device Development Tools requests, Accessory Classification Requests, requests for recognition of publicly accessible genetic variant database requests, combination product agreement meeting requests, and requests for waivers under 21 C.F.R. § 812.28. This section focuses on Pre-Subs and Informational Meetings as well as other types of engagement that fall outside the Q-Sub process.

These meetings can provide an opportunity for the sponsor to share information about the preclinical data gathered to date (i.e., bench and animal testing), for the FDA to provide advice on the investigational plan (i.e., clinical protocol), and for the sponsor and FDA to reach agreement on the next phase of development. Sponsors typically use the end of feasibility studies to plan for their pivotal trial or trials for a medical device.

A. Pre-Subs

Submitters may obtain feedback from FDA prior to an intended premarket submission (e.g., a de novo request or 510(k)) through a Pre-Sub. A Pre-Sub includes a formal written request from a submitter for feedback from FDA that is provided in the form of a written response or, if the submitter wishes, formal written feedback followed by a meeting in which any additional feedback or clarifications are documented in meeting minutes. The Pre-Sub meeting can be in person or via teleconference. A Pre-Sub also provides an avenue to request agency clarification, request more information, or to request meetings with the agency. The Pre-Sub process is not associated with any user fees. In terms of overall timeline, a Pre-Sub process takes between 75 to 90 days, with 21 days for urgent public health issues.

The Pre-Sub should include specific questions regarding review issues relevant to a planned market submission.[27] Feedback generated from the Pre-Sub process is not binding, and issues raised by FDA in its feedback do not obligate submitters to addressing or resolving those in a future submission, though any future submission related to that topic should discuss why a different approach was chosen or an issue left unresolved. However, this process is most appropriate for a company that intends to make a future premarket submission.

For example, the de novo classification process exists for medical devices that would otherwise be automatically classified as Class III medical devices because there is no available predicate device enabling it to be classified as a Class I or Class II device.[28] The requester must be able to describe why the device is low-to-moderate risk and would more appropriately be classified as Class I or II. When seeking de novo classification, Pre-Subs are strongly recommended for devices not previously reviewed under a 510(k) application.

B. Informational Meetings

Companies may also request an Informational Meeting with FDA. FDA may ask clarifying questions. The degree of direction and feedback provided may depend on the seniority of the attendees and the issues for which the company requests feedback. These meetings tend to be most beneficial if the company wants to establish a relationship with FDA, position itself as a thought leader on a specific product-related issue, or if the product may evolve over time or involve multiple use cases. However, this information sharing can be helpful in providing an overview of ongoing product development and in familiarizing FDA staff about new devices. Although FDA is not obligated to grant such meetings, many companies have success scheduling these Informational Meetings within two weeks to 30 days of a request. The meetings typically last one hour and FDA controls or dictates who attends the meeting from FDA. While FDA may ask clarifying questions during an Informational Meeting, it is possible they may not provide any feedback, and any feedback provided is not binding.

---

27. *See Requests for Feedback and Meetings for Medical Device Submissions: The Q-Submission Program: Guidance for Industry and Food and Drug Administration Staff*, FDA (May 7, 2019), Appendix 1, https://www.fda.gov/media/114034/download for more information on what should be included in a Pre-Sub request.

28. *See* 21 U.S.C. § 360c(f)(2).

C. 513(g) Requests for Information

Companies may make a 513(g) Request for Information to obtain information regarding the class in which a device has been classified or the requirements applicable to a device under the FDCA. The Request for Information should include a description of the product, intended uses, and the product's proposed labeling. FDA will respond to indicate whether a product is a device within the meaning of the FDCA and, if applicable, whether it may be another type of product regulated by FDA. The agency issues a response to a 513(g) Request for Information within 60 days of receipt, provided the submitter has paid all user fees owed, including all required establishment registration fees. Thus, the 513(g) Request for Information process is most appropriate for a company whose product is likely to be regulated as a medical device.

Unlike a formal Request for Designation, the agency's response to a 513(g) Request for Information is not binding. However, to the extent a company disagrees with FDA's feedback, having undergone the 513(g) Request for Information process increases the likelihood of enforcement if the company does not take the appropriate premarket clearance or approval steps required to introduce its product to the market.

D. Informal Digital Health Submissions

For digital health products, companies may submit questions regarding interpretation of digital health guidance to FDA's Division of Digital Health at DigitalHealth@fda.hhs.gov. FDA indicates this would be appropriate for questions such as "Can you help me determine whether the FDA would consider my digital health product to be an actively regulated product?" or "Can you help me understand the FDA definition of a low-risk product, as referenced in the General Wellness guidance document?"[29] There are benefits to informally engaging FDA in a discussion, particularly because any feedback the agency provides is not binding. However, because there is no formal guidance or procedure that governs these types of inquiries, there is no guarantee of a response or of a timely response from the agency. However, FDA typically responds to these requests in 30 to 60 days.

29. *See Ask a Question About Digital Health Regulatory Policies*, FDA, https://www.fda.gov/medical-devices/digital-health/ask-question-about-digital-health-regulatory-policies (last visited Sept. 21, 2020).

CHAPTER 2

FDA Regulation of Digital Health Care Products

Jeffrey N. Gibbs and Allyson B. Mullen[1]

I. Overview of Digital Health Products: Proliferation of Products and Services

The Food and Drug Administration (FDA) regulates a wide variety of devices. An increasing proportion of these products fall into the realm of "digital health." Digital health products include, for example, devices that incorporate artificial intelligence, mobile medical applications, digital therapeutics, and software that integrates medical data and provides a diagnosis.

Digital health products offer many potential advantages, including the ability of consumers to generate health or wellness information remotely. The importance and value of better access to health care has been powerfully illustrated by the disruptions caused by COVID-19. By allowing consumers to diagnose or treat themselves without visiting health care facilities, digital health products can be invaluable tools when consumer mobility is sharply curbed. Digital health products have also been used by health care professionals to aid in diagnosing COVID-19.

For example, in June 2020, FDA granted authorization to an artificial intelligence tool to identify COVID-19 patients who are at higher risk of respiratory failure or hemodynamic instability. The diverse, proliferating set of digital health products has created regulatory challenges for FDA, not least of which is the fundamental question of when a health product

1. Veronique Li, Senior Medical Device Regulation Expert and a former reviewer at the FDA, assisted with this chapter.

crosses the statutory line to become a device, subject to FDA's jurisdiction. This, in turn, raises a second question: which digital health devices *should* be regulated, given the relatively low risks many present? Given the rapid evolution of technology, how can FDA develop a regulatory framework that is—and will remain—flexible and appropriate? Then-Commissioner Gottlieb summarized these issues in a 2017 statement:

> FDA's traditional approach to medical devices is not well suited to these [digital health] products. We need to make sure our approach to innovative products with continual updates and upgrades is efficient and that it fosters, not impedes, innovation. Recognizing this, and understanding that the potential of digital health is nothing short of revolutionary, we must work toward establishing an appropriate approach that's closely tailored to this new category of products. We need a regulatory framework that accommodates the distinctive nature of digital health technology, its clinical promise, the unique user interface, and industry's compressed commercial cycle of new product introductions.[2]

A fundamental question is easy to frame and hard to answer: What is digital health? This chapter will treat digital health as *technologies that are electronic products that enable consumers to make data-driven decisions about their own health, provide alternatives for treating, managing or detecting conditions outside of traditional care settings, or electronic products intended to assist physicians in providing health care.*

Underscoring the breadth of this field, FDA has identified ten different types of digital health products or features, each of which we describe in more detail next. Note that many of these product categories would not have been technologically or commercially viable in the recent past, further illustrating the rapid pace of development in this area.[3]

1. **Software as a Medical Device (SaMD)**—*software intended for one or more medical uses that may run on different operating systems or in virtual environments.*

   This can include stand-alone software designed to operate on general purpose computers or mobile platforms (e.g.,

---

2. Scott Gottlieb, *FDA Announces New Steps to Empower Consumers and Advance Digital Healthcare* (July 27, 2017), https://www.fda.gov/news-events/fda-voices-perspectives-fda-leadership-and-experts/fda-announces-new-steps-empower-consumers-and-advance-digital-healthcare.

3. *Digital Health Criteria*, FDA (Mar. 23, 2018), https://www.fda.gov/medical-devices/digital-health/digital-health-criteria.

smartphone or tablet). It does *not* include software that controls a medical device (e.g., an MRI machine or laboratory instrument).

2. **Advanced Analytics**—*a device or product that can identify, analyze, and use big data and large complex data sets from a variety of sources.*

   Advanced analytics may take multiple forms, including statistical modeling and analytical techniques to provide insights, predictions, recommendations, and other outputs. Such outputs are increasingly available due to the expansive data sets provided by technology. Advanced analytics techniques are often used for medical purposes to analyze large, varied datasets to discover new patterns in data. Notably, advanced analytics was deployed by many companies to help diagnose COVID-19 or monitor the impact of the disease on patients.

3. **Artificial Intelligence**—*a device or product that can imitate intelligent behavior or mimics human learning and reasoning.*

   One rapidly growing area of artificial intelligence is "machine learning," used to advance clinical care. Machine learning can design an algorithm or model without explicit programming, but rather through the use of automated training based on received data. Because machine learning results in continuing changes in the algorithm or model, it provides particular challenges to FDA's review process, which has historically focused on final, static products.

4. **Cloud**—*a device or product with Internet-based computing that provides computer processing resources and data on demand. The cloud is a shared pool of configurable resources (e.g., computer networks, servers, storage, applications, and services).*

   The cloud is used for a rapidly growing suite of services, including clinical and diagnostic data. Many products now transmit data directly to the cloud. This technology allows for increased storage potential and efficiency, but creates new risks and challenges regarding the privacy and security of the stored information. This risk creates the need for the next category, cybersecurity.

5. **Cybersecurity**—*a device or product that can prevent unauthorized access, modification, misuse, or denial of use, or the unauthorized use of information that is stored, accessed, or transferred from a medical device to an external recipient.*

   With the rise of digital health, there is a corresponding need for cybersecurity products to protect the devices and their data.

FDA has placed much more emphasis evaluating the cybersecurity features of a device. This includes not only the protection of private information but also the mitigation of vulnerabilities to hackers who can remotely manipulate software-based medical devices.

6. **Interoperability**—*a device or product that can exchange and use information through an electronic interface with another medical/nonmedical product, system, or device.*

   Interoperability becomes an increasingly important issue as devices need to be able to "talk" to each other to be functional and achieve their full clinical potential. It likewise presents additional risks in terms of security and reliability.

7. **Medical Device Data System (MDDS)**—*hardware or software that can transfer, store, convert data formats, or display medical device data without controlling or altering the functions or parameters of any connected medical device.*

   These types of software products are ubiquitous. Originally considered moderate risk by FDA, the agency now recognizes they are low risk and mostly falling outside the definition of a device.[4]

8. **Mobile Medical App (MMA)**—*A software application that meets the definition of a medical device.*

   Having an MMA can transform a mobile platform into a regulated medical device or to an accessory to a regulated medical device.

9. **Wireless**—*a device or product that uses wireless communication of any form (e.g., Wi-Fi, Bluetooth, NFC) to perform at least one function.*

   Wireless, of course, is becoming more common. The incorporation of wireless can change the regulatory status. For example, while hearing aids were generally exempt from marketing review, the first wireless hearing aid needed to go through the de novo review process and receive FDA marketing authorization.[5]

4. Medical Devices; Medical Device Data Systems, 76 Fed. Reg. 8,637 (Feb. 15, 2011); Medical Devices; Medical Device Classification Regulations To Conform to Medical Software Provisions in the 21st Century Cures Act, 86 Fed. Reg. 20278 (Apr. 19, 2021).

5. 21 C.F.R. § 874.3325.

10. **Novel Digital Health**—*a device or product that includes new, unfamiliar, or unseen digital health technology never submitted, cleared, or approved by FDA.*

    With the heavy investment in digital technology and the rapid technological strides, there will be increasing numbers of novel digital health devices.

These broad elements result in a digital landscape that covers a large swath of products, including wearable devices, telehealth and telemedicine, mobile health, health information technology, and electronically based personalized medicine. As discussed later in the chapter, FDA is reviewing more marketing applications for digital health devices. Concurrently, far more digital health products have entered the market without undergoing FDA review as general wellness products or unregulated devices.

FDA's review of the Apple's ECG App (DEN180044) illustrates some of the complexities and challenges of digital health. Because the app's intended use was to identify possible atrial fibrillation, FDA considered it to be intended for a medical purpose, and therefore subject to review. In contrast, the watch used to generate the single lead data for analysis by the app appears to have been considered general purpose hardware, outside the scope of FDA's review. By taking this approach, FDA effectively allocated resources to review the medical apps and software that sit on top of the general-purpose hardware, while not regulating the hardware itself. This focus on the software has afforded greater regulatory flexibility for companies introducing these types of products.

The Apple ECG App may have seemed like science fiction not long ago, but it is now routine in digital health products. For example, FDA granted 510(k) clearance to Ultromics for an image analysis system that automates cardiac analysis to aid in the early detection of cardiovascular disease.[6] Ultromics' system, known as EchoGo Core, employs AI analysis to automate echocardiography and help clinicians interpret echocardiograms. Another example is Pear Therapeutics' reSET device (DEN160018), intended to increase abstinence from a patient's substances of abuse during treatment and increase retention in an outpatient treatment program for individuals with substance use disorder.[7] reSET was the first software-only therapeutic authorized by the FDA, creating a new classification for prescription digital therapeutics. Since then, there have

6. Ultromics Ltd., 510(k) Premarket Notification, K191171 (Nov. 13, 2019).
7. Pear Therapeutics, Inc., De Novo Petition, DEN160018 (Sept. 14, 2017).

been several others, including Somryst for chronic insomnia,[8] NightWare for sleep disturbance related to nightmares due to post-traumatic stress disorder (PTSD),[9] and Parallel for Irritable Bowel Syndrome (IBS).[10] By the time this book is published, there will undoubtedly be multiple additional examples.

Digital health offers many potential advantages. Developers claim that it facilitates patient engagement with both clinicians and developers, can help manage chronic conditions, reduce inefficiencies in the health care system, enhance flexibility in health care delivery, improve access, reduce costs, and increase quality through frequent modifications and updates. The importance of some of these attributes has been highlighted by the COVID-19 pandemic.

At the same time, while digital health products undeniably offer advantages and efficiencies to an inherently complex system, it can be difficult, especially in the medical context, to distinguish hype from reality. It remains to be seen what digital health's actual impact will be on the U.S. health care system. However, the increasing reliance on technology presents its own risks, including erroneous results, unforeseen interoperability issues, security breaches and hacking, and more. For FDA, one of the greatest challenges is efficiently deploying its resources in developing a regulatory framework that allows digital health the opportunity to generate benefits while minimizing risks to patients and the health care system.

II. Overview of FDA Authority over Software

FDA regulates digital health products pursuant to authority granted under the Federal Food, Drug, and Cosmetic Act (FDCA).[11] Under that statute, FDA has the authority to regulate medical devices that enter into interstate commerce in the United States, including those manufactured within the U.S. or imported into the U.S.[12] The FDCA, in relevant part, defines a "device" as an article

8. Pear Therapeutics, Inc., 510(k) Premarket Notification, K191716 (Mar. 23, 2020).

9. NightWare, Inc, De Novo Petition, DEN200033 (Nov. 6, 2020).

10. Mahana Therapeutics, Inc., De Novo Petition, DEN200029 (Nov. 25, 2020).

11. 21 U.S.C. §§ 321, *et seq.*

12. *Id.*

> intended for use in the diagnosis of disease or other conditions, or in the cure, mitigation, treatment, or prevention of disease, in man or other animals . . . and which does not achieve its primary intended purposes through chemical action within or on the body of man or other animals and which is not dependent upon being metabolized for the achievement of its primary intended purposes.[13]

This definition can encompass all types of software applications, which then run on a desktop computer, laptop computer, remotely on a website or cloud, or on a mobile device. The location or embodiment of the software plays little to no role in whether it is subject to regulation as a "device." The far more important statutory prong is whether the software is "intended for use in the diagnosis . . . or in the cure, mitigation, treatment, or prevention of disease."[14] The Center for Devices and Radiological Health (CDRH), a division within FDA, has jurisdiction over most devices.[15] Following Congress's direction, CDRH has generally used a risk-based approach in regulating devices.[16] While FDA has the authority to regulate all devices, the agency has chosen to exercise enforcement discretion with respect to many devices, including digital devices.

In particular, during the COVID-19 public health emergency, FDA elected to exercise enforcement discretion regarding many uses of digital devices. For example, the agency waived the premarket and certain postmarket regulatory requirements for certain digital therapeutic products used to treat mental health conditions.[17] These digital therapeutics have the potential to bring therapies to many patients who may not have access to a qualified provider during the pandemic. FDA noted that its granting of enforcement discretion would expand the availability of these digital

---

13. *Id.* § 321(h).

14. *Id.*

15. *Center for Devices and Radiological Health*, FDA, (July 12, 2019), https://www.fda.gov/about-fda/fda-organization/center-devices-and-radiological-health. The Center for Biologic Evaluation and Research regulates some devices, including software used in blood banking.

16. Scott Gottlieb, *Fostering Medical Innovation: A Plan for Digital Health Devices*, FDA (June 28, 2018), https://www.fda.gov/news-events/fda-voices-perspectives-fda-leadership-and-experts/fostering-medical-innovation-plan-digital-health-devices.

17. *Enforcement Policy for Digital Health Devices for Treating Psychiatric Disorders during the Coronavirus Disease 2019 (COVID-19) Public Health Emergency*, FDA (Apr. 2020), https://www.fda.gov/media/136939/download.

therapeutics and reduce user and health care provider contact and thereby minimize potential exposure to COVID-19.

A. Historical Position on Software as a Device

Medical devices have been utilizing software for decades. In fact, FDA guidance on the "General Principles of Software Validation" was first drafted in 1997 and then finalized in 2002.[18] Briefly, the guidance describes how certain provisions of the Quality System Regulation[19] apply to software. For instance, it recommends an integration of software life-cycle management and risk management activities. This recommendation has largely been carried forward to today as FDA contemplates a somewhat similar regulatory approach for many digital health products.

The late 1990s also marked the introduction of guidance documents for the content of premarket submissions for software contained in medical devices, as well as guidance for a premarket notification submission for blood establishment computer software.[20] A 2005 version of the "Guidance for the Content of Premarket Submissions for Software Contained in Medical Devices"[21] supersedes both documents and is discussed in the next section.

Prompted by technological changes, FDA more recently developed additional digital health guidance for products. FDA first issued a "Mobile Medical Applications" (MMA guidance) in 2013,[22] later updating it in 2015[23] and 2019 to describe the agency's oversight of device software functions. In 2019, the guidance was renamed "Policy for Device Software Functions and Mobile Medical Applications."[24] The guidance informs distributors, manufacturers, and other stakeholders that FDA

---

18. *Guidance for Industry, General Principles of Software Validation*, FDA (Jan. 11, 2002), https://www.fda.gov/media/73141/download.

19. 21 C.F.R. pt. 820.

20. *Guidance for Industry, Blood Establishment Computer System—Validation in the User's Facility*, FDA (Apr. 2013), https://www.fda.gov/media/72533/download. Software used in blood banks is regulated as a device; but the Center for Biologic Evaluation and Research is responsible for regulating these products.

21. *Guidance for Industry, Guidance for the Content of Premarket Submissions for Software Contained in Medical Devices*, FDA (May 11, 2005), https://www.fda.gov/media/73065/download.

22. *Guidance for Industry, Mobile Medical Applications*, FDA (Sept. 25, 2013).

23. *Guidance for Industry, Mobile Medical Applications*, FDA (Feb. 9, 2015).

24. *Guidance for Industry, Policy for Device Software Functions and Mobile Medical Applications*, FDA (Sept. 27, 2019), https://www.fda.gov/media/80958/download.

will focus on software that presents a greater risk to patients if it does not work as intended and on software that causes smartphones, computers, or other mobile platforms to affect the functionality or performance of traditional medical devices. FDA also issued the final guidance in July 2020, "Multiple Function Device Products: Policy and Considerations," addressing design and review considerations for products containing both software delivering device functions and software delivering non-device function.[25] The scenario is quite common, particularly after the statutory changes to what constitutes a device from a software perspective. The guidance states that "FDA may assess the impact that the software non-device function has on the device function when assessing the safety and effectiveness of the device function."

B. Clinical Decision Support Software (CDSS)

As noted earlier, the statutory definition of a device is quite broad. Read literally, the definition could potentially encompass software that helps automate the analysis of data generally conducted by health care professionals. While physicians have long used tools to assess multiple variables to help make diagnoses and prognoses, new software has enabled health care professionals to receive analyses of enormous, complex data sets that could not be evaluated efficiently—or at all—by any single physician. Thus, while the output is not necessarily novel, the calculation speed and complexity certainly are—but does this function serve as a medical device? In response to ambiguities regarding the reach of the definition of device as applied to these types of programs, as part of the 21st Century Cures legislation, Congress carved out so-called CDSS from the definition of a device.[26]

Section 520(o) of the FD&C Act excludes from the definition of a device, software functions that meet all of the following criteria:

1. Not intended to acquire, process, or analyze a medical image or a signal from an in vitro diagnostic device or a pattern or signal from a signal acquisition system;
2. Intended for the purpose of displaying, analyzing, or printing medical information about a patient or other medical information

25. *Guidance for Industry and FDA Staff, Multiple Function Device Products: Policy and Considerations, FDA* (July 29, 2020), https://www.fda.gov/media/112671/download.

26. 21st Century Cures Act, Pub. L. No. 1145-255, § 3060, 130 Stat. 1033 (2016).

(such as peer-reviewed clinical studies and clinical practice guidelines);

3. Intended for the purpose of supporting or providing recommendations to a health care professional about prevention, diagnosis, or treatment of a disease or condition; and
4. Intended for the purpose of enabling such health care professional to independently review the basis for such recommendations that such software presents so that it is not the intent that such health care professional rely primarily on any of such recommendations to make a clinical diagnosis or treatment decision regarding an individual patient.

Notwithstanding the statutory attempt at clarity, understanding what constitutes CDSS can be challenging. In response, FDA published a draft guidance in 2017 to provide greater clarity,[27] which it later updated in September of 2019.[28] Unsurprisingly, FDA's revised draft guidance elicited some criticisms due to scope and clarity.[29]

One portion of the draft guidance provides an expanded discussion of FDA's interpretation of criterion (1) of the Cures Act, specifically with respect to the phrase "a signal from an in vitro diagnostic device or a pattern or signal from a signal acquisition system." Software utilizing such a "signal" is disqualified from being CDSS. The draft guidance states that FDA considers "physiological signals" to be included within this definition, and defines "physiological signals" as those signals that require use of:

- An in vitro diagnostic device, which typically includes an electrochemical or photometric response generated by an assay and instrument that may be further processed by software to generate a clinical test result, or
- A signal acquisition system that measures a parameter from within, attached to, or external to the body for a medical purpose and often includes:
    - use of sensors (e.g., electrocardiogram (ECG) leads) along with electronics and software function that is used for signal generation (e.g., ECG);

---

27. *Draft Guidance for Industry, Clinical and Patient Decision Support Software*, FDA (Dec. 8, 2017).

28. *Draft Guidance for Industry, Clinical and Patient Decision Support Software*, FDA (Sept. 27, 2019).

29. Comments of AdvaMed, Docket No. FDA-2017-D-6569 (Dec. 20, 2019); Comments of Resmed Docket No. FDA-2017-D-6569 (Dec. 26, 2019).

- collections of samples or specimens such as tissue, blood, or other fluids, (e.g., conducting a pathological study using software such as digital pathology); or
- use of radiological imaging systems (e.g., computed tomography (CT)) and a software function for image generation.[30]

There are, however, many other inputs that could potentially be considered "signals" that are not addressed in FDA's guidance, creating uncertainty for industry.

The second and third criteria of the statutory CDSS definition tend to be easier to apply. The fourth one—often referred to as the "primary reliance" requirement—though has resulted in more uncertainty. Trying to provide more clarity, FDA reframed this element as a question: "Can the User Independently Review the Basis?" To meet this criterion, the software must contain a function that enables the user to independently review the basis for the recommendations, so that it is not the intent that the user relies primarily on any such recommendation.

CDSS comprises a large and rapidly growing type of medically related software. The boundaries between CDSS—unregulated by FDA—and software that is a device remain fluid. To date, FDA has not taken public enforcement action against a company claiming that its software is CDSS when FDA believes it to be a regulated device. The statutory exemption for CDSS enabled many companies to introduce software related to COVID-19 diagnoses and monitoring without the need to go through FDA review.

C. Software Incorporated in Devices

FDA characterizes software that functions as a device as "device software functions." This includes both Software in a Medical Device (SiMD) and Software as a Medical Device (SaMD). Examples of software incorporated in devices include an enteral feeding pump to alert users of alarms[31] and a software program to notify dialysis personnel of an increased risk of access site stenosis for hemodialysis patients.[32]

---

30. *Draft Guidance for Industry, Clinical and Patient Decision Support Software*, FDA, at 10 (Sept. 27, 2019).

31. *Guidance for Industry, Guidance for the Content of Premarket Submissions for Software Contained in Medical Devices*, FDA (May 11, 2005), https://www.fda.gov/regulatory-information/search-fda-guidance-documents/guidance-content-premarket-submissions-software-contained-medical-devices.

32. *Id.*

These products have enjoyed a more predictable regulatory approach than many other digital health products. Not only are there device-specific guidances for certain products; FDA has also issued broader generic guidances that advise applicants on what to consider and include in marketing applications.

In its "Guidance for the Content of Premarket Submissions for Software Contained in Medical Devices,"[33] FDA noted that the emergence of consensus standards has provided greater consistency and quality of software documentation. The guidance applies to devices that contain one or more software components, parts, or accessories, or are composed solely of software as "software devices," as well as firmware and other means for software-based control of medical devices of software.[34] The guidance takes a risk-based approach, classifying the risks into low, moderate, or major. The level of risk is initially self-determined by the company, but that determination is subject to FDA review. The degree of risk affects the level of documentation required. Generally speaking, documentation for SiMD is expected to include a description of the device design; documentation of design implementation; a demonstration of how the device produced by design implementation was evaluated; a demonstration that hazards have been identified appropriately and risks managed effectively; and traceability to link together design, implementation, testing, and risk management.[35]

D. Stand-alone Software

Software as a Medical Device was previously referred to as "stand-alone software," "medical device software," and/or "health software." There are now numerous examples of SaMD. Two illustrative examples of SaMD are software that allows a user to view images obtained from a magnetic resonance imaging (MRI) via a smartphone[36] and a Computer-Aided Detection (CAD) software that aids radiologists in interpreting mammograms.[37] SaMD can be used across a broad range of technology platforms.

Recognizing the dynamic characteristics of SaMD, regulators from around the world saw the need to develop a shared framework to promote

33. *Id.*
34. *Id.* at 2.
35. *Id.* at 8.
36. Ultromics Ltd., 510(k) Premarket Notification, K191171 (Nov. 13, 2019).
37. ICAD, Inc., Premarket Approval, P010034 (Jan. 31, 2002).

innovation and protect public health.[38] Chaired by FDA, the International Medical Device Regulators Forum (IMDRF) is a group of global medical device regulators who convened to reach agreement on medical device regulation.[39] In 2013, IMDRF formed the Software as a Medical device Working Group (WG) to develop guidance supporting innovation and timely access to safe and effective SaMD. IMDRF defined SaMD as software intended to be used for one or more medical purposes that performs these purposes without being part of a hardware medical device.[40] In 2014, the WG developed a framework for risk categorization and related considerations, application of the Quality Management System, and clinical evaluation for Software as a Medical Device. FDA has utilized these principles in developing its own regulatory regime.

FDA's guidance "Software as a Medical Device (SaMD): Clinical Evaluation"[41] adopts the principles agreed upon by the IMDRF. The guidance explains that clinical evaluation should be a repeated and uninterrupted process as part of the Quality Management System; that SaMD may be subject to independent review of the results of the clinical evaluation to provide clinical values to users; and that encourages continuous monitoring of the SaMD for its safety, effectiveness, and performance.

E. Software as a Service

A different category—software as a service (SaaS)—is meant "to include any 'server software application' that provides a service to a client software application on a mobile platform."[42] This, too, is a broad and growing category. FDA intends to regulate only those software functions that are medical devices and could pose a risk to the patient if the device does not function as intended. These are software functions that "are an extension of one or more medical devices by connecting to such device(s) for purposes of controlling the device(s) or analyzing medical device data"; transform the mobile platform into a regulated medical device by using

---

38. https://www.fda.gov/medical-devices/digital-health/software-medical-device-samd.

39. *Software as a Medical Device (SaMD)*, FDA (Dec. 4, 2018), https://www.fda.gov/medical-devices/digital-health/software-medical-device-samd.

40. http://www.imdrf.org/docs/imdrf/final/technical/imdrf-tech-131209-samd-key-definitions-140901.pdf, page 6

41. *Guidance for Industry, Software as a Medical Device (SAMD): Clinical Evaluation*, FDA (Dec. 8, 2017), https://www.fda.gov/media/100714/download.

42. *Guidance for Industry, Policy for Device Software Functions and Mobile Medical Applications*, FDA, at 7 (Sept. 27, 2019), https://www.fda.gov/media/80958/download.

attachments, display screens, or sensors or by including functionalities similar to those of currently regulated medical devices"; or "become a regulated medical device by performing patient-specific analysis and providing patient-specific diagnosis, or treatment recommendations."[43]

Conversely, FDA does not intend to expand its resources on low-risk SaaS. For example, software functions that assist patients with self-management of their diseases without offering specific treatments or suggestions, or that automate straightforward tasks for clinicians, are products FDA does not intend to regulate. Other low-risk, unregulated functions include software that provides coaching to aid patients in their day-to-day activities, that helps patients and clinicians communicate with one another by documenting or transmitting images, or that performs simple calculations.

Software as a service may also have regulatory implications beyond FDA. For example, companies offering software as a service to clinical laboratories may find themselves subject to regulation as clinical laboratories even though their facilities consist only of servers. The College of American Pathologists (CAP) has required accreditation of bioinformatics facilities when such data is needed to generate a reportable result.

F. Unregulated Software

There are many other types of software products related to clinical management that FDA is not currently regulating. For example, FDA has not historically considered software functions such as processing and maintenance of financial records, appointment schedules, and analysis to predict patient utilization to be software functions of devices. Many of these functions should not be subject to device regulation. Even if they affect clinical management, they do not fall within the device definition.

Additionally, Laboratory Information Systems (LIS) and Laboratory Information Management Systems (LIMS) functions intended for administrative support are not considered device functions. Transferring, storing, or displaying clinical laboratory test data and results are also not considered to be within the definition of a device.[44]

Moreover, software functions that are intended to transfer, store, convert formats, or display electronic patient records that are the equivalent of a paper medical chart are not devices if the following criteria are met:

---

43. *Id.* at 11–12.

44. *Guidance for Industry, Changes to Existing Medical Software Policies Resulting from Section 3060 of the 21st Century Cures Act*, FDA, at 4 (Sept. 27, 2019), https://www.fda.gov/media/109622/download.

1. Such records were created, stored, transferred, or reviewed by health care professionals (HCPs), or by individuals working under supervision of such professionals, (section 520(o)(1)(C)(i) of the FD&C Act);
2. Such records are part of information technology certified under a program of voluntary certification kept or recognized by the Office of the National Coordinator for Health Information Technology (ONC) under section 3001(c)(5) of the Public Health Service Act ("ONC Health IT Certification Program") (section 520(o)(1)(C)(ii) of the FD&C Act); and
3. Such software functions are not intended for interpretation or analysis of patient records, including medical image data, for the purpose of the diagnosis, cure, mitigation, prevention, or treatment of a disease or condition (section 520(o)(1)(C)(iii) of the FD&C Act).

On the other hand, functions that extend beyond those intended to transfer, store, convert formats, or display the equivalent of a paper medical chart—such as by using a mobile device's camera to document or transfer images to in lieu of what would otherwise be an in-person consultation between a patient and health care provider—would be deemed devices. However, these uses would also be subject to FDA's exercise of enforcement discretion.

As part of its update to the *Mobile Medical Applications* guidance document,[45] FDA increased the number of examples it does *not* consider medical devices from five to 21. FDA also changed one of its examples to better define the distinction between apps that provide clinical input versus those that document a clinical determination. Specifically, whereas the example of what was not a device previously said, "assessing the need for immunization," FDA's updated guidance changed the example of "documenting the need for immunization."[46] FDA revised the example because "assessing the need" connotes clinical input, while "documenting" is simply recording of a clinician's action. This example highlights how seemingly small semantic differences can materially change regulatory status for digital products.

One of the biggest challenges for FDA is that the world of digital health changes rapidly. This is underscored by FDA's evaluation and its

45. *Guidance for Industry, Policy for Device Software Functions and Mobile Medical Applications*, FDA (Sept. 27, 2019), https://www.fda.gov/media/80958/download.

46. *Id.* at 20.

approach to Medical Device Data Systems (MDDS). Initially, FDA considered MDDS high risk,[47] and, as a result, required product marketing applications. As FDA became more comfortable with this category, however, it began to exercise enforcement discretion and no longer required premarket applications.[48] Now, because of changes resulting from the 21st Century Cures Act, software functions that meet the definitions of MDDS are no longer even devices.[49]

As a result, the "Medical Device Data Systems, Medical Image Storage Devices, and Medical Image Communications Devices" guidance document has been modified to clarify that software functions that are solely intended to transfer, sore, convert formats, and display medical device data and results are not devices and therefore not subject to FDA regulatory requirements.[50] This is true regardless of whether they affect or result in immediate clinical action.

III. FDA Regulation of General Wellness Products

Historically, products intended for use for general health and wellness that are intended to help change a person's lifestyle in a healthy way have not been subject to FDA regulation *unless* they are intended for medical purposes. Once again, applying this distinction can be challenging for both FDA and industry.

Products intended to benefit a user's overall health and wellness, and that do not make claims about disease prevention, treatment, mitigation, or cure, would not be regulated as medical devices. When FDA issued the draft guidance "General Wellness: Policy for Low Risk Devices,"[51] it defined a "general wellness product" as a product that has:

1. An intended use that relates to maintaining or encouraging a general state of health or a healthy activity, or

---

47. *See* 76 Fed. Reg. 8637 (Feb. 15, 2011).

48. *Guidance for Industry, Medical Device Data Systems, Medical Image Storage Devices, and Medical Image Communications Devices*, FDA, at 11 (Sept. 27, 2019), https://www.fda.gov/media/88572/download.

49. Medical Devices; Medical Device Classification Regulations to Conform to Medical Software Provisions in the 21st Century Cures Act, 86 Fed. Reg. 20278 (Apr. 19, 2021).

50. 21 U.S.C. § 360j(o)(1)(D); *Guidance for Industry, Medical Device Data Systems, Medical Image Storage Devices, and Medical Image Communications Devices*, FDA, at 2 (Sept. 27, 2019), https://www.fda.gov/media/88572/download.

51. *Guidance for Industry, General Wellness: Policy for Low Risk Devices*, FDA (Sept. 27, 2019), https://www.fda.gov/media/90652/download.

2. An intended use that relates the role of healthy lifestyle with helping to reduce the risk or impact of certain chronic diseases or conditions and where it is well understood and accepted that healthy lifestyle choices may play an important role in health outcomes for the disease or condition.[52]

Elaborating further, FDA states that this second category includes two subcategories:

1. Intended uses to promote, track, and/or encourage choice(s), which, as part of a healthy lifestyle, *may help to reduce the risk of* certain chronic disease or conditions; and
2. Intended uses to promote, track, and/or encourage choice(s) which, as part of a healthy lifestyle, *may help living well with* certain chronic diseases or conditions.[53]

FDA's guidance provides examples. One example is a product that promotes physical activity, which, as part of a healthy lifestyle may help reduce the risk of high blood pressure.[54] Another example is a product that tracks caloric intake and helps manage a healthy eating plan to maintain a healthy weight and balanced diet, which in turn may help living well with high blood pressure and type 2 diabetes.[55] Based on this framing of utility, neither product is regulated as a device, even though the product is promoted for its ability—through general wellness—to improve a clinically diagnosed condition. In other words, the manufacturer may say more about the product than that it merely helps achieve a healthy lifestyle or may help aid in weight loss. FDA has included the caveat that it must be well-known that the healthy lifestyle choices are associated with improved outcomes for those diseases or conditions. There is a second important limitation: the general wellness product must present a low risk. FDA's guidance makes clear that products are not low risk if CDRH actively regulates products of the same type in question. Companies positioning their product as general wellness need to be careful in framing their claims and associated promotional materials.

It is not always easy to determine whether a product meets the definition of a general wellness product. FDA's guidance document states that FDA "does not intend to examine low risk general wellness products to determine whether they are devices within the meaning of" the

52. *Id.* at 3.
53. *Id.* at 4.
54. *Id.* at 5.
55. *Id.*

Federal Food, Drug, and Cosmetic Act.[56] Thus, manufacturers may self-determine that they believe the product they intend to market meets the definition of a general wellness product. FDA, though, has the power to disagree with the manufacturer's classification and initiate compliance action.

As discussed earlier, many digital health products do not need FDA review to enter prior to entering the market. Other products, though, must navigate the FDA review process to enter the U.S. market. Such digital health products include, for example, software that connects to or controls a medical device, digital therapeutics, and software used in active patient monitoring to analyze patient-specific medical device data.

Digital devices can go through any of the typical premarket review pathways: 510(k) premarket notification, de novo authorization, and premarket approval (PMA). The statutory requirements for completing FDA review are no different for digital devices than for other devices. However, the specific data requirements will differ, reflecting the need for different kinds of data to ensure safety and effectiveness.

The list of digital health products that have successfully completed that review process is constantly growing. A few examples that illustrate the breadth of the field are provided here.

- Denture identification is commonly used to match dentures that have been misplaced with their owners. The DentureID Microchip is an implantable radiofrequency transponder system that provides access to patient identification and health information when used with removable oral appliances.[57]
- The Omron Avail TENS device delivers Transcutaneous Electrical Nerve Stimulation technology and microcurrent therapy through the Omron TENS iOS or Android app to treat chronic muscle and joint pain on multiple body locations.[58]
- The GoSpiro is a single-patient use device intended to be used to conduct basic lung function and spirometry testing. It can be used in traditional clinical settings such as the physician's office or clinic and can also be used in the home. Real-time lung

56. *Id.* at 2.

57. CMP Industries LLC, Premarket Notification, K170423 (Oct. 25, 2017), https://www.accessdata.fda.gov/cdrh_docs/pdf17/K170423.pdf.

58. Omron Healthcare, Inc., Premarket Notification, K172079 (Oct. 19, 2017), https://www.accessdata.fda.gov/cdrh_docs/pdf17/K172079.pdf.

function data is transmitted via Bluetooth to computers, tablets, or smartphones for telemedicine applications to the physician.[59]

- Cleared in February 2020, the Canon Aquilion Prime SP incorporates deep learning to distinguish true signal from noise to generate a detailed visualization of a patient's tissue composition at a faster speed.[60]
- Provided de novo authorization to Akili Interactive Labs Inc.'s EndeavorRx, a digital therapeutic indicated to improve attention function as measured by computer-based testing in children ages 8 to 12 years old with primarily inattentive or combined-type ADHD, who have a demonstrated attention issue.[61]
- In May 2021, FDA cleared Overjet's Dental Assist software. "Dental Assist uses deep-learning algorithms to measure bone loss in dental X-rays. Those measurements are then used to diagnose periodontal disease, which is estimated to affect nearly half of all U.S. adults."[62]

IV. Pre-Certification Program

FDA has applied its general device regulatory framework to digital health products. However, the arrival and rapid evaluation of digital health has posed a challenge to the existing paradigm.

One key distinction between digital health and the types of devices FDA has historically regulated is that software-based medical technologies iterate more quickly in terms of design, development, and modification. Software products much more readily lend themselves to changes than do physical devices. Updates are rapidly pushed out directly to users on their smartphones, tablets, and other mobile platforms. By design, machine learning software is dynamic, not static. The traditional FDA approach of reviewing a locked-down version of a device does not work well for constantly evolving software products. For a device that has undergone review through the 510(k) premarket notification process, a change that could significantly affect intended use or safety or effectiveness

59. Monitored Therapeutics, Inc., Premarket Notification, K163249 (Mar. 24, 2017), https://www.accessdata.fda.gov/cdrh_docs/pdf16/K163249.pdf.

60. Canon Medical Systems Corporation, Premarket Notification, K192832 (Feb. 21, 2020).

61. Akili Interactive Labs Inc., De Novo Petition, DEN200026 (June 15, 2020).

62. https://www.fiercebiotech.com/medtech/overjet-nets-fda-clearance-for-gum-disease-spotting-deep-learning-software.

requires a new submission.[63] For devices that have entered the market via a PMA, some changes require prior approval, some prompt notification, and some need to be described in the annual report.[64] The upshot is that rapid revision to marketed devices is inhibited by the need for new FDA reviews. Applying the same approach to digital devices can stifle innovation. At the same time, allowing digital health manufacturers unfettered freedom to change their software presents its own risks.

To try to address these challenges, in August 2017, FDA introduced the concept of a Digital Health Software Precertification (Pre-Cert) program.[65] The Pre-Cert program is a novel, creative approach intended to create a streamlined regulatory process for software as a medical device, potentially replacing the need for a traditional premarket submission for some software-based medical devices. FDA plans to accomplish this by examining companies who develop digital health products and their processes to leverage postmarket opportunities unique to software to verify the continued safety, effectiveness, and performance of these digital health products. Significantly, this includes a review of *the processes* within the company to assure FDA of continued quality of output.

FDA said it would test the Pre-Cert process through a pilot program. The test plan will include retrospective tests of SaMD submissions that have been previously reviewed and prospective tests. For prospective tests, Pre-Cert company volunteers will not only undergo the Pre-Cert process but will also submit a full premarket submission. FDA will compare results of the current review process to the streamlined review process. For example, FDA states they will "consider the Pre-Cert model to be confirmed when the program framework remains static over multiple premarket submissions." There is no communicated endpoint or duration for this pilot program. In March 2020, FDA cleared Pear Therapeutics' Somryst, a prescription digital therapeutic for the treatment of patients with chronic insomnia.[66] According to the company's press release, Somryst was "the first product submitted through FDA's traditional 510(k)

63. 21 C.F.R. § 807.81(a)(3).

64. *See id.* §§ 814.39, 814.84.

65. *Digital Health Software Precertification (Pre-Cert) Program*, FDA (July 18, 2019), https://www.fda.gov/medical-devices/digital-health/digital-health-software-precertification-pre-cert-program.

66. Pear Therapeutics, Somryst, 510(k) Premarket Notification, K191716 (Mar. 23, 2020).

pathway while simultaneously reviewed through FDA's Software Precertification Pilot Program."[67]

Should FDA implement this program beyond the pilot phase, it is possible that lower risk software will not require premarket product review. On the other hand, developers of software identified to present moderate and higher risk would submit product-specific information and follow a streamlined FDA premarket review if the company receives a prior third-party certification for engaging in high-quality software design and testing (validation) and ongoing maintenance. FDA has stated its intention to leverage the IMDRF framework, to the extent consistent with current statutory authority, to help determine the risk categorization of a SaMD product. The agency will consider the SaMD medical purpose and the seriousness of the medical condition that the SaMD is intended to treat.

According to FDA, the goal of the Pre-Cert program is to:

> have tailored, pragmatic, and least burdensome regulatory oversight that assesses organizations (large and small) to establish ***trust*** that they have a culture of quality and organizational excellence such that they can develop high quality SaMD products, leverages ***transparency*** of organizational excellence and product performance across the entire life cycle of SaMD, uses a tailored streamlined premarket review, and leverages unique postmarket opportunities available in software to ***verify*** the continued safety, effectiveness and performance of SaMD in the real world.[68]

The Pre-Cert program thus proposed a novel concept: evaluating corporate culture as part of the regulatory process. While FDA officials have *implicitly* considered a device company's regulatory history in making compliance decisions, the Pre-Cert program is the most explicit statement of the use of corporate culture in the product review process.[69]

Ultimately, according to FDA, the Pre-Cert aims to:

- **Benefit** a participating organization based on its "precertified" status by offering the ability to participate in a streamlined premarket review and opportunities to collect and leverage

67. https://peartherapeutics.com/pear-therapeutics-obtains-fda-authorization-for-somryst-a-prescription-digital-therapeutic-for-the-treatment-of-adults-with-chronic-insomnia/.

68. *Developing a Software Precertification Program: A Working Model*, FDA, at 7 (Jan. 2019), https://www.fda.gov/media/119722/download.

69. *See* https://www.fda.gov/media/135703/download.

real-world postmarket data, which encourages innovation, timely patient access, and safety and effectiveness over the product life cycle.

- **Leverage and use information and data** from all available sources allowing FDA and SaMD manufacturers to be more efficient and streamlined without compromising safety and effectiveness of SaMD products.
- **Enable a modern and tailored approach** that allows software iterations and changes to occur in a timely fashion under appropriate controls.
- **Ensure high-quality software products** throughout the life of the product by enabling companies to demonstrate their embedded culture of quality and organizational excellence and ability to monitor real-world performance.
- **Adapt** key elements and measure based on the effectiveness of the program.[70]

If the Pre-Cert program is successfully adopted, it will affect not only digital health but also other types of FDA-regulated devices. At this point, it is not clear whether the Pre-Cert program will be adopted and, if so, when. This uncertainty is due in part to numerous questions having been raised by members of Congress as to FDA's statutory authority to implement the program.[71]

V. Special Considerations for Software Submissions

In addition to the typical contents for a device premarket submission, sponsors of digital health premarket submissions must also address specific topics, including cybersecurity and interoperability.

A. Cybersecurity

FDA has two separate guidance documents related to cybersecurity: (1) Cybersecurity for Networked Medical Devices Containing Off-The-Shelf (OTS) Software and (2) Content of Premarket Submissions

70. *Digital Health Software Precertification (Pre-Cert) Program*, FDA (July 18, 2019), https://www.fda.gov/medical-devices/digital-health/digital-health-software-precertification-pre-cert-program.

71. *See* https://www.warren.senate.gov/imo/media/doc/2019.10.30%20Letter%20with%20Senators%20Murray%20and%20Smith%20to%20FDA%20requesting%20additional%20information%20on%20the%20agency's%20software%20pre-certification%20pilot%20program.pdf.

for Management of Cybersecurity in Medical Devices. Next, we discuss each.

1. Cybersecurity for Networked Medical Devices Containing Off-The-Shelf (OTS) Software

Vulnerabilities, such as viruses or worms, may jeopardize the operation of networked medical devices. As a result, constant maintenance is required to safeguard against unauthorized access to the network or medical device. Device manufacturers that incorporate OTS software in their medical devices are expected to be vigilant; FDA has stated they are responsible for cybersecurity vulnerabilities under 21 C.F.R. § 820.100. Pursuant to this regulation, each manufacturer is expected to regularly analyze sources of data and implement necessary corrective and preventive actions relating to cybersecurity.

This guidance[72] applies to medical devices that use OTS software, connect to networks, and need updates. That is because the OTS software has been found to be vulnerable to threats. The guidance aids in understanding this complex, crucially important aspect of security. As such, the guidance is useful to manufacturers of a wide range of devices, such as picture archiving and communications systems on networks within health care facilities, systems that monitor patient activity, and those responsible for ensuring the protection of networked devices from threats.

Once a vulnerability is spotted, it is unlikely that a software patch will require a new 510(k) submission. For a product with an approved PMA, a supplement is required if the software patch results in a change to the approved indications for use or is deemed to have an adverse effect on the device's safety and effectiveness.[73] Regardless of whether a new submission is needed, software changes should be validated to address cybersecurity vulnerabilities.

2. Content of Premarket Submissions for Management of Cybersecurity in Medical Devices

Much like the guidance for software in a medical device, this guidance outlines the documentation to be included in premarket submissions for

72. *Guidance for Industry, Cybersecurity for Networked Medical Devices Containing Off-the-Shelf (OTS) Software*, FDA (Jan. 14, 2005), https://www.fda.gov/media/72154/download.

73. 21 C.F.R. § 814.39.

devices with cybersecurity risk.[74] The security of software-based devices is of increasing concern to FDA, and to the broader health care community. For example, in January 2020, FDA issued a safety communication warning that attackers could "remotely take control of the medical device and to silence alarms, generate false alarms and interfere with alarms of patient monitors connected to these devices."[75]

Reflecting the increasing risks and the heightened need for precaution, FDA's 2018 draft guidance[76] expands significantly upon a draft guidance issued in 2014. FDA clarified the draft guidance is applicable for "devices that contain software (including firmware) or programmable logic as well as software that is a medical device." It further defines two tiers of devices according to the cybersecurity risk, noting that the device's cybersecurity risk is different from the overall risk of the device in determining the classification.

Tier 1 is for devices with higher cybersecurity risk where the following criteria are met:

1. The device can connect to another product, or to a network, or to the Internet; and
2. "A cybersecurity incident affecting the device could directly cause harm to multiple patients."[77]

A Tier 2 device is one that does not meet the criteria for Tier 1. For a Tier 2 device, the guidance recommends that sponsors include Tier 1 documentation or "provide a risk-based rationale for why specific cybersecurity design controls" are not appropriate.[78]

Device applicants need to adequately address FDA's cybersecurity requirements or risk the rejection of their marketing application.[79] FDA's draft guidance provides definitions, discussion of general principles related to cybersecurity controls and cybersecurity functions, and the cybersecurity documentation that should be included in a premarket submission. The guidance also contains recommendations for the content

---

74. *Draft Guidance for Industry, Content of Premarket Submissions for Management of Cybersecurity in Medical Devices*, FDA (Oct. 18, 2018), https://www.fda.gov/media/119933/download.

75. https://www.fda.gov/medical-devices/safety-communications/cybersecurity-vulnerabilities-certain-ge-healthcare-clinical-information-central-stations-and.

76. https://www.fda.gov/media/119933/download.

77. *Id.* at 10.

78. *Id.* at 11.

79. *Guidance for Industry, Refuse to Accept Policy for 510(k)s*, FDA (Sept. 13, 2019).

of device labeling. According to the draft guidance, detailed design and risk management documentation related to cybersecurity should be submitted in a premarket submission, as well as detailed system diagrams that show how the specific device design elements are incorporated into a system-level and holistic picture. For a large, complex software system, the amount of documentation will be extensive. Even though draft guidances are not legally binding,[80] applicants are well-advised to carefully consider the elements of this draft guidance. The failure to address these elements can result in delays in—or the failure to successfully complete—the FDA review process.

B. Interoperability

Interoperable devices are those "that have the ability to exchange and use information[81] through an electronic interface with another medical/non-medical product, system, or device." In 2016, FDA released a draft guidance entitled "Design Considerations and Pre-market Submission Recommendations for Interoperable Medical Devices." A final version was released in 2017.[82] The guidance is not limited to the addressing unidirectional sending of patient data; it includes complex interactions, including the control of medical devices. It addresses three principal areas: (1) design considerations for interoperable devices, including testing and risk management of interoperable devices; (2) the content of premarket submissions for interoperable devices; and (3) labeling considerations for interoperable devices. The guidance elaborates in detail on each of these elements.

FDA further states that to ensure the safe performance of the interoperable devices, manufacturers must establish "appropriate functional, performance, and interface requirements."[83] According to FDA, failure to do so may lead to device malfunction, patient injury, and possibly death. To illustrate the point, FDA gives a simple example: the transmitting

80. Nor are final guidances legally binding. 21 C.F.R. § 10.115(d). Nevertheless, as a practical matter the failure to meet the expectations set out in a guidance can result in an applicant's rejection.

81. With respect to interoperable devices, exchange of information is defined as the "transmission, reception or both," that may be accomplished by means of wired or wireless methods that may exist on a local network, or through the internet. *Guidance for Industry, Design Considerations and Pre-market Submission Recommendations for Interoperable Medical Devices*, FDA, at 2 (Sept. 6, 2017), https://www.fda.gov/media/95636/download.

82. *Id.* at 1.

83. *Id.* at 3.

of patient weight in kilograms when the receiving device assumes the weight is in pounds.

VI. FDA's Approach to Algorithms and Deep Learning[84]

Some digital health products can be easily accommodated by FDA's traditional device regulatory scheme. Others cannot. AI and, to an even greater degree, machine learning, are examples of the latter.

AI has been considered the science and engineering of making intelligent machines. It employs different methods, such as models incorporating statistical analyses, use of "if-then" statements, and, sometimes, machine learning. Machine learning (ML) is a subset of AI that can design and inform software algorithms so that they learn from new data. Algorithms can be "locked" so their function remains unchanged or they can be "adaptive," allowing their behavior to change over time, even after undergoing FDA review to gain access to the market. An adaptive algorithm changes its behavior using a defined learning process. It may be that for a given set of inputs, the output will vary over time. In other words, a fixed set of input might give different diagnoses than it did before due to changes in the algorithm.[85]

Because ML is adaptive to real-world use and experience, FDA is considering when a continuously learning AL/ML-based SaMD should require a premarket submission for an algorithm change. FDA released a discussion paper "Proposed Regulatory Framework for Modifications to Artificial Intelligence/Machine Learning (AI/ML)-Based Software as a Medical Device (SaMD)—Discussion Paper and Request for Feedback" on a potential approach to premarket review for AI and ML-driven modifications to software.[86] In this discussion paper, FDA describes a process that takes a Total Product Life Cycle (TPLC) approach to the regulation of AI/ML-based SaMD. For example, FDA suggests that the following categories of software modification may require a premarket submission:

84. https://www.fda.gov/medical-devices/software-medical-device-samd/artificial-intelligence-and-machine-learning-software-medical-device.

85. Esther Abels et al., *Computational Pathology Definitions, Best Practices, and Recommendations for Regulatory Guidance: A White Paper from the Digital Pathology Association*, 249(3) J. PATHOLOGY 286–94 (NOV. 2019).

86. *Proposed Regulatory Framework for Modifications to Artificial Intelligence/Machine Learning (AI/ML)-Based Software as a Medical Device (SaMD)—Discussion Paper and Request for Feedback*, FDA, https://www.fda.gov/media/122535/download.

- A change that introduces a new risk or modifies an existing risk that could result in significant harm;
- A change to risk controls to prevent significant harm; and
- A change that significantly affects clinical functionality or the performance specifications of the device.
- For higher-risk PMA devices, a supplement would be required for changes that could affect safety or effectiveness, such as new indications for use, new clinical effects, or significant technology modifications that affect performance. That standard is largely consistent with the existing regulation for when a PMA supplement is needed.[87]

While FDA has cleared or approved some AI/ML-based SaMD,[88] to date nearly all of these appear to have been for locked algorithms. Locked algorithms are algorithms that are designed to provide the same result each time the same input is provided. For adaptive algorithms, FDA has indicated that the TPLC approach should be used to keep up with the rapid nature of product enhancements. FDA proposed a framework based on the IMDRF risk categorizations, FDA's benefit-risk framework, risk management principles embodied in the software modifications guidance, and FDA's TPLC approach.

FDA anticipates that modifications to AI/ML-based SaMD would typically fall into three categories: performance, inputs, and intended use.

- Performance refers to both clinical and analytical performance.[89] This may include retraining with new sets of data. If the retraining identifies issues, for example, the modified algorithm now provides erroneous answers, the manufacturer can notify users.
- Inputs used by the algorithm can be modified without changing the product use. For example, expanding the SaMD's ability to use new sources of the same type of input data or adding different

---

87. 21 C.F.R. § 814.39.

88. *See*, *e.g.* EchoGo Pro, Premarket Notification, K201555 (Dec. 18, 2020); Accelerate Pheno System, Premarket Notification, K192665 (Sept. 15, 2020); Caption Guidance, De Novo Petition, DEN190040 (Feb. 7, 2020).

89. FDA, Proposed Regulatory Framework for Modifications to Artificial Intelligence/Machine Learning (AI/ML)-Based Software as a Medical Device (SaMD)—Discussion Paper and Request for Feedback, 14, https://www.fda.gov/media/122535/download. "Analytical performance" refers to parameters that help underlie the clinical performance, such as reportability, i.e., do the same inputs always yield the identical outputs.

input data types could be modifications related to inputs that do not affect the intended use.
- Intended use refers to a change in the significance of information provided by the SaMD. For example, the manufacturer could claim an expanded intended patient population, for example, all patients, not just adults, or the intended disease population, for example, all solid tumors, not just breast cancer.

Under this framework, following commercialization, the agency will expect manufacturers to monitor the AI/ML device performance and incorporate a documented risk management approach. To maintain continued assurance of safety and effectiveness, FDA also will expect transparency both to users and the agency through reporting of postmarket, realworld performance. If performance no longer meets expectations and problems arise, companies may need to notify users and FDA. This, of course, requires a defined system for learning about and systematically evaluating problems in the field as they arise, as well as reasonably well-defined criteria as to what is to be reported, in what format, and what circumstances prompt reporting.[90] Generally, device manufacturers do not have systems for accessing real world data in real time.

As is the case for traditional devices, the data necessary for FDA to weigh the safety and effectiveness of a device during premarket review will depend on the function of the potential AI/ML, the risks it poses, and its intended uses. Currently, devices that rely on AI/ML are expected to follow the Clinical Evaluation Guidance by the IMDRF.[91] There, AI/ML-based SaMD manufacturers are offered the option to submit a plan for post-clearance/post-approval modifications as part of the premarket review of their product. FDA's premarket review would examine "the SaMD's performance, the manufacturer's plan for modifications, and the ability of the manufacturer to manage and control resultant risks of the modifications."[92] This framework relies on what FDA is calling a "predetermined change control plan." The predetermined change control plan includes two elements:

90. 21 C.F.R. pt. 803 (general requirements of reporting device malfunctions and adverse events).

91. http://www.imdrf.org/docs/imdrf/final/technical/imdrf-tech-170921-samd-n41-clinical-evaluation_1.pdf.

92. https://www.fda.gov/media/122535/download, at 10.

1. SaMD Pre-Specifications (SPS)—anticipated modifications to "performance" or "inputs," or changes related to the "intended use" of AI/ML-based SaMD
2. Algorithm Change Protocol (ACP)—a step-by-step delineation of the data and procedures to be followed so that the modification achieves its goals and the device remains safe and effective after the modification.

FDA listed three examples that demonstrate this concept of establishing an SPS and its corresponding ACP:

1. "[c]hanges that involve improvements in performance, or changes in input, without affecting the intended use of the SaMD,"
2. "an increase in the significance of the information provided to the user for the same healthcare situation or condition," and
3. "certain changes related to the intended use."[93]

In the first two examples, an ACP could be created, reviewed, and agreed on between the FDA and manufacturer. This would require an appropriate level of pre-specifications, which would be no trivial task. In the third example, a manufacturer might want to broaden the patient population for its SaMD. This might be for a new patient population where there was not enough information to originally support a proposed indication for use. That manufacturer may show the clinical association between the disease and input data type in the broader patient population. The manufacturer may also include a data collection plan and algorithm testing for this new population. This concept has potential applicability for other types of devices; the concept of device evolution or expanded utility is not unique to software-based products. In fact, the concept of a change protocol is not entirely novel and has been used in some software and diagnostic products previously.[94]

If the modification is beyond the intended use for which the SaMD was previously approved or cleared, manufacturers are expected to submit a new marketing application. FDA says it may then do a "focused review" of the proposed SPS and ACP for a particular SaMD. Manufacturers can

93. *Id.* at 11–12.

94. *See*, *e.g.* EyeArt, Premarket Notification, K200667 (Aug. 3, 2020). Caption Guidance, De Novo Petition, DEN190040 (Feb. 7, 2020). FDA, Guidance for Industry and FDA Staff, Infectious Disease Next Generation Sequencing Based Diagnostic Devices: Microbial Identification and Detection of Antimicrobial Resistance and Virulence Markers (May 2016).

engage with FDA through the pre-submission process,[95] obtain concurrence from the review division,[96] or submit a premarket submission.

Central to FDA's approach for AI/ML-based SaMD, as with its regulation of all devices, is assuring the safety and effectiveness of products. Implementing mechanisms that provide transparency and allow for the monitoring of real-world performance are critical. For instance, FDA maintains it is essential that device modifications be communicated to stakeholders so that they know about the change. These customer communications could take a variety of forms, including software notifications, e-mails, and letters. Companies will need to decide whether these communications constitute corrections or removals that must be reported to FDA.[97]

Real-word performance monitoring will require developers to gather data in a manner that device companies have not traditionally done. They will need to learn about how their products are used, identify areas for improvement opportunities, and respond to safety or usability concerns. Given that these products differ from conventional devices by evolving through design, it is not surprising that FDA will expect more in the way of monitoring real-world performance than for traditional devices.

Based on feedback to the 2019 discussion paper, in January 2021, FDA issued an additional documents: an "Artificial Intelligence/Machine Learning (AI/ML)-Based Software as a Medical Device (SaMD) Action Plan" (AI/ML Action Plan).[98] The AI/ML Action Plan sets forth a five part plan that includes (1) creating a tailored regulatory framework for AI/ML-based software, which the Agency appears to plan to do through guidance; (2) encourage harmonized development of Good Machine Learning Practice (GMLP) through additional FDA participation in collaborative communities and consensus standards development efforts; (3) create a patient-centered approach to AL/ML-transparency, which the agency said it will do by holding a public workshop on how device labeling supports transparency to users and enhances trust in AI/ML-based devices; (4) "support regulatory science efforts to develop methodology for the evaluation and improvement of machine learning algorithms, including for the identification and elimination of bias, and for the evalu-

95. *See Guidance for Industry and FDA Staff, Requests for Feedback and Meetings for Medical Device Submissions: The Q-Submission Program*, FDA (May 7, 2019), https://www.fda.gov/media/114034/download.

96. https://www.fda.gov/files/medical%20devices/published/US-FDA-Artificial-Intelligence-and-Machine-Learning-Discussion-Paper.pdf.

97. *See* 21 C.F.R. pt. 806.

98. https://www.fda.gov/media/145022/download.

ation and promotion of algorithm robustness" through the agency's work with centers of excellence; and (5) establish and support a voluntary pilot program for real-world performance monitoring of AI/ML SaMD.[99]

VII. Conclusion

FDA's regulation of devices has never been static. The statutory and regulatory requirements have shifted dramatically since enactment of the Medical Device Amendments of 1976.[100] Yet, if the law has changed materially over the past four decades, the devices have changed far more. Digital health, by assuming so many different forms at such a rapid pace, presents significant challenges to the existing regulatory regime. Devices that exist now would have seemed fantastical 15 years ago, and it is hard to envision what new products that will be developed in the next few years will be capable of accomplishing.

FDA is well aware of those challenges. In its conclusion to the AI/ML Action Plan FDA noted how that this is a rapidly changing field. That comment applies to the field of digital health care product generally. How FDA addresses the explosion of digital health products will have a major impact on the agency, manufacturers, the health care industry, patients and consumers, and the growth of the digital health industry.

99. AI/ML Action Plan at 3-6.

100. https://www.govinfo.gov/content/pkg/STATUTE-90/pdf/STATUTE-90-Pg539.pdf.

CHAPTER 3

Data, Clinical Trials, and Good Clinical Practices

Gerard Prud'homme, Kristin Zielinski Duggan, Megana Sankaran[1]

I. Clinical Trials Generally

Medical device companies developing submissions to FDA must first determine whether clinical data is required to demonstrate the safety and effectiveness of an investigational device. Clinical data is essentially always necessary to support the safety and effectiveness of Class III devices and may also be needed to support market applications for Class II devices. FDA uses the term "sponsor" to describe a person who takes responsibility for and initiates a clinical investigation.

A. Clinical Studies Supporting Premarket Applications

The type of device and the attendant marketing approval pathway dictate significantly different potential approaches to designing clinical studies. The type of submission shapes variables such as number of patients and complexity of study design, for example, whether the "gold standard" double-blind randomized-controlled trial (RCT) must be conducted, or if a simpler open-label observational approach is all that is required.

Higher-risk and innovative moderate-risk devices in particular will necessitate clinical evidence. However, these frequently do not require large randomized trials—small trials and use of data sources such as registries, clinical experience, and modeling techniques are often sufficient to reach FDA's threshold for valid scientific evidence.

1. The authors would like to acknowledge the assistance of Sandra Milena McCarthy and Eriko Yoshimaru in preparing this chapter.

1. Studies Supporting 510(k) Premarket Notifications

The vast majority of devices reach the market via application for clearance through the 510(k) pathway. From 2010 through 2019, on average, 3,000 devices a year received 510(k) marketing clearance.

Devices utilizing the 510(k) pathway must demonstrate that a new device is substantially equivalent to a predicate device (a device that is already cleared or approved). Compared to the predicate device, the new device must have the same intended use and the same technological characteristics, or must show that differences in technological characteristics do not raise novel questions regarding safety and effectiveness.

In recent years, approximately 10 percent of 510(k) submissions require clinical data. Clinical studies are most likely to be necessary when there are important differences with the predicate device, such as a significant change in technology. Study types will be determined by questions that cannot be addressed in bench and animal testing and the amount of difference that exists between the new device and the predicate. In addition, depending on the device type, clinical data may also be required if a predicate device's submission was supported by clinical data.

From 2010 to 2019, only about 2 percent of cleared 510(k) devices included a clinical trial registered on clinicaltrials.gov. This suggests that a relatively small proportion of clinical studies carried out for 510(k) submissions may be large-scale robust clinical studies.

2. Studies Supporting De Novo Applications

The De Novo submission pathway is available for novel devices of low or moderate risk, where there is no appropriate predicate and whose type has not been classified previously. Rather than submit the more time- and resource-intensive premarket approval (PMA) application, a company may request De Novo down classification for such a device. If granted, the De Novo request establishes a new "device type," along with its classification, regulation, necessary controls, and product code.

Unlike 510(k)'s, in virtually all cases in recent years, clinical studies have been required to support De Novo applications due to the lack of a predicate device on which to base an assessment of safety and effectiveness. Clinical studies will generally focus on device performance and may be determined largely by the questions that are not easily addressed by bench and animal studies.

Although use of the relatively new De Novo mechanism has increased steadily,[2] the amount and type of clinical data the agency requires appears

2. In the first 15 years following the creation of the classification process by the Food and Drug Administration Modernization Act (FDAMA) of 1997, there

to be quite variable. The type of study and amount of data required is highly dependent on the type of product and the level of risk. For example, in 2019, a De Novo granted for a novel diagnostic required several thousand prospective samples (https://www.accessdata.fda.gov/cdrh_docs/reviews/DEN180056.pdf), and a De Novo for a software device to control insulin delivery involved a prospective, controlled, multicenter pivotal study with 168 patients, in addition to analyses of human factors and other safety issues (https://www.accessdata.fda.gov/cdrh_docs/reviews/DEN190034.pdf). Conversely, a De Novo granted in 2018 for software to triage intracranial hemorrhage cases in a radiologist's worklist was supported by an analysis of 300 retrospectively collected CT images (https://www.accessdata.fda.gov/cdrh_docs/reviews/DEN170073.pdf).

3. Studies Supporting PMA Applications

Marketing authorization of the highest risk devices (Class III) requires submission of a premarket approval (PMA) application, the most rigorous approval pathway for medical devices. Devices that must be authorized through PMAs support or sustain human life, are substantially important to preventing impairment of human health, or have potential for unreasonable risk of illness or injury.

For a PMA application to be approved by FDA, the applicant must provide reasonable assurance of the safety and effectiveness of the investigational device that is the subject of the application. Although manufacturers may submit any form of evidence to FDA in an attempt to substantiate the safety and effectiveness of a device, the agency only relies on valid scientific evidence to determine whether there is reasonable assurance that the device is safe and effective. See 21 C.F.R. § 860.7(c)(1). Valid scientific evidence is defined in 21 C.F.R. § 860.7(c)(2) as evidence from

- well-controlled investigations,
- partially controlled studies,
- studies and objective trials without matched controls,
- well-documented case histories conducted by qualified experts, and
- reports of significant human experience with a marketed device, from which it can fairly and responsibly be concluded by

---

were only 76 total completed submissions. After the process was revamped in 2012 (FDASIA) to allow for direct submissions, annual numbers of classification requests increased significantly. From 2013 to 2019, there were a total of 417 classification requests.

qualified experts that there is reasonable assurance of the safety and effectiveness of a device under its conditions of use. Clinical studies are almost always required to provide such assurance of safety and effectiveness for PMA devices.

Because PMA devices present significant potential for benefit or harm, requirements for PMA clinical studies supporting PMA applications are typically more complex and extensive than for the other approval pathways.

Most PMAs will involve first-in-human studies and/or feasibility or pilot studies prior to initiating a pivotal study. Pivotal studies are often multicenter randomized control trials, but depending on the nature of the subject device and the available data, historical controls and use of standard of care as a control can be acceptable.

Sample sizes need to be statistically justified and tend to be several hundred patients. Pivotal studies are hypothesis-driven, which necessitates careful statistical considerations in initial design to assure that a study is sufficiently powered to show that results for endpoints are not due to chance.

Depending on the nature of the device and indication for use, pivotal studies must carefully control the data input for factors such as length of follow-up, number of visits, and procedures and assessments at each visit.

4. Studies Supporting HDE Applications

The humanitarian device exemption (HDE) is a marketing approval pathway designed to provide incentives for device developers to address the needs of small patient populations. Designation as a humanitarian use device (HUD) requires that the device be targeted to treat conditions that affect "not more than 8,000" people in the United States per year.

Of 36 HDE approvals from 2007 to 2019, 25 (69 percent) included at least one prospective clinical study, whereas 11 (31 percent) relied exclusively on analysis of retrospective data or case experiences. Of the 25 prospective studies, 21 (or 84 percent) were single-arm studies and only three were randomized studies.

Devised to reach a small population, HDE studies typically rely on small sample sizes. Prospective trials can range from as few as 20 to slightly over 200, although sample sizes of 30 to 50 have been the most common.

B. Medical Device Clinical Study Phases

1. First-in-Human Studies

A first-in-human (FIH) study is a one in which a device for a specific indication is evaluated for the first time in human subjects.[3] These studies are typically small, and are used to determine whether the device is suitable for clinical use and whether changes are needed. In this way, an FIH study may be viewed as a type of design validation. Typically, only devices with novel technology require FIH studies.

2. Early Feasibility Studies

Designed to increase the efficiency of the device development process and promote initiation of early studies in the United States instead of overseas, Investigational Device Exemption (IDE) applications for early feasibility studies (EFS) of significant-risk devices allow for clinical evaluation of devices early in development, typically before the device design has been finalized.[4] An early feasibility study may be intended to assess, for example, whether the device can be successfully delivered, implanted, or used; operator technique; patient characteristics that may impact device performance; or aspects of device design.

An EFS may be supported by less nonclinical data than generally required for a traditional feasibility or pivotal study. FDA guidance[5] describes a device evaluation strategy (DES) methodology that should be followed, and provides a detailed table for presenting the DES information, which is based on a risk-benefit assessment.

3. Pilot Studies

A pilot study is usually performed in a small number of patients (<20) and can accomplish preliminary objectives such as providing initial safety and efficacy evidence. A pilot study can provide insight on the appropriate treatment schedule, patient population, and outcome measures for the investigational device. The results of a pilot study are then used to design

3. *Investigational Device Exemptions (IDEs) for Early Feasibility Medical Device Clinical Studies, Including Certain First in Human (FIH) Studies* (Oct. 1, 2013), https://www.fda.gov/regulatory-information/search-fda-guidance-documents/investigational-device-exemptions-ides-early-feasibility-medical-device-clinical-studies-including.

4. *Id.*

5. *Id.* at 15–16.

a pivotal study with a larger number of patients. If studies have been performed with similar devices, a pilot study may not be needed.

Pilot studies often provide sufficient preliminary evidence of the safety of a device to justify studying the device in a larger pivotal study where more patients will be exposed to the investigational device. They can also provide preliminary evidence of the degree of effectiveness of the device, and its relative performance to a control, which may be used in a pivotal study, so that better assumptions underlying sample size calculations can be made.

4. Pivotal Studies

For clinical studies that support medical device marketing applications, a pivotal study provides the primary clinical evidence. Although FDA will review a pilot study for safety data, it generally focuses on the safety and efficacy data from a pivotal study in making a decision on a marketing application. Pivotal clinical studies are usually required to support approval of PMA applications.

5. Other Premarket Studies

As part of the premarket clearance or approval process, FDA may request that data from studies that evaluate the device-user interface be submitted in order to ensure and maximize the likelihood that new medical devices, or changes to a device, are safe and effective for the intended users, uses, and use environments.[6] Human factors and usability studies are conducted during an original premarket approval or clearance process for a new device. Confirmatory studies are generally conducted to validate safety, efficacy, and data integrity associated with changes introduced to a device, or to an existing clinical study in effect.

a. Human Factors

As part of a device's design validation, FDA sometimes recommends that manufacturers conduct human factors studies or simulated-use human factors studies. Human factors refer to human behavior, abilities, limitations, and other characteristics of medical device users. The goal of these smaller-scale studies is to ensure that human factors and any limitations have been applied to the design and development of the device,[7] such

6. *Applying Human Factors and Usability Engineering to Medical Devices—Guidance for Industry and Food and Drug Administration Staff* (Feb. 3, 2016), https://www.fda.gov/media/80481/download.

7. Molly Follette Story, *FDA Perspectives on Human Factors in Device Development—RAPS Webinar* (June 7, 2012), https://www.fda.gov/media/84709/download.

that errors that could cause harm or degrade medical treatment are either eliminated or reduced to the extent possible. This type of study is generally designed after the manufacturer conducts a preliminary analysis and evaluation to identify any potential risks and issues associated with the device.[8]

Human factors studies or validation testing are designed to include:[9]

- The test participants that represent the intended (actual) users of the device.
- All critical tasks are performed during the test.
- The device user interface represents the final design.
- The test conditions are sufficiently realistic to represent actual conditions of use.

FDA has recognized standards for human factors testing and published these standards in *Applying Human Factors and Usability Engineering to Medical Devices Guidance* (2016).[10] Protocols and results for this type of testing are generally included in premarket clearance or premarket approval applications under the performance testing section.

b. Usability

Similarly to human factors studies, usability studies are also designed to evaluate the interactions between the devices and their users. These types of studies evaluate effectiveness, efficiency, ease of user learning, user satisfaction, and intended user interface with the device, as those occur without serious use errors or problems.

For these studies, participants are provided with a series of tasks related to the use of the device, and a facilitator will observe and document use errors, failures, and difficulties associated with the tasks, task success, and task failure.[11] Protocols and results for this type of testing are generally included, along with human factors testing, in premarket clearance or premarket approval applications.

c. Confirmatory

Confirmatory studies are generally designed and conducted to confirm the efficacy and safety of a device after such device has undergone a

8. *Id.*

9. *Premarket Information—Device Design and Documentation Process* (July 2018), https://www.fda.gov/medical-devices/human-factors-and-medical-devices/premarket-information-device-design-and-documentation-processes.

10. *Applying Human Factors, supra* note 6.

11. Story, *supra* note 7.

change; or in a situation where a clinical study is underway and a change to the study protocol has been made, for which FDA has expressed concerns regarding the data collected prior to such change taking effect. These studies generally mirror pre-approved study protocols for the device, with respect to data collection and analysis; provided that such studies will be of a smaller scale, enrolling a fraction of the subjects that participated in the original study.

Plans for confirmatory studies are generally developed through interactive discussions with FDA after the manufacturer communicates the change to FDA through a protocol change notice discussed in Chapter 3.III.H, or in an Interim Report as discussed in Chapter 3.III.J.

Clinical studies supporting 510(k) premarket notifications are often confirmatory in nature.

C. Postmarket Clinical Studies

One of FDA's main concerns when evaluating premarket approvals (PMAs) is ensuring the continued safety and effectiveness of an approved device. FDA employs different tools and enforcement mechanisms to ensure that safety questions and concerns are addressed by the manufacturer after a device has been approved.

1. Post-Approval Studies

One such tool is the requirement that a post-approval study (PAS) be conducted for original PMAs, as a condition of approval under 21 C.F.R. § 814.82(a)(2). FDA requires that post-approval studies be conducted for many but not all PMAs. If such studies are required, FDA notifies the device sponsor prior to PMA approval and obtains the sponsor's agreement to conduct such a study along with agreement on the goals and basic elements of the study. Post-approval studies are intended to gather specific information to address unresolved questions about the performance or experience with an approved medical device as they transition out of a controlled clinical trial environment and enter real world utilization.[12]

FDA may approve a device even when there is some uncertainty regarding certain benefits or risks if this uncertainty is sufficiently balanced by other factors, including the overall benefit/risk profile and the extent of postmarket controls. Examples from FDA's 2015 Guidance on

12. *Procedures for Handling Post-Approval Studies Imposed by PMA Order—Guidance for Industry and FDA Staff* (June 15, 2009), https://www.fda.gov/media/71327/download.

pre/postmarket balance include mature technology, urgent public health need, assay migration studies for IVDs, long-term performance, and rare adverse events among others.[13] Post-approval studies have been required by FDA for various reasons, including long-term follow-up of implantable devices (e.g., six- to eight-year postmarket follow-up, whereas two-year follow-up is required premarket), studies assessing the impact of serious adverse events identified during the pivotal studies, and real-world experience in the United States with the device (outside of a controlled clinical trial environment) under a developed training program.

Post-approval studies are designed and finalized through joint collaboration between the manufacturer and FDA during the PMA review process. The agreed upon PAS protocol is communicated in the PMA approval order[14] and it includes the following elements: (1) primary and secondary endpoints (including success criteria); (2) follow-up schedule and assessments; (3) statistical analysis methods; and (4) expected study milestone dates. Changes to the protocol by the manufacturer must be requested of FDA through a PMA supplement.

2. Postmarket Surveillance

Another tool utilized by FDA, which stems from authority granted by Congress to the agency, is the postmarket surveillance study required under section 522 of the Federal Food Drug, and Cosmetic (FD&C) Act, also referred to as "522 studies." FDA has the authority to order, either at the time of approval or clearance or at any time thereafter during the life cycle of a device, postmarket surveillance for any Class II or Class III device: (1) for which failure of the device would be reasonably likely to have a serious adverse health consequence;[15] (2) is expected to have significant use in pediatric populations;[16] (3) is intended to be implanted in the human body for more than one year;[17] (4) is intended to be a life-sustaining or life-supporting device used outside of a user facility.[18]

---

13. *Balancing Premarket and Postmarket Data Collection for Devices Subject to Premarket Approval—Guidance for Industry and Food and Drug Administration Staff* (Apr. 2015), https://www.fda.gov/media/88381/download.

14. PMA approval orders are published on FDA's PMA searchable database, https://www.accessdata.fda.gov/scripts/cdrh/cfdocs/cfPMA/pma.cfm.

15. Section 522(a)(1)(A)(i) of the act, 21 U.S.C. § 3601.

16. Section 522(a)(1)(A)(ii) of the act, 21 U.S.C. § 3601.

17. Section 522(a)(1)(A)(iii)(I) of the act, 21 U.S.C. § 3601.

18. Section 522(a)(1)(A)(iii)(II) of the act, 21 U.S.C. § 3601.

FDA is authorized to order prospective 522 studies for a duration of up to 36 months unless the manufacturer and FDA agree to extend that timeframe or, if the device is expected to have significant use in pediatric populations, and an extended period is necessary in order to assess the impact of the device on growth and development, or the effects of growth, development, activity level, or other factors on the safety or efficacy of the device. These studies must commence no later than 15 months after the day the order is issued. In its *2016 Postmarket Surveillance Guidance*,[19] FDA describes different postmarket surveillance study designs that may be used depending on the particular public health question.

Examples of concerns or inquiries that may require postmarket surveillance include:

- To understand the nature, severity, or frequency of suspected problems reported in adverse event reports or in the published literature.
- To obtain more information on device performance associated with real-world clinical practice.
- To address long-term or infrequent safety and effectiveness issues for implantable and other devices for which the premarket testing provided more limited information.
- To better define the association between problems and devices when unexpected or unexplained serious adverse events occur after a device is marketed.

Some highly publicized devices for which their manufacturers have been ordered to conduct 522 studies include:

- *Urogynecological surgical mesh devices.* On January 3, 2012, the FDA ordered 522 studies by manufacturers of urogynecologic surgical mesh devices to address specific safety and effectiveness concerns related to mini-sling devices for SUI and surgical mesh used for transvaginal repair of pelvic organ prolapse. This order was based on the FDA's evaluation of the published literature, analysis of adverse events reported to the FDA, and feedback from the Obstetrics and Gynecology Devices Panel of the Medical Device Advisory Committee.[20]

19. *Postmarket Surveillance under Section 522 of the Federal Food, Drug, and Cosmetic Act—Guidance for Industry and Food and Drug Administration Staff* (May 2016), https://www.fda.gov/media/81015/download.

20. *FDA's Activities: Urogynecologic Surgical Mesh* (Oct. 2019), https://www.fda.gov/medical-devices/urogynecologic-surgical-mesh-implants/fdas

- *Metal on Metal (MoM) total hip replacement devices.* In May 2011, the FDA issued 522 orders instructing all five U.S. manufacturers of MoM total hip replacement devices on the market at that time to conduct a postmarket surveillance study of their devices. These postmarket studies consisted of a clinical study of patient ion levels and clinical outcomes, as well as a separate explant analysis study of failed devices.[21]

Manufacturers will submit a postmarket surveillance plan to FDA for its approval. Once approved and postmarket surveillance has commenced, manufacturers must submit interim and final postmarket surveillance reports as required in the approval of the postmarket surveillance plan. Interim reports are submitted every six months for the first two years, and annually thereafter, unless otherwise negotiated with FDA. 522 studies are published in FDA's searchable database.[22]

A failure to comply with a postmarket surveillance requirement under 522 is a prohibited act under the FD&C Act and renders the device misbranded, which may lead to enforcement actions, including warning letters, seizure of products, injunction, prosecution, and/or civil money penalties.

3. Postmarket Studies

While post approval studies and postmarket surveillance studies are mandated by FDA, postmarket studies are not mandated by FDA and are undertaken by the manufacturer voluntarily. A manufacturer may initiate a voluntary study for different reasons, which may include a manufacturer seeking to gain additional information for the launch of a related product; a manufacturer seeking to expand the claims for an approved device; a manufacturer gathering information for a future publication; or a manufacturer seeking to learn about the commercial experience and performance of the device.

It is important to note that postmarket clinical investigations of devices must have an approved IDE or be exempt from IDE regulations. If a manufacturer decides to undertake a voluntary clinical study that is exempt from IDE requirements under 21 C.F.R. § 812.2(c), IDE approval

-activities-urogynecologic-surgical-mesh.

21. *Metal-on-Metal Hip Implants: The FDA's Activities* (Mar. 2019), https://www.fda.gov/medical-devices/metal-metal-hip-implants/metal-metal-hip-implants-fdas-activities.

22. FDA 522 Postmarket Surveillance Studies Database, https://www.accessdata.fda.gov/scripts/cdrh/cfdocs/cfpma/pss.cfm?s=a.

is not necessary (e.g., where the study is being conducted completely on label or is a nonsignificant risk study). Similarly, if a manufacturer decides to undertake a voluntary study to expand the uses of a significant risk device that was previously indicated for other uses, or is conducting testing to assess safety or effectiveness of the device, the manufacturer must first obtain IDE approval prior to enrolling any patients in the study. IDE-exempted studies and significant-risk devices are further described in Chapter 3.III.

4. Investigator-Initiated Studies

After approval or clearance, physicians may perform their own studies of a device. These studies are called investigator-initiated studies or trials, or sponsor-investigator studies under 21 C.F.R. § 812.3(o). Physicians typically perform these studies separate to and independent from device manufacturers. Investigators in these studies are responsible for both investigator and sponsor duties, as described later. Depending on the device and indication, an IDE may be needed for the study.

II. Good Clinical Practices

A. Generally

Good clinical practices (GCPs) are an ethical and scientific quality standard for the design, conduct, performance, monitoring, auditing, recording, analyses, and reporting of **clinical** trials. The goals of GCPs are to protect the rights, safety, and welfare of humans participating in research; to ensure the quality, reliability, and integrity of data collected; and to provide standards and guidelines for the conduct of clinical research.

While there is a single, unified regulation for good manufacturing practices (namely, the quality system regulation found in 21 C.F.R. Part 820), there is no single GCP regulation. Rather, GCPs refer to the collection of regulations and requirements that must be complied with while conducting a clinical study. These regulations apply to manufacturers, sponsors, clinical investigators, and IRBs. Although the Center for Devices and Radiological Health (CDRH) has not historically codified GCPs, the agency adopted the International Conference on Harmonization (ICH) *E6(R2) Good Clinical Practice: Integrated Addendum to ICH E6(R1)* in February of 2018.

FDA regulations that essentially comprise the current state of GCPs for medical device clinical studies in the United States are:

- Electronic Records; Electronic Signatures (21 C.F.R. Part 11)
- Protection of Human Subjects (Informed Consent) (21 C.F.R. Part 50)[23]
- Financial Disclosure by Clinical Investigators (21 C.F.R. Part 54)
- Institutional Review Boards (21 C.F.R. Part 56)
- Investigational Device Exemptions (21 C.F.R. Part 812)

Important aspects of each of these regulations are described more fully later in the chapter.

Further to the requirements placed on medical device clinical study sponsors by these good clinical practice regulations, sponsors must ensure the quality of their clinical trial data during the conduct of the study. Given the scrutiny with which FDA is currently evaluating clinical trial practices, a sponsor should consider implementing a quality system for its clinical studies, to ensure the integrity of the data, ease the premarket review process, and prevent any clinical holds on the company's submissions. Please see Section 3.V.E for further detail on clinical study quality systems.

B. Electronic Records and Electronic Signatures (21 C.F.R. § 11)

This regulation sets forth the criteria under which the agency considers electronic records, electronic signatures, and handwritten signatures executed to electronic records to be trustworthy, reliable, and generally equivalent to paper records and handwritten signatures executed on paper. Additional information regarding the use of electronic records can be found in *Guidance for Industry: Computerized Systems Used in Clinical Trials* (April 1999); *Guidance for Industry: Electronic Source Data in Clinical Investigations* (September 2013); and *Guidance for Industry—Part 11, Electronic Records; Electronic Signatures—Scope and Application* (September 2003) (https://

23. *See also* the following Federal Register notices with respect to 21 C.F.R. pt. 50: 71 Fed. Reg. 32827, 32834 (June 7, 2006), https://www.govinfo.gov/content/pkg/FR-2006-06-07/html/E6-8790.htm; 76 Fed. Reg. 256–270 (Jan. 4, 2011), https://www.govinfo.gov/content/pkg/FR-2011-01-04/html/2010-33193.htm; 83 Fed. Reg. 57378–57386 (Nov. 15, 2018), https://www.govinfo.gov/content/pkg/FR-2018-11-15/html/2018-24822.htm; 83 Fed. Reg. 65322–65323 (Dec. 20, 2018), https://www.govinfo.gov/content/pkg/FR-2018-12-20/html/2018-27519.htm; and 84 Fed. Reg. 5968–5969 (Feb. 25, 2019,) https://www.govinfo.gov/content/pkg/FR-2019-02-25/html/2019-03195.htm.

www.fda.gov/regulatory-information/search-fda-guidance-documents/part-11-electronic-records-electronic-signatures-scope-and-application).

C. Informed Consent, Protection of Human Subjects (21 C.F.R. § 50)

This regulation provides the requirements and general elements of informed consent. The foundations for the ethical conduct of clinical research are found in the Nuremberg Code, the Declaration of Helsinki, the Belmont Report, and the International Conference on Harmonization (ICH-GCP). Thus, GCP compliance provides public assurance that the rights, safety, and well-being of human subjects involved in research are protected.

All clinical research that involves humans as subjects must be performed ethically and in accordance with federal and state regulations. Prior to engaging in research involving human subjects, an investigator must obtain informed consent from the subject. The subject must be given all of the necessary information that a reasonable person would want to have in order to make a decision to participate. The subject must also be given sufficient opportunity to consider whether or not to participate in the study. Informed consent must follow the proscribed format included in 21 C.F.R. § 50.20. The regulation explicitly requires that informed consent be communicated in language and at a reading level that can be understood by the subject. In addition, the informed consent cannot include any form of exculpatory language that appears or suggests the waiver of any of the subjects' legal rights or releases, or appears to release the investigator, the sponsor, the institution, or its agents from liability for negligence.

Another explicit requirement for informed consent is the need to satisfy a specific set of key elements described as follows:

- A statement that the study involves research
- The expected duration of the subject's participation
- A description of the procedures to be followed
- Identification of any procedures that are experimental
- A description of any reasonably foreseeable risks or discomforts to the subject
- A description of any benefits to the subject or to others that may reasonably be expected from the research
- A disclosure of appropriate alternative procedures or courses of treatment, if any
- A statement describing the extent to which confidentiality of records identifying the subject will be maintained

- For research involving more than minimal risk, an explanation as to whether any compensation if injury occurs
- An explanation of whom to contact for answers to questions about the research and in the event of a research-related injury
- A statement that participation is voluntary and may be discontinued at any time, and any refusal to participate will not result in penalty or loss of benefits to which the subject is otherwise entitled[24]
- If the study will be registered on ClinicalTrials.gov,[25] the following statement must be included in the informed consent: "A description of this clinical trial will be available on http://www.ClinicalTrials.gov, as required by U.S. Law. This Web site will not include information that can identify you. At most, the Web site will include a summary of the results. You can search this Web site at any time."

The regulation also sets forth additional elements to include in the informed consent when it is appropriate. See also Questions and Answers on Informed Consent Elements, 21 CFR § 50.25(c)—Small Entity Compliance Guide—Guidance for Sponsors, Investigators, and Institutional Review Boards (February 2012) (https://www.fda.gov/regulatory-information/search-fda-guidance-documents/questions-and-answers-informed-consent-elements-21-cfr-ss-5025c); and Informed Consent—Draft Guidance for IRBs, Clinical Investigators, and Sponsors (July 2014) (https://www.fda.gov/regulatory-information/search-fda-guidance-documents/informed-consent).

1. Exception from Informed Consent

FDA has developed regulations that explicitly list a few instances in which informed consent from a subject is not required in emergency circumstances. In order to be accepted under § 50.23, both the investigator and an unrelated physician must certify in writing all of the following:

- The research study must involve subjects that are confronting a life-threatening situation that necessitates the use of the test article.

24. Informed Consent Checklist, HHS.gov, https://www.hhs.gov/ohrp/regulations-and-policy/guidance/checklists/index.html; *see also* 21 C.F.R. § 50.25.

25. ClinicalTrials.gov is a web-based resource that provides patients, their family members, health care professionals, researchers, and the public with access to information on publicly and privately supported clinical studies.

- Informed consent cannot be obtained from the subject because of an inability to communicate with, or obtain legally effective consent from, the subject.
- Time is not sufficient to obtain consent from the subject's legal representative.
- No alternative method of approved or generally recognized therapy that provides an equal or greater likelihood of saving the life of the subject.[26]

If immediate use of the test device is, in the investigator's opinion, required to preserve the life of the subject, and time is not sufficient to obtain the independent determination required in advance of using the test device, this must be done and submitted to the IRB within five working days after the use of the device.

Another exception to informed consent requirements pertains to the use of the device for emergency research (§ 50.24). "Emergency Research," as explained by the FDA in its guidance, refers to investigation that involves human subjects who have a life-threatening medical condition that necessitates urgent intervention (for which available treatments are unproven or unsatisfactory), and who, because of their condition cannot provide informed consent.[27] An example of such a device would be a device intended to resuscitate subjects following a heart attack. Additional responsibilities imposed on parties involved with emergency research studies include a consultation with representatives of the community(ies) in which the research will be conducted and from which the subjects will be drawn, public notice to the community and subject pool of information regarding the study before the start and following its completion, and the establishment of an independent monitoring committee to oversee the study.[28]

Additional guidance regarding informed consent can be found in Questions and Answers on Informed Consent Elements (21 CFR § 50.25(c)—Guidance for Sponsors, Investigators, and Institutional Review Boards (February 2012); Guidance on Exculpatory Language in Informed Consent (August 19, 2011); and Impact of Certain Provisions of the Revised Common Rule on FDA-Regulated Clinical Investigations

---

26. 21 C.F.R. § 50.23.

27. *Exception from Informed Consent Requirements for Emergency Research—Guidance for Institutional Review Boards, Clinical Investigators and Sponsors* (Apr. 2013), https://www.fda.gov/regulatory-information/search-fda-guidance-documents/exception-informed-consent-requirements-emergency-research.

28. *Id.*

(October 2018). In addition to obtaining informed consent, an overview of the responsibilities of a person who conducts a clinical investigation to protect human subjects and ensure the integrity of the data can be found in Investigator Responsibilities—Protecting the Rights, Safety, and Welfare of Study Subjects—Guidance for Industry (October 2009).

D. Institutional Review Board (IRB) Review (21 C.F.R. § 56)

As defined by FDA, Institutional Review Boards (IRBs) are "appropriately constituted group[s] that have been formally designated to review and monitor biomedical research involving human subjects. IRBs are tasked with conducting an initial and continuing review of research to approve the research, determine modifications, or disprove the research" proposed by a particular applicant.[29]

The purpose of the IRB is to ensure both in advance and by periodic review, that appropriate steps are taken to protect the rights and welfare of humans participating as subjects in the research. To accomplish this purpose, IRBs use a group process to review research protocols and related materials (e.g., informed consent documents and investigator brochures) to ensure protection of the rights and welfare of human subjects of research.[30] Each IRB that reviews FDA-regulated studies is required to register with the Department of Health and Human Services (HHS).[31] Registration information must be renewed every three years.

No clinical investigation, unless otherwise exempted under 21 C.F.R. § 54.104 or waived by FDA, in support of a marketing application with the FDA, can be initiated unless the investigation has been reviewed and approved by the IRB.

It is important to note that an institution does not need to establish its own IRB. FDA regulations permit an institution without an IRB to arrange for an "outside" IRB to be responsible for initial and continuing review of studies conducted at the non-IRB institution. Such arrangements should be documented in writing.[32]

---

29. *See IDE Institutional Review Boards*, https://www.fda.gov/medical-devices/investigational-device-exemption-ide/ide-institutional-review-boards-irb.

30. *Id.*

31. *IRB Registration—Guidance for Institutional Review Boards (IRBs) Frequently Asked Questions* (July 2009), https://www.fda.gov/media/77059/download.

32. *Frequently Asked Questions—Information Sheet Guidance for Institutional Review Boards and Clinical Investigators* (Jan. 1998), https://www.fda.gov/regulatory-information/search-fda-guidance-documents/institutional-review-boards-frequently-asked-questions#IRBMember; *see also IRB Continuing Review after Clinical Investigation Approval—Guidance for Institutional Review Boards*

Further, the 21st Century Cures Act passed in 2016 provides for centralized IRBs for medical device trials.[33] The law eliminated the previous requirement that the sponsor of a medical device trial must use a local IRB. The rationale for using local IRBs had been that they not only approve trial protocols but also perform various site-specific tasks for clinical trials, such as training staff, and ensuring compliance with research protocols and HIPAA privacy rules.

1. IRB Approval

In order to approve research under the purview of FDA, the IRB must determine that all of the following requirements are satisfied:

- Risks to subjects are minimized by using procedures that are consistent with research design and that do not unnecessarily expose subjects to risk; and whenever appropriate, by using procedures already being performed on the subjects.
- Risks to subjects are reasonable in relation to anticipated benefits, if any, to subjects, arising only from the research and the importance of the knowledge that may be expected to result.
- Selection of subjects is equitable. In making this assessment, the IRB should take into account the purposes of the research and the setting in which the research will be conducted and should be aware of the special problems of research involving vulnerable populations, such as children, prisoners, pregnant women, handicapped or mentally disabled persons, or economically or educationally disadvantaged persons.
- Informed consent will be sought from each prospective subject or the subject's legally authorized representative, and properly documented.
- Where appropriate, the research plan makes adequate provision for monitoring the data collected to ensure the safety of subjects.
- Where appropriate, there are adequate provisions to protect the privacy of subjects and to maintain the confidentiality of data.[34]

Clinical Investigators, and Sponsors (Feb. 2012), https://www.fda.gov/regulatory-information/search-fda-guidance-documents/irb-continuing-review-after-clinical-investigation-approval.

33. *See Using a Centralized IRB Review Process in Multicenter Clinical Trials—Guidance for Industry* (Mar. 2006), https://www.fda.gov/regulatory-information/search-fda-guidance-documents/using-centralized-irb-review-process-multicenter-clinical-trials.

34. 21 C.F.R. § 56.111.

Furthermore, as explained in Section 3.III.B, an IRB initially determines if an investigation involves a significant risk (SR) or nonsignificant risk (NSR) study device.

In order to comply with FDA regulations, IRBs must follow written procedures and must also maintain certain records and reports. The composition of IRBs is described in Section 3.IV.C.1.c regarding study Organizational Units.

FDA has several documents relating to IRBs in clinical studies, including the following:

- *Institutional Review Board (IRB) Written Procedures—Guidance for Institutions and IRBs* (May 2018) (checklist) (https://www.fda.gov/regulatory-information/search-fda-guidance-documents/institutional-review-board-irb-written-procedures)
- *FDA Institutional Review Board Inspections—Information Sheet Guidance for IRBs, Clinical Investigators, and Sponsors* (January 2006) (https://www.fda.gov/media/75192/download)
- *Sponsor–Investigator–IRB Interrelationship—Information Sheet Guidance for Institutional Review Boards and Clinical Investigators* (January 1998) (https://www.fda.gov/regulatory-information/search-fda-guidance-documents/sponsor-investigator-irb-interrelationship)

E. Ethics—The Common Rule

The Federal Policy for the Protection of Human Subjects was originally promulgated as the Common Rule in 1991. On January 18, 2017, HHS issued a final rule to update the Common Rule. This regulation sets forth requirements for IRBs, informed consent, and other provisions that are critical in ensuring the ethical conduct of human subjects' research. The regulation applies to federally funded clinical studies.[35]

The Common Rule proposes to promote uniformity, understanding, and compliance with human subject protections and to create a uniform body of regulations across the federal departments and agencies.

The 2017 Common Rule revisions were intended to better protect human subjects involved in research, while facilitating valuable research and reducing burden, delay, and ambiguity for investigators. Some of these revisions, relevant to device investigations included the following:

35. *Federal Policy for the Protection of Human Subjects ("Common Rule")*, HHS.gov, https://www.hhs.gov/ohrp/regulations-and-policy/regulations/common-rule/index.html.

- Authorization of a single IRB to be used for cooperative site studies.
- Removal of the requirement to conduct continuing review of ongoing research studies that undergo expedited review and for studies that are merely analyzing study data or are conducting observational follow up.
- Changes related to the requirements of informed consent, including changes relating to the content, organization, and presentation of information included in the consent form and process to facilitate a prospective subject's decision about whether to participate in research as well as changes to the basic and additional elements of consent.[36]

The promulgation of these revisions created certain differences between the FDA and HHS human subject regulations. FDA clarified in 2018 that it is actively working to harmonize its human subject protection regulations consistent with recent changes in the Common Rule.[37] As of the date of publication of this book, no updated guidance on harmonization of the Common Rule with FDA regulations has been finalized.

F. Financial Disclosure by Clinical Investigators (21 C.F.R. § 54)

This regulation covers the disclosure of financial compensation to clinical investigators, which is part of FDA's assessment of the reliability of the clinical data.

The financial disclosure regulation requires applicants who submit a marketing application for a device to submit certain information concerning the compensation to, and financial interests and arrangements of, any clinical investigator conducting clinical studies covered by the regulation. A clinical investigator means a listed or identified investigator or sub-investigator who is directly involved in the treatment or evaluation of research subjects, including the spouse and each dependent child of the investigator or sub-investigator.[38] The rationale behind this regulation is that investigators with a financial interest in the product may, either consciously or unconsciously, act in a way that would make the study more

36. *See Impact of Certain Provisions of the Revised Common Rule on FDA-Regulated Clinical Investigations—Guidance for Sponsors, Investigators, and Institutional Review Boards* (Oct. 2018), https://www.fda.gov/regulatory-information/search-fda-guidance-documents/impact-certain-provisions-revised-common-rule-fda-regulated-clinical-investigations.

37. *Id.*

38. *See* 21 C.F.R. § 54.2(d).

likely to be successful for the device. Ideally, investigators would have no financial interests that go beyond those that are required to be disclosed, described later.

The regulation applies to clinical studies submitted in premarket notification submissions under section 510(k) of the FD&C Act, reclassification petitions under section 513 of the FD&C Act, premarket approval applications (PMAs) under section 515 of the FD&C Act, or that the applicant or FDA relies on to establish that the product is effective (including studies that show equivalence to an effective product), or any study in which a single investigator makes a significant contribution to the demonstration of safety. IDE sponsors are not required to submit information regarding clinical investigator financial interests or arrangements in IDE applications. They are, however, required to collect this information before a clinical investigator participates in a clinical study.[39]

Financial disclosures are required in order for applicants to certify the absence of certain financial interests and arrangements of clinical investigators that could affect the reliability of data submitted to FDA. If there are such interests, the disclosures are made along with identification of steps taken to minimize the potential for bias (21 C.F.R. § 54.4(a).[40] Such steps might include blinded assessments, assessments by centralized study units (e.g., core lab), or objective (versus subjective) assessments, which would help ensure the device was not treated preferentially over the control, for example.

1. Disclosable Financial Interests and Certification

Applicants are required to submit to FDA a list of all clinical investigators who conducted covered clinical studies and to identify those who are full-time or part-time employees of the sponsor of each covered study (21 C.F.R. § 54.4). A disclosure statement in Form FDA 3455 must be included with a marketing application and must include detailed information about disclosed financial interests and arrangements.

Applicants are required to specifically disclose financial interests in the following scenarios:

- The value of compensation of the clinical investigator could be affected by the outcome of the investigations;

---

39. *See id.* §§ 312.53(c)(4), 812.20(b)(5), 812.43(c)(5).

40. *Financial Disclosure by Clinical Investigators—Guidance for Clinical Investigators, Industry, and FDA Staff* (Feb. 2013), https://www.fda.gov/media/85293/download.

- The clinical investigator has any proprietary interest in the tested product, such as a patent;
- The clinical investigator has any equity interest in the sponsor of the covered study;
- The clinical investigator has any equity interest in a publicly held company;
- The clinical investigator has received payments of other types that exceed $25,000 or payments are made by sponsor to investigator or investigator's institution exclusive of the costs of the clinical study or other clinical studies.

If there are no disclosable financial interests or arrangements as described above, the applicant must only include a certification in Form FDA 3454 that certifies that the clinical investigator has no disclosable financial interests.

If the applicant does not include a certification and/or disclosure, or does not certify that it was unable to obtain the information despite exercising due diligence, the agency may refuse to file the application.[41]

In cases where clinical investigator deliberately submits false information to a sponsor, including information regarding financial disclosures, FDA may disqualify the clinical investigator and will render him or her not eligible to receive investigational devices or to conduct any clinical investigation that supports a marketing application.[42]

Additional information regarding financial disclosure can be found in Guidance for Clinical Investigators, Industry, and FDA Staff: Financial Disclosure by Clinical Investigators (February 2013).

G. IDE Regulations (21 C.F.R. Part 812)

This regulation covers the procedures for the conduct of clinical studies with medical devices including application, responsibilities of sponsors and investigators, labeling, records, and reports. It is described more fully in the next section (Section III).

III. Investigational Device Exemptions (IDEs)

A. Regulations and Guidance

The IDE regulations, found in 21 C.F.R. Part 812, exist to encourage the discovery and development of useful devices intended for human use, while ensuring that such discovery and development remain consistent

41. *Id.*; *see also* 21 C.F.R. § 54.4(c).
42. 21 C.F.R. § 812.119.

with the protection of public health and safety, and with ethical standards.[43] The IDE regulations apply to all clinical investigations of medical devices to determine the safety and effectiveness of such devices. IDE applications are needed for clinical studies of unapproved devices or new intended use of approved devices even if no future marketing application is planned (e.g., investigator-sponsored studies). Regulation of clinical studies is dependent on the risk that the device and the study presents to human health. Depending on the classification of the device (significant risk versus nonsignificant risk), either full IDE requirements or abbreviated requirements will apply to the clinical studies. Certain studies are also exempt, as explained further later in the chapter.

An approved IDE permits a device to be shipped in interstate commerce to be used in a clinical study in order to collect safety and effectiveness data required to support a marketing submission to the FDA. Specifically, it exempts the device from misbranding, registration and listing, premarket notification, performance standards, banned device regulation, records and reports, restricted device requirements, good manufacturing practices, color additive requirements, and unique device identifier requirements. However, IDE devices remain subject to adulteration prohibitions; labeling requirements; import and export requirements; prohibitions on promotion, marketing, and commercialization; as well as prohibitions on representing that the device is safe and effective for the use that is being studied.

The regulations covering IDEs in Part 812 also grant oversight to FDA of the conduct of studies, use of the device, protection of human subjects, institutional review boards, and financial disclosure by clinical investigators. Interpreted together with FDA's guidance documents, these regulations provide the primary regulatory framework for sponsors, clinical investigators, and IRBs engaged in clinical studies for the development of medical devices.

B. Study Risk Determination

The IDE regulation describes three types of studies: significant risk (SR), nonsignificant risk (NSR), and exempt. The agency uses this classification system to determine commensurate levels of regulatory control over these medical device investigations.

A study's classification as SR or NSR ultimately dictates whether an IDE application and FDA approval is required prior to initiating the study and establishes requirements that must be followed during the study.

43. 21 C.F.R. § 812.1.

The sponsor of a clinical study is an individual or organization that initiates and/or finances a clinical trial but often does not actually conduct the investigation. It is the sponsor who makes the initial risk determination and presents that recommendation to the various institutional review boards (IRBs). Each reviewing IRB, after conducting its own review of whether the proposed use of a device in an investigation presents significant risk, must determine whether it agrees with the sponsor's determination, or whether the determination must be modified. A sponsor can proceed to treat a study as an NSR study only if all reviewing IRBs render an NSR decision. However, FDA is the final arbiter on whether a specific device is a significant or nonsignificant risk device and may disagree with the reviewing IRBs.

1. Significant Risk (SR) Device

A significant risk device, as defined in 21 C.F.R. § 812.3(m), is an investigational device that:

> (1) Is intended as an implant and presents a potential for serious risk to the health, safety, or welfare of a subject;
>
> (2) Is purported or represented to be for a use in supporting or sustaining human life and presents a potential for serious risk to the health, safety, or welfare of a subject;
>
> (3) Is for a use of substantial importance in diagnosing, curing, mitigating, or treating disease, or otherwise preventing impairment of human health and presents a potential for serious risk to the health, safety, or welfare of a subject; or
>
> (4) Otherwise presents a potential for serious risk to the health, safety, or welfare of a subject.

For these devices, a full IDE application must be approved by FDA; the protocol and informed consent form must also be approved by IRBs for all participating clinical sites. Examples of devices that are considered SR are surgical lasers for use in various medical specialties, tissue adhesives, breathing gas mixtures, cardiac assist devices, cochlear implants, hemodialyzers, sutures, implantable joint replacement devices, implanted spinal cord stimulators, antepartum home uterine activity monitors, and intraocular lenses.

2. Nonsignificant Risk Devices

Nonsignificant risk devices are those devices that do not present significant risk to subjects, and do not otherwise meet the definition of significant risk device. For these devices, FDA does not require a full review and approval of the clinical study. However, clinical studies for these devices must be approved by an IRB. For these devices, the IRB essentially acts as a surrogate for FDA for review, approval, and continuing review of the NSR device studies.[44] These devices continue to be subject to requirements related to monitoring, records, reporting, and prohibition against promotion.

Examples of devices that are considered NSR are caries removal solution, conventional laparoscopes, digital mammography, and non-implantable electrical incontinence devices. For detailed examples, see FDA's guidance on this issue.[45]

A summary of the requirement differences between NSR and SR studies is presented in Table 3.1.

Table 3.1 Summary of Requirements

	Significant Risk	Nonsignificant Risk
FDA Approval	Yes	No
IRB Approval	Yes	Yes
Informed Consent	Yes	Yes
Reporting	Yes	Limited
Recordkeeping	Yes	Limited

3. IDE-Exempt Devices

Not all clinical investigations are subject to the IDE regulations. In accordance with 21 C.F.R. § 812.2(c), the following types of investigations are exempted from the IDE regulations, with the exception of 21 C.F.R. § 812.119 (disqualification of a clinical investigator):

- Devices in commercial distribution prior to the 1976 Medical Device amendments and those determined to be substantially equivalent to pre-1976 devices when used in accordance with its cleared indications for use
- Certain types of diagnostic devices (if testing is noninvasive, does not require invasive sampling that presents significant risk,

44. *Significant Risk and Nonsignificant Risk Medical Device Studies—Information Sheet Guidance for Institutional Review Boards and Clinical Investigator, and Sponsors* (Jan. 2006), https://www.fda.gov/media/75459/download.

45. *Id.*

does not introduce energy into the subject, and is not used for diagnosis without confirmation by an established diagnostic device/procedure)

- Testing of consumer preference, of a modification, or of a combination of devices in commercial distribution, when not determining safety or effectiveness and not putting subjects at risk
- Veterinary devices or research on/with laboratory animals and labeled as such (per 21 C.F.R. § 812.5(c))
- Custom devices (as defined in 21 C.F.R. § 812.3(b))

Importantly, testing for a *new use* of a previously cleared or approved device is *not* exempted from complying with IDE requirements. Examples of changes of an approved device where a new IDE application would be required include expanding the indication for use of a device with respect to function, target population, organ or organ system, tissue type, disease entity, or analyte. In making such determinations, FDA evaluates the risk profile of the new use, and the public health impact of such use.

C. IDE Application

1. Pre-submission Filings

FDA has established a pre-submission process to allow sponsors to get early feedback prior to formal submission of an IDE application. The success of the IDE pre-submission program (then called the pre-IDE program), which was initiated in 1995, led the agency to expand the program to cover interactions prior to PMAs, HDEs, De Novo requests, and 510(k) submissions.

This voluntary program allows sponsors to get early agency input on clinical studies, which can improve the quality of the submission and shorten subsequent review times. There is a formal submission process (Q-Submission) that provides a mechanism for receiving informal advice from FDA. Interaction with the agency can be through written feedback only or also include a meeting.

Agency feedback is nonbinding on the agency, but it does create a record with meeting minutes. The pre-submission process can be used to ask FDA for a formal Study Risk Determination, that is, whether a planned medical device clinical study is SR, NSR, or exempt. Study Risk Determination requests receive a formal letter response within 90 days. Other appropriate topic areas for pre-submission filings include investigational plans—both in the United States and outside the United States (OUS), particularly for devices that require complex testing, or for novel devices where the data requirements are not well understood. For studies that are NSR or will be conducted entirely OUS, the pre-submission is the only mechanism for obtaining feedback on the study protocol. For SR studies, sponsors are encouraged to submit a full protocol if available in order to obtain the most useful feedback.

The sponsor requesting the meeting or written feedback must prepare a submission identifying the purpose of the meeting, the device description, proposed indications for use, and regulatory history, and include concrete proposals for discussion. The sponsor is encouraged to identify three to four substantial topics for discussion with FDA to enable focused meetings. In addition, FDA recommends that the pre-submission include clear specific questions regarding review issues relevant to a planned IDE.[46] Depending on the type of pre-submission request, the agency allows for a 75- to 90-day review schedule.[47]

Some sponsors of SR studies choose to proceed directly to an IDE without first reviewing the protocol with the agency as part of the pre-submission process. Depending on the circumstances, such an approach may not give FDA adequate opportunity to consider some complex device, testing or clinical study issues given the very short review time for an IDE (30 days), and can result in more rounds of review prior to IDE approval than if the sponsor had filed a pre-submission.

2. IDE Submission

An IDE application must be submitted to FDA when a sponsor intends to use a significant risk device in a clinical study. The required elements of an IDE application are specified in § 812.20(b). IDE applications often take a considerable time to compile and include detailed information regarding the device (including manufacturing) and study protocol, including informed consent, monitoring procedures, and so on. The principal components of the application include:

- *A cover letter.* This typically sets forth a general overview of the IDE application and provides any regulatory history of the device that FDA should be made aware.

46. *Requests for Feedback and Meetings for Medical Device Submissions: The Q-Submission Program—Guidance for Industry and Food and Drug Administration Staff* (May 7, 2019), https://www.fda.gov/media/114034/download.

47. The process is detailed in FDA's guidance document, *id. See also Early Collaboration Meetings Under the FDA Modernization Act (FDAMA); Final Guidance for Industry and for CDRH Staff* (Feb. 2001), https://www.fda.gov/regulatory-information/search-fda-guidance-documents/early-collaboration-meetings-under-fda-modernization-act-fdama-final-guidance-industry-and-cdrh.

- *Name and address of the sponsor*
- *Report of prior investigations.* The report of prior investigations (§ 812.27) compiles reports of all prior clinical, animal, and biocompatibility and other laboratory testing. A bibliography of all publications, adverse or supportive, and copies of all published and unpublished adverse information must be provided. Additionally, the submitter must include statements of compliance with good laboratory practices (GLP) (Part 58) human subject protection requirements (Part 50), and IRB regulations (Part 56).
- *Investigational plan.* Section 812.25 requires the investigational plan to detail the purpose (objectives and duration of the investigation), protocol (methodology), risk analysis, description of the device (components, ingredients, properties, and principles of operation), monitoring procedures, labeling, consent materials, IRB information, and additional records and reports that will be maintained beyond those required in § 812.40.
- A description of the methods, facilities, and controls used for the manufacture, processing, packing, storage, and installation of the device.
- Sample investigator agreement and certification that investigators signed agreement.
- The names, addresses, and chairpersons of all IRBs, and investigators.
- The name and address of any other institution where a part of the investigation may be conducted, for example, a core lab.
- Justification for amount charged for device and an explanation of why sale does not constitute commercialization.
- *Labeling.* This includes adequate directions for use, as well as the following caution statement: "Caution—investigational device, limited by Federal Law to Investigational Use." Under no circumstances can the device be promoted as safe/effective for investigational use.
- *Informed consent forms and materials.* The informed consent must not include any exculpatory language, and must contain language that the participation in the study is voluntary. Informed consent requirements are further explained in Section 3.II.C.

Although an environmental assessment (or claim for categorical exclusion) was required in the past, this is no longer necessary for an IDE application.

FDA reports that the three most common areas that are deficient in IDE applications are (1) an inadequate report of prior investigations (ROPI); (2) an inadequate investigational plan; and (3) an inadequate/incomplete design and manufacturing section. Common deficiencies include:

- ROPI: the methods are not well described or the data does not support the conclusions.
- Investigational plan: that the study objectives are not developed or that risks are not identified and addressed.
- Device/manufacturing: the rationale for the device design is missing, and that sufficient information is not provided regarding the controls in place to ensure the device is manufactured consistently and reliably.

Clear communication of each IDE component is a key element to a successful IDE application, and the sponsor should take care to provide accurate and concise information to the agency.

D. FDA Interactions and IDE Review Process

Once an IDE application is filed, FDA sends an acknowledgment that contains an IDE number (GXXXXXX). FDA will route the application to the appropriate division based on intended use. FDA's action on IDE applications is outlined in § 812.30. The agency may grant full approval; approval with modifications, conditions, or limitations; staged approval; or disapprove an IDE application. FDA may also request additional information. Unless FDA notifies the sponsor that the investigation may not begin, the sponsor may initiate the study 30 days after FDA receives the IDE application, as long as IRB approval has been secured. In practice, however, the agency always sends a letter and it is highly advisable to wait to initiate a study until receiving FDA approval. The IDE approval (or approval with conditions) letter will specify the maximum number of U.S. subjects and sites that can be enrolled.

1. Approval

The investigation may begin immediately upon receipt of an order from FDA of full IDE approval (and following IRB approval).

Although FDA may not disapprove an IDE solely because the study would not support clearance or approval of a medical device, it will generally outline the changes it would recommend to the study design to support a marketing application in the form of advisories, additional considerations, or study design considerations at the end of the IDE approval letter. Although sponsors may conduct a study without addressing those considerations, they should give serious consideration to implementing them if they do intend the study to be the primary support for a marketing application.

2. Approval with Conditions

If FDA grants approval with conditions, the study may begin enrollment once IRB approval is in place and subject to any limitations the agency describes in its decision letter. The sponsor must provide FDA with information addressing the issues identified as conditions within 45 days of FDA's letter. Referred to as an "IDE amendment," the response must include specific information on modifications, or scientifically valid alternatives or rationale for why a response is not needed for each of the issues raised in the approval with conditions letter. FDA informs the sponsor of its decision within 30 days of receipt of the IDE amendment. If all the issues are adequately resolved, then the agency will grant full approval; however, if issues remain, the agency will again grant approval with conditions, requiring an additional IDE amendment filing within 45 days.

In its guidance, FDA offers the following examples of outstanding issues that may lead to approval with conditions:

- Requests for additional information or data involving nonclinical testing issues that do not need to be resolved prior to initiation of subject enrollment;
- Late-stage follow-up procedures and assessments that relate to the care of study subjects but, because they occur late in the study, can likely be addressed in response to FDA's letter prior to subjects reaching that point in the study;
- Minor issues related to the informed consent document that must be corrected before initiation of subject enrollment but FDA can review after implementation;
- Other minor clarifications, corrections, or modifications (not related to study design) that do not need to be resolved prior to initiation of subject enrollment.[48]

48. *FDA Decisions for Investigational Device Exemption Clinical Investigations—Guidance for Sponsors, Clinical Investigators, Institutional Review Boards, and Food and Drug Administration Staff* (Aug. 19, 2014) at 7, https://www.fda.gov/regulatory-information/search-fda-guidance-documents/fda-decisions-investigational-device-exemption-clinical-investigations.

In some cases, the agency will grant "staged approval," with or without conditions, allowing the trial to enroll a portion of the intended cohort while outstanding questions are addressed. Once supplemental information has been filed and found adequate, the agency may then allow expansion of study enrollment.

3. Disapproval

The IDE regulations state clear grounds for disapproval of an IDE application, as described in § 812.30(b), including:

- Failure to comply with regulatory requirements
- An untrue statement of material fact is contained in the application or a report
- Failure to timely respond to an agency request for additional information
- Risk to subjects outweighs benefits
- Inadequate informed consent
- Proposed investigation is scientifically unsound
- There is reason to believe the device is ineffective
- Otherwise unreasonable to conduct study given the way in which the device is used or there is inadequate
    - Report of prior investigations,
    - Methods, facilities or controls for manufacture, processing, packing or storage of device
    - Monitoring[49/50]

The Food and Drug Administration Safety and Innovation Act (FDASIA) of 2012 modified the criteria for disapproving an IDE. Specifically, FDA could no longer disapprove an IDE solely because the study would not support clearance or approval of a medical device. Since that time, disapproval of IDEs has primarily been due to risk or safety concerns for subjects.

---

49. *FDA Decisions for Investigational Device Exemption Clinical Investigations—Guidance for Sponsors, Clinical Investigators, Institutional Review Boards, and Food and Drug Administration Staff* (Aug. 19, 2014), https://www.fda.gov/regulatory-information/search-fda-guidance-documents/fda-decisions-investigational-device-exemption-clinical-investigations.

50. *Factors to Consider When Making Benefit-Risk Determinations for Medical Device Investigational Device Exemptions—Guidance for Industry and Food and Drug Administration Staff* (Jan. 13, 2017), https://www.fda.gov/regulatory-information/search-fda-guidance-documents/factors-consider-when-making-benefit-risk-determinations-medical-device-investigational-device.

E. Sponsor Responsibilities and Recordkeeping

The sponsor is an individual or organization that initiates and/or finances a clinical trial but often does not actually conduct the investigation. FDA has set forth clear responsibilities of the sponsor in regulations and subsequent guidance.[51]

1. Sponsor Obligations

Sponsor obligations for SR studies include the following:

- Requirements prior to clinical trial
  - Select qualified investigators (§§ 812.40 and 812.43(a))
  - Ship investigational devices only to qualified investigators participating in investigation (§ 812.43(b))
  - Obtain signed investigator agreements (§ 812.43(c))
  - Ensure FDA approval of IDE (for significant risk study) (§§ 812.20(a)(1) and 812.42)
  - Ensure IRB review and approval of protocol and informed consent materials (§ 812.40)
  - Select monitors (§ 812.43(d))
  - Develop and ensure proper monitoring procedures (§ 812.46)
  - Conduct pre-investigational site visit
  - Develop, produce, and distribute Case Report Forms (CRFs)
  - Provide investigators with information necessary to start study and to conduct investigation properly (CRFs, protocol, investigational plan, study procedures, schedule of forms and visits, etc.) (§§ 812.40 and 812.45)
  - Coordinate investigator meetings
- Requirements during clinical trial
  - Maintain records relating to the investigation (§ 812.140(b))
  - Conduct periodic monitoring visits
  - Monitor compliance by investigators, and secure compliance by or terminate participation of noncompliant investigators (§ 812.46(a))
  - Evaluate any unanticipated adverse device effects (§ 812.46(b))
  - Ensure IRBs and FDA are informed of significant new information about the investigation (§ 812.40)
  - Ensure continuing IRB approval (§ 812.64)

---

51. *Sponsor's Responsibilities for Significant Risk Device Investigations* (Nov. 1995), https://www.fda.gov/medical-devices/investigational-device-exemption-ide/sponsors-responsibilities-significant-risk-device-investigations-nov-1995.

    - Receive data and data processing (including data entry, edits, etc.)
    - Terminate investigators that present unreasonable risks to subjects (§ 812.46(b)(2))
    - Permit entry and inspection by authorized FDA employees (§ 812.145)
    - Submit reports about unanticipated adverse device effects, withdrawal of IRB or FDA approval, current investigator lists, progress, recall and device disposition, informed consent, and significant risk device determination (§ 812.150(b))
- Requirements after clinical trial
    - Record retention for two years (§ 812.140(d))
    - Permit entry and inspection by authorized FDA employees (§ 812.145)
    - Submit final reports (§ 812.150(b)(7))
    - Termination/site closeout monitoring visits

Sponsors of NSR studies are subject to the abbreviated IDE requirements set forth in § 812.2(b).

F. Investigator Responsibilities and Recordkeeping

An investigator is the individual under whose immediate direction a test article is administered, or dispensed to, or used involving a subject or the responsible leader (principal investigator) of a team of investigators.

Investigator responsibilities for SR studies include the following:[52]

- Requirements prior to clinical trial
    - Submit signed investigator agreement to sponsor regarding prior experience and commitment to investigation (§ 812.43(c))
    - Submit financial disclosure to sponsor (§ 812.110(d))[53]
    - Await IRB and FDA approval before allowing subjects to participate in investigation (§ 812.110(a))

52. *Investigator Responsibilities—Protecting the Rights, Safety, and Welfare of Study Subjects—Guidance for Industry* (Oct. 2009), https://www.fda.gov/regulatory-information/search-fda-guidance-documents/investigator-responsibilities-protecting-rights-safety-and-welfare-study-subjects; and *Investigators' Responsibilities for Significant Risk Device Investigations* (Nov. 1995), https://www.fda.gov/medical-devices/investigational-device-exemption-ide/investigators-responsibilities-significant-risk-device-investigations-nov-1995.

53. *Financial Disclosure by Clinical Investigators—Guidance for Clinical Investigators, Industry, and FDA Staff* (Feb. 2013), https://www.fda.gov/regulatory-information/search-fda-guidance-documents/financial-disclosure-clinical-investigators.

- Requirements during clinical trial
    - Conduct investigation in accordance with sponsor agreement, investigational plan, IRB requirements, and FDA regulations (§§ 812.100 and 812.110(b))
    - Supervise all human testing of the device and ensure rights, safety, and welfare of subjects (§ 812.100)
    - Ensure requirements for obtaining informed consent are met (§ 812.100)[54]
    - Restrict use of investigational device only to subjects under investigator's supervision (§ 812.110(c))[55]
    - Maintain records related to participation in investigation (§ 812.140(a))
    - Permit entry and inspection by authorized FDA employees (§ 812.145)
    - Submit reports about unanticipated adverse device effects, withdrawal of IRB approval, progress, deviations from the investigational plan, and use without informed consent (§ 812.150(a))
- Requirements after clinical trial
    - Return any remaining supply of device to sponsor or dispose of device as instructed by sponsor (§ 812.110(e))
    - Record retention (§ 812.140(d))
    - Permit entry and inspection by authorized FDA employees (§ 812.145)
    - Submit final reports (§ 812.150(a)(6))

Investigators of NSR studies are subject to abbreviated IDE requirements set forth in § 812.2(b).

Tables 3.2, 3.3, and 3.4 summarize the recordkeeping and reporting requirements for SR and NSR studies.

---

54. *A Guide to Informed Consent—Guidance for Institutional Review Boards and Clinical Investigators* (Jan. 1998), https://www.fda.gov/regulatory-information/search-fda-guidance-documents/guide-informed-consent.

55. *Recruiting Study Subjects—Information Sheet Guidance for Institutional Review Boards and Clinical Investigators* (Jan. 1998), https://www.fda.gov/regulatory-information/search-fda-guidance-documents/recruiting-study-subjects; *Preparing Notices of Availability of Investigational Medical Devices and for Recruiting Study Subjects—Guidance for Industry and FDA Staff* (Mar. 1999), https://www.fda.gov/regulatory-information/search-fda-guidance-documents/preparing-notices-availability-investigational-medical-devices-and-recruiting-study-subjects.

Table 3.2 Responsibilities for Maintaining Records (§ 812.140)

	Records	Maintained by	
		Investigator	Sponsor
Significant Risk Device	All Correspondence Pertaining to Investigation	X	X
	Shipment, Receipt and Disposition	X	X
	Device Administration and Use	X	
	Subject Case Histories	X	
	Informed Consent	X	
	Protocols and Reason for Deviations from Protocol	X	
	Adverse Device Effects and Complaints	X	X
	Signed Investigator Agreements		X
Nonsignificant Risk Device	Name and Intended Use of Device		X
	Brief Explanation of Why Device Does Not Involve Significant Risk		X
	Name and Addresses of Investigator(s) and IRBs		X
	Degree GMPs Followed		X
	Informed Consent	X	
	Adverse Device Effects and Complaints		X

Table 3.3 Responsibilities for Preparing and Submitting Reports for Nonsignificant Risk Devices (§ 812.150)

Type of Report	Reports Prepared by Investigators for:	Report Prepared by Sponsors for:
Unanticipated Adverse Effect Evaluation	Sponsors and IRBs	FDA, Investigators, and IRBs
Withdrawal of IRB Approval	Sponsors	FDA, Investigators, and IRBs
Progress Report	N/A	IRBs
Final Report	N/A	IRBs
Inability to Obtain Informed Consent	Sponsors and IRBs	FDA
Withdrawal of FDA Approval	N/A	Investigators and IRBs
Recall and Device Disposition	N/A	FDA and IRBs
Significant Risk Determinations	N/A	FDA

Table 3.4: Responsibilities for Preparing and Submitting Reports for Significant Risk Devices (§ 812.150)

Type of Report	Reports Prepared by Investigators for:	Report Prepared by Sponsors for:
Unanticipated Adverse Effect Evaluation	Sponsors and IRBs	FDA, Investigators, and IRBs
Withdrawal of IRB Approval	Sponsors	FDA, Investigators, and IRBs
Progress Report	Sponsors, Monitors, and IRBs	FDA and IRBs
Final Report	Sponsors and IRBs	FDA, Investigators, and IRBs
Emergencies (Protocol Deviations)	Sponsors and IRBs	FDA
Inability to Obtain Informed Consent	Sponsors and IRBs	FDA
Withdrawal of FDA Approval	N/A	Investigators and IRBs
Current Investigator List	N/A	FDA
Recall and Device Disposition	N/A	FDA and IRBs
Records Maintenance Transfer	FDA	FDA
Significant Risk Determinations	N/A	FDA

See Data Retention When Subjects Withdraw from FDA-Regulated Clinical Trials—Guidance for Sponsors, Clinical Investigator, and Institutional Review Boards (October 2008), https://www.fda.gov/media/75138/download.

G. Study Monitoring Requirements

A study monitor is an individual designated by a sponsor or contract research organization to oversee the progress of the clinical investigation. The sponsor's written procedures for monitoring the investigation are required to be included in the IDE application.

Study monitoring requirements include the following:

- Requirements prior to clinical trial
  - Establish written procedures to assure study quality and individual duties
  - Perform clinical site initiation visits
  - Ensure the clinical investigator (CI) understands investigational status of test article, nature of the investigational plan, and requirements for a well-controlled study
  - Ensure the CI will conduct investigation in accordance with FDA regulations
  - Ensure the CI has access to adequate number of test subjects
  - Ensure the CI has adequate facilities and time to conduct investigation

- Requirements during clinical trial
    - Make periodic visits throughout investigation to ensure communication with and compliance by investigator
    - Ensure the CI facilities continue to be acceptable
    - Ensure protocol or investigational plan is followed
    - Ensure protocol changes are approved by and/or reported to sponsor or IRB
    - Ensure proper maintenance of records
    - Ensure data sets are complete
    - Ensure that information and data conveyed to sponsor are identical to data recorded in source documents
    - Ensure submission of proper reports to sponsor and IRB
    - Ensure investigational activities are not delegated to unspecified persons
- Requirements after clinical phase
    - Possible close-out visits

For more information on study monitoring, see Sections 3.IV.C.1.d and 3.V.D.

H. Modifications to IDE Studies

IDE supplements may be required when there are significant post-application changes to IDE studies. Section 812.35(a) regulates when a change requires prior approval from FDA.[56] It is also in the sponsor's interest to report changes to the study to FDA. Post-IDE approval modifications to clinical studies can complicate the subsequent marketing review for the device. If these changes are not properly reported and communicated, the review cycle could be longer and/or lead to unfavorable decisions down the road.

During the course of an investigational study, changes to the investigational plan, including to the device or to the clinical protocol, may become necessary. The sponsor is responsible for assessing the effect any changes to the investigational plan may have on the clinical investigation and the data resulting from the study.

Changes in the investigational plan that require prior FDA approval include any modifications, including manufacturing changes, involving basic principles of operation or significant design changes. Additionally,

56. *Changes or Modifications during the Conduct of a Clinical Investigation; Final Guidance for Industry and CDRH Staff* (May 29, 2001), https://www.fda.gov/regulatory-information/search-fda-guidance-documents/changes-or-modifications-during-conduct-clinical-investigation-final-guidance-industry-and-cdrh.

changes must be approved that may affect the validity of the data from the study; the risk to benefit relationship for enrolled subjects; the scientific soundness of the investigational plan; or patients' rights, safety, or welfare.

Examples of changes requiring an IDE supplement include the following:

- Change in indication
- Change in type or nature of study control
- Change in primary endpoint
- Change in method of statistical evaluation
- Early termination of the study (except for reasons related to patient safety)
- Increasing the number of investigational sites
- Increasing the number of study subjects
- Significant change in device design or basic principles of operation not based on study information

This requirement does not apply to changes effected to protect the life or physical well-being of a subject in an emergency. However, any emergency-related change must be reported to FDA within five working days after the sponsor learns of it (§ 812.35(a)(2)).

1. Five-Day Notice of IDE Change

Certain changes may be made without prior approval if the sponsor submits notice to FDA within five working days after making the change (§ 812.35(a)(3)). Changes that do not affect data validity; the risk benefit relationship to the patient; the scientific soundness of the investigational plan; or the rights, safety, or welfare of human subjects do not require filing of an IDE supplement. The sponsor must determine that the changes meet these criteria based on "credible information" as defined in § 812.35(a)(3)(iii). Examples of credible information for developmental (including manufacturing) changes include data generated under design control procedures or preclinical testing results. For clinical protocol modifications, documentation supporting the conclusion that the change presents no significant impact on study design or analysis, and will not affect human subject safety, is required.

Although responsibility for determining that a change does not require prior approval rests with the sponsor, FDA reserves the right to question the sponsor's determination based on the contents of the Notice of IDE Change or other information, and to require prior approval, if the agency has reason to believe that the modification could jeopardize patient safety, the scientific soundness of the investigation, or the validity of the data.

For purposes of determining timeliness of the notice, changes to devices are deemed to occur on the date the device—manufactured incorporating the design or manufacturing change—is distributed to the clinical investigator or upon notification to the investigator of a change in study protocol (§ 812.35(a)(3)(iv)). In its guidance, the agency emphasizes that sponsors must complete "assessment of the change and any supporting testing . . . before the change is implemented, and the Notice of IDE Change must be submitted to the agency within 5 days of implementation."[57]

Examples of changes appropriate for a 5-Day Notice include the following:

- Developmental changes in the device that do not constitute a significant change in design or basic principles of operation and that are made in response to information gathered during the course of the investigation
- Certain changes to clinical protocol that do not affect
  - The validity of the data or information in the approved protocol, or the patient risk to benefit relationship relied upon to approve the protocol
  - The scientific soundness of the investigational plan
  - The rights, safety, or welfare of the human subjects involved in the investigation
- Extension of shelf life
- Change in design found not to impact safety/effectiveness
- Modification of inclusion/exclusion criteria to better define the target patient population
- Increasing the frequency at which data or information is gathered
- Inclusion of additional patient observations or measurements
- Modifying the secondary endpoints

The Notice of IDE Change should contain a description of the change to the device, manufacturing process, or protocol, with the relevant information supporting the determination that prior approval is not required.

I. Termination of IDE Studies

An IDE study may be discontinued, either by a sponsor or by withdrawal of IRB or FDA approval, prior to completion (§ 812.3(q)). Further, in the

57. *Id.*

case of an unanticipated adverse device effect that presents an unreasonable risk to subjects, the sponsor must terminate the investigation as soon as possible and (1) no later than five working days after the sponsor makes this determination and (2) no later than 15 working days after the sponsor first received notice of the effect (§ 812.46).

J. IDE Annual Reports

Sponsors are required to provide progress reports to all reviewing IRBs, and to FDA for SR devices, at least annually. The report should include the following contents:

- Basic elements. The IDE number, device name and indication(s) for use, and contact information.
- Study progress. A summary of the study progress in relation to the investigational plan, including numbers of investigators and subjects enrolled, devices shipped, and a summary of results including adverse events and protocol deviations.
- Risk analysis. Any information that would change the risk analysis, published articles, and a new risk analysis if needed.
- Other changes. Changes to the device, manufacturing, or investigational plan not required to be submitted in an IDE supplement.
- Future plans. Progress and timelines toward product approval/clearance, and any plans to change the investigation.

Changes may be reported in the annual progress report for the IDE if the changes do not affect the validity of the data or information resulting from the completion of the approved protocol; the scientific soundness of the investigational plan; or the rights, safety, or welfare of the human subjects involved in the investigation (§ 812.150(b)(5)). Examples include minor changes to the labeling or monitoring procedures.

K. Expanded Access

Expanded access is a means by which patients may obtain access to medical products before approval, outside of the confines of a traditional IDE study. For example, if a patient does not meet the inclusion and exclusion criteria for a particular study, they may still be able to obtain treatment with the device, subject to certain restrictions. There are several mechanisms for expanded access, as described next.

1. Emergency Use (§ 812.35(a))

This covers emergency situations where an investigational device may be used in a manner inconsistent with the approved investigational plan.

Criteria for emergency use are: the patient has a life-threatening condition that needs immediate treatment, no generally acceptable alternative treatment for the condition exists, and because of the immediate need to use the device, there is no time to use existing procedures to get FDA approval for the use. In such an event, the investigator should try to obtain informed consent and concurrence of the institution, IRB chairperson, an independent physician, and the device manufacturer, if possible. Depending on whether there is an IDE, the sponsor or the physician should report the emergency use to FDA within five days.

2. Compassionate Use

Pursuant to section 402 of the Food and Drug Administration Modernization Act of 1997 (FDAMA), FDA may permit compassionate use of an investigational device for treatment of a patient who does not meet the requirements for inclusion in a clinical study, but for whom the treating physician believes the device will be beneficial for treating the patient's disease or condition. Compassionate use of an investigational device is permitted only for patients who are faced with a serious disease or condition for which no suitable alternative treatment exists. This mechanism typically applies to individual patients but can be used to treat a small group, if the request is made under an IDE.

FDA approval is required before an investigational device can be used under the compassionate use provision. If there is an ongoing IDE, the sponsor needs to submit an IDE supplement requesting approval to deviate from the approved study protocol.

> If there is no ongoing IDE, a physician or the manufacturer can make a compassionate use request to FDA for a single patient, including the preceding information as well as a device description.

FDA will review and make a decision (approval, approval with conditions, disapproval) on a compassionate use request. There is a 30-day review timeline for requests submitted under an IDE, but, in practicality, they are typically reviewed significantly faster, sometimes in one day, depending on the need.

3. Treatment IDE

A Treatment IDE is used when no approved or cleared comparable or satisfactory alternative treatment exists, a patient does not meet the eligibility requirements of any clinical trial, and the device is not approved for marketing but is under clinical investigation by a company seeking clearance or approval to treat a serious or immediately life threatening condition. This provision is intended to facilitate the availability of promising new devices to desperately ill patients as early in the device development process as possible, and to obtain additional data on the device's safety and effectiveness.

As described under section 812.36, FDA requires meeting the following four conditions to consider the use of an investigational device under a treatment IDE:

- The device is intended to treat or diagnose a serious or immediately life-threatening disease or condition (defined as a stage of a disease in which there is a reasonable likelihood that death will occur within a matter of months or in which premature death is likely without early treatment);
- There is no comparable or satisfactory alternative device or other therapy available to treat or diagnose that stage of the disease or condition in the intended patient population;
- The device is under investigation in a controlled clinical trial for the same use under an approved IDE, or such clinical trials have been completed; and
- The sponsor of the investigation is actively pursuing marketing approval/clearance of the investigational device with due diligence.

The contents of a treatment IDE application are spelled out in § 812.36(c). After a sponsor obtains FDA approval for a treatment IDE, the investigator should apply for IRB approval and must obtain informed consent. The sponsor of a treatment IDE must also submit semi-annual progress reports to FDA until the marketing application is filed.

4. Continued Access

Continued access allows doctors to access a medical device while the premarket approval (PMA) application is under review, if there is:

- A public health need for the device; or
- Preliminary evidence that the device is likely to be effective and no significant safety concerns have been identified for the proposed indication.

The request should be submitted as IDE supplement, containing: a justification for the extension; a summary of the preliminary safety and effectiveness data from the IDE; a brief discussion of the risks posed by the device; the proposed rate of continued enrollment; the clinical protocol as well as the proposed objectives for continued study; and a brief discussion of the sponsor's progress in obtaining marketing approval/clearance for the device.

It is noted that continued access no longer appears on FDA's website as a means of expanded access and the guidance on this topic (Continued Access to Investigational Devices during PMA Preparation and Review July 15, 1996 (Blue Book Memo)) was withdrawn in August of 2017. However, we understand from FDA staff that these documents were outdated and are in the process of being updated; continued access remains an option in the interim until new guidance can be developed.

IV. Study Design and Analysis

A. Types of Studies

1. Observational versus Interventional

Clinical studies are categorized as "observational" or "interventional." In an observational study, a patient population with a particular condition is defined and followed, but specific treatments or "interventions" are not assigned to patients. A registry is one example of an observational study, typically in which patients' health data is collected on a consistent basis for a particular condition or treatment according to the standard of care. Conversely, in an interventional study, patients are assigned to groups specified in the protocol to receive a particular treatment. For clinical studies supporting a marketing application, FDA generally prefers interventional studies with two or more arms in order to differentiate the treatment effect.

2. Prospective versus Retrospective

A prospective study is one in which a protocol is developed before the data is collected. Once the protocol is finalized and necessary approvals are received, a study starts to enroll patients according to the eligibility criteria and collects their appropriate health data moving forward as outlined in the protocol. In a retrospective study, a protocol is developed to analyze data that has already been collected. A protocol for a retrospective study defines a patient population and certain health data to collect similar to a prospective study, but collects data from preexisting sources. For example, this can be done through a review of medical records. Both prospective and retrospective studies can include one or more treatment arms.

Sponsors often prefer retrospective studies as they are less costly and faster to perform compared to prospective studies. Prospective study costs typically include patient treatment procedures and assessments, expenses for follow-up visits, as well as expenses associated with retaining clinical sites, study monitoring, and database development and maintenance. Time requirements for prospective clinical studies include the time for possible feasibility or pilot studies, IDE approval of the various studies, contracting with clinical sites, and conduct of the study itself, including enrollment, treatment, and follow-up of patients. Nevertheless, FDA generally recommends sponsors perform prospective studies as they typically have fewer confounding variables and potential biases. In a prospective study, a protocol can strictly define a patient population, their treatments, and schedule for follow-up. Although a retrospective study protocol aims to define the same variables, it is harder to confirm since only certain data have been collected. In certain cases, the agency is amenable to a retrospective clinical study supporting a marketing application, for example, where the rate of enrollment is too slow to make the study feasible in a prospective manner (e.g., rare conditions).

3. Real-World Evidence (RWE)

On August 17, 2017, FDA finalized its guidance, *Use of Real-World Evidence to Support Regulatory Decision-Making for Medical Devices.* The guidance is part of the agency's recent efforts to take creative approaches to the evidence required to support regulatory decision making. Real-world evidence (RWE) includes "data relating to patient health status and/or the delivery of health care routinely collected from a variety of sources" such as electronic health records, claims and billing data, data from product and disease registries, patient-generated data including in home-use settings, among other sources. As noted in the guidance, RWE may be used to support regulatory applications, including PMA, HDEs, and De Novo requests. For RWE to be acceptable, the agency recommends a prospectively defined protocol to eliminate bias in data collection, with the protocol having similar elements as a traditional clinical study. Despite the desire to use RWE in premarket and postmarket settings, industry has seemingly had little success with the agency accepting RWE in lieu of formal clinical studies, especially as the main source of evidence in the premarket setting.

4. Reader Studies

Depending on the device type and indication, FDA sometimes requires sponsors to conduct reader studies to evaluate physician ("reader") performance when the device is used. Reader studies are typically required when the output from the device has the potential to change physician performance, and to measure physician performance with and without the device. The agency has required reader studies for some in vitro diagnostic devices and computer-assisted detection (CADe) software devices, since the device output can change the way physicians interpret standard of care data. Reader studies can be conducted with prospective or retrospectively collected data, and generally do not involve any direct interaction between patients and the device. That is, patients provide their data for use in reader studies (e.g., MRI images), but patient data is analyzed by the device separate to patients' usual care. Because of this separation, reader studies are sometimes classified as performance studies rather than clinical studies.

5. Single-Arm and Crossover Studies

The agency generally prefers two-arm studies with concurrent controls, but in certain situations accepts single-arm studies with subjects used as their own control (i.e., comparing measurements pre- and post-intervention), historical control, objective performance criteria (OPC), or a performance goal (PG). Further information on OPCs and PGs is included in Section 3.IV.B.10.h.

An historical control group uses data from a completed study as a comparison in a subject treatment study. Patient line-item data is typically needed in order to utilize this option. The key concern with an historical control is whether the historical patients are sufficiently comparable to the treatment group in terms of (1) demographics and baseline characteristics and (2) study protocol (e.g., study procedures and follow-up schedule), in order to make an appropriate comparison and draw conclusions from the analysis.

B. Essential Study Design Parameters

For FDA's overview of the elements of trial design relevant to premarket submissions, see Design Considerations for Pivotal Clinical Investigations for Medical Devices—Guidance for Industry, Clinical Investigators, Institutional Review Boards and FDA Staff (November 2013) https://www.fda.gov/regulatory-information/search-fda-guidance-documents/design-considerations-pivotal-clinical-investigations-medical-devices ("Design Guidance"). Additional FDA guidance with regard to IVD studies can be found later.[58]

---

58. *See In Vitro Diagnostic (IVD) Device Studies—Frequently Asked Questions—Guidance for Industry and Food and Drug Administration Staff* (June 2010), https://www.fda.gov/regulatory-information/search-fda-guidance-documents/vitro-diagnostic-ivd-device-studies-frequently-asked-questions.

1. Clinical Centers/Sites

A clinical study can be performed at one clinical center or at several clinical centers. The decision whether to include one or more clinical centers in a study is generally based on the study phase, number of patients to be enrolled, and type of FDA marketing application. For example, a pilot study with 20 patients and one treatment arm is typically performed at one or two centers, whereas a pivotal study with 200 patients is usually performed at several centers to facilitate faster recruitment and to evaluate the reproducibility of device results. For a pivotal study supporting a marketing application, the agency generally prefers a multicenter design to analyze whether the treatment can be administered consistently across a range of physician and patient populations. A multicenter study is also preferred in order to ensure the study population is representative of the U.S. population with respect to age, sex, race, ethnicity, socioeconomic status, and other variables. FDA will require a poolability analysis in a multicenter study to confirm that the study results are consistent across clinical centers.

Sponsors should carefully review clinical centers that may participate in a study. Centers should have sufficient staff and resources to perform the study as specified in the protocol. The investigator (physician) at the center should have the appropriate experience with the patient population and preferably with performing clinical studies in general.

Clinical studies can be performed in the United States, outside the United States (OUS), or include a combination of U.S. and OUS sites. Although FDA wants to ensure that all of the clinical pivotal study data is applicable to the U.S. population, the agency is open to partial or complete OUS data in certain situations. For studies that include partial OUS data, the agency typically expects at least 50 percent of the patients be U.S. patients from U.S. sites. In addition, if an IDE is required for the study, the IDE approval letter will specify the maximum number of U.S. patients and U.S. sites that can be enrolled in the study, as FDA does not have jurisdiction over OUS sites. OUS data may be included in IDE studies if the sponsor demonstrates that the patient population is comparable to the U.S. intended use population, the same protocol is used in the US and OUS, and the standards of care (including concomitant medications and other therapies) are the same between countries. A poolability analysis is also generally required to determine that the OUS and U.S. data can be combined for analysis purposes. This analysis between OUS and U.S. data is applicable for all clinical studies submitted to FDA for clearance or approval purposes, regardless of whether an IDE is needed for the study.

For more information, please see FDA's Guidance, *Acceptance of Clinical Data to Support Medical Device Applications and Submissions.*[59]

2. Eligibility Criteria

Clinical study protocols must include eligibility criteria for patients in the study. Eligibility criteria are typically comprised of both inclusion and exclusion criteria, where patients must meet all inclusion criteria and no exclusion criteria to be included in the study. 21 C.F.R. § 860.7(f)(1)(ii) describes the eligibility criteria as follows:

> A method of selection of the subjects that:
>
> (a) Provides adequate assurance that the subjects are suitable for the purposes of the study, provides diagnostic criteria of the condition to be treated or diagnosed, provides confirmatory laboratory tests where appropriate and, in the case of a device to prevent a disease or condition, provides evidence of susceptibility and exposure to the condition against which prophylaxis is desired;

The criteria are designed primarily to reflect the target, or intended use, population. For example, if the device is intended only for adult (which FDA defines as age ≥22 years) females with a certain condition, the criteria should reflect that only those individuals are to be included in the study. This is important to ensure the correct patients are included in the study and that the data collected in the study support the proposed intended use of the device. If the criteria are too broad or incorrectly defined, the sponsor risks not having a successful study. Sponsors should also pay particular attention to the eligibility criteria in the study, as these typically mirror what the agency will require to be stated in the device's labeling. For example, if the study exclusion criteria include patients with pacemakers, then the device will need to be contraindicated in the labeling for patients with pacemakers.

3. Controls

In a clinical outcome study, a control group is needed in a majority of study designs to properly characterize the effect of the investigational

59. Acceptance of Clinical Data to Support Medical Device Applications and Submissions—Guidance for Industry and Food and Drug Administration Staff (Feb. 2018), https://www.fda.gov/regulatory-information/search-fda-guidance-documents/acceptance-clinical-data-support-medical-device-applications-and-submissions-frequently-asked.

device. Options for controls in clinical studies are described in 21 C.F.R. § 860.7 as follows:

> A comparison of the results of treatment or diagnosis with a control in such a fashion as to permit quantitative evaluation. The precise nature of the control must be specified and an explanation provided of the methods employed to minimize any possible bias of the observers and analysts of the data. Level and methods of "blinding," if appropriate and used, are to be documented. Generally, four types of comparisons are recognized;
>
> (a) No treatments. Where objective measurements of effectiveness are available and placebo effect is negligible, comparison of the objective results in comparable groups of treated and untreated patients;
>
> (b) Placebo control.* Where there may be a placebo effect with the use of a device, comparison of the results of use of the device with an ineffective device used under conditions designed to resemble the conditions of use under investigation as far as possible;
>
> (c) Active treatment control. Where an effective regimen of therapy may be used for comparison, e.g., the condition being treated is such that the use of a placebo or the withholding of treatment would be inappropriate or contrary to the interest of the patient;
>
> (d) Historical control. In certain circumstances, such as those involving diseases with high and predictable mortality or signs and symptoms of predictable duration or severity, or in the case of prophylaxis where morbidity is predictable, the results of use of the device may be compared quantitatively with prior experience historically derived from the adequately documented natural history of the disease or condition in comparable patients or populations who received no treatment or who followed an established effective regimen (therapeutic, diagnostic, prophylactic).
>
> *In most device studies, inactive control devices are called "sham" devices.

In addition to the preceding, FDA also recognizes subjects used as their own control (i.e., comparing measurements pre- and post-intervention), as well as study-wide controls based on objective performance criteria (OPC) and performance goals (PGs) in single-arm studies, as discussed in Section 3.IV.B.10.h.

For FDA Guidance regarding control groups in clinical studies, see *Choice of Control Group and Related Issues in Clinical Trials—Guidance for Industry* (May 2001 ICH) (https://www.fda.gov/media/71349/download).

4. Randomization

When there are multiple arms in a study, a randomized allocation methodology is preferred to ensure the groups are similar at baseline before an intervention is administered. Randomization is helpful in balancing groups with respect to known variables such as "sex and other demographic variables, severity or duration of the disease, prior therapies, professional user biases and/or preferences, and use of interventions other than the investigational device" as well as unknown variables.[60] As noted in the referenced Design Guidance, FDA acknowledges there are situations in device studies where randomization is "impossible, difficult, or potentially inappropriate." While randomization is the "gold standard," other allocation methods for patients such as alternate allocation (where sequential patients are assigned to treatments in alternate order) may be considered with caution to avoid any biases.

For all clinical studies, the agency recommends discussing a study design before initiation. This is especially true if there are open questions regarding the adequacy of a study aspect.

5. Blinding

Whenever feasible, treatment assignments in a clinical study should be blinded to the subject and physician performing clinical assessments ("double blind"). As described in the Design Guidance, "knowledge of the intervention assignment can influence the behavior and decisions of the subject, clinician, investigator, care-givers and third-party evaluators, whether consciously or unconsciously."[61] However, the agency recognizes that blinding may not be possible for some medical device studies where the device is worn or otherwise obvious. In these cases, FDA recommends blinding patients ("single blind") and including evaluators in the study who are separate to the staff assigning and performing treat-

60. *Design Considerations for Pivotal Clinical Investigations for Medical Devices—Guidance for Industry, Clinical Investigators, Institutional Review Boards and Food and Drug Administration Staff* (Nov. 7, 2013), https://www.fda.gov/media/87363/download.

61. *Id.*

ments, and utilizing objective criteria. This way, even if it is difficult or impossible to blind a treating provider because of a certain device configuration or appearance, evaluators are blinded and should not be biased with knowledge regarding treatment assignment.

If applicable to the primary endpoint, an outside review body (see Section 3.IV.C.2) that does not have knowledge of the treatment assignment may be employed to review the data in a "blinded" fashion. Where subjects are blinded to the treatment, a study often includes a blinding assessment either at the same time as the primary endpoint measurement or later in order to evaluate the effectiveness of the blinding procedure and determine if there may be any influence on the results.

It should also be noted that some clinical study designs plan for unblinding subjects at a certain time point. For example, in crossover studies, typically sham or control subjects have the option of using the investigational treatment after the primary endpoint is measured. At this time, they would be unblinded to their treatment assignment. Sponsors use a crossover study design to obtain unblinded, long-term safety data and incentivize subjects to stay in the study if they are assigned a sham or control treatment.

6. Endpoints

The endpoints in a study should be prespecified in a protocol to evaluate the safety and effectiveness of a device in the proposed intended use population. Safety and effectiveness endpoints are typically separated with their own individual success criteria, but sometimes one study endpoint can include both safety and effectiveness criteria (known as a "composite" endpoint).

Careful consideration should be made in determining the appropriate endpoints for a clinical study. The device type, desired indications for use, and intended patient population are key aspects of the endpoint design process. For example, in cancer studies, overall survival or progression-free survival are commonly used primary effectiveness endpoints. A decrease in pad weight or number of pads used are recommended in urinary incontinence studies. In addition, sensitivity and specificity are common primary endpoints for diagnostic devices.

The primary endpoint specifically is used to characterize the treatment effect of the device and often is the sole determinant of study success. Secondary endpoints are used to analyze other clinically meaningful aspects of the device, and often include quality of life and other patient-reported outcomes. For all endpoints, the protocol should prespecify the methodology for evaluating a primary endpoint, including the particular assessment, timing for the measurement, person or committee that will evaluate the endpoint, and statistical analysis.

7. Hypothesis and Success Criteria

In a statistically powered study, the primary endpoint must have an associated prespecified hypothesis and success criteria. In a two-arm design, the hypothesis should reflect whether the study is designed to test superiority or non-inferiority of the investigational device's performance and/or safety compared to a control group. Superiority and non-inferiority are commonly used designs for marketing approval. Superiority and non-inferiority studies are designed to demonstrate that the effectiveness or safety of an investigational device is better or not worse within a specific margin compared to the control group, respectively.

The success criteria for the primary endpoint should be prespecified in a protocol before the study initiates, and should reflect a clinically meaningful effect for the device. For superiority, the criterion is often referred to as the minimally clinically important difference (MCID) (i.e., the amount of improvement needed with investigational device use to be clinically meaningful to patients). Success criteria should be prespecified for the primary effectiveness endpoint in a pivotal study, as MCIDs are often established in the literature, medical or scientific society documents, or FDA guidance documents. If an MCID is not established in the medical community, FDA generally advises sponsors to formulate one at the outset of a study with the assistance of key opinion leaders and medical experts for the indicated condition. In terms of non-inferiority, the non-inferiority margin is generally considered to be a clinically insignificant difference between an investigational device and control group. This "non-inferiority margin" is typically between 5 percent and 15 percent, but varies by device and condition.

If a sponsor wishes to make claims on one or more secondary endpoints, hypotheses for these secondary endpoints must be prespecified in a manner similar to the preceding. Statistical considerations when there are multiple hypotheses in a study are described in Section 3.IV.B.10.

As noted earlier, in a single-arm study, the investigational data is often compared to an historical control, OPC or PG in certain situations. These analyses also require a statistical hypothesis, with the OPC or PG used as the success criteria.

8. Follow-up Visits and Duration

In clinical outcome studies, patients are typically followed for a prespecified amount of time to evaluate the device's safety and efficacy.

The amount of follow-up varies based on device type and condition. For example, a device that is indicated for cancer will typically follow a patient until death, whereas a device that is indicated for postoperative pain will follow a patient for a short period after surgery. Studies evaluating investigational in vitro diagnostic devices may have no or little follow-up. In a clinical study, patients are enrolled during a visit at the clinical center. If the device is indicated for use by a physician, treatment is also administered in the office, hospital, or outpatient setting. If the device is indicated for home use, patients may use the device at home. In either case, studies typically include visits in the office or some other medical setting during and after a treatment period. For example, a clinical study with a device that is indicated for ten weeks of treatment may include weekly in-office visits to administer treatments and collect clinical and safety assessments, followed by five weeks of follow-up by telephone for patients to report any adverse events (complications) with the device. Again, the frequency, duration, and type of study visits (e.g., in-office or telephone) will depend on the studied device, indicated condition, and study endpoints.

All efforts should be made to retain patients in the study. Specifically, study staff at clinical centers may utilize automated reminders or personal telephone calls to patients to remind them of study visits. If patients drop out during a study (also known as "lost to follow-up"), the visits and assessments not completed will be counted as missing. A substantial amount of missing data raises questions about the tolerability of the device, and may also compromise the reliability of the final analysis and results.

9. Procedures and Assessments

The clinical protocol should specify and describe all clinical procedures to be performed in the study from baseline until the final follow-up visit. Procedures performed at baseline should be sufficient to determine whether a patient is eligible for a study (e.g., general physical, condition-specific assessments) and include procedures related to the study endpoints, as applicable (e.g., if change from baseline is an endpoint in the study). All assessments utilized in a study should be validated for use in the subject patient population. For example, FDA requires many outcome studies to include quality of life questionnaires for patients to complete throughout the duration of the study. This questionnaire must be validated in peer-reviewed literature for use in the subject patient population.

FDA has guidance documents on its website to help sponsors design studies for certain indications. Where available, these guidance documents describe the clinical assessments that should be included in a study.

10. Statistical Considerations

a. Statistical Analysis

The analysis section of a protocol should explain what methodology will be used to analyze the data collected from procedures and assessments in the study. For example, in pivotal clinical studies, primary endpoints are almost always analyzed with a statistical test as they are typically associated with a hypothesis. The statistical test should be determined prospectively during the design phase of the clinical study and is primarily based on the type of data (continuous, proportion, etc.) and expected data distribution. As noted earlier, a study may include a few hypothesis-driven secondary endpoints as well; the statistical methodology for analyzing these endpoints should be prespecified in the protocol as well. Protocols often include additional secondary and/or exploratory endpoints that a sponsor wishes to study for internal or publication purposes, separate to a regulatory submission. The protocol should explain how a sponsor will analyze these data as well; generally, descriptive statistics (mean, median, standard deviation, proportions, etc.) are used. In addition, the strategy for handling missing data for each endpoint should be prespecified.

A clinical study protocol typically includes an overview of the statistical analyses in a study. A separate document called a statistical analysis plan (SAP) includes more detailed information for the analyses. It is important for the analysis methods to be determined before the data is available. Certain post-hoc analyses (i.e., unplanned analyses selected after the data is available) may be presented to FDA to support a regulatory application, but may inflate the type I error if not handled properly. Generally, post-hoc analyses are appropriate only to complement prespecified analyses, as long as they are interpreted correctly as post-hoc.

b. Demographic and Baseline Characteristics

As described earlier, a sponsor should ensure the eligibility criteria in a study reflect the intended use population. To confirm that the study population is representative of the intended use population, demographic and baseline characteristics must be collected for each subject. At a minimum, this includes age and gender and generally also includes relevant medical history.

c. Analysis Populations

"Analysis populations" are prospectively defined subsets of enrolled subjects that are used to assess the robustness of the results. In superiority studies, the intent-to-treat (ITT) analysis population is usually the primary subset used to analyze the primary endpoint. The ITT population includes all randomized subjects, regardless of whether the subject received treatment or completed the study. Thus, the ITT population typically provides a conservative estimate of a treatment effect in superiority studies and one that may be realistic of real-world use since patients sometimes do not finish treatment. A "per protocol" (PP) analysis generally includes subjects who completed treatment, attended all follow-up visits required in the protocol, and did not have major protocol deviations (i.e., strictly adhered to the protocol). A PP analysis is used as the primary population for non-inferiority studies as it is a more conservative estimate of performance for non-inferiority, and is often also used to confirm ITT results. Other analysis populations that are modifications of the ITT or PP analysis populations are sometimes used depending on the nature of the study and investigational treatment.

d. Multiplicity

As noted earlier, a study can include one or multiple hypotheses to test with the collected data. If the study includes one primary endpoint, the overall significance level in the study (known as "alpha") can be used to test that primary endpoint hypothesis. If there are two co-primary endpoints or secondary endpoints with hypotheses, then the overall significance level of the study must be adjusted to protect the overall type error 1 (i.e., chance of an erroneous conclusion). For example, the alpha in a study (typically 0.05) may be split between two endpoints so that each one is tested at a 0.025 level. Or, a hierarchy may be established such that a subsequently tested endpoint's hypothesis is tested only if a prior hypothesis is rejected. The strategy for multiplicity adjustments must be prespecified in the study protocol.

For FDA's overview of handling multiple endpoints in a study, see *Multiple Endpoints in Clinical Trials—Guidance for Industry—Draft Guidance* (January 2017) (https://www.fda.gov/media/102657/download).

e. Sample Size

A clinical study protocol must prospectively define number of subjects to include in a study. A sample size is calculated to have sufficient power to achieve the hypothesis-driven endpoints in a study. In order to calculate a sample size, the statistical power (typically 80 percent or 90 percent), overall alpha (i.e., 0.05), success criteria, and expected performance for each treatment arm in a study (i.e., difference between study arms in a multi-arm study or "treatment effect") are used. The last factor relates to the hypothesis-driven primary endpoint. If there are multiple hypothesis-driven primary endpoints in a study, the sample size is calculated for each endpoint and the largest sample size is used. Expected performance is derived from pilot studies or studies with similar devices. In a clinical outcome study, the calculated sample size must be increased by 10 to 15 percent to account for the proportion of patients who are expected to be lost to follow-up.

f. Frequentist versus Adaptive Design

A frequentist study design is one that prospectively defines all aspects of the study before the study is initiated. An adaptive design is a design that allows for prospectively planned modifications based on accumulating study data without undermining the trial's integrity and validity. Adaptive designs are most useful when there are uncertainties about certain aspects of the study design, such as the device or control performance or even whether the study as designed will be successful. For fixed (or non-adaptive) designs, sample size calculations are based on assumed values of certain parameters (made prior to study conduct), but the sponsor may not have confidence in the choice of those parameter values (possibly leading to an under- or over-powered study).

The decision whether to employ an adaptive versus a frequentist design may depend on a sponsor's confidence in their ability to estimate certain study parameters and their willingness to possibly risk a frequentist study when using a fixed study design. If planned and implemented correctly, an adaptive study design may enable timelier device development decision making, and therefore more efficient investment in resources in a clinical study.[62]

An adaptive design includes at least one interim analysis at a pre-defined time point, for example, when a certain number of events have been collected or when a portion of subjects have completed a certain amount of follow-up. The interim analysis may be designed to reassess the sample size, or stop the study early for efficacy or futility. The interim analysis is performed by a statistician independent from the company. Firewalls must be in place to ensure that only certain individuals have access to the data while the study is ongoing. Depending on the type of interim analysis performed and whether the study data must be unblinded, certain adjustments may be needed to the overall alpha in a study to account for multiple looks at the data.

---

62. Prud'homme, Gerard J., et al., *New Draft Guidance Outlines FDA's Key Considerations for Adaptive Designs in Clinical Studies*, Hogan Lovells (May 22, 2015), https://ehoganlovells.com/cv/168e710a02bab3f92a978dc0747ff9c223eb03d7.

For several adaptive design options and the pros and cons of such design, see *Adaptive Designs for Medical Device Clinical Studies—Guidance for Industry and Food and Drug Administration Staff* (July 2016) (https://www.fda.gov/regulatory-information/search-fda-guidance-documents/adaptive-designs-medical-device-clinical-studies).

g. Crossover Study Design

A crossover study is another design that may be considered for prospective clinical studies. In crossover studies, typically subjects initially assigned to the sham or control arm have the option of using the investigational treatment (or "crossing over" to the investigational treatment arm) after the primary endpoint is measured. At that time, they would be unblinded to their treatment assignment and given the option of receiving the investigational device. Sponsors use a crossover study design to obtain unblinded, long-term safety data and incentivize subjects to stay in the study if they are assigned a sham or control treatment.

h. Considerations for Single-Arm Study

As noted earlier, an OPC or PG may be used as a "comparison" in single-arm studies. An OPC is a "numerical target value derived from historical data clinical studies and/or registries." An OPC must be validated for use with the studied device and its current technology. Because device technology is constantly evolving, there are very few OPCs used to support regulatory applications. OPCs are typically not developed by FDA or a sponsor alone, and will have greater support if adopted by a medical or scientific society or standards organization, or is cited in a guidance document released by the agency.

A PG is similar to an OPC, but is typically derived from literature and is considered to be a lower level of evidence than an OPC because less information is available. As such, PGs are sometimes used for newer technologies.[63]

---

63. Greg Campbell, PhD, *FDA Guidance: "Design Considerations for Pivotal Clinical Investigations for Medical Devices"* (Dec. 4, 2013), https://www.fda.gov/media/87225/download; *Design Considerations for Pivotal Clinical Investigations for Medical Devices, supra* note 60.

C. Organizational Units

1. Mandatory

a. Sponsor

The sponsor of a clinical study is an individual or organization that initiates and/or finances a clinical trial but often does not actually conduct the investigation. A sponsor's responsibilities from before a clinical trial is initiated to after the trial is completed are outlined in 21 C.F.R. § 812, and are discussed in detail in Section 3.III.E.

b. Clinical Investigators

Per 21 C.F.R. § 812.3(i), an investigator is "an individual who actually conducts a clinical investigation, i.e., under whose immediate direction the test article is administered or dispensed to, or used involving, a subject, or, in the event of an investigation conducted by a team of individuals, is the responsible leader of that team." A clinical investigator's responsibilities from before a clinical trial is initiated to after the trial is completed are outlined in 21 C.F.R. § 812, and are discussed in detail in Section 3.III.F. In any clinical site, the principal investigator in that site must supervise all human testing of the device and ensure the rights, safety, and welfare of subjects. Investigators may designate sub-investigators to perform study-related procedures under their supervision.

c. IRB

As explained in Section 3.II.D, the agency's regulations regarding IRBs are outlined in 21 C.F.R. § 56 and § 812. All clinical studies must be reviewed by an IRB.

FDA defines an IRB as follows:

> An IRB is an appropriately constituted group that has been formally designated to review and monitor biomedical research involving human subjects. In accordance with FDA regulations, an IRB has the authority to approve, require modifications in (to secure approval), or disapprove research. This group review serves an important role in the protection of the rights, safety and welfare of human research subjects.[64]

An IRB is composed of at least five members with varying backgrounds. The members must be diverse, including in race, gender, and cultural backgrounds, and sensitive to such issues as community attitudes.

64. *IDE Institutional Review Boards,* https://www.fda.gov/medical-devices/investigational-device-exemption-ide/ide-institutional-review-boards-irb.

At least one member of the IRB must evaluate concerns in the scientific areas, at least one member must evaluate concerns in nonscientific areas, and one member must not be affiliated with the institution. Most IRBs include physicians and PhD level physical or biological scientists. Such members satisfy the requirement for at least one scientist. When an IRB encounters studies involving science beyond the expertise of the members, the IRB may use a consultant to assist in the review, as provided by 21 C.F.R. § 56.107(f). One member can satisfy more than one membership category.[65] Any member of the IRB must be sufficiently qualified through experience and expertise. Members that have conflicting interests cannot participate in the review of a research proposal.[66]

d. Monitor

A monitor is utilized in a study to ensure the investigator understands the investigational device and nature of the investigation, and ensure the site has proper facilities, staff, and record retention. Monitors make periodic visits to all clinical sites throughout the study, from before the study is initiated to after it is completed. A monitor may be a sponsor employee or contracted to a third party organization.

See Section 3.III.G for a description of monitoring requirements, and Section 3.V.D for sponsor responsibilities regarding monitoring.

For FDA's guidance on monitoring *see Oversight of Clinical Investigations – A Risk-Based Approach to Monitoring—Guidance for Industry* (August 2013) (https://www.fda.gov/regulatory-information/search-fda-guidance-documents/oversight-clinical-investigations-risk-based-approach-monitoring).

2. Optional

a. Contract Research Organization (CRO)

A contract research organization (CRO) is a contracted third-party organization that may monitor a clinical study (see prior section). Depending on a sponsor's needs, certain CROs may also be able to maintain the electronic database of clinical data, perform the statistical analyses at the end of a study, and produce the final clinical study report. CROs are almost always utilized for large pivotal studies that include several clinical sites. For a smaller study, a sponsor may have adequate internal resources or contract a few individuals to perform the same role as a CRO. As a "unit" in a clinical study, CROs are also subject to inspection by authorized

65. *Id.*
66. 21 C.F.R. § 56.107(e).

FDA employees. Many of the abovementioned requirements for investigators (e.g., record retention) are also applicable to CROs.

b. Data Monitoring Committee

In a clinical trial, a data monitoring committee (DMC, also known as data monitoring board (DMB)) is a group of individuals with pertinent expertise that reviews on a regular basis accumulating data from one or more ongoing clinical trials. Trials where a DMC can be useful (but is not required) include those with a study endpoint with a highly favorable or unfavorable result, or even a finding of futility, as an interim analysis might ethically require termination of study before planned completion. In addition, there may be a priori reasons for a particular safety concern, for example, if the procedure for administering the treatment is particularly invasive or possibly has serious toxicity, that warrant a DMC's ongoing review of safety data in a study. An ongoing DMC review may also be necessary for vulnerable study populations (i.e., pediatrics, subjects with an elevated risk of death or other serious outcome).

For FDA's guidance on DMCs, see *Establishment and Operation of Clinical Trial Data Monitoring Committees—Guidance for Clinical Trial Sponsors* (March 2006) (https://www.fda.gov/media/75398/download).

c. Clinical Events Committee (CEC)

A clinical events committee (CEC) may be delegated by a sponsor to monitor certain aspects of study. For example, a CEC may be tasked with reviewing important endpoints reported by investigators to determine if they meet protocol defined criteria. A CEC is valuable when endpoints are "subjective or require application of complex definition and when intervention is not delivered in a blinded fashion."[67] Examples of CEC duties include judging of adverse events (severity, relatedness to investigational device, etc.) and subjective data related to primary endpoints. All multicenter clinical studies will have some level of variability between physician investigators and, specifically, how they assess patients. This variability may be low when objective criteria are used to determine endpoints, and may be higher for subjective or complex endpoint definitions. In cases where variability between clinical sites may be higher, a CEC is recommended to "standardize" review of the results. CECs are typically masked to assigned study arm when performing assessments.

67. *Establishment and Operation of Clinical Trial Data Monitoring Committees—Guidance for Clinical Trial Sponsors* (Mar. 2006), https://www.fda.gov/media/75398/download.

d. Core Laboratories

Core laboratories ("labs") are centralized centers used to provide a "standardized" review of imaging data from a study. For example, a study with an investigational orthopedic implant may require radiographs to evaluate a primary endpoint. A core lab is often utilized in this case to provide an independent and centralized review of the radiographs using protocol-defined criteria.

D. Clinical Study Reports

If a clinical study is performed to support a regulatory application, the marketing application should include a clinical study report (CSR) that summarizes the protocol and presents the key results from a study. The results and analyses presented in the CSR generally follow the protocol and SAP. Based on the submission type and the FDA review team's preference, the raw data from a study and the statistical programs used to create the CSR may need to be provided to the agency.

For a guideline to clinical study reports, see *Structure and Content of Clinical Study Reports—Guideline for Industry* (July 1996) (https://www.fda.gov/media/71271/download).

V. Study Conduct

When designing a clinical study, sponsors should pay careful attention to considerations to ensure procedures are in place to maintain a high level of study conduct and data quality. Many of these considerations have been previously described in Sections 3.II and 3.III, and including adhering to GCP principles of record retention, informed consent, IRB approval, and financial disclosures in addition to the agency's regulations for IDEs. The following sections include further specific recommendations for sponsors.

A. Investigator and Site Selection

As described in Section 3.IV.B.1, sponsors should carefully review clinical centers that may participate in a study. Centers should have sufficient staff and resources to perform the study as specified in the protocol. The investigator (physician) at the center should have the appropriate training (e.g., board certification) and experience with the patient population and preferably with performing clinical studies in general. Investigators with a poor clinical trial history (i.e., issued untitled or warning letters, previously terminated for a clinical study) should not be included. In order for clinical study patients to meet eligibility criteria and represent the larger patient population in the United States, it is often helpful to include a mix of academic and community centers in geographically diverse locations. Thought leaders and key opinion leaders can help in determining the appropriate center types for a clinical study.

Sponsors should establish study-specific selection criteria for investigators and sites and may consider forming site selection committees and disseminating study-specific questionnaires to select the appropriate clinical study sites.

B. Investigator and Clinical Trial Agreements

Two separate agreements are needed for clinical trials, investigator agreements and clinical trial agreements. Per 21 C.F.R. § 812.43(c), a sponsor must obtain from each participating investigator a signed agreement ("investigator agreement") that includes the investigator's curriculum vitae, a statement of relevant experience if applicable, explanation of participation in any termination investigations, and a statement of the investigator's commitment to (1) conduct the investigation in accordance with the agreement, investigational plan, regulations, and conditions of approval from IRB and FDA, (2) supervise all testing of the device with human subjects, and (3) ensure that requirements for obtaining informed consent are met.

A clinical trial agreement (CTA) is a business agreement and separate to the investigator agreement. A CTA is typically between a sponsor and institution, principal investigator, and sub-investigators, and outlines the scope of work and applicable laws and regulations (FDA, HIPAA, and state laws). Compensation and financial arrangements, intellectual property ownership, publication and disclosure, representation and warranties, and insurance and indemnity are typically covered in a CTA.

C. Patient Recruitment

A sponsor may advertise for research subjects to participate in a clinical study. Promotional material must characterize the device as investigational, and cannot include claims related to the safety or effectiveness of the device. Advertisements should be reviewed and approved by the IRB before distribution to ensure they are not unduly coercive, do not promise a certainty of treatment or cure beyond what is outlined in the consent and protocol, and do not include claims regarding device performance compared to another device or treatment.[68]

---

68. *Recruiting Study Subjects—Information Sheet Guidance for Institutional Review Boards and Clinical Investigators* (Jan. 1998), https://www.fda.gov/regulatory-information/search-fda-guidance-documents/recruiting-study-subjects.

Investigators must carefully screen patients to ensure patients meet all eligibility criteria in a protocol and are broadly reflective of the disease or condition being studied. The study population should include an appropriate distribution of gender, age, race, ethnicity, and specific factors related to a disease (e.g., a range of disease severity as applicable).

D. Study Monitoring

Along with selecting qualified investigators and ensuring they are provided with the information they need to conduct the investigation, the sponsor is also responsible for selecting qualified monitors and ensuring proper monitoring of the investigation. Effective monitoring of clinical investigations by sponsors is critical to the protection of human subjects and the conduct of high-quality studies, while protecting the rights, welfare, and safety of human subjects and the quality of the clinical trial data submitted to FDA. FDA requires that a sponsor fulfill the following responsibilities:

- *Secure compliance.* A sponsor who discovers that an investigator is not complying with the signed agreement, the investigational plan, or other applicable FDA regulations, or any conditions of approval imposed by the reviewing IRB or FDA, shall promptly either secure compliance, or discontinue shipments of the device to the investigator and terminate the investigator's participation in the investigation. A sponsor shall also require such an investigator to dispose of or return the device, unless this action would jeopardize the rights, safety, or welfare of a subject.
- *Evaluate unanticipated adverse device effects.* A sponsor shall immediately conduct an evaluation of any unanticipated adverse device effect. An unanticipated adverse device effect that presents an unreasonable risk to subjects must be identified and all investigations or parts of investigations presenting that risk must be terminated not later than 5 working days after the sponsor makes this determination and not later than 15 working days after the sponsor first received notice of the effect.
- *Resumption of terminated studies.* If the device is a significant risk device, a sponsor may not resume a terminated investigation without IRB and FDA approval. If the device is not a significant risk device, a sponsor may not resume a terminated investigation without IRB approval.

In recent years, FDA has recommended a risk-based monitoring approach, encouraging sponsors to develop monitoring plans that manage important risks to human subjects and data quality, and address the challenges of oversight in part by taking advantage of the innovations in modern clinical trials. A risk-based approach to monitoring focuses on oversight activities that prevent or mitigate important and likely risks to data quality and to processes critical to human subject protection and trial integrity.[69]

See Section 3.III.G for monitoring requirements and Section 3.IV.C.1.d for a description of the study monitor. *See also Draft Guidance for Industry—A Risk-Based Approach to Monitoring of Clinical Investigations Questions and Answers* (March 2019) (https://www.fda.gov/regulatory-information/search-fda-guidance-documents/risk-based-approach-monitoring-clinical-investigations-questions-and-answers).

E. Quality Systems Approach to Clinical Trials

Medical device clinical study sponsors must ensure the quality of their clinical trial data via the conduct of the study. Given the scrutiny with which FDA is currently evaluating clinical trial practices, a sponsor should consider implementing a quality system for its clinical studies, to ensure the integrity of the data, ease the premarket review process, and prevent any clinical holds on the company's submissions. Quality systems for clinical studies are akin to quality system regulation for manufacturing.

Generally, clinical quality control systems should include (1) developing clinical trial standard operating procedures ("clinical SOPs") and written procedures for all elements of the study, including corrective actions, (2) conducting internal audits, (3) engaging in constant data quality monitoring, and (4) following the recording and reporting requirements of the GCP regulations mentioned earlier. Specifically, however, quality control methods should incorporate techniques for data measurement, recording, transfer to computer databases, editing, verification, and the modification of incorrect or missing data. The procedures should define the roles and responsibilities of study personnel and ensure proper training of all study personnel and investigators.

F. Standard Operating Procedures

Standard operating procedures (SOPs) are written procedures, with detailed instructions to record routine operations, daily processes and practices followed to conduct investigational tasks according to a clinical

69. *Draft Guidance for Industry—A Risk-Based Approach to Monitoring of Clinical Investigations Questions and Answers* (March 2019) (https://www.fda.gov/regulatory-information/search-fda-guidance-documents/risk-based-approach-monitoring-clinical-investigations-questions-and-answers).

protocol, institutional, and applicable state and federal regulations. SOPs should be written in a uniform manner and should provide step-by-step clear and concise guidance to research staff regarding a specific procedure or operation. Furthermore, it is helpful for SOPs to include the following elements: definition of acronyms, reference to applicable guidance and regulations, date of approval, and revision history.

A set of SOPs can be created for a variety of clinical study tasks and procedures. Following are examples of commonly used SOPs in device clinical trials:

- Recruitment and retention of participants
- Informed consent process
- Filing and recordkeeping
- IRB review: initial, modification, and continuing review
- Study monitoring procedures
- Documenting, resolving, and reporting protocol deviations and violations
- Adverse events, and unanticipated adverse device effects
- Regulatory document submission process
- Preparing for FDA audits
- Study closure

G. Bioresearch Monitoring Audits

FDA's Bioresearch Monitoring (BIMO) Program[70] conducts audits of clinical data contained in PMA and some De Novo and 510(k) submissions, ordinarily prior to approval, to verify the quality and integrity of the data, and to protect the rights and welfare of human research subjects. These inspections can target clinical sites and investigators, clinical research organizations (CROs), and IRBs. Factors for selection of inspected sites include studies with a large number of subjects, multiple sites, data concerns, protocol deviations, or problems identified during sponsor monitoring visits. If FDA determines a BIMO adult is necessary, the visit may be unannounced or planned with advance notice. A pre-inspection conference is conducted before an on-site inspection. Records may be reviewed from the sponsor, physician's office, hospital, nursing home, laboratories, and other sources. During these visits,

70. See contents of Bioresearch Monitoring Program (BIMO), https://www.fda.gov/inspections-compliance-enforcement-and-criminal-investigations/fda-bioresearch-monitoring-information/bioresearch-monitoring-program-information.

inspectors compare submitted data with data at the sites. Auditors will provide inspection feedback and issue an establishment inspection report (EIR), which is also reviewed by the appropriate center at FDA. Potential consequences of site visits include:

- Inspection expanded to include other submissions
- Integrity hold on submissions
- Warning letters and/or AIP
- Clinical investigator disqualification
- Data thrown out from violative sites
- Re-analysis of data
- Third-party audit
- SOP development
- Ethics training
- Supplementary study could be required
- Delays in time to approval/clearance (or non-approval/clearance)

See FDA Inspections of Clinical Investigators—Information Sheet Guidance for Institutional Review Boards, Clinical Investigators, and Sponsors (June 2010) (https://www.fda.gov/media/75185/download).

H. Reimbursement and Coverage Considerations

See Chapter 10 for reimbursement and coverage considerations for clinical studies.

VI. Conclusions

In sum, there are numerous considerations that must be taken into account when considering conducting a clinical study of a medical device. Applicable good clinical practice regulations must be followed and careful attention made to numerous pertinent FDA guidance documents. First, sponsors should determine whether a clinical study is needed to support regulatory approval, which is related to the level of risk posed by the device and partially the type of regulatory application needed to support clearance or approval. If clinical data is needed to support a regulatory submission, an FIH and/or EFS may be needed for a device with a novel technology before proceeding to pilot and pivotal studies.

Depending on the type of study, there are several considerations regarding the design and analysis plan for the study. Thought and key opinion leaders for the specific disease or condition should be consulted to design a study that is appropriate for the device and intended use patient population and statistically valid. Before a study is initiated, IRB approval must be obtained and informed consent developed. In addition, for significant risk studies, FDA must also approve the study protocol in an IDE before study initiation. There are numerous responsibilities sponsors, investigators, and IRBs must comply with before, during, and after conducting a clinical study, all of which contribute to protect the rights, safety, and welfare of humans participating in research and to ensure the quality, reliability, and integrity of data collected.

Logistically, the conduct and monitoring of a clinical trial is often a significant undertaking. There are also business and reimbursement considerations that should be taken into account. Responsibilities with respect to clinical data do not end when a clinical study is completed. Sponsors must then prepare the data for submission to FDA in a regulatory application, prepare for potential audits, answer any questions from the agency regarding the clinical data during the clearance or approval process, and conduct post-approval or postmarket studies as appropriate.

Navigating the world of clinical trials requires significant time and resources, as well as expertise in the rules that must be followed. Regardless of the device type and specific regulatory submission required, early engagement with FDA before a clinical study is initiated is strongly recommended to ensure the study design is appropriate to support a regulatory submission.

CHAPTER 4

Intellectual Property Protections for Medical Devices

Ed Buthusiem, Jeffrey Klenk, and Eric Carlson

I. Initial Considerations of a Patent's Value

Before considering the economic value of a patent, it is first necessary to assess some of the basic characteristics of the patent itself, as well as the rights that may be granted for that patent in a license. One important consideration is the effort needed to commercialize the invention disclosed in the patent. Obviously, for patents that cover products that have already been brought to market, such considerations are less relevant. Also, some patents disclose an invention in something close to the final form of the product to be sold. However, other patents disclose more of a vague idea that may require additional research before a product can be developed using that idea. If such research requires significant sums of money or a significant amount of time, that would tend to have a depressing effect on the value of the patent, since commercializing the patent would require an upfront capital expenditure compared to an uncertain payoff at some point in the future.[1]

1. It is a well-recognized financial principle that a dollar today is worth more than a dollar tomorrow. To account for both a future payout, and the uncertainty of that payout, future cash flows need to be brought back to present value using a discount rate. *See, e.g.*, RICHARD BREALEY, ET AL., FUNDAMENTALS OF CORPORATE FINANCE 115–16, (6th ed. 2009). The choice of discount rates can vary, but should reflect the length of time into the future of the cash flows and the riskiness of those cash flows. *See, generally* Joseph Galanti, *Estimating the Cost of Capital*, *in* LITIGATION SERVICES HANDBOOK: ROLE OF THE FINANCIAL EXPERT (5th ed. 2012).

Particularly for products in the medical space, commercialization can be an uncertain process due to the need, in at least some cases, to conduct clinical trials and, ultimately, to obtain regulatory approval. Furthermore, the process of conducting clinical trials and obtaining regulatory approval could extend the time necessary to bring a product to market, especially if there are adverse outcomes in the clinical trial. Both this uncertainty and the added time would tend to have a depressing effect on the value of a patent that has not yet been commercialized.

When analyzing what might be required to commercialize a patent, it is also important to consider what other technologies may be necessary to bring a product to market. If, for example, the patent covers just a limited component of a much more complex product, that patent may be worth significantly less than a patent covering the entirety of the product. This is particularly true if the company commercializing the product needs to obtain rights to a number of additional patents and needs to pay royalties or other fees to do so. Of course, even a patent covering just a limited component of a product could be of tremendous value if that component is the primary driver of the product's value.[2]

In addition to the efforts and risks associated with commercializing a patent, the rights granted for a patent can affect the patent's value. Exclusive rights to a patent can offer tremendous benefits to the licensee but could limit the licensing revenues recognized by the licensor. Also, some technologies benefit from so-called network effects, in which case the widespread diffusion of the technology enhances its value. This is particularly so for technologies that are part of an ecosystem and the more broadly that ecosystem is adopted the more valuable the technology becomes.[3] In such instances, offering a reduced licensing fee to encourage

2. Understanding the relationship between the patented invention and the product into which that invention is incorporated is particularly important in the litigation context. Case law indicates that damages cannot be assessed on the entire value of a product unless it can be shown that the "infringing components [are] the basis for customer demand for the entire machine including the parts beyond the claimed invention." Cornell Univ. v. Hewlett-Packard Co., 609 F. Supp. 2d 279, 286 (N.D.N.Y. 2009). For a more general discussion of this issue, see RICHARD TROXEL & WILLIAM KERR, ASSETS AND FINANCES: CALCULATING INTELLECTUAL PROPERTY DAMAGES § 5.8 (2016).

3. One economics text defines the network effect as a "consumer's willingness to pay for a good or service increases as the number of other consumers buying the product rises." *See* LYNNE PEPALL ET AL., INDUSTRIAL ORGANIZATION: CONTEMPORARY THEORY AND PRACTICE 77–78 (3d ed. 2005).

adoption of the patented technology could actually enhance the technology's value and the revenue recognized from licensing the patent.[4]

Some patent licenses may also limit the geographic scope of where the patent can be practiced or the fields of use in which the patent can be practiced. In the medical space, a licensor may grant a license for the development of a product to treat a specific disease or condition but expressly limit the rights of a licensee to develop a product to treat other diseases or conditions. Such granting of limited patent rights allows a patent holder to monetize its technology in areas where it may not compete while protecting its hegemony in areas where it does compete.

With these considerations in hand, it is then possible to begin assessing what economic value a patent might have. The discussion that follows generally assumes that a product embodying a patented technology has already been developed, obtained any necessary regulatory approval, and brought to market. To the extent that has not yet happened, then for the reasons just discussed any economic assessment of a patent must be tempered by the inherent uncertainty that surrounds the development and commercialization of a technology.

II. The Economic Value of a Patent

When thinking about the economic value of a patent (as opposed to the strategic value or some other consideration) it is useful to keep in mind that economics is fundamentally the study of trade-offs: what must be given up to obtain the desired result. In economic parlance, this is known as opportunity cost and is measured as the cost of not pursuing the next-best alternative. Every decision has some cost associated with it. Hence the saying, "There's no such thing as a free lunch." If nothing else, simply the time spent attending an otherwise free lunch represents a cost. Because every decision has a cost associated with it, economics looks at the incremental, or marginal, difference between two decisions and measures the extra benefit or extra cost associated with making one decision versus another.

---

4. David Teece, a noted scholar on innovation, contends that in some industries reaching a common standard may be necessary for the widespread diffusion of a product. In those industries, Teece notes that a "firm may need to license-out its technology widely, and often must do so on liberal terms" and that such licenses "are often negotiated for minimal royalties." As Teece observes, however, while the "innovator shares the market," the "total market size is larger." David Teece, Managing Intellectual Capital § 8.4 (2002).

Assessing the value of a patent is grounded in this fundamental economic principle of incremental benefit or incremental cost. Often, the technology embodied by a patent will result in a more desirable product that generates a higher level of revenue (either because the product commands a higher price or captures a greater share of sales) relative to a product not containing that technology. Alternatively, the technology embodied by a patent may reduce a firm's costs of production. Either way, the use of the technology embodied in a particular patent would be expected to generate an incrementally higher level of profitability for a firm compared to that firm adopting an alternative technology. This incremental profitability forms the basis of a patent's value.

A focus on the incremental profitability of a patent is also enshrined in U.S. case law. One of the guiding cases on evaluating damages stemming from patent infringement is *Georgia-Pacific*.[5] That case lays out 15 factors that the court found to be "seemingly more pertinent" to the evaluation of a royalty for a license to a patent.[6] Many of these factors specifically address the value of the patent relative to the next-best alternative for that patent. For example, Factor 9 relates to the "utility and advantages of the patent property under the old modes or devices, if any, that had been used for working out similar results."[7] Likewise, Factor 13 relates to the "portion of the realizable profit that should be credited to the invention as distinguished from non-patented elements, the manufacturing process, business risks, or significant features or improvements added by the infringer."[8]

As Factor 13 emphasizes, the focus on assessing a patent's incremental value needs to isolate just the contributions of the patented technology, separate from other drivers of a product's value.[9] With respect to medical devices, this means that when assessing the value of a patented technology incorporated within the device it is first necessary to identify the other aspects of that device that contribute to its value. These other aspects could include other patented technology embodied in the device, the regulatory risks overcome in bringing the device to market, and the marketing efforts undertaken to create demand for the device.

Given the economic value created by a particular technology, patents serve an important role in protecting that value and ensuring that the

5. Georgia-Pacific Corp. v. U.S. Plywood Corp., 318 F. Supp. 1116 (S.D.N.Y. 1970).

6. *Id.* at 1120.

7. *Id.*

8. *Id.*

9. This implications of this is discussed more fully in footnote 2.

inventor receives compensation for the efforts spent developing the patented technology. In this regard, patents are no different from any other mechanism which allows a property holder to benefit from the ownership of that property, except that patents protect intellectual, as opposed to real, property. As explained by one economist, the "patent system was perceived by the framers of the Constitution as a system of incentives and rewards" with the patent "offer[ing] the statutory right to exclude as a means of inducing creative activity."[10] This statutory right to exclude provides a "reward to those who invest their time and money in technological invention and innovation" and allows an inventor to recoup any sunk costs that he or she incurred.[11]

III. Three Principle Valuation Approaches

Three valuation approaches are generally used to identify the incremental value of a patent.[12] These are (1) the income approach, (2) the cost approach, and (3) the market approach. Each of these three approaches provides a quantitative framework for assessing a patent's value. It should be noted, however, that not all approaches will necessarily be viable for any given patent or any given product. The application of any particular valuation approach will be dependent on the specific facts and circumstances of the patent and how that patent has been incorporated into a product.

A. Income Approach

As its name implies, the income approach is predicated on isolating the incremental income generated by the inclusion of a patented technology in a particular product. Income here can be viewed as synonymous with profit, which is simply the revenue earned by a firm on its sales of a product minus the costs incurred by that firm in making those sales. Although a simple concept, determining a firm's profits on a particular product can

---

10. Stanley Besen & Leo Raskind, *An Introduction to the Law and Economics of Intellectual Property*, 5(1) J. ECON. PERSPECTIVES 8, 3–27 (Winter 1991). *See also* Roger Blair & Thomas Cotter, *An Economic Analysis of Damages Rules in Intellectual Property Law*, 39(5) WM & MARY L. REV. 1585–1694.

11. F.M. SCHERER & DAVID ROSS, INDUSTRIAL MARKET STRUCTURE AND ECONOMIC PERFORMANCE 621–22 (3d ed. 1990).

12. These approaches can also be used more broadly to assess the value of a wide range of both tangible and intangible assets. For a comprehensive overview of these approaches, see JAMES HITCHNER, FINANCIAL VALUATION: APPLICATIONS AND MODELS (2d ed. 2006).

be difficult in practice. In particular, there can be a question over which costs are relevant to consider for the purposes of identifying the profits attributable to a patent (e.g., should one consider development costs, fixed costs of production, sales and marketing costs, etc.) and, even once it has been decided which costs are relevant for consideration, measuring those costs (as distinct from other costs) can require complex calculations.[13]

A necessary first step in determining the incremental profitability contributed by a patented technology's inclusion in a product is isolating the additional revenue generated by that patented technology. This additional revenue could manifest itself in the form of either a higher price or a greater quantity of sales. Very rarely, will all the revenue associated with a product be attributable to just the patented technology.[14] More likely, a number of different aspects of the product will contribute to its revenue-generating capacity.

One common way to isolate the incremental revenue generated by the inclusion of a particular patented technology is to compare the price and sales volume of a product including that technology to the price and sales volume of a product not including that technology. Such comparisons could involve a comparison of the same product over time, to the extent that older versions of the product did not incorporate the patented technology, or could involve a comparison of two different products that are primarily differentiated by whether they include the patented technology or not. Of course, any such comparison needs to be cognizant of other factors that could be driving differences in price and sales volumes. For example, a newer version of the same product could command a higher price both because of its inclusion of the patented technology and also because marketplace conditions have become more favorable to the sale

---

13. One way of estimating relevant costs can be through the use of econometrics; namely, regression analysis. A regression is a statistical tool used to measure the effects of one or more economic factors on another economic factor thought to be dependent on those factors. These are known as the independent and dependent variables, respectively. For a basic explanation of regression analysis, see ABA, ECONOMETRICS: LEGAL PRACTICAL, AND TECHNICAL ISSUES, ch. 1 (2005). A more technical discussion can be found in JEFFREY WOOLDRIDGE, INTRODUCTORY ECONOMETRICS, A MODERN APPROACH (4th ed. 2009). In the context of cost estimation, a regression could be used to measure the relationship, for instance, between a firm's volume of output and a particular cost. *See, e.g.*, Jeffrey Kinrich, *Cost Estimation*, *in* LITIGATION SERVICES HANDBOOK: THE ROLE OF THE FINANCIAL EXPERT § 7.6 (3d ed. 2001).

14. See *supra*, note 2.

of that product. Various techniques exist to control for such intertemporal changes.[15]

After isolating the incremental revenue associated with the inclusion of a patented technology in a product, it is necessary to determine the profitability of that revenue. This can be done by applying some measurement of costs (either the monetary amount of those costs or some percentage reflecting those costs) to the measurement of revenue, as discussed earlier.

Often, the income approach will be used as the basis for determining a possible royalty rate for the purposes of licensing a patented technology. Such royalty rates can be structured in multiple forms but typically take the form of an upfront payment, a per unit amount, or a percentage of revenue. To arrive at such a royalty rate, it is often necessary to apportion the incremental profitability generated by a patented technology between the patent holder (the licensor) and the entity seeking to use the patented technology (the licensee). Certain industry heuristics might exist for conducting such an apportionment but frequently a consideration of the licensor's and licensee's relative bargaining positions are considered.[16] Various economic theories can be used to inform the evaluation of each side's bargaining position, but the application of any particular theory needs to conform to the specific facts of the negotiation at hand.[17]

---

15. As discussed in footnote 13, regression analysis could be used to isolate the incremental value of a product with the patented technology versus a product without the patented technology, while also controlling for other differences between the products and other changes that may have occurred in the marketplace.

16. Historically, one commonly used rule-of-thumb was the so-called 25 percent rule which assigned 25 percent of a patent's estimated value to the licensor while the licensee was assigned the remaining 75 percent. However, in its *Uniloc* decision, the federal circuit severely restricted, if not outright prohibited, the use of the 25 percent rule for litigation purposes stating: "This court now holds as a matter of Federal Circuit law that the 25 percent rule of thumb is a fundamentally flawed tool for determining a baseline royalty in a hypothetical negotiation." Uniloc USA, Inc. v. Microsoft Corp., 632 F.3d 1292, 1315 (Fed. Cir. 2011). Outside of litigation purposes, anecdotal exists that some licensing professionals still rely on the 25 percent rule as a general check on a licensing outcome. *See* TROXEL & KERR, *supra* note 2, §§ 5.24 & 5.25.

17. An economic theory of bargaining that has gained some traction in case law is known as the Rubinstein bargaining model, named after Ariel Rubinstein. See Ariel Rubinstein, *Perfect Equilibrium in a Bargaining Model*, 50 ECONOMETRICA (1982). In essence, Rubinstein's model favors the more "patient" party in a negotiation, where patience could be viewed as the parties' respective costs of capital. The implication of this model is that the party that can better afford to wait before consummating a license agreement will likely be able to extract better terms from the other party. Although courts have been open to this general line of argumentation, they have noted

B. Cost Approach

In contrast to the income approach, the cost approach measures the incremental cost savings associated with a patented technology. In some instances, use of a patented technology will reduce the costs of production. As an example, use of a patented technology may improve the yield of finished product given the same level of inputs. In other instances, infringement of a patented technology can be avoided by adopting an alternative design, albeit at a higher cost. This is known as a non-infringing alternative. In either instance—the costs saved or the higher costs avoided—the monetary value of those savings can provide insight into what a particular patent is worth.

Reduced costs of production are in many ways analogous to the increased profitability measured in the income approach. Often, reduced costs of production flow right to the bottom line (i.e., directly contribute to a firm's profitability) and so provide a direct indication of a patented technology's economic value to a firm. Also similar to the income approach, one could think of converting a reduced cost of production into a royalty amount, such as the percentage of a good's selling price represented by those cost savings or the per-unit value of those cost savings. Again, it may be necessary to engage in an apportionment exercise to determine an appropriate allocation of the cost savings between the patent holder and the user of the patented technology.

Rather than seeking to license a patented technology, some firms will instead seek to find an alternative to that technology that would not be deemed as infringing.[18] However, there is usually some cost associated with pursuing that alternative: the product at issue might need to be redesigned, the manufacturing process might need to be altered, additional regulatory approval might need to be obtained, and so on. In addition to the out-of-pocket expenditures a firm may incur to avoid infringement, the time necessary to implement a non-infringing alternative can often result in a delay in bringing a product to market. For some products,

---

that its application must be specifically tied to the "facts of the case." See Limelight Networks, Inc. v. XO Comm'cns, LLC & Akamai Technologies, Inc., 2018 WL 678245 (E.D.V.A. 2018). It may also be possible to apply a different form of bargaining theory, based on the work of John Nash, to evaluating the relative bargaining positions of the parties to a licensing negotiation. *See* Richard Higgins & Jeffrey Klenk, *An Application of Nash Bargaining to Intellectual Property Negotiations*, 25 FED. CIR. B.J. (2015).

18. In a litigation context, opinions by qualified experts may be necessary to establish whether a particular alternative is truly infringing or not.

where arriving on the market in a timely manner is crucial to a product's success, such a delay could impose additional costs on a firm.[19]

Particularly if avoiding infringement of a particular patent is a relatively costless endeavor, the value of that patent may be capped. This is consistent with the economic principle articulated earlier that economic value can be derived by analyzing the difference between the economic outcome resulting from one decision versus the economic outcome resulting from pursuing the next-best alternative. If the difference in economic outcomes between using the patented technology versus implementing a non-infringing alternative are not too different, then it may be difficult to convince a potential licensee to pay a significant amount to access that patented technology. In many instances, the value of a patent may be capped by the cost of implementing a non-infringing alternative as a prospective user of a patented technology would not pay more for access to that technology than the cost of using the next-best alternative.[20]

---

19. Often, the first firm to bring a product to market can establish the standards for subsequent products to follow (see footnotes 3 and 4) or can establish a reputation for success that subsequent entrants find difficult to match. See DAVID BESANKO, ET AL., ECONOMICS OF STRATEGY 554–58 (1996). In the generic pharmaceutical industry, the first manufacturer to challenge an innovator's patent is, under certain conditions, awarded a period of 180 day exclusivity during which time it is the only manufacturer allowed to market a generic version of the innovator's drug. During this period, the sole generic manufacturer can accrue sizable profits. *See, e.g.*, David Korn, et al., *A New History and Discussion of 180-Day Exclusivity*, 64(2) FOOD & DRUG L.J., 335–90 (2009). Also in the pharmaceutical space, the first entrant may be able to obtain more favorable formulary placement relative to later entrants.

20. The existence, or potential existence, of a non-infringing alternative is often cited in the litigation context as well as a cap on possible damages. One economic article, though, has pointed to the potential adverse public policy outcome from allowing a non-infringing alternative to serve as a cap on damages. According to the authors, the non-infringing alternative may serve as a so-called free option to the party accused of infringement since that party could theoretically choose to infringe by not expending the time or money to develop the non-infringing alternative but, if subsequently accused of infringement, then rely on the potential existence of the non-infringing alternative as a cap on damages. Arguably, then, the party accused of infringement is rewarded for its infringement since, at worst, its act of infringement is no more costly to it than if it had developed the non-infringing alternative in the first place. See Jerry Hausman & Gregory Leonard, *Real Options and Patent Damages: The Legal Treatment of Non-Infringing Alternatives, and Incentives to Innovate*, 20(4) J. ECON. SURVEYS 493–512 (2006).

C. Market Approach

For some patents, it may be possible to glean their economic value from licensing agreements previously entered into for similar technologies and in similar industries. This process is analytically similar to, say, gleaning the economic value of a house by looking at sales of comparable houses in the same neighborhood. Since no two houses are ever exactly the same, adjustments often must be made to ensure that comparisons are occurring on as nearly equal of a basis as possible. With patents, a similar process can often be undertaken of identifying existing licensing agreements that reflect a similar technology, being used for a similar purpose, as the patent-at-issue. Provided that the economic conditions are sufficiently similar between the existing licensing agreements and the patent-at-issue, the royalty rates in those existing licensing agreements can provide insight into the economic value that a patent holder and a licensee previously assigned to similar technology.

When attempting to determine a patent's value from licensing agreements for other, similar patents, the key is, of course, ensuring not only the comparability of the technology embodied by the patents but also ensuring the comparability of the economic circumstances under which the licenses are negotiated. Even if a previously consummated licensing agreement is for a technology generally comparable to the patent-at-issue, that agreement may reflect idiosyncratic factors unique to the negotiation that resulted in that agreement. It may be that access to a patented technology was especially valuable to one firm, perhaps because of its particular manufacturing process, and less valuable to other firms. The passage of time may also result in differing values, even for generally comparable technology, as over time the novelty of a particular invention may fade or additional non-infringing alternatives may become available. Understanding the economic factors underpinning the negotiations resulting in previous licensing agreements for comparable technology thus can be quite important in ensuring the applicability of those agreements in benchmarking the potential value of the patent-at-issue.

It is also important to note whether prior licensing agreements for the patent-at-issue, or for similar technology, were the result of arms-length negotiations (i.e., negotiations between unrelated firms) and whether they were consummated under duress (such as the threat of litigation). Negotiations between a parent company and one of its subsidiaries, for instance, may not reflect the same outcome that two completely independent companies would have achieved in their negotiations. Likewise, in litigation, resolution of disputed patent claims is mandatory, meaning that the licensee may not have been free to walk away from a negotiation over royalty rates and hold out for a better outcome.[21] This would reduce the bargaining power of the licensee and may result in a royalty rate for the patent-at-issue different from what would have resulted had the bargaining power of both parties been more evenly split.

In addition to the previously consummated agreements for the patent-at-issue (or for similar technology), those agreements that *failed* to be consummated also provide valuable insight. It may be that the inventor (or patent holder) had an overly optimistic view of the patented technology and placed inflated valuations on that technology. To the extent those inflated valuations were then rejected by potential licensees, it may be useful to investigate the reasons why those licensees rejected previous licensing offers. As just one example, industry participants may have realized that commercializing a patented technology, or obtaining regulatory approval for a product containing that technology, would be more difficult than the inventor realized and so factored those risks into their own assessment of the patented technology's value.

D. Patent Valuation in the Context of Litigation

Often, two parties will find themselves attempting to determine the value of a patent in the midst of litigation. Case law envisions that if a patent is found to be both valid and infringed, the patent holder is entitled to no less than a reasonable royalty to compensate it for the use of its patent.[22] The three principle valuation techniques just discussed would still

---

21. Courts have historically disfavored reliance on licenses consummated as part of the litigation process. However, in a 2010 decision, while affirming its previous hesitation to accept as evidence royalty rates stemming from litigation, the federal circuit observed "that the most reliable license in this record arose out of litigation," and noted that the defendant was "entitled to rely on that record evidence to show a royalty rate reasonably related to the technology in this litigation." ResQNet.com, Inc. v. Lansa, Inc., 594 F.3d 860, 872–73 (Fed. Cir. 2010). *See also* TROXEL & KERR, *supra* note 2, § 5:30.

22. A patent holder may also be entitled to a damages award based on lost profits if it can show that absent the infringement it would have made those sales. A number of conditions must be met, however, to establish the basis for a lost profits award, including demand for the patented product; absence of acceptable non-infringing alternatives; manufacturing and marketing capability on the part of the patent holder to exploit the demand; and the amount of profit the patent holder would have earned. These are known as the *Panduit* factors, stemming from the eponymous case. Panduit Corp. v. Stahlin Bros. Fibre Works, 575 F.2d 1152, 1156 (6th Cir. 1978). A note of caution is in order, that when analyzing potential lost profits damages, one needs to

be applicable in such a situation. In fact, the *Georgia-Pacific* construct envisions that each side's damages experts will reconstruct a hypothetical negotiation modeling what would have happened had the patent holder and the infringer reached a licensing agreement just prior to the first act of infringement.[23] The primary difference between such a hypothetical negotiation and what may have happened in actuality is that in the hypothetical negotiation it is assumed with complete certainty that the patent-at-issue is both valid and infringed.[24] Uncertainty, as would likely have existed in the real world, would tend to have a depressing effect on the negotiated value.

IV. Market Dynamics Play an Important Role in Determining a Patent's Value

The value of any particular patent will be crucially dependent on the dynamics of the market in which products embodying the patented technology will be sold. Medical devices are complex tools that are integral to the performance of medical procedures, many of a life-sustaining or life-saving nature. They can range in cost from a few hundred dollars, or less, to hundreds of thousands dollars and more. Net spending on medical devices in the United States is anticipated to grow at a significant rate. In 2017, net spending on medical devices in the United States was

---

consider the relationship between possible price erosion and the quantity of the product that would have been sold absent the infringement. *See, e.g.*, James Nieberding, *Lost Profits and Price Erosion in Patent Infringement Cases: Implications of* Crystal Semiconductor, 16(1) J. FORENSIC ECONOMICS 37–49 (2003).

23. *Georgia-Pacific Corp.*, 318 F. Supp. at 1120. Determining the date of first infringement can often be difficult as a dispute may exist over what conduct on the part of the alleged infringer constitutes infringement. However, the outcome of a hypothetical negotiation could be crucially dependent on when that negotiation would have occurred. *See, e.g.*, John Jarosz & Michael Chapman, *The Hypothetical Negotiation and Reasonable Royalty Damages: The Tail Wagging the Dog*, 16(3) STAN. TECH. L. REV. 803–07, 769–832 (Spring 2013).

24. In addition, the hypothetical negotiation generally relies on what information would have been available to both parties at that point in time. However, case law affirms that information subsequent to the hypothetical negotiation can also be relied upon with one court observing that the hypothetical negotiation date "does not rigidly foreclose the factfinder from considering subsequent events." Honeywell Int'l, Inc. v. Hamilton Sunstrand Corp., 378 F. Supp. 2d 459, 464 (D. Del. 2005). Reliance on information subsequent to the hypothetical negotiation is known as the "Book of Wisdom." *See also* Jarosz & Chapman, *supra* note 23, at 802–03.

approximately $156 billion and is expected to grow to $432.6 billion by 2025.[25] Thus, it should come as no surprise that payors, such as health plans and government insurers, constantly seek ways to control health care costs. Two common reimbursement models for medical devices are so-called fee-for-service (FFS) arrangements and value-based payments (VBP). Understanding these reimbursement models can be critical to assessing the value of a patent for a medical device.

A. Reimbursement Mechanisms for Medical Devices

Traditionally, FFS arrangements have been the prevailing payment model in the pharmaceutical and medical device reimbursement environment. Under the FFS payment model, health care providers are reimbursed based upon the quantity of services they provide, rather than the quality of care. With the focus on quantity over quality, health care providers often purchased medical devices and medical technology equipment themselves in an effort to increase their own profits. For example, many physician practices purchased their own MRIs and other imaging equipment, rather than sending a patient to an imaging center for testing. For medical device manufacturers, this translated into a marketing model focused on selling to customers based on a negotiated price that often included volume-based and other discounts to list price. As the cost associated with the use of these devices increased, private and public payors alike have sought to encourage cost containment through increased governmental pressure and economic incentives which seek to tie costs to outcomes.

In contrast, in VBP models the price of a drug or medical device is directly linked to the economic and therapeutic value it provides to patients, payers, and the health care system. As a result, such models have gained traction as a mechanism to better align payments with efforts to reduce the costs of health care while continuing to prioritize safety and quality. These arrangements can take many forms, such as health plans requiring clinical results for patients in exchange for an agreed-upon price; giving refunds for adverse events caused by the drug or device; and encouraging patient compliance by lowering the cost of a drug for

25. Jeff Lagasse, *United States Remains the Largest Market for Medical Devices, at More than $150 Billion*, HEALTHCARE FINANCE (May 13, 2019), https://www.healthcarefinancenews.com/news/united-states-remains-largest-market-medical-devices-more-150-billion; and Medical Device Market Report: Trends, Forecast and Competitive Analysis, https://www.researchandmarkets.com/research/42d8b9/global_medical?w=5.

each subsequent prescription refill. As VBP models have become commonplace in the pharmaceutical industry in recent years, payors are now seeking to apply similar value-based approaches to the purchase of medical devices.

B. Recent Shift in the Medical Device and Technology Industry toward Value-Based Payments

While VBP models have become well-established in the pharmaceutical industry, adoption in the medical device industry has been much slower due to differences in the reimbursement landscape between drugs and devices. Because reimbursement payments for drugs are primarily based upon the cost of that product, cost plays a large role in formulary placement, which can influence the usage of a drug.[26] With regard to devices, however, insurers rarely reimburse providers separately for the cost of devices. Rather, providers are reimbursed based upon the total cost of the procedure in which the device was used. As further explained in a report published in the Health Affairs Journal:[27]

> A medication's price is usually the primary driver of its overall cost of use. For this reason, modifying a drug's price based on outcomes can significantly affect treatment cost-effectiveness; all else held equal, halving a drug's price should make it twice as cost-effective. For devices, the device itself represents a smaller and more variable percentage of its overall use cost. For example, while a coronary artery stent costs around $1,000 (less if purchased in bulk and after discounts), a hospital receives $10,000

---

26. A formulary is a list of prescription drugs or medical devices that a committee, usually made up of physicians, pharmacists, and administrators, have determined offer the greatest overall value and should be available to patients. In a typical formulary, usually only one or two drugs in a given therapeutic class are listed. Health plan formularies dictate which drugs are covered by insurance, while hospital formularies dictate which drugs a doctor may prescribe to a patient. The aim of the formulary is to include products that are safe, effective, and affordable while maintaining or improving patient care. If a drug or device with a high cost is not perceived to have a significant benefit over other drugs or devices for the same use, it is unlikely that the product will have favorable formulary placement. Thus, drug companies have been well aware of the need to demonstrate to payors and providers how their product is different and why their product deserves to be paid the price set by the company.

27. Daniel Blumenthal et al., *Using Outcomes-Based Pricing for Medical Devices to Improve Cardiovascular Disease Treatment Value*, Health Affairs (March 29, 2018), https://www.healthaffairs.org/do/10.1377/hblog20180326.318510/full/.

or more in reimbursement for outpatient PCI (and more for inpatient procedures).

Thus, because reducing the price of a device to reflect its value to patients has little impact on cost-effectiveness, device manufacturers had little incentive to engage in the same negotiations with payors as their counterparts in the pharmaceutical industry.[28] Nevertheless, recent government initiatives are now leaving device manufacturers with little choice but to transition to value-based pricing.

As just one example of this transition, on April 1, 2016, the Centers for Medicare and Medicaid Services (CMS) implemented a first-of-its-kind mandatory bundled-payment model for hip or knee replacements performed in randomly selected metropolitan areas.[29] At the outset of the program, approximately 800 hospitals were required to participate in the program, wherein Medicare provides a bonus payment to participating providers whose aggregate fee-for-service costs for a hip- or knee-replacement episode were lower than the predetermined benchmark cost for that service. Conversely, if the aggregate fee-for-service costs were higher than the targeted benchmark, the hospital would owe the difference in cost to CMS.[30]

This initiative, along with other CMS initiatives,[31] were designed to reverse the incentives inherent in the FFS model—that is, the potential financial bonuses and the use of bundled payments promoted a decrease in unnecessary procedures and medical services in hospitals while encouraging coordinated care between hospitals and other providers to cut costs. As potentially unnecessary services decrease, the overall volume of the medical devices market has decreased as well. For example, a

---

28. *Id.*

29. Michael Barnett et al., *Two-Year Evaluation of Mandatory Bundled Payments for Joint Replacement*, 380 New Eng. J. Med. 252–62 (Jan. 17, 2019), *available at* https://www.nejm.org/doi/full/10.1056/NEJMsa1809010.

30. Aaron Glickman et al., *The Current State of Evidence on Bundled Payments*, Issue Brief, 22(3) Leonard Davis Inst. of Health Econ., U. Pa. (Oct. 8, 2018), *available at* https://ldi.upenn.edu/brief/current-state-evidence-bundled-payments.

31. On January 9, 2018, CMS announced the Bundled Payments for Care Improvement Advanced payment model, a voluntary program that provides physicians with the opportunity to earn financial incentives when an episode of care is under a certain cost metric which factors in quality (*The Effect of Value-Based Care on the Medical Devices Industry*, Med. Device Network (Jan. 17, 2018), https://www.medicaldevice-network.com/comment/effect-value-based-care-medical-devices-industry/). Medicare provides participating providers with bonuses or penalties based on Medicare spending per episode (BPCI Advanced, CMS.gov, https://innovation.cms.gov/innovation-models/bpci-advanced).

2017 study analyzing spending for lower extremity joint replacements at a health system participating in the BPCI initiative revealed a decrease of 20.8 percent of spending per procedure.[32] Reductions in medical device costs (e.g., implants) contributed the greatest proportion of savings, down an average of 29 percent per case.[33] Moreover, as these programs increased the pressure on hospitals to control costs, the hospitals in turn are putting more pressure on medical device manufacturers to differentiate themselves and deliver higher value. More and more frequently, value committees are driving hospitals' purchasing decisions, including being more selective about which technologies they choose.[34] To meet these new expectations, more device manufacturers are feeling the pressure to shift to VBP models to remain competitive in the market.

C. Design and Implementation of Value-Based Payment Systems for Medical Devices

To adapt to the shift from FFS to VBP models, medical device manufacturers have been pursuing a variety of different strategies. These include the following:[35]

1. Outcome guarantee approach. Manufacturers give providers discounts or rebates on the product if certain clinical or economic outcomes are not met.
2. Gain sharing approach. Manufacturers furnish product at a lower price if the providers agree to share a portion of the cost savings from the use of product with the manufacturer.
3. Access service approach. Manufacturers allow providers to access technologies through a subscription service, rather than purchasing the technology outright.
4. Management service approach. Providers outsource the management and operation of a laboratory or clinic to the manufacturer, rather than administering it themselves.

---

32. Amol Navathe et al., *Cost of Joint Replacement Using Bundled Payment Models*, 177(2) JAMA INTER. MED. 214–22 (2017), *available at* https://jamanetwork.com/journals/jamainternalmedicine/fullarticle/2594805.

33. *Id.*

34. Jay Zhu et al., *New Payment Models in Medtech: Regulatory, Technology, and Marketplace Trends Converging to Create New Opportunities for Manufacturers*, DELOITTE INSIGHTS (Mar. 2, 2020), https://www2.deloitte.com/us/en/insights/industry/life-sciences/medical-device-business-model-payments.html.

35. *Id.*

The facilitation of these arrangements necessitates a reliance on data to drive sales and insights to an extent that is unprecedented in the medical device and technology industries. Under these various VBP arrangements, data is needed to establish baselines, design solutions, measure performance, and inform consumer decisions.[36] As was the case in the pharmaceutical industry, payors and medical device manufacturers can expect to spend significant amounts of time collaborating to develop and implement VBP agreements, due to the large amounts of health systems data and the complex data collection and analysis.

Despite the added complexity, VBP models are particularly suited to medical device and technology companies as they often are inherently data-driven—indeed, according to AdvaMed, medical device manufacturers function as "the backbone of the data ecosystem."[37] Medical device companies can harness their resources, data infrastructure, and availability of product-related information to collect, analyze, and share patient and operational data in a manner that is compliant with health information security and privacy regulations. Nevertheless, even with their often advanced data collection and reporting capabilities, the monitoring and analysis of the patient data needed to facilitate VBP arrangements is more complex than most companies are accustomed to, and therefore has proven challenging for manufacturers to execute. To keep up with the increasing focus on VBP frameworks, companies must sharpen their abilities to measure outcomes, improve data systems and interoperability, and expand the real-world evidence base for their products to inform value propositions.

D. Implications of Value-Based Payment Systems for Valuing Medical Device Patents

Under VBP models of reimbursement and coverage, the ways in which manufacturers engage with health care providers, payors, and patients will necessarily evolve to support a more fluid exchange of information and a heightened focus on patient experience and outcomes. This means that medical device companies can no longer be focused solely upon developing and commercializing products, but must also design and market solutions combining technology and service to enhance clinical,

---

36. Letter from AdvaMed to Ms. Joanne Chiedi, Acting Inspector General, Department of Health and Human Services, dated December 24, 2019, *available at* https://www.advamed.org/sites/default/files/resource/advamed_comments_re_oig_vb_aks_sh_nprm_2019-12-24.pdf (p. 2).

37. *Id.*

economic, and patient-centered outcomes. This suggests that those patents facilitating products that enhance patient outcomes will have particular economic value in a world of VBP systems.

As discussed earlier, the economic value of a patent often is determined by the incremental profitability of a product containing the patented technology relative to a product that does not. In the context of reimbursement for a medical device based on a VBP system, it will be important to understand how the patented technology is likely to improve a patient's outcome.[38] Codifying this improvement and measuring the enhanced reimbursement stemming from that improvement would likely form the basis of assessing a medical device patent's economic value. Patents simply providing an alternative method of treatment, without providing the possibility of improved patient outcomes, are likely to have less economic value when reimbursement is tied to a VBP system.

V. Monetization of a Medical Devices Patent

In some instances, a patent may have some intrinsic value "sitting on the shelf" of a patent owner. These instances may include defensive value (e.g., in the case of an operating company looking to block others from entering a market) and value in helping to secure funding and/or otherwise legitimize research efforts or company operations (e.g., in the case of a startup looking to raise capital and grow). However, more typically, to unlock the potential value of a patent a patent owner must take affirmative steps vis-à-vis third parties. This is particularly true because a patent is generally regarded as a "wasting asset." That is, a patent has a fixed expiration date in the future and generally decreases in value as the point in time where the exclusionary rights provided by the patent cease to exist draws closer.

At the outset, it is important to note that many patents have little value from a monetization standpoint. This is particularly true where the patented technology has not been adopted commercially, the patented technology would be difficult to commercialize and/or is unlikely to be commercialized in the future, and/or there exist legal deficiencies with respect to how the patent was prosecuted that prevent it from being commercially valuable. Numerous patents fall into one or more of these buckets. Indeed, one only need to look the sheer volume of patents that exist to reach the conclusion that most do not have significant monetization

38. This likely could be assessed using the same data collected by the medical device company to justify enhanced reimbursements under a VBP regimen.

potential. To get a sense of this number, as of the beginning of 2019, the U.S. had issued over 10.65 million patents in total,[39] with 370,434 patents newly issued and 616,852 patents newly filed in 2019 alone.[40] However, for the relative minority of patents with commercial value, patent monetization is potentially very lucrative for the patent owner. To this end, there are three primary avenues that a patent owner can pursue to monetize its patent.

A. Sale of a Patent

The first monetization option is for a patent owner to sell its patent. A patent sale is a transfer of ownership of a patent from the patent owner to a third party. Patents are intangible intellectual property assets that are freely transferrable from one entity to another, the same way that a parcel of land or a piece of machinery are. As part of a sale, a patent owner gives up *all* rights and ownership to its patent, assigning them to the buyer, usually in exchange for some form of monetary compensation.

Generally speaking, there are several types of entities that might be interested in buying a patent. These entities include operating companies, patent assertion entities (PAEs), or other investors. An operating company, that is, one that is actively developing, manufacturing, and/or selling a product, might be interested in buying a patent because it plans to invest in and bring to market the patented technology, it is interested in leveraging the patent rights for "defensive" purposes, and/or to help it attract investors and raise capital. Another type of entity that might be interested in buying a patent is a PAE. PAEs are companies that generate most of their revenue from the acquisition and subsequent monetization (typically, through licensing and/or litigation) of patents.[41] Finally, more broadly, there exists a robust secondary market for patent sales comprised of various brokers, investors, and other others looking to acquire patent assets for various purposes.

The sales price for patents can vary significantly and is dependent on a variety of factors, including the technology field of the patent, the extent to which the patented technology has been commercially adopted, the

39. *See* Table of Issue Years and Patent Numbers, for Selected Document Types Issued since 1836, USPTO, *available at* https://www.uspto.gov/web/offices/ac/ido/oeip/taf/issuyear.htm.

40. *See* Performance and Accountability Report, FY 2019, USPTO, *available at* https://www.uspto.gov/sites/default/files/documents/USPTOFY19PAR.pdf.

41. PAEs range in size from one-person LLCs set up to hold and monetize a small group of patents to large, sophisticated corporate entities, some even publicly traded, that own thousands of patents.

strength of a patent from a legal perspective, the identity of the buyer and seller, and the type of deal structure that is sought. Furthermore, while a sales price is informed by the methods of measuring the economic value of a patent discussed earlier, any price will likely reflect a discount to those measures of value, as the seller is effectively transferring the risk of potentially realizing that value—either through commercial exploitation of the underlying technology or by subsequent monetization efforts—to the buyer.[42]

In terms of dollar amounts, it can be difficult for sellers and buyers to determine a "market" price because most sales are done in private and the sales prices are not made public in the normal course. One recent study found, though, that in 2016 the average sales price per U.S. patent was $215,000 and the median sale price was $203,000.[43] Anecdotally, in practice patent sales might range from tens of thousands of dollars to multiple millions of dollars. A patent sale might be structured as a one-time payment of cash, a "backend" deal whereby the seller becomes entitled to a percentage of the "value" that the buyer ultimately creates with the patent, or some combination of these two models (e.g., a modest up-front payment coupled with more backend upside in the form of a royalty).

Effectuating a patent sale may be difficult for a patent owner, as there is no central clearinghouse or marketplace where patent sales are conducted. In certain instances, the patent owner, by virtue of its work in a technological field, will know the most likely buyers and may be in position to attempt a sale on its own. In other instances, a patent owner may need assistance and might opt to tap into the network of patent brokers, attorneys, and other patent professionals that exists.

B. Licensing of a Patent

Another potential monetization option is for a patent owner to license its patent. A patent license is fundamentally different from the sale of a patent in that, when granting a license, the patent owner retains ownership (and

---

42. It should be noted that in a litigation context, often such risks are assumed not to exist (i.e., it is assumed that the contested patent is both valid and infringed).

43. *See* Brian J. Love, Kent Richardson, Erik Oliver & Michael Costa, *An Empirical Look at the "Brokered" Market for Patents*, 83 Mo. L. Rev. (2018), *available at* https://scholarship.law.missouri.edu/mlr/vol83/iss2/7. Note that, this study was limited to the "brokered market" for patents, as the authors of the study were able to access some amount of sales data from the participants of this market. Also note that the "brokered market" more typically involves the sale of larger portfolios of patents and is one where the brokers involved have likely done some work to initially determine that the patents for sale have market potential.

likely other rights) of the patent and grants only limited rights under the patent to a third party. A patent license is an agreement whereby a patent owner, or licensor, grants certain rights to a third party, a licensee, for a period of time in exchange for payment. These rights might include the right to manufacture a patented invention, the right to use a patented invention, the right to sell a patented invention, and the right to sublicense the patent. These rights may be specific to a particular field of use and/or geography.

There are two primary types of patent licenses: exclusive and nonexclusive. An exclusive license is a patent license in which the licensor grants the licensee the sole right to practice the invention. That is, the grantor of an exclusive patent license agrees not to grant the same patent rights to any other entity. An exclusive license is more common in situations where the licensee seeks to acquire and invest in commercializing a patented technology, as an exclusive licensee effectively guarantees that a licensee is the *only* entity that can practice the patented technology (without infringing). On the other hand, a nonexclusive license grants rights to use a patented technology, but it does not provide any exclusivity—the licensor is free to grant the same rights to any number of other licensees. A nonexclusive license is more common in a setting where a licensee seeks to acquire a license to avoid infringing a patent (and thus being exposed to a patent infringement lawsuit), particularly where the licensee is already using the patented technology.

A patent owner might seek to license its patent on its own, or it might seek legal and/or business assistance in doing so. As in the context of a patent sale, there exists an ecosystem of attorneys, licensing professionals, and other intermediaries that can help patent owners in their licensing efforts. Negotiating and executing a license is often a time-consuming, difficult process. Successfully licensing a patent typically involves several meetings with both business and legal personnel at the licensor, in an attempt to persuade the licensor that it should either adopt the patented technology (and take a license for commercialization purposes) or that it is already using the patented technology (and needs to acquire a license so as to avoid infringement).

Since a patent license is simply a contract between the patent licensor and the patent licensee, it, and the payment terms contained therein, can be structured in nearly any way.[44] In terms of payment to the licensor, a

44. For illustrative purposes, the Harvard Office of Technology Development makes available sample template patent licensing agreements, and examples of both an exclusive patent license and a nonexclusive license can be found at https://otd.harvard.edu/industry-investors/sample-agreements/licensing/.

patent license sometimes includes a one-time, up-front cash payment in exchange for the rights granted under the patent license. Alternatively, a patent license might provide for royalty payments to be paid to the licensor by the licensee over time, either on a predetermined schedule or as a function of sales or other activity of the licensor. Or, as is fairly common, a patent license might provide for a hybrid approach, whereby the licensor receives an up-front payment and also additional royalty payments over time. Other key economic terms that may be contained in a patent license include a time duration, license scope (e.g., which of the licensees products are covered), minimum payments, maximum payments, and reporting requirements (i.e., the licensee is obligated to share information with the licensor sufficient to allow the licensor to confirm the accuracy of the licensees royalty payments).

When a patent owner believes that a potential licensee is already practicing the patented technology, licensing efforts are often a precursor to litigation. That is, if a potential licensee refuses to pay a patent owner for a license (i.e., acquire the legal right to practice the patented technology), a patent owner may elect to initiate litigation and file a patent infringement lawsuit against the potential licensee. Indeed, the threat of litigation is the key point of leverage that a paten owner has over a potential licensee. If litigation were not an option for a patent owner, potential licensees could, with impunity, continue to use the patented technology for "free."

C. Litigation of a Patent

The final option for monetization of a patent is litigation. Litigation is the process of taking legal action against a third party, in this instance filing a lawsuit against a third party alleging infringement of a patent. Litigation is by far the costliest and most resource-intensive route for monetization, but it is also potentially the most lucrative for a patent owner. Put differently, patent litigation can be a high risk, high reward proposition. As mentioned earlier, a patent owner may choose to litigate if its licensing negotiations with a third party fail to bear fruit. However, it is equally common for a patent owner to initiate patent litigation in the first instance without first engaging a party in licensing discussions.

The first step a patent owner seeking to initiate patent litigation must take is to retain patent litigation counsel. Patent litigation is a particularly specialized area of the law, as it requires both legal and technical expertise. Thus, the universe of lawyers that can effectively litigate a patent case is relatively small. In most circumstances, patent litigation counsel will charge by the hour for their legal services, with hourly rates ranging from $300 to $2,000 or more, depending on the law firm and its geography. In some circumstances, patent litigation counsel may be willing to take a case on contingency, in which counsel is paid if and only if the case generates proceeds. The market for contingency representation in a patent case is subject to significant variation, but a patent owner should reasonably expect to pay litigation counsel between 30 and 50 percent of any proceeds generated by the case.

Once a patent owner has selected litigation counsel, a patent owner initiates a patent case by filing a lawsuit alleging patent infringement in a U.S. district court.[45] A patent lawsuit begins with a complaint, which sets forth the basic details of the patent owner's allegations of patent infringement, including identification of the patents that are infringed and basic facts about how the defendant infringes. The parties then embark on several months of discovery, motion practice, and hearings, eventually culminating in a trial, likely before a jury. This entire process can take anywhere between 18 months and as much as four or five years. Any final decision at the district court is then subject to potential appeals, which could add another year and a half to three years to the time necessary to reach a final decision on the merits of the case. The vast majority of patent cases do not proceed through this entire process, however, as they typically either settle or are lost at an interim stage.

Generally speaking, the cost of patent litigation is notoriously high. The cost associated with patent litigation come in the form of attorney fees and hard costs (e.g., filing fees, expert fees, discovery-related costs, etc.). A recent study released by the American Intellectual Property Law Association reports that the median range of the cost of patent litigation in the United States is between $700,000 and $4 million.[46] For cases with tens or hundreds of millions at stake, the total cost could be many multiples of these average figures—legal budgets of $10 to $20 million or more are not uncommon. This high cost is a critical consideration for

45. Patent law in the United States is governed by federal law, namely, Title 35 of the United States Code. Thus, patent infringement lawsuits must be filed in federal court. The U.S. district courts that handle the most patent lawsuits include the District of Delaware, the Central District of California, the Eastern District of Texas, and the Western District of Texas. *See* Docket Navigator 2019 Year in Review Report, https://brochure.docketnavigator.com/2019-year-in-review/.

46. *See* 2019 Report of the Economic Survey, American Intellectual Property Law Association, https://www.aipla.org/detail/journal-issue/2019-report-of-the-economic-survey.

patent owners potentially pursuing litigation. For litigation to be profitable from a return-on-investment perspective, the litigation proceeds must exceed this cost, perhaps significantly so after factoring in the cost to obtain the patent, ongoing maintenance fees, and any other patent-related investments made by the patent owner. Thus, before a patent owner elects to pursue litigation, it must carefully weigh the strength and potential value of its case in consultation with patent litigation counsel against the associated costs.

There are several ways that a patent owner might seek to defray the costs needed to maintain litigation, as there exists a robust ecosystem of attorneys and investors willing to partner with patent owners and invest in litigation in the appropriate circumstances. As mentioned earlier, counsel may be willing to represent a patent owner in litigation in exchange for a contingency fee, reducing or eliminating the out of pocket costs required to litigate. Additionally, there are several types of investors that may be willing to provide funding for patent litigation in exchange for a share of the proceeds, alone or in conjunction with contingency counsel.

A patent infringement case may be resolved in a number of different ways. First, a patent owner, or plaintiff in a patent infringement lawsuit, could lose the litigation, resulting in zero dollars flowing to it and a loss of any capital expended on the litigation. A plaintiff may lose at the preliminary pleading stage, at the pretrial motion stage (e.g., summary judgment), or at the jury trial stage. Assuming a loss is not overturned on appeal, it could not only result in no money for the patent owner, but it could also result in a funding that the subject patent is invalid and unenforceable as to any other potential infringers/licensing targets. Such a finding would thereby preclude any subsequent litigation or licensing with respect to that patent. On the other hand, a plaintiff could win a litigation, resulting in money flowing to it. There are two primary ways a patent infringement lawsuit might result in a win for the patent owner—a settlement or a final judgment. The most common form of positive resolution, by far, is settlement. The parties to litigation could enter into a settlement at any point in time, early in the litigation or late in the litigation, including after a favorable jury verdict. A settlement is essentially a contractual agreement whereby the plaintiff agrees to cease litigation in exchange for some form of payment by the defendant. A settlement of patent litigation typically involves the patent owner granting a nonexclusive patent license to the defendant, so that the defendant can continue to practice the patented technology.

The amount of a settlement typically reflects a discount to the damages that the plaintiff would ultimately seek at trial. For instance, a settlement very early in the life of the case, before too many substantive cards have turned over, might reflect 80 to 90 percent of the amount that would have been sought by plaintiff at trial. The other way a lawsuit might resolve favorably for a patent owner is by a court's entry of a final judgment, which the defendant is legally obligated to pay. A final judgment payable to plaintiff would occur if a plaintiff took its case to trial, was awarded a verdict, and then that verdict withstood any appeals filed by the defendant. This is exceedingly rare in patent litigation, as most cases either lose or settle prior to a final judgment, even if they reach the trial stage. For the time period between 2013 and 2017, the median damages award of all patent cases that went to trial and resulted in a verdict was approximately $9.2 million.[47] That said, in particularly high value cases, trial verdicts can be several hundreds of millions—or even billions—of dollars.[48]

47. PwC 2018 Patent Litigation Study, https://www.pwc.com/us/en/forensic-services/publications/assets/2018-patent-litigation-study.pdf.

48. By way of exceptional example in the medical device space, Edwards Lifesciences won a $393mm jury verdict against Medtronic in 2017 in a case related to transcatheter heart valves. This case later settled for $750mm plus ongoing royalties. The largest patent jury verdict in the U.S. ever was $2.54B, in a 2016 case Merck brought against Gilead related to hepatitis C drugs (it was overturned during post-trial motions, however).

CHAPTER 5

Business Arrangements and Contractual Agreements

David Hatch and Robert Miller

I. Business Arrangements

One of the first things to consider in structuring a business that intends to bring a medical device to market is the type of entity to form for carrying out the business and engaging in the various arrangements and transactions. The most common types of entities used in forming a business are general corporations, limited liability companies, and partnerships, each having its own benefits. In this section, the differences between the types of entities are discussed and some of the considerations for deciding what kind of entity to form are considered.

A. Corporations and Limited Liability Companies

1. Formation Documents

When it comes to forming a business entity, limited liability companies and corporations follow similar paths to establishment, but the underlying structures are slightly different. Both types of entities are formed by filing a document with the Secretary of State, Division of Corporations, or other applicable agency in the state in which the entity is being formed. For corporations, this document is typically called the Articles of Incorporation or Certificate of Incorporation, depending on the jurisdiction. The Articles of Incorporation is used to declare fundamental information about the operation of the entity and to opt in or out of some default statutes that the corporation would otherwise be subject to (these statutes vary by state). Each state's corporation statutes set forth the minimum governing provisions that must be included in the Articles of Incorporation. For a limited liability company, the document filed with the Secretary of State or other applicable governmental agency is usually called the Articles of Organization, or Certificate of Organization, depending on the jurisdiction. It serves the same purpose as the Articles of Incorporation in setting forth the foundational information about the structure of the entity, but it typically does not require as much detail as that of the corporation's articles. The Articles of Incorporation or Articles of Organization, as applicable, are public documents. If there is certain information that the founders of the entity do not want to be made public at the early stage of operations, a limited liability company may be more advantageous by allowing the founders to keep some of that information out of the initial filing, while being addressed in the Operating Agreement (as discussed later), which is not generally publicly available.

In addition to the Articles of Incorporation, each corporation should have bylaws that lay out the governance of the corporation in more detail than that contained in the Articles of Incorporation. Not every state requires a corporation to have bylaws, but it is typically a good idea to avoid confusion among the shareholders or leadership of the corporation about the logistics of governance. As mentioned earlier, each state has its own default governance procedures in the applicable corporation statutes. Many of these statutes can be overruled by the corporate bylaws as long as the applicable provisions so state. In the event that the bylaws are silent on any such governing procedures, the default state statutes would apply, so it is important to review the state corporations statute in detail.

The equivalent of bylaws for a limited liability company is a document called the Operating Agreement or Limited Liability Company Agreement, depending on the jurisdiction. The Operating Agreement is a contract that is entered into by the owners of the limited liability company (the owners are called "members"). Like the bylaws, the Operating Agreement is where the members lay out in detail how the entity is to be governed, as well as other agreements amongst the members. Also, like corporations, the state laws governing limited liability companies (often the "Limited Liability Company Act") provide governance defaults that, except for a small subset of required defaults, can be superseded by agreeing to alternative terms in the Operating Agreement.

2. Management

Another consideration in determining what type of entity to form is how the entity will be managed and how involved the owners want to be in the management of the entity. Corporate shareholders have differing levels of power based upon shares (as discussed later), but they elect a board of directors to manage the overall affairs of the business, and the directors then appoint officers or executives to handle the day-to-day operations. Beyond electing the directors and making certain major business decisions, shareholders typically have limited involvement in the operational management of the business. A limited liability company, on the other hand, may be member managed (meaning the owners manage the business) or manager managed (where the members appoint one or more managers, similar in function to directors). For owners that wish to be heavily involved in the management of the business, a member-managed limited liability company would provide the desired level of control. A manager-managed limited liability company may be more akin to a corporation with respect to owner control, but the operating agreement frequently reserves authority to the members for those decisions that are important to the members.

The management structure of the entity is set forth in the Articles of Incorporation and bylaws for a corporation and the Articles of Organization and operating agreement for limited liability companies, but as discussed earlier, there are typically a limited number of default minimum standards dictated by the applicable state statutes. For example, corporations are typically required to hold annual shareholder meetings, and corporations and limited liability companies may be required to fill certain officer positions (e.g., president, secretary, and treasurer). One key benefit that often leads owners of smaller entities to choose limited liability companies over corporations is the greater flexibility in governance and logistics. For example, corporations typically require greater governance formalities, such as meeting and documentation requirements. Corporations, for example, are required to hold annual shareholder meetings with specific notice requirements, and directors may not be corporate entities themselves and may not be able to vote by proxy. Limited liability companies are given greater flexibility in these governance logistics (i.e., the statutes have fewer requirements), and business entities can serve as managers and may vote by proxy.

3. Ownership

Terminology involving ownership of corporations and limited liability companies is often mixed up. Shareholders of a corporation hold their ownership interests through ownership of shares of stock, which is represented by stock certificates. Members of limited liability companies do not own shares of stock, rather they own membership interests often referred to as "units" in the company; these units may be certificated or uncertificated. Corporate stock certificates can be tedious in terms of recordkeeping, such as tracking the ownership history of each share through stock ledgers. The membership interests in a limited liability company are typically recorded in the operating agreement, which can be amended to keep the ownership records current (though membership interests can also be certificated and treated just like corporate stock certificates). Uncertificated membership interests in limited liability company can ease the corporate recordkeeping burden, which can be one less thing to worry about for early-stage startup company owners.

4. Taxation

Corporations are typically taxed at the entity level and the shareholders are again taxed individually on dividends. To avoid this double-taxation, qualifying corporations (not all entities are eligible, such as those that issue multiple classes of stock or those owned by other business entities or non-resident aliens) may choose to be designated as S corporations, whereby the entity is not taxed, but only the shareholders are taxed on dividends received. LLCs on the other hand, are pass-through entities by default. The LLC is not taxed and the tax liabilities reside solely with the members of the LLC. LLCs may file requests to be treated as S corporations or C corporations for tax purposes, but this is relatively uncommon. There may be additional nuanced differences between standard pass-through, C corporation and S corporation treatment to be considered, such as impacts on employment and social security taxes. It is therefore wise to get accountants involved to determine what the most advantageous tax treatment would be for the business's specific purpose and operational structure.

For those businesses that will eventually look to recruit top-notch talent, employment benefits may be a factor in selecting an entity type. Corporations have more flexibility in crafting benefit plans, including stock options and stock purchase options, and may enjoy certain related tax benefits for shareholder-employees. LLCs can of course also structure attractive benefit plans, but may not have as large of a pallet from which to draw. As with accountants, employee benefits counsel may provide valuable insight in mapping out a successful plan for business growth with respect to human relations.

B. Partnerships

It is also worth noting that some businesses are formed as partnerships. Unlike corporations and LLCs, partnerships are not separate entities that are distinct from their owners. Partnerships are automatically created when two or more individuals go into business together without the need for specific filings or documents (more on this later). With the exception of limited partners discussed later, the individual partners are personally liable for the business's obligations and creditors can go after personal assets to satisfy those obligations. Furthermore, one partner can be held liable for obligations arising from other partners' decisions related to the business. This lack of corporate liability shield available to owners and officers of corporations or limited liability companies may be unattractive for growing businesses developing complex technologies in a heavily regulated industry like health care. From a tax perspective, however, partnerships are pass-through entities like LLCs.

Though many of the formalities just discussed with respect to corporations and LLCs (such as board meetings, filings, stock/interests, etc.) are not required of partnerships, it does make sense for partners to enter into a partnership agreement. This is not required, but it allows the partners to select the ground rules of the business operations instead of relying on the statutory defaults. It also ensures that the partners set expectations for all of the important aspects of running a business that may cause friction at some point during the life of the partnership.

The foregoing describes a general partnership. There is another type of partnership called a limited partnership that is more practical for business partnerships that will be looking to add investors. In a limited partnership, a general partner controls the day-to-day operations of the business and other "limited partners" contribute assets to the partnership without having the same level of control over the business. The upshot for the limited partners is that their liability for the partnership's obligations is capped at the amount of their investment. So the amounts that were contributed can be used to settle the business's debts, but the limited partners' personal assets aren't at risk.

For a startup company that is going to be raising capital and expanding, a limited partnership is likely more applicable, but can be complicated like corporations and LLCs, especially where limited partnership interest sales/transfers are concerned.

C. Choosing the Type of Entity

The analysis for deciding what type of entity to use should consider short- and long-term goals of the business and planned-for growth. The corporate form is often attractive to early-stage businesses looking to obtain funding and planning for considerable growth, because they provide more flexibility in the ownership structure by offering multitiered stock classes that can allow stakeholders to maintain control while involving additional investors. They also provide a more streamlined and direct path to an initial public offering (IPO) exit. LLCs, on the other hand, offer more flexibility in the management of the company. Because there will not just be one limited set of facts that make the decision immediately obvious, involve experts early on in mapping out these strategies, such as accountants, as well as business, tax, and employee benefits attorneys.

II. Common Agreements

A medical device manufacturer is likely to encounter a variety of agreement types based on the specific product being brought to market and the entities involved, but the following types of agreements are fairly common. Very basic form samples of each are also included for general reference, but these forms will need to be tailored to your particular situation and may not address the various regulatory considerations that may apply (e.g., fraud and abuse, governmental approvals, etc.). It is useful to review the forms for familiarity with the concepts and structures that might be needed and to serve as a starting point in developing more detailed templates. We recommend that medical device businesses consult with legal counsel in developing any agreements for use with their business.

A. Letter of Intent

Before the agreements discussed next are negotiated, the parties to an arrangement may want to negotiate a letter of intent, commonly referred to as an "LOI." An LOI allows the parties to agree at a high level on the most important terms and conditions of the relationship. The parties can decide which of the terms and conditions of the LOI are contractually binding, but during the earlier stages of a transaction, such as diligence, many of the key business terms to are typically nonbinding, except for terms to protect the parties if the deal is terminated, such as nondisclosure. LOI's often include a binding obligation to negotiate in good faith, as well as binding exclusivity obligations. An LOI can also vary in the granularity that is included, but at this early stage, much of the nitty gritty details will be reserved for the substantive agreement, as the parties are more interested in obtaining each other's general commitment to do the deal. A sample LOI is included in [______________________].

B. Nondisclosure Agreement (NDA)

A nondisclosure agreement, often referred to as an "NDA," aims to protect sensitive or proprietary information by preventing its disclosure. Mutual NDAs are often entered into by two or more parties to an arrangement, such as a joint venture, vendor-client relationship, and so on. In addition to functioning during the term of the arrangement, NDAs may also be entered into prior to consummating a transaction to protect the parties' information and the terms of the potential deal as they work through diligence or negotiations. One-sided NDAs are also used with employees or independent contractors where the main concern is protection of the employer's confidential information, which typically includes the terms of the employment itself. Some important things to be addressed by an NDA are (1) how the information to be protected is defined; (2) the time period in which the information is to be protected; (3) how the information may be appropriately used or disclosed; and (4) remedies for breach. A sample NDA is included in [____________].

C. Licensing Agreement

Under a licensing agreement, the owner of property, such as a technology or other intellectual property, allows another person or entity to use the property and sets the parameters on its use. Some important considerations in drafting a licensing agreement are the restrictions on the use of the licensed property (e.g., geographic, length of time, manner of use), whether the licensee will have the exclusive right to use it, and how the licensee will pay for the right to use the property. Each of these considerations can be critical business terms and are often heavily negotiated between a licensor and licensee. A sample licensing agreement is included in [____________].

D. Business Associate Agreement

It is possible that some party to an arrangement involving medical devices may have access to personal health information of ultimate end-users of the device. Those who receive health information in the provision of professional services (e.g., health care providers), referred to under HIPAA (as defined later) as "covered entities," and those who receive such information in performing services as contractors of those covered entities, referred to under HIPAA as "business associates," it is important to understand the duties of each and the limitations on and appropriate use of such health information. A business associate agreement is entered into by the covered entity and the business associate and outlines the business associate's use of and obligations in handling such health information. Business associate agreements are required under HIPAA if federal health care programs are involved, but each state may have its own privacy and security laws that may have additional requirements and may or may not apply depending on the circumstances of the arrangement.

Like most other agreements, business associate agreements can be tailored to be more friendly to the business associate or covered entity. Note, however, that HIPAA or particular state laws may require specific language to be included, so it may be helpful to consult a privacy expert. We refer to "HIPAA" collectively as the Health Insurance Portability and Accountability Act of 1996; 45 C.F.R. Part 160 and Part 164, subparts A and E; 45 C.F.R. Part 160 and subparts A and C of Part 164; and the Health Information Technology for Economic and Clinical Health Act. A sample BAA is included in [____________].

E. Distribution Agreement

In many cases, an early-stage supplier may lack the resources necessary to fully distribute and market its products to consumers and may need to get outside help. In such cases, a distribution agreement is advisable to map out the distributor's/marketer's responsibilities. As with a licensing agreement, exclusivity is an important consideration, and there are many possibilities for setting the boundaries on the distribution (e.g., certain regions, stores, online vs. retail, etc.). Other important considerations are how much control the supplier will have over marketing materials and strategy, product training for the distributor, and the distributor's forecasting and data reporting requirements. Lastly, there are a number of ways to structure compensation, such as basing it on a commission or percentage of sales, but as discussed next and in Chapter ___, there may be additional regulatory considerations when structuring a distribution arrangement in the health care industry. A sample distribution agreement is included in [____________].

In bringing a new medical device to market, a device manufacturer is likely to encounter all or any combination of these concepts, among various others that may be needed depending on the situation. Some of these concepts may be included in several of the agreements, and sometimes several agreements can be combined into one overarching agreement. For example, many of the agreements are likely to address nondisclosure requirements, so a stand-alone nondisclosure agreement may not be needed if adequately addressed elsewhere. Additionally, in a hypothetical joint venture between a manufacturer and a distributor, a joint venture agreement may define a number of important aspects of the relationship, including licensing and distribution activities. There is a great deal of flexibility in structuring these contractual relationships. Though we are including a few very basic samples of for reference purposes, each agreement should be carefully tailored to reflect the nature and goals of each relationship. Lastly, in forming and operating a medical device company there are numerous health care regulatory laws that the organization will need to carefully consider to ensure compliant operations and reduce the risk of costly enforcement investigations or actions. In particular, organizations should be familiar with state and federal anti-kickback laws, state and federal self-referral and disclosure laws, as well as the Physician Payments Sunshine Act. These laws are discussed in detail in Chapter 9.

APPENDIX A

Effective Date: [Date]

VIA EMAIL ONLY to [address]

[Address]

Re: [Description of Proposed Transaction]

Dear [Contact Name]:

This letter (this "**Letter**") is intended to summarize the principal terms of the proposed transaction by which [Counterparty name] ("**you**" or "**your**") and [Company name] (the "**Company**") would [description of Proposed Transaction] (the "**Proposed Transaction**" You and the Company are referred to herein collectively as the "**Parties**." Except as expressly set forth herein, this Letter constitutes a nonbinding expression of the mutual intention of the Parties to pursue the Proposed Transaction on the terms and subject to the conditions described herein.

1. Proposed Transaction. Subject to the satisfaction of the conditions described in this Letter, [description of essential terms of the Proposed Transaction, including purchase price/consideration, term, transaction structure, *etc.*)]. Notwithstanding anything to the contrary, the Parties recognize that all of the terms and structure of the Proposed Transaction are subject to the Company's continuing review and analysis and that it may be necessary or appropriate to restructure the form and the terms of the Proposed Transaction as a result of due diligence investigation or regulatory, compliance, tax, accounting or other considerations.
2. Proposed Definitive Agreement. As soon as reasonably practicable after the execution of this Letter, the Company shall instruct its legal counsel to draft, and the Parties shall commence to negotiate, one or more definitive agreements relating to the Proposed Transaction (the "**Definitive Agreements**"). The Definitive Agreements would include the terms summarized in this Letter and such other representations, warranties, conditions, covenants, indemnities and other terms that are customary for transactions of this kind.

3. Conditions. The Company's obligation to proceed with the Proposed Transaction will be subject to customary conditions, including without limitation the following: (i) the Company's satisfactory completion of due diligence; (ii) the governing body of the Company approving the Proposed Transaction; (iii) the Parties' execution of the Definitive Agreements; (iv) the receipt of any regulatory approvals and third-party consents, on terms satisfactory to the Company; (v) there being no material adverse change in the business, results of operations, prospects, condition (financial or otherwise) or assets of the Company; and (vi) satisfaction of conditions and covenants at the closing as are customary in similar transactions and agreements.
4. Access to Information. During the period from the signing of this Letter through the termination of this Letter pursuant to paragraph 6 (the "**Diligence and Negotiation Period**"), you will provide the Company and its designated officers and employees, and its accountants, lawyers, manager, and other representatives, reasonable access during normal business hours, to all information relating to your operations for the purpose of performing the Company's due diligence review. The due diligence investigation may include, but is not limited to, a review of the legal, tax, intellectual property and labor records and agreements relating to you, and any other matters as the Company's accountants, tax and legal counsel, and other advisors deem relevant in connection with the Proposed Transaction.
5. Exclusive Dealing. Until such date as may be provided in the executed Definitive Agreements or, if no Definitive Agreements are executed, until the termination of the Diligence and Negotiation Period, neither you nor any person acting on your behalf shall solicit offers from, or enter into negotiations, discussions or agreements with, any other person regarding a similar transaction to the Proposed Transaction, or any transaction that could prohibit you from entering into or consummating the Proposed Transaction. You represent that as of the Effective Date and thereafter neither you nor person acting on your behalf is party to any existing discussions or negotiations with any person or group of persons other than the Company and its affiliates regarding the Proposed Transaction or bound by any agreement with respect to a transaction similar to the Proposed Transaction other than under this Letter.

6. Termination. This Letter will automatically terminate and be of no further force and effect upon the earlier of (i) execution of the Definitive Agreements by the Parties; (ii) the Company's delivery of written notice to you that the Company has determined not to proceed with the Proposed Transaction or (ii) mutual agreement of the Parties. Notwithstanding anything in the previous sentence, the preamble and paragraphs 5–12 shall survive the termination of this Letter and the termination of this Letter shall not affect any rights any Party has with respect to the breach of this Letter by another Party prior to such termination.
7. GOVERNING LAW. **THIS LETTER SHALL BE GOVERNED BY AND CONSTRUED IN ACCORDANCE WITH INTERNAL LAWS OF THE STATE OF [STATE] WITHOUT GIVING EFFECT TO ANY CHOICE OR CONFLICT OF LAW PROVISION OR RULE THAT WOULD CAUSE THE APPLICATION OF LAWS OF ANY JURISDICTION OTHER THAN THOSE OF THE AFOREMENTIONED STATE.**
8. Confidentiality. This Letter is confidential to the Parties and their representatives and the Parties hereto agree that, so long as this Letter is in effect, without the prior written consent of the other Parties, no Party shall disclose to any third party (other than attorneys, accountants, agents, representatives and governmental agencies involved in the Proposed Transaction) the existence or terms of this Letter or any confidential data, information, documents or other materials provided by the other Parties or developed in connection with the transactions contemplated hereby unless (a) such disclosure is consented to by the other Parties, (b) the disclosure is required by law, rule or regulation or (c) the information is independently available to such third party through no fault of the Parties.
9. No Third-Party Beneficiaries. Except as specifically set forth or referred to herein, nothing herein is intended or shall be construed to confer upon any person or entity other than the Parties and their successors or assigns, any rights or remedies under or by reason of this Letter.
10. Expenses. The Parties will each pay their own transaction expenses, including the fees and expenses of legal counsel and other advisors, incurred in connection with the Proposed Transaction. Notwithstanding the foregoing or anything else to the

contrary, if any dispute arises between you and the Company concerning the enforcement or declaration of any right under this Letter, then the prevailing party shall be entitled to receive from the non-prevailing party any and all of the costs, expenses, and fees incurred by the prevailing party in connection therewith, including, without limitation, reasonable attorneys' fees and all costs and expenses associated with such dispute.

11. No Binding Agreement. Each Party agrees to negotiate the terms and conditions of the Definitive Agreement in good faith, it being understood and agreed that (i) this Letter does not purport to set forth all of the terms and conditions of the Proposed Transaction, (ii) with respect to those terms and conditions of the Proposed Transaction addressed in this Letter, this Letter does not purport to set forth all matters with respect to such terms and conditions, and (iii) the terms and conditions of the Proposed Transaction set forth in this Letter may change as a result of, among other things, the Company's due diligence review. This Letter reflects the intention of the Parties, but for the avoidance of doubt neither this Letter nor its acceptance shall give rise to any legally binding or enforceable obligation on any Party, except with regard to the preamble and paragraphs 5–12 hereof.
12. Miscellaneous. This Letter may be executed in counterparts, each of which shall be deemed to be an original, but all of which together shall constitute one agreement. Signature pages transmitted by facsimile or email shall be deemed original signatures for all purposes. The headings of the various sections of this Letter have been inserted for reference only and shall not be deemed to be a part of this Letter.

[End of Text; Signature Page Follows]

This Letter will be void and the terms contained herein revoked unless accepted and returned by 5:00 p.m. (Pacific Standard Time) on [Expiration Date]. If you agree with the terms set forth in this Letter and desire to proceed with the Proposed Transaction on that basis, please sign this Letter in the space provided below and return an executed copy to me at the address indicated on the letterhead.

Very truly yours,

[COMPANY NAME]

____

Title:________________________

Agreed to and accepted:

[COUNTERPARTY NAME]

____

Title:________________________________

Print Name:___________________________________

APPENDIX B

DISTRIBUTION AGREEMENT

This Distribution Agreement ("**Agreement**"), is entered into as of [Date] (the "**Effective Date**") by and between [Name] ("**Distributor**"), with its principal corporate address at [Address] and [Name] ("**Supplier**"), with its principal corporate address at [Address].

RECITALS

Distributor desires to purchase certain Products (as defined below) from Supplier from time to time and Supplier desires to sell certain Products to Distributor in accordance with the terms and conditions set forth in this Agreement.

Supplier desires to appoint Distributor as a non-exclusive distributor to market Products within the Territory (as defined below) and Distributor accepts such appointment on the terms set forth in this Agreement. Under the terms of this Agreement, Distributor will function as a distributor and reseller of the Products.

NOW, THEREFORE, in consideration of the recitals above and the mutual covenants and conditions contained in this Agreement and other good and valuable consideration, Distributor and Supplier hereby agree as follows:

ARTICLE I DEFINITIONS, APPOINTMENT AND TERM OF AGREEMENT

1.1 Definitions. When used in this Agreement, the following terms shall have the meanings set forth below (all defined terms not defined in this Section 1.1 shall have the meanings set forth elsewhere in this Agreement):

(a) "Confidential Information" means confidential information, proprietary information and trade secrets relating to the operations, transactions, relationships, customers, claims, assets, liabilities and future plans of each party's business, including without limitation, technical, financial, business, commercial, operational and strategic information and data, know-how, trade secrets, customer lists, pricing policies, computer programs or software, inventions (whether patentable or not), operational methods, marketing studies, plans or strategies, product development techniques or plans, business plans, new personnel designs and design projects, invention and research projects, forecasts, financial projections, sales projections and all records containing or otherwise reflecting information which are not available to the general public, regardless of form or medium. Confidential Information shall not include any information that: (i) at the time of disclosure is generally available to the public through no act of any person in violation of a confidentiality obligation, (ii) a disclosing party has obtained lawfully from an independent source not subject to a confidentiality obligation or (iii) is lawfully in the possession of a disclosing party at the time of disclosure, as evidenced by the receiving party's files and records.

(b) "**Customers**" of Distributor shall include health care providers, distributors, resellers, and other entities that acquire the Products from Distributor.

(c) "**Documentation**" shall mean user manuals, training materials, product descriptions and specifications, brochures, technical manuals, supporting materials and other printed information relating to the Products, whether distributed in print, electronic, or video format.

(d) "**Effective Date**" shall mean the date on which this Agreement is signed and dated by a duly authorized representative of Distributor and each Supplier party.

(e) "**End Users**" shall mean the final purchasers who have acquired Products for their own use and not for redistribution to other persons.

(f) "**Non-Saleable Products**" shall mean any Product that has been returned to Distributor by its Customers for any reason, including, without limitation, any of the following reasons: (i) because of a Product defect or non-conformity with specifications; (ii) because any component of the original package are missing, damaged or modified; or (iii) because the Product is otherwise not fit for resale.

(g) "**Products**" shall mean, individually or collectively as appropriate, those medical devices, products, implants or instruments, Documentation, supplies, accessories, and other items related to any of the foregoing currently produced or sold, or produced in the future or sold by Supplier, in each case listed on Exhibit A attached hereto.

(h) "**Return Credit**" shall mean a credit to Distributor in an amount equal to the price paid by Distributor for Products for any Products returned by Distributor.

(i) "**Services**" means any warranty, maintenance, advertising, marketing or technical support and any other services performed or to be performed by Supplier.

(j) "**Territory**" shall mean [Define Territory].

1.2 Term of Agreement. The term of this Agreement (the "**Term**") shall commence on the Effective Date and, unless terminated by either party as set forth in this Agreement, shall remain in full force and effect until [_________ (__)] years after the Effective Date; provided, however, that this Agreement shall automatically renew for [_________ (__)] additional term of [_________ (__)] years, unless either party provides the other party with at least [_________ (__)] days prior written notification of its intent to allow this Agreement to terminate after the initial [_________ (__)] year term.

1.3 Appointment of Distributor. Supplier hereby appoints Distributor to act as a non-exclusive distributor in the Territory during the term of this Agreement. Distributor shall not sell or offer to sell Products outside the Territory. Supplier, in its sole discretion, may sell Products to any other person, including distributors, retailers, and customers in and outside the Territory. Distributor hereby accepts such appointment and Distributor will use reasonable efforts to promote sales of the Products. Supplier agrees that Distributor may obtain Products in accordance with this Agreement for the benefit of its parent, affiliates and subsidiaries of Distributor pursuant to this Agreement.

1.4 Distributor Obligations. Distributor shall:

(a) market, advertise, promote, and sell Products to Customers in a manner that reflects favorably at all times on all Products and the good name, goodwill and reputation of Supplier and consistent with good business practice, in each case using its best efforts to maximize the sales volume of the Products;

(b) maintain a place or places of business in the Territory, including adequate office, storage, and warehouse facilities and all other facilities as required for Distributor to perform its duties under this Agreement;

(c) purchase and maintain at all times a representative quantity of Products sufficient for and consistent with the Distributor's Customers' needs;

(d) have sufficient knowledge of the industry and products competitive with each Product (including specifications, features, and benefits) so as to be able to explain in detail to Customers:

(i) the differences between the Products and competing products; and

(ii) information on standard protocols and features of each Product;

(e) observe all directions and instructions given to it by Supplier in relation to the marketing, advertisement, and promotion of the Products, including Supplier's sales, marketing, and merchandising policies as they currently exist or as they may hereafter be changed by Supplier;

(f) not use any promotional and marketing materials, whether prepared by Distributor or others, without the prior written consent of Supplier;

(g) establish and maintain a sales and marketing organization sufficient to develop the market potential for the sale of the Products, and independent sales representatives, facilities, and a distribution organization sufficient to make the Products available for shipment by Distributor to each Customer immediately on receipt of order;

(h) develop and execute a marketing plan sufficient to fulfill its obligations under this Agreement;

(i) not make any materially misleading or untrue statements concerning Supplier or the Products, including any product disparagement or "bait-and-switch" practices;

(j) promptly notify Supplier of any complaint or adverse claim about any Product or its use of which Distributor becomes aware;

(k) submit to Supplier complete and accurate monthly reports regarding inventory, marketing, and sales of the Products in a computer-readable format and containing the scope of information acceptable to Supplier, maintain books, records, and accounts of all transactions and permit full examination thereof by Supplier in accordance with this Agreement;

(l) not resell Products to any federal, state, local, or foreign government or political subdivision or agency thereof, without express written approval from Supplier; and

(m) only resell any software or accessories sold, bundled, or packaged with any Product on those terms and conditions as Supplier may require at that time.

1.5 Seller Obligations. Seller shall:

(a) provide any information and support that may be reasonably requested by Distributor regarding the marketing, advertising, promotion, and sale of the Products;

(b) allow Distributor to participate, at its own expense, in any marketing, advertising, promotion and sales programs or events that

Supplier may make generally available to its authorized distributors of Products in the Territory, provided that Supplier may alter or eliminate any program at any time;

(c) approve or reject, in its discretion, any promotional information or material submitted by Distributor for Supplier's approval; and

(d) in Supplier's discretion provide promotional information and material for use by Distributor in accordance with this Agreement.

ARTICLE II PURCHASE ORDERS

1.6 Issuance of Purchase Order.

(a) This Agreement shall not obligate Distributor to purchase any Products or Services except as specifically set forth in a written purchase order.

(b) Distributor may issue to Supplier one or more purchase orders identifying the Products Distributor desires to purchase from Supplier. By issuing a purchase order, Distributor makes an offer to purchase Products under the terms and conditions listed on Supplier's purchase order, Supplier's website and this Agreement, and no other terms. Notwithstanding any terms or conditions on Distributor's purchase orders, the terms and conditions of this Agreement shall apply to and govern all purchase orders accepted or shipped by Supplier hereunder, except that purchase orders may include other terms and conditions which are consistent with the terms and conditions of this Agreement, or which are mutually agreed to in writing by Distributor and Supplier. Purchase orders will be placed by Distributor by fax, email or other electronic communication.

(c) Distributor will include in each purchase order at least the following information: (i) the Products to be purchased, including information sufficient for Supplier to identify the specific type of Product, (ii) the quantities ordered and (iii) the requested delivery date.

1.7 Supplier's Right to Accept or Reject Purchase Orders. Supplier, in its sole discretion, may accept or reject any purchase order. Supplier may accept any order by confirming the order (whether by written confirmation, invoice, or otherwise) or by delivering the Products, whichever occurs first. If Supplier does not accept the order under the terms of this Agreement within [Number] days of Supplier's receipt of the order, the order will lapse. No order is binding on Supplier unless accepted by Supplier as provided in this Agreement.

ARTICLE III DELIVERY AND ACCEPTANCE OF PRODUCTS

1.8 Acceptance of Products. Distributor shall inspect all Products received under this Agreement. On the [Ordinal number] day after delivery of the Products, Distributor shall be deemed to have accepted the Products unless it earlier notifies Supplier in writing and provides a written explanation and other documentation as required by Supplier showing that the Products: (i) are damaged, defective or otherwise do not conform to the purchase order or (ii) were delivered to Distributor as a result of Supplier's error. If Distributor notifies Supplier in accordance with the foregoing sentence, then Supplier, in its sole discretion, may either repair or replace the Products or refund the price Distributor paid supplier for the Products. Distributor shall ship at its expense and risk of loss all goods to be returned, repaired or replaced to a location designated by Supplier. Distributor agrees and acknowledges that Distributor's rights under this Section 3.1 are exclusive of all other remedies and that, except as provided in this Section 3.1, all sales of Products to Distributor are made on a one-way basis and Distributor has no other right to return Products purchased from Supplier.

1.9 Title and Risk of Loss; FOB Origin. Title and risk of loss or damage to Products shall pass to Distributor at the time the Products are made available for pickup at Supplier's facility (*i.e.*, FOB Supplier's facility). As collateral security for the payment of the purchase price of the Products, Distributor hereby grants to Supplier a lien on and security interest in and to all of the right, title and interest of Distributor in, to and under the Products, wherever located, and whether now existing or hereafter arising or acquired from time to time, and in all accessions thereto and replacements or modifications thereof, as well as all proceeds (including insurance proceeds) of the foregoing. The security interest granted under this provision constitutes a purchase money security interest under the [State] Uniform Commercial Code.

1.10 Transportation of Products. Supplier shall select the method of shipment of and the carrier for the Products. Supplier, in its sole discretion and without liability or penalty, may make partial shipments of the Products, each of which constitutes a separate sale and Distributor shall pay for the Products shipped. Supplier shall deliver the Products using Supplier's standard methods for packaging and shipping. Any time quoted for delivery is only an estimate and is not binding on any person.

ARTICLE IV PAYMENT TO GS MEDICAL

1.11 Charges, Prices and Fees for Products. All charges, prices, quantities and discounts, if any, for Products shall be determined as set forth in Exhibit A. All prices are exclusive of all sales, use and excise taxes, and any other similar taxes, duties, and charges of any kind imposed by any governmental authority on any amounts payable by Distributor under this Agreement. Distributor is responsible for all charges, costs, and taxes. Distributor shall pay interest on all late payments, calculated daily and compounded monthly, at the lesser of the rate of [percent (__%)] per month or the highest rate permissible under applicable law. Distributor shall perform its obligations under this Agreement without setoff, deduction, recoupment or withholding of any kind for amounts owed or payable by Supplier, whether relating to Supplier or Supplier's affiliates' breach, bankruptcy, or otherwise and whether under this Agreement, any purchase order, any other agreement between (i) Distributor or any of its affiliates and (ii) Supplier or any of its affiliates, or otherwise. Distributor shall be solely responsible for the prices it charges the Customers.

1.12 Payment. Supplier shall issue periodic invoices to Distributor for all Products ordered in the previous time period. Distributor shall pay all invoiced amounts due to Seller within [Number] days after Distributor's receipt of such invoice, except for any amounts disputed by Distributor in good faith. Distributor shall make all payments in US dollars by check, wire transfer, or automated clearing house in accordance with the instructions received from Supplier from time to time.

1.13 Availability/Changes in Products. Supplier, in its sole discretion, may add or make changes to Products from Exhibit A on notice to Distributor, in each case without obligation to modify or change any Products previously delivered or to supply new goods meeting earlier specifications. Additionally, Supplier shall have the right to increase or decrease prices from time to time upon written notice to Distributor.

ARTICLE V WARRANTIES, INDEMNITIES AND OTHER OBLIGATIONS

1.14 Authority. Each party hereto represents and warrants to the other party that: (i) it has the right, power and authority to enter into this Agreement and to perform all of its obligations hereunder; (ii) this Agreement, when executed and delivered by such party, will be a legal, valid and binding obligation of such party enforceable against it and any entity to which it is an agent in accordance with its terms; and (iii) neither the execution of this Agreement nor such party's performance of its obligations hereunder conflicts with or contravenes any other contract, agreement or instrument to which such party is a party or by which such party or its assets or property is bound or any law, rule or regulation to which such party or its assets are subject.

1.15 Limited Warranty. Supplier hereby represents and warrants that the Products are free from defects in material and workmanship under normal use and service with proper maintenance for [Number] months. The term for such warranties shall begin upon Customer's receipt of the Product. Distributor or Customer shall promptly notify Supplier of any known warranty claims and shall cooperate in the investigation of such claims. If any Product is proven to not conform with this warranty during the applicable warranty period, Supplier, at its exclusive option, shall either repair or replace the Product or refund the purchase price paid by Distributor for each non-conforming Product. Supplier agrees that Distributor shall be entitled to pass through to Customers of Distributor and End Users of the Products all Product warranties granted by Supplier under this Agreement. Distributor shall have no authority to alter or extend any of the warranties of Supplier expressly contained or referred to in this Agreement without prior approval of Supplier. Supplier shall have no obligation under any warranty if Distributor or Customer: (i) fails to notify Supplier in writing during the warranty period of a non-conformity; or (ii) uses, misuses or neglects the Product in a manner inconsistent with the Documentation, modifies the Product or improperly installs, handles or maintains the Product. Except as explicitly authorized in this Agreement or in a separate written agreement with Supplier, Distributor shall not service, repair, modify, alter, replace, reverse engineer, or otherwise change the Products. Distributor shall not provide its own warranty regarding any Product.

1.16 Disclaimer. EXCEPT FOR THE WARRANTIES SET OUT UNDER SECTION 5.2, NEITHER SUPPLIER NOR ANY PERSON ON SUPPLIER'S BEHALF HAS MADE OR MAKES FOR DISTRIBUTOR'S BENEFIT ANY EXPRESS OR IMPLIED REPRESENTATION OR WARRANTY WHATSOEVER, INCLUDING ANY WARRANTIES OF: (i) MERCHANTABILITY; (ii) FITNESS FOR A PARTICULAR PURPOSE; (iii) TITLE; OR (iv) NON-INFRINGEMENT; WHETHER ARISING BY LAW, COURSE OF DEALING, COURSE OF PERFORMANCE, USAGE OF TRADE OR OTHERWISE, ALL OF WHICH ARE EXPRESSLY DISCLAIMED. DISTRIBUTOR

ACKNOWLEDGES THAT IT HAS NOT RELIED ON ANY REPRESENTATION OR WARRANTY MADE BY SUPPLIER, OR ANY OTHER PERSON ON SUPPLIER'S BEHALF.

1.17 Compliance With Laws. Distributor shall at all times comply with all federal, state and local laws, ordinances, regulations and orders that are applicable to the operation of its business, and this Agreement and its performance hereunder. Without limiting the generality of the foregoing, Distributor shall at all times, at its own expense, obtain and maintain all certifications, credentials, authorizations, licenses, and permits necessary to conduct its business relating to the exercise of its rights and the performance of its obligations under this Agreement.

1.18 Indemnification.

(a) Supplier. Subject to the terms and conditions of this Agreement, Supplier agrees to indemnify and hold harmless Distributor, its parent, affiliates and subsidiaries and their officers, directors, members, managers, and employees from and against any and all claims, damages, costs, expenses (including, but not limited to, reasonable attorneys' fees and costs) or liabilities that result, in whole or in part, from Supplier's breach of any of the warranties contained in this Agreement.

(b) Distributor. Subject to the terms and conditions of this Agreement, Distributor agrees to indemnify and hold harmless Supplier, its parent, affiliates and subsidiaries and their officers, directors, members, managers and employees from and against any and all claims, damages, costs, expenses (including, but not limited to, reasonable attorneys' fees and costs) or liabilities that result, in whole or in part, from Distributor's gross negligence or willful misconduct in the distribution of the Products pursuant to this Agreement or breach of Distributor's obligations under this Agreement.

1.19 Limitation of Liability. EXCEPT FOR OBLIGATIONS TO MAKE PAYMENT UNDER THIS AGREEMENT, LIABILITY FOR INDEMNIFICATION, LIABILITY FOR BREACH OF CONFIDENTIALITY, OR LIABILITY FOR INFRINGEMENT OR MISAPPROPRIATION OF INTELLECTUAL PROPERTY RIGHTS, IN NO EVENT (i) IS SUPPLIER OR ANY SUPPLIER REPRESENTATIVE LIABLE FOR CONSEQUENTIAL, INDIRECT, INCIDENTAL, SPECIAL, EXEMPLARY, PUNITIVE, OR ENHANCED DAMAGES, LOST PROFITS OR REVENUES, OR DIMINUTION IN VALUE, ARISING OUT OF OR RELATING TO ANY BREACH OF THIS AGREEMENT, REGARDLESS OF WHETHER THE DAMAGES WERE FORESEEABLE, WHETHER SELLER WAS ADVISED OF THE POSSIBILITY OF THE DAMAGES OR THE LEGAL OR EQUITABLE

THEORY (CONTRACT, TORT, OR OTHERWISE) ON WHICH THE CLAIM IS BASED; (ii) SHALL SELLER'S LIABILITY FOR EACH CLAIM ARISING OUT OF OR RELATED TO THIS AGREEMENT, WHETHER ARISING OUT OF OR RELATED TO BREACH OF CONTRACT, TORT (INCLUDING NEGLIGENCE), OR OTHERWISE, EXCEED THE TOTAL OF THE AMOUNTS PAID AND AMOUNTS ACCRUED BUT NOT YET PAID TO SELLER UNDER THIS AGREEMENT IN THE SIX-MONTH PERIOD PRECEDING THE EVENT GIVING RISE TO THE CLAIM. THE FOREGOING LIMITATIONS APPLY EVEN IF THE DISTRIBUTOR'S REMEDIES UNDER THIS AGREEMENT FAIL OF THEIR ESSENTIAL PURPOSE.

1.20 Insurance.

(a) During the term of this Agreement, Distributor, at its own expense, shall maintain Commercial General Liability or Comprehensive General Liability Insurance in such amounts as is reasonable and standard for the industry with limits no less than $[Amount] for each occurrence and $[Amount] in the aggregate. Either policy form should contain the following coverages: Personal and Advertising Injury, Broad Form Property Damage, Products and Completed Operations, Contractual Liability, employees as Insured and Fire Legal Liability.

(b) Upon request by Supplier, Distributor will provide evidence of the existence of insurance coverages referred to in this Agreement by certificates of insurance, which should also provide for at least [Number] days' notice of cancellation, non-renewal or material change of coverage to Supplier. The certificates of insurance shall name Supplier as an additional insured for the purpose of insuring claims arising pursuant to this Agreement or related to Distributor's sale or distribution of the Products. Except where prohibited by law, Distributor shall require its insurer to waive all rights of subrogation against Supplier's insurers, Supplier and the other indemnified parties.

1.21 Trademark Usage. Distributor is hereby granted a limited, non-transferable, non-sublicensable, non-exclusive license and is authorized to use the trademarks and trade names of Supplier and third parties licensed by Supplier, if any, solely for use in advertising, promoting and distributing the Products in accordance with this Agreement in the Territory during the Term. Distributor acknowledges and agrees that it shall have no other rights whatsoever in the trademarks or trade names of Supplier and third parties licensed by Supplier and that Supplier or such other third parties shall at all times remain the owners all trademarks, trade names and patents associated with the Products. Distributor will act consistent with such rights, and Distributor shall comply with all of Supplier's guidelines related to such trademark or trade name usage, which may be amended from time to time in Supplier's sole discretion. Distributor will promptly discontinue the display or use of any trademark or trade names and change the manner in which a any trademark or trade name is displayed or used with regard to the Products when requested by Supplier. Distributor will notify Supplier of any infringement or misuse of any trademark or trade name. Distributor immediately shall discontinue use of Supplier's trademarks or trade names upon termination of this Agreement.

1.22 Fair Value Warranty. Each party represents and warrants on behalf of itself, that the aggregate benefit given or received under this Agreement has been determined in advance through a process of arms-length negotiations that were intended to achieve an exchange of goods and/or services consistent with fair market value under the circumstances, and that any benefit given or received under this Agreement is not intended to induce, does not require, and is not contingent upon, the admission, recommendation or referral of any customer, directly or indirectly, and further, is not determined in any manner that takes into account the value of business generated between the parties.

ARTICLE VI TERMINATION; EXPIRATION

1.23 Termination.

(a) Termination With Cause. In the event that either party fails to perform any of its obligations set forth in this Agreement, and such default is not cured to the satisfaction of the non-defaulting party within [Number] days after written notice is given to the defaulting party specifying the default, then the non-defaulting party, by giving written notice thereof to the defaulting party and in its sole discretion, may terminate either this Agreement or the applicable purchase order relating to such default as of the date specified in such notice of termination.

(b) Termination by Agreement. In the event Distributor and Supplier shall mutually agree in writing, this Agreement may be terminated on the date specified in such written agreement.

(c) Termination for Insolvency or Bankruptcy. Either party at its option may terminate this Agreement and any purchase orders immediately by giving written notice to the other party in the event of (i) the liquidation or insolvency of the other party, (ii) the appointment of a receiver or similar officer for the other party, (iii) an assignment by the other party for the benefit of all or substantially all of its creditors, (iv) entry by the other party into an agreement for the composition, extension, or readjustment of all or substantially all of its obligations, or (v) the filing of a petition in bankruptcy by or against a party under any bankruptcy or debtors' law for its relief or reorganization that is not dismissed within [Number] days.

1.24 Rights Upon Termination or Expiration.

(a) Termination or expiration of this Agreement shall not affect Supplier's right to be paid for all amounts payable to Supplier hereunder.

(b) Upon termination or expiration of this Agreement for any reason, Distributor shall discontinue holding itself out as, and acting as, a distributor of the Products.

1.25 Survival of Terms. Termination or expiration of this Agreement for any reason shall not release either party from any liabilities or obligations set forth in this Agreement which (i) the parties have expressly agreed shall survive any such termination or expiration, or (ii) remain to be performed or by their nature would be intended to be applicable following any such termination or expiration. The termination or expiration of this Agreement shall not affect any of Distributor's representations, warranties, indemnification obligations or obligations relating to any other matters set forth in this Agreement that should survive termination or expiration to carry out their intended purpose, all of which shall survive the termination or expiration of this Agreement.

ARTICLE VII MISCELLANEOUS

1.26 Binding Nature, Assignment, and Subcontracting. This Agreement shall be binding on the parties and their respective permitted successors and assigns. Distributor shall not have the right to assign this Agreement, except upon the prior written consent of Supplier. Any change of control of Distributor shall be deemed an assignment of this Agreement. Any assignment in violation of this provision shall be null and void.

1.27 Counterparts. This Agreement may be executed in several counterparts, including by electronic means or otherwise, all of which taken together shall constitute one single agreement between the parties.

1.28 Headings. The Article and Section headings used in this Agreement are for reference and convenience only and shall not affect the interpretation of this Agreement.

1.29 Independent Contractors; Relationship of Parties. The Parties are performing pursuant to this Agreement only as independent contractors. Nothing set forth in this Agreement shall be construed to create the relationship of principal and agent between Distributor and Supplier.

Neither party shall act or represent itself, directly or by implication, as an agent of the other party.

1.30 Confidentiality. Distributor acknowledges that in the course of performance of its obligations pursuant to this Agreement, it may obtain certain Confidential Information of Supplier. This Confidential Information may or may not be marked as confidential. Distributor hereby agrees that all Confidential Information communicated to it by Supplier, its parent, affiliates, subsidiaries or agents, whether before or after the Effective Date, shall be and was received in strict confidence, shall be used only for purposes of this Agreement, and shall not be disclosed without the prior written consent of Supplier, except as may be necessary by reason of legal, accounting or regulatory requirements beyond Distributor's reasonable control. The provisions of this section shall survive termination or expiration of this Agreement.

1.31 Investigation. Each party agrees that it has read all provisions of this Agreement and any other documents, instruments or certificates delivered in connection with this Agreement in full, has reviewed those provisions with counsel, understands such provisions, and voluntarily agrees to be bound hereby and thereby. Each party has made such investigation and inquiry into the matters among the parties to this Agreement as such party deems adequate and appropriate under the circumstances and such party is satisfied that it is informed sufficiently to execute and deliver this Agreement and all documents, certificates and instruments contemplated hereby. Each party acknowledges that it has been adequately represented by or has had the opportunity to be represented by counsel of its choice with respect to the matters relating to this Agreement and the transactions contemplated by this Agreement.

1.32 Arbitration. Each dispute, controversy or claim arising out of or relating to this Agreement shall be settled by arbitration in [Location] in accordance with [State] law and the [Arbitration Rules], which shall apply except as modified by this section, including the rules applicable to selection of an arbitrator. Judgment on the award rendered by the arbitrator may be entered in any court having competent jurisdiction. The arbitrator shall not have the power to alter, amend or revise the Agreement or commit errors of law. Each party shall pay an equal share of the fees and expenses of any arbitrator and any administrative fee of the arbitrator and the costs of the arbitration shall be borne equally by the parties until a ruling is made, at which time the prevailing party shall be entitled to recover its attorney's fees and other litigation expenses, including without limitation expert witness fees and investigation expenses.

1.33 Notices. Wherever one party is required or permitted to give notice to the other party pursuant to this Agreement, such notice shall be deemed given when actually delivered by hand, by telecopier or electronic communication (if and when immediately confirmed in writing by any of the other means provided herein ensuring acknowledgment of receipt thereof for purposes of providing notice of default or termination), via overnight courier, or when mailed by registered or certified mail, return receipt requested, postage prepaid, and addressed as follows:

Supplier: ______________________________
____
____
____

Distributor: ______________________________
____
____
____

Either party may from time to time change its address for notification purposes by giving the other party written notice of the new address and the date upon which it will become effective.

1.34 Force Majeure. The term "**Force Majeure**" shall be defined to include fires or other casualties or accidents, acts of God, pandemics, severe weather conditions, strikes or labor disputes, war or other violence, or any law, order, proclamation, regulation, ordinance, demand or requirement of any governmental agency. If a Force Majeure condition prevents a party from performance of any obligation other than payment of amounts from Distributor to Supplier, such performance is excused so long as the excused party provides prompt written notice describing the Force Majeure condition and immediately continues performance once the Force Majeure condition is removed.

1.35 Severability. If any provision of this Agreement is declared or found to be illegal, unenforceable or void, then both parties shall be relieved of all obligations arising under such provision, it being the intent and agreement of the parties that this Agreement shall be deemed amended by modifying such provision to the extent necessary to make it legal and enforceable while preserving its intent.

1.36 Waiver. A waiver by either of the parties of any covenants, conditions or agreements to be performed by the other party or any breach thereof shall not be construed to be a waiver of any succeeding breach thereof or of any other covenant, condition or agreement herein contained.

1.37 Remedies. All remedies set forth in this Agreement shall be cumulative and in addition to and not in lieu of any other remedies available to either party at law, in equity or otherwise, and may be enforced concurrently or from time to time.

1.38 Legal Compliance. The parties shall conduct themselves in an ethical, lawful, businesslike, and professional manner in performance of this Agreement and shall comply with all applicable laws, regulations and directives that may apply to them in the United States or elsewhere. Each party shall reasonably assist the other party to assure such compliance at all times during the term of this Agreement. Notwithstanding anything to the contrary contained in any other provision of this Agreement, if any federal, foreign, state or local government or agency or judicial body passes, issues or promulgates any law, rule, regulation, standard, decision or interpretation, or materially changes its current position as to the interpretation of any existing law, rule, regulation or standard, at any time while this Agreement is in effect in a manner that would prohibit, render unlawful, or materially restrict or limit the relationship described herein or would materially affect a party's ability to meet its legal compliance obligations, or if any governmental entity issues a written allegation or otherwise provides notice to either party to the effect that the relationship described herein is in violation of any law, rule, regulation or otherwise will adversely affect a party's legal compliance (in any case, an "**Adverse Event**"), then either party may give the other party notice of intent to amend this Agreement to bring it into conformity with applicable laws, and the parties shall negotiate in good faith to so amend this Agreement. In conducting such good faith negotiations to amend this Agreement, the parties agree to use their commercially reasonable efforts to avoid the Adverse Event and, to the extent possible, to preserve the existing financial and business relationships between the parties. If this Agreement is not amended in writing by mutual agreement within thirty (30) days after said notice is given, and the party giving notice submits to the other party (or its counsel) a written legal opinion of its counsel or a written determination of any government agency or judicial body that continuation of this Agreement without modification would render the relationship described hereunder unlawful or present a material risk that it would be found unlawful, or trigger an Adverse Event, then the party giving notice shall have the right to terminate the Agreement upon submission of such opinion or determination.

1.39 Entire Agreement. This Agreement, including any schedules and documents referred to in this Agreement or attached hereto, constitutes the entire and exclusive statement of Agreement between the parties with respect to its subject matter and there are no oral or written representations, understandings or agreements relating to this Agreement which are not fully expressed herein. The parties agree that unless otherwise agreed to in writing by the party intended to be bound, the terms and conditions of this Agreement shall prevail over any contrary terms in any purchase order, sales acknowledgment, confirmation or any other document issued by either party affecting the purchase or sale of Products hereunder.

1.40 Governing Law; Venue. This Agreement shall be governed by and construed in accordance with the laws of the State of [State], without reference to choice of laws. The parties agree that this Agreement excludes the application of the 1980 United Nations Convention on Contracts for the International Sale of Goods, if otherwise applicable.

1.41 Time of Performance. Time is hereby expressly made of the essence with respect to each and every term and condition of this Agreement.

[End of Text; Signature Page Follows]

IN WITNESS WHEREOF, the parties have each caused this Agreement to be signed and delivered by its duly authorized officer or representative as of the Effective Date.

"Distributor"		**"Supplier"**	
By:	________________	By:	________________
Name:	________________	Name:	________________
Its:	________________	Its:	________________

Exhibit A

PRODUCTS

[Parties to provide.]

APPENDIX C

TECHNOLOGY LICENSING AGREEMENT

This Technology Licensing Agreement ("**Agreement**") is entered into as of [Date] (the "**Effective Date**") by [Name] ("**Licensor**"), and [Name] ("**Licensee**"). Licensor and Licensee are referred to collectively herein as the "**Parties.**"

1. <u>License and Related Rights and Duties</u>. Subject to the terms and conditions of this Agreement and expressly conditioned on Licensee's timely payment of all fees hereunder, Licensor hereby grants to Licensee during the Term a nontransferable, nonsublicensable, non-exclusive right and license under the licensed rights and technology set forth on Exhibit A (the "**Licensed Technology**") to make, use, offer to sell, sell, and import Licensed Products in [Territory] (the "**Territory**"); provided, however, that the right and license granted in this Agreement is expressly limited to Licensed Products that (i) are designed by Licensee; (ii) sold, offered for sale, or distributed under a trademark owned by Licensee. For the avoidance of doubt, no "have made' rights are granted hereunder and Licensee has no right to permit any third party to make any Licensed Products. Licensed Products means the products set forth on Exhibit B.

2. Limited Grant. Except for the rights and licenses granted by Licensor under Section 1, this Agreement does not grant to Licensee or any other Person any right, title, or interest by implication, estoppel, or otherwise. Without limiting the foregoing, nothing in this Agreement grants by implication, estoppel, or otherwise, any right, title, or interest in, to, or under any patents, trademarks, copyrights or other intellectual property rights owned or controlled by Licensor other than the Licensed Technology. All rights, titles, and interests not specifically and expressly granted by Licensor hereunder are hereby reserved.

3. <u>Know-How; Improvements. Upon reasonable request of Licensee from time-to-time, Licensor agrees to provide guidance on the know-how and processes necessary to successfully utilize the Licensed Technology.</u> Licensee hereby grants to Licensor a non-exclusive, worldwide, royalty-free, license, with the right to grant sublicenses, to any of its modifications of or improvements or enhancements to any Licensed Technology.

4. Royalties. In consideration of its license to the Licensed Technology under this Agreement, Licensee shall pay to Licensor, concurrently with the execution of this Agreement, an initial payment of $[____________] (the "**Upfront Payment**") by wire transfer to a bank account to be designated in writing by Licensor. The Upfront Payment is not refundable and is in addition to and not a prepayment of any Royalties under this Agreement. Licensee shall report monthly to Licensor the total gross revenues received by Licensee in connection with the Licensed Technology (the "**Revenues**"), and shall pay Licensor [________] percent ([___]%) of the Revenues as the royalty license fees (the "**Royalty License Fees**") by the end of each month. If the Royalty License Fees for any month are less than $[Minimum Royalty Amount] (the "**Minimum Royalty**"), Licensee shall pay Licensor the difference between the actual amount already paid to Licensor for such month and the Minimum Royalty.

5. Records and Audit. Licensee shall keep and maintain complete and accurate books of accounts and records with respect to the Revenues. Such books and records must be made known and copies thereof must be made available to the person appointed by Licensor for the purposes of enabling Licensor to access the actual figures and amount of the Revenues. Licensee shall provide copies of such books and records to Licensor within three (3) days following Licensor's written request.

6. Term. This Agreement shall have a [duration] term and shall automatically renew for additional [duration] terms, unless one Party provides the other Party with at least thirty (30) days' advance written notice of non-renewal prior to the renewal date. This Agreement may be terminated at any time upon the mutual agreement of the Parties. Either Party may terminate this Agreement if the other Party materially breaches this Agreement and, if such breach is curable, fails to cure such breach within ten (10) days of receipt of written notice of such breach.

7. Effect of Termination. The termination or expiration of this Agreement will not affect the rights of the Parties with respect to any obligations or liabilities arising from this Agreement prior to such termination or expiration, including any liability for damages resulting from the breach of this Agreement or otherwise, and the obligation of Licensee to pay any amounts to Licensor. For the determination of such rights, Sections 4 through 16 of this Agreement shall survive any termination or expiration of this Agreement. Upon the termination or expiration of this Agreement for any reason Licensee shall (i) immediately cease using the Licensed Technology, (ii) return all documents and materials relating to the Licensed Technology to Licensor._

8. Representations and Warranties.

(a) Each Party hereby represents and warrants to each other Party that it has full right, power, legal capacity and authority to execute, deliver and perform its obligations under this Agreement, and once executed and delivered this Agreement shall be valid and fully binding on such Party.

(b) Licensee represents and warrants that it has not received any notice or threat of any claim, suit, action, or proceeding, and has no knowledge or reason to know of any information, that could adversely affect any of Licensor's right, title or interest in the Licensed Technology.

9. Compliance with Law. The Parties intend for the Agreement to comply with all applicable laws. Each Party agrees that the aggregate benefit given or received under this Agreement has been determined in advance through a process of arms' length negotiations that were intended to achieve an exchange of goods and/or services consistent with fair market value under the circumstances, and is not determined in any manner that takes in to account the value of business generated among the parties. The Parties further represent and warrant and certify that, with respect to performance of this Agreement, they shall not violate the Anti-kickback Statute, the Stark Law or any other federal or state laws applicable to any business operating in the health care industry.

10. Relationship of the Parties. The relationship between the Parties is that of independent contractors. Nothing contained in this Agreement creates any agency, partnership, joint venture, or other form of joint enterprise, employment, or fiduciary relationship between the parties, and neither Party has authority to contract for or bind the other party in any manner whatsoever.

11. Amendment; Modification; Waiver. This Agreement may only be amended, modified, or supplemented by an agreement in writing signed by each Party. No waiver by any Party of any of the provisions hereof will be effective unless explicitly set forth in writing and signed by the waiving Party. Except as otherwise set forth in this Agreement, no failure to exercise, or delay in exercising, any rights, remedy, power, or privilege arising from this Agreement will operate or be construed as a waiver thereof; nor will any single or partial exercise of any right, remedy, power, or privilege hereunder preclude any other or further exercise thereof or the exercise of any other right, remedy, power, or privilege.

12. Assignment. Licensee shall not assign or otherwise transfer any of its rights, or delegate or otherwise transfer any of its obligations or performance, under this Agreement, in each case whether voluntarily, involuntarily, by operation of law, or otherwise, without Licensor's prior

written consent. For purposes of the preceding sentence, and without limiting its generality, any merger, consolidation, change of control or reorganization involving Licensee (regardless of whether Licensee is a surviving or disappearing entity) will be deemed to be a transfer of rights, obligations, or performance under this Agreement for which Licensor's prior written consent is required. No delegation or other transfer will relieve Licensee of any of its obligations or performance under this Agreement. Any purported assignment, delegation, or transfer in violation of this Section is void. Licensor may freely assign or otherwise transfer all or any of its rights, or delegate or otherwise transfer all or any of its obligations or performance, under this Agreement without Licensee's consent. This Agreement is binding upon and inures to the benefit of the Parties and their respective permitted successors and assigns.

13. Confidentiality. Each Party and its agents and representatives shall not disclose any knowledge or information concerning the business, affairs and financial records of each other Party obtained or furnished pursuant to this Agreement ("**Confidential Information**"). Each Party shall exercise the same degree of care in maintaining the secrecy of Confidential Information that it uses in maintaining the secrecy of its own proprietary and confidential information but in no event less than a reasonable degree of care. Licensee agrees to maintain the secrecy of Licensor's proprietary methods and intellectual property rights and other confidential information related to the Licensed Technology, and to use such knowledge and information only as expressly permitted under this Agreement. Confidential Information shall not include: (i) information that is in the public domain as of the date of this Agreement; (ii) information that becomes part of the public domain subsequent to the date of this Agreement through no fault of either Party or its directors, officers, employees, representatives or agents (including its accountants and attorneys); (iii) information that becomes available to either Party from a source other than the discloser or their agents; (iv) information that is required to be disclosed by either Party by order of a governmental agency or court of competent jurisdiction so long as such Party uses reasonable efforts to limit disclosure and to obtain confidential treatment or a protective order; or (v) information that is developed by the recipient independently from and without access to Confidential Information, as evidenced by prior written records or other evidence in the possession of such Party.

14. Choice of Law. This Agreement shall be construed in accordance with and governed by the internal laws of the state of [State], except choice of law rules that would require the application of the laws of any

other jurisdiction. Each Party hereby consents to the exclusive jurisdiction of the state and federal courts sitting in [City, State] in any action on a claim arising out of, under or in connection with this Agreement or the transactions contemplated by this Agreement. Each Party further agrees that personal jurisdiction over a Party may be made by service of process by registered or certified mail addressed to the address of such Party provided in connection with this Agreement, and that when so made shall be as if served upon such Party personally within the aforementioned state.

15. Entire Agreement. This Agreement, including the Exhibits attached hereto, constitutes the entire understanding and agreement of the Parties regarding the subject matter hereof and supersedes any prior oral or written agreements, representations, understandings or discussions between the Parties. If any term or provision of this Agreement is invalid, illegal, or unenforceable in any jurisdiction, such invalidity, illegality, or unenforceability will not affect any other term or provision of this Agreement or invalidate or render unenforceable such term or provision in any other jurisdiction. Upon a determination that any term or other provision is invalid, illegal, or unenforceable, the Parties shall negotiate in good faith to modify this Agreement so as to effect the original intent of the Parties as closely as possible in a mutually acceptable manner in order that the transactions contemplated hereby be consummated as originally contemplated to the greatest extent possible.

16. Counterparts. This Agreement may be executed in counterparts, each of which shall be deemed to be an original, but all of which together shall constitute one agreement. Signature pages transmitted by facsimile or email shall be deemed original signatures for all purposes. The headings of the various sections of this Agreement have been inserted for reference only and shall not be deemed to be a part of this Agreement.

[End of Text; Signature Page and Exhibits Follow]

IN WITNESS WHEREOF, the Parties have caused this Agreement to be executed as of the Effective Date.

[LICENSOR]
By ______________________________
Name: ___________________________
Title: ____________________________

[LICENSOR]
By ______________________________
Name: ___________________________
Title: ____________________________

Exhibit A

Licensed Technology

[Licensor to describe.]

Exhibit B

Licensed Products

[Licensee to describe.]

APPENDIX D

NON-DISCLOSURE AGREEMENT

THIS NON-DISCLOSURE AGREEMENT (this "**Agreement**") is made as of [Date] (the "**Effective Date**"), by and between [Recipient] ("**Recipient**") and [Discloser] ("**Discloser**").

In connection with Recipient's evaluation of a possible business relationship (the "**Relationship**") with Discloser, Discloser desires to provide Recipient with access to Confidential Information (as defined below) to aid Recipient in evaluating the Relationship. In consideration thereof, and as a condition to the disclosure of the information, Recipient hereby agrees as follows:

1. Discloser may disclose and reveal to Recipient certain "**Confidential Information**" which is not generally available to the public. Subject to the limitations set forth in Section 3 of this Agreement, "**Confidential Information**" means all information directly or indirectly concerning Discloser, in whatever form, that Discloser delivers or discloses to Recipient, whether on or after the date of this Agreement, including, but not limited to, information relating to Discloser's concepts, business, operations, finances, products, services, marketing methods and plans, prospects, pricing, supplier lists, market studies, business plans, business opportunities, product and service costs, personnel practices, and all other similar information disclosed to Recipient or any of Recipient's partners, directors, officers, employees, agents, contractors, affiliates, attorneys and other advisors or representatives (collectively, "**Representatives**").
2. Upon receipt of any Confidential Information, Recipient shall: (a) only disclose such Confidential Information to those of its Representatives with a need to have access to and knowledge of the Confidential Information and not disclose any portion thereof to any other person except with the prior written approval of Discloser in each instance and (b) advise any of its Representatives who receive the Confidential Information of the existence and terms of this Agreement and of the obligations of confidentiality and non-disclosure herein, and bind each such Representative

to comply with all such obligations to the extent such Representative is not already so bound by previous agreement or professional conduct standards. Recipient and its Representatives will use the Confidential Information solely for the purpose of evaluating the Relationship and in no way for their own use or benefit, for the use or benefit of any third party, or in any other way detrimental to Discloser or its business.

3. Recipient shall not be obligated to preserve the confidentiality of any Confidential Information that Recipient can demonstrate: (a) prior to any disclosure by Discloser was known by Recipient or any of its Representatives, free of any known obligation to keep it confidential; (b) is or becomes publicly available by other than unauthorized disclosure by Recipient or any of its Representatives; (c) was developed by Recipient or any of its Representatives independently of any of the Confidential Information or (d) is publicly disclosed by a third party, which disclosure does not violate any confidential obligation of such third party to Discloser that is known to Recipient. Recipient may disclose the Confidential Information pursuant to a valid order issued by a court or governmental agency, provided that Recipient provides Discloser with: (a) prior written notice of such obligation; and (b) reasonable opportunity to oppose such disclosure or obtain a protective order or similar relief.
4. At any time upon written demand by Discloser, Recipient shall, and shall cause its Representatives to, immediately return all Confidential Information disclosed or delivered by any media to Recipient or any of its Representatives, along with all copies, extracts and reproductions thereof. Recipient agrees to destroy, and shall cause its Representatives to destroy, all notes, analyses, compilations, studies, designs, plans, and all other works prepared by Recipient or any of its Representatives, on any media, that are generated from or based on any of the Confidential Information, immediately upon request by Discloser. Recipient further agrees to provide Discloser written certification of Recipient's satisfaction of the terms of this Section.
5. All Confidential Information disclosed under the terms of this Agreement shall remain the property of Discloser. Nothing contained in this Agreement shall be construed as granting or conferring to Recipient or its Representatives any rights by license or otherwise in any Confidential Information, or under any trademark, design work, copyright, trade secret or any other property

right now owned or hereafter owned or controlled by Discloser. Recipient agrees that it shall not, and shall cause its Representative not to, remove, overprint or deface any notice of confidentiality, copyright, trademark, logo, legend or other notices of ownership or confidentiality from any original or copies of the Confidential Information it obtains in connection with this Agreement, or authorize any third party to do any of the foregoing. Neither Discloser nor any other person makes any representations or warranties regarding the completeness or accuracy of the Confidential Information. The provision of Confidential Information pursuant to this Agreement shall not obligate Discloser to enter into any transaction or relationship with Recipient, nor shall it prevent Discloser from providing the same or different Confidential Information to any third party upon terms and conditions determined at its discretion.

6. The obligations of the parties contained in this Agreement shall terminate upon the second anniversary of the date first set forth above; provided, however, that Recipient's obligations under Paragraph 2 shall continue with respect to the Confidential Information until such Confidential Information (or relevant portion thereof) falls into an exception contained in Paragraph 3. Recipient acknowledges that disclosure of the Confidential Information would cause irreparable harm to Discloser, the value of which may be difficult to determine. Recipient agrees that in the event of any breach or threatened breach by Recipient of its obligations hereunder, Discloser shall be entitled to injunctive relief, restraining orders or such other relief as Discloser determines appropriate, and Recipient waives the defense that a remedy in damages would be adequate and any requirement of a posting of a bond.
7. Recipient agrees that for a period of two (2) years following the date of this Agreement, Recipient neither shall solicit nor hire any employee of Discloser with whom Recipient came into contact or became aware of as a result of disclosure of Confidential Information or its analysis thereof to terminate his or her employment with Discloser; except Recipient shall not be (i) restricted in any general solicitation for employees or public advertising of employment opportunities (including the use of employment agencies) not specifically targeted at such persons, or (ii) precluded from hiring any such person whose employment has been terminated by Discloser prior to commencement of employment discussions between Recipient and such person.

8. This Agreement shall be governed and construed in accordance with the laws of the state of [State], without giving effect to the principles of conflict of laws thereof. Any claim or proceeding arising out of or in connection with this Agreement shall be brought exclusively in state or federal courts located in [City, State]. This Agreement constitutes the entire agreement of the parties with respect to its subject matter. This Agreement may be waived, amended, or modified only by an instrument in writing signed by the party against which such waiver, amendment or modification is sought to be enforced. The term "person" as used in this Agreement shall be broadly interpreted to include, without limitation, any individual, group or entity. No failure or delay in exercising any right, power or privilege hereunder shall operate as a waiver thereof, nor shall any single or partial exercise thereof preclude any other or further exercise thereof or the exercise of any right, power or privilege hereunder. Recipient may not assign this Agreement without the advance written consent of Discloser. If any provision of this Agreement is for any reason adjudged to be void, invalid or unenforceable, then the remainder of this Agreement shall continue and remain in full force and effect. This Agreement may be executed in counterparts, each of which shall constitute an original of this Agreement and all of which shall constitute one and the same Agreement. Facsimile or electronically transmitted signatures shall be accepted by the parties and binding thereon.

[End of Text; Signature Page Follows]

IN WITNESS WHEREOF, the undersigned has duly executed this Non-Disclosure Agreement on behalf of Recipient and delivered it to Discloser as of the Effective Date.

RECIPIENT:

[RECIPIENT]

By: ____
Title:

____
Print Name of Signatory

Discloser:

[DISCLOSER]

By: ____
Title:

APPENDIX E

BUSINESS ASSOCIATE AGREEMENT

This Business Associate Agreement ("**Agreement**") is entered into as of [Date] (the "**Effective Date**") by and between [Name] ("**Business Associate**") and [Name] ("**Covered Entity**"), which is a covered entity under the Health Insurance Portability and Accountability Act of 1996 ("**HIPAA**"). The parties are entering into this Agreement to assist the Covered Entity in complying with HIPAA, and to set forth Business Associate's obligations under the Health Information Technology for Economic and Clinical Health Act of 2009 (the "**HITECH Act**"), and 45 CFR Parts 160 and 164, Subpart C (the "**Security Rule**"), Subpart D (the "**Data Breach Notification Rule**"), and Subpart E (the "**Privacy Rule**" and, collectively, the "**HIPAA Regulations**") and applicable state law. Terms used in this Agreement have the meanings given them in the HIPAA Regulations. This Agreement applies to any Protected Health Information Business Associate receives from Covered Entity, or creates, receives or maintains on behalf of Covered Entity, under its agreements with Covered Entity (the "**Principal Agreements**").

AGREEMENT

1. Business Associate may use and disclose Covered Entity's Protected Health Information to provide Covered Entity with the goods and services contemplated by the Principal Agreements. Except as expressly provided below, this Agreement does not authorize Business Associate make any use or disclosure of Protected Health Information that Covered Entity would not be permitted to make.

2. Business Associate will:

(a) Not use or further disclose Covered Entity's Protected Health Information except as permitted or required by law, including without limitation performance of Business Associate's obligations under the Principal Agreements or this Agreement;

(b) Use appropriate safeguards, and comply, where applicable, with the HIPAA Security Rule with respect to electronic protected health information, to prevent use or disclosure of Covered Entity's Protected

Health Information other than as provided for by the Principal Agreements or this Agreement;

(c) Report to Covered Entity any use or disclosure of Covered Entity's Protected Health Information not provided for by the Principal Agreements or this Agreement of which it becomes aware, including breaches of unsecured Protected Health Information as required by the Data Breach Notification Rule (45 CFR § 164.410), and any security incident of which Business Associate becomes aware. Notwithstanding the foregoing, Covered Entity and Business Associate hereby agree that Business Associate receives frequent, routine, unsuccessful attempts to penetrate or compromise its systems, including without limitation pings, port scans and log on attempts, and that this constitutes Business Associate's report and notification to Covered Entity of such events, and no further reporting of any such security incidents is required unless these attempts result in an unauthorized access to, use, disclosure, destruction or loss of electronic Protected Health Information;

(d) Ensure that any of Business Associate's subcontractors that create, receive, maintain, or transmit Protected Health Information on behalf of the Business Associate agree in writing to the same restrictions and conditions that apply to Business Associate with respect to such information, including compliance with the HIPAA Security Rule with respect to electronic Protected Health Information;

(e) Make any Protected Health Information in a designated record set available to Covered Entity to enable Covered Entity to meet its obligation to provide access to the information in accordance with 45 CFR § 164.524;

(f) Make any Protected Health Information in a designated record set available for amendment and incorporate any amendments to Protected Health Information as directed by Covered Entity pursuant to 45 CFR § 164.526;

(g) Make available to Covered Entity the information concerning disclosures that Business Associate makes of Covered Entity's Protected Health Information required to enable Covered Entity to provide an accounting of disclosures in accordance with 45 CFR § 164.528;

(h) To the extent that Business Associate carries out Covered Entity's obligations under the Privacy Rule, comply with the requirements of the Privacy Rule that apply to Covered Entity in the performance of such obligations;

(i) Make Business Associate's internal practices, books, and records relating to Business Associate's use and disclosure of Protected Health Information received from Covered Entity, or created or received by Business Associate on behalf of Covered Entity, available to the Secretary of the United States Department of Health and Human Services for purposes of determining Covered Entity's compliance with the HIPAA Regulations;

(j) Upon termination of the Principal Agreements, return or destroy all Covered Entity's Protected Health Information that Business Associate still maintains in any form and retain no copies of such information or, if return or destruction is not feasible or contemplated under the Principal Agreements, extend the protections of this Agreement to that information;

3. If Covered Entity determines that Business Associate has violated a material term of this Agreement, and if Business Associate fails to cure such violation within thirty (30) days of delivery of written notice thereof, Covered Entity may immediately terminate this Agreement.

4. Business Associate may use Covered Entity's Protected Health Information for the management and administration of Business Associate's company and to carry out Business Associate's own legal responsibilities, and Business Associate may disclose the information for these purposes if Business Associate is required to do so by law, or if Business Associate obtains reasonable assurances from the recipient of the information (1) that it will be held confidentially, and used or further disclosed only as required by law or for the purpose for which it was disclosed to the recipient, and (2) that the recipient will notify Business Associate of any instances of which the recipient is aware in which the confidentiality of the information is breached.

5. Business Associate may use Covered Entity's Protected Health Information for data aggregation, as permitted by the Privacy Rule.

6. Business Associate may de-identity Covered Entity's Protected Health Information, in compliance with the requirements of 45 C.F.R. Section 164.514. Business Associate shall be the owner of such de-identified data.

7. This Agreement is to be interpreted in accordance with HIPAA, the HITECH Act, and the regulations promulgated thereunder, as amended from time to time.

IN WITNESS WHEREOF this Business Associate Agreement is executed as of the Effective Date.

"BUSINESS ASSOCIATE"

[Name]

By: ______________________________
Title: ____________________________

"COVERED ENTITY"

[Name]

____
By:
Its:

CHAPTER 6

Postmarket Requirements

Paul Gadiock and Jamie Ravitz

I. Postmarket Requirements

The Food and Drug Administration (FDA) takes a total product life cycle approach to medical device regulation. This means that regulated industry is responsible for complying with requirements after a device has been authorized for marketing by the FDA. Postmarket regulatory expectations take many forms, some of which overlap with the Quality System Regulation (QSR). Records of device modifications must be maintained, certain device failures must be reported to FDA, or clinical studies or monitoring may need to be conducted, among other potential requirements. Companies that lack adequate postmarket policies or otherwise fail to satisfy applicable requirements can be subject to monetary penalties or withdrawal of device approval or clearance, as discussed further in the chapter on Compliance and Enforcement.

In contrast to premarket requirements that are largely completed for advice iteration once it has been authorized for marketing by FDA, the postmarked regulation of medical devices is ongoing throughout an individual device's life. Additionally, even organizations that maintain postmarket compliance need to remain vigilant of emerging regulatory developments. One such example is the mandate for unique device identification (UDI), authorized in the Food and Drug Administration Safety and Innovation Act (FDASIA) of 2012.[1] Virtually all medical devices were expected to affix a label under and be reflected into a database under UDI, even approvals and clearances that occurred prior to 2012. As discussed later in this chapter, UDI's implementation is ongoing with

1. Pub. L. No. 112-144.

enforcement discretion in effect for certain devices. However, its enactment underscores that compliance with postmarket requirements is an ongoing process with goalposts that do not necessarily stay constant.

II. Device Modifications

Device modifications are generally required to be maintained under a device's QSR.[2] The QSR requires manufacturers of finished medical devices to review and approve changes to device design and production and document changes and approvals in the device's master record.[3] Beyond the fundamental QSR framework for device modifications are classification-specific requirements described in the 510(k) and premarket approval (PMA) regulations.

A. 510(k) Modifications

If a manufacturer modifies their device with the intent to significantly affect the safety or effectiveness of the device (for example, to significantly improve clinical outcomes, to mitigate a known risk, in response to adverse events, etc.), submission of a new 510(k) is likely required. Devices are typically refined and sometimes improved approval or clearance. Typical changes to Class I reserved and Class II devices marketed under a 510(k) must be evaluated to determine whether they are so significant that submission of a 510(k) is triggered for the new device iteration. If clearance of a new 510(k) is not required based on the type of change(s) being made to the device, the rationale for not submitting a new regulatory clearance must be documented by the manufacturer and maintained in the records.

The regulatory standard for whether a 510(k) clearance is required for device changes is distinct from the premarket regulatory standard of substantial equivalence. Instead, significantly changed or modified in design, components, method of manufacture, or intended use are the standards by which to judge the necessity of a 510(k) clearance. More specifically, a new 510(k) is required for any modification that could significantly affect the device's safety or effectiveness, or that would constitute a major change in its intended use. Given how demanding the premarket requirements are for obtaining 510(k) clearance, whether a new regulatory submission is required is a critical consideration.

2. 21 C.F.R. § 820.186.
3. *Id.* §§ 820.30, 820.70, 820.181.

The 510(k) decision-making process is complex with numerous decision points related to device aspects such as labeling, technology, and materials, with special considerations for in vitro diagnostic devices (IVDs). The decision-making policy is detailed in two FDA guidances, one of which addresses medical devices generally and the other of which specifically targets software devices. The guidance, "Deciding When to Submit a 510(k) for a Change to an Existing Device" was issued by the FDA in 2017 and replaced the agency's previous policy on 510(k) modifications, which was, at the time, approximately 20 years old.[4] Its software counterpart, "Deciding When to Submit a 510(k) for a Software Change to an Existing Device," is a companion document that issued simultaneously. Both guidances share the same basis in regulation and similar guiding principles but the latter layers in considerations largely unique to software such as cybersecurity or whether a change could affect the software's architecture. For software device changes that affect a non-software device aspect such as labeling, the conventional 510(k) Modifications Guidance should be consulted as the relevant considerations would generally not be specific to software. Examples are used throughout the guidances to illustrate how device modifications may or may not trigger a new 510(k).

Savvy manufacturers consult the guidances not only before changes are seriously considered, but also for direction when exploring the types of device modifications that may be instituted without a new regulatory submission. In addition, early planning can help establish data collection methods and endpoints for verification and validation testing that must demonstrate to the manufacturer that the modification would not significantly affect the safety or effectiveness of the device. Other times, the guidances are consulted ex post facto when a device change is necessary rather than elective. For example, the guidances are also intended to

4. FDA Guidance, *Deciding When to Submit a 510(k) for a Change to an Existing Device* (Jan. 10, 1997). In 2011, FDA issued a draft guidance intended to replace the 1997 guidance regarding changes to existing devices. However, the draft guidance entitled, *Guidance for Industry and FDA Staff—510(k) Device Modifications: Deciding When to Submit a 510(k) for a Change to an Existing Device*, was met with significant industry opposition as the policy in the draft guidance, if finalized, was expected to trigger the submission of significantly more 510(k)s for device changes. Prior to its finalization, section 602(b) of FDASIA formally legislated the draft guidance's withdrawal in 2012. FDA did not issue a revised draft of its policy concerning changes to existing devices until August 8, 2016. The policy in this draft more closely resembled the policy in the 1997 guidance that was in effect at the time and was met with far less resistance, ultimately being finalized October 27, 2017.

apply to situations where a legally marketed existing device is the subject of a recall, correction, or removal, and a change in the device or its labeling is necessary.

Changes must be evaluated against the original device, that is, the device described in their most recently cleared 510(k) for the device, their legally marketed preamendments device, or their device that was granted marketing authorization via the de novo classification process. This regulatory position prevents successive minor changes that would cumulatively affect device safety or effectiveness. Many simultaneous changes may be considered at once, so each change should be assessed separately, as well as in the aggregate.

FDA may assess the risk that a medical device will cause direct or indirect patient harm by considering a variety of factors including severity of harm, likelihood of risk, distribution of nonconforming devices, duration of exposure to population, false-positive or false-negative results, patience tolerance of risk, and risk factors for health care professionals or caregivers. These factors, when relevant, should be considered in aggregate. Each factor may be considered early in the medical device product life cycle and reassessed as the device is used more widely. Changes in risk should be noted in the manufacturer's risk management documentation. Changes in risk may occur due to, among other things, observed unanticipated harm to patients exposed to the device or to device users, changes in the medical device use environment, identified medical device nonconformities, and issues related to the design or manufacturing of the device. It should be noted that all devices have some level of anticipated risk, even without device nonconformities or regulatory noncompliance, and hazards can occur both when a device functions normally and if it malfunctions. Medical device nonconformities may increase risk or introduce new risks.

Failure to comply with applicable statutes or regulations also may be a negative indicator of a manufacturer's ability to consistently manufacture high quality medical devices, even if a device made by such a manufacturer still performs as expected. Postmarket data may also show that risk is higher than anticipated, even in the absence of a medical device nonconformity or regulatory noncompliance. Therefore, the risk factors account for considerations related to nonconforming devices, failure to comply with applicable statutes or regulations, and harm potentially unrelated to compliance with legal requirements or device nonconformities

When prioritizing compliance and enforcement efforts to maximize medical device quality and patient safety, FDA may assess the extent of benefit of a device alongside its risks, in the aggregate. The benefit-risk factors may be considered when device manufacturers evaluate appropriate responses to nonconforming product or regulatory compliance issues, such as determining whether to limit the availability of a medical device (e.g., a voluntary recall or market withdrawal). FDA may consider the benefit-risk factors during, for example, evaluation of device shortage situations, selection of the appropriate regulatory engagement mechanism following an inspection during which regulatory noncompliance was observed, evaluation of recalls, and consideration of petitions for variance from those sections of the QSR for which there were inspectional observations during a PMA pre-approval inspection.

1. 510(k) Modification Decision-Making Process

If a manufacturer modifies their device with the intent to significantly affect the safety or effectiveness of the device (for example, to significantly improve clinical outcomes, to mitigate a known risk, in response to adverse events, etc.), submission of a new 510(k) is likely required. The manufacturer should also consider whether the change could have unintended consequences. For example, changes in sterilization may unintentionally affect device materials, or changes to materials may unintentionally affect the performance of the device. The FDA's current approach for the Special 510(k) Program focuses on whether the method(s) to evaluate the change(s) are well-established, and whether the results can be sufficiently reviewed in a summary or risk analysis format.

In the event a new 510(k) is triggered, manufacturers may have the option to submit it under the Special 510(k) framework and take advantage of a briefer FDA review timeline. The program was intended to create an efficient review process for certain changes subject to 510(k) submission requirements. If a new 510(k) is needed for the change, then summary information that results from the design control process may serve as the basis for substantial equivalence along with the required elements of a 510(k) found in 21 C.F.R. § 807.87. A design or labeling change to an existing device (including certain changes to the indications for use) may be appropriate for a Special 510(k) when the proposed change is submitted by the manufacturer legally authorized to market the existing device, performance data are unnecessary, or if performance data are necessary, well-established methods are available to evaluate the change, and all performance data necessary to support substantial equivalence can be reviewed in a summary or risk analysis format.

Special 510(k)s allow the FDA and industry to rely on previous agency review of detailed information, where appropriate, without altering any statutory or regulatory requirements related to the premarket notification process under sections 510 and 513 of the FD&C Act, and 21 C.F.R. § 807 subpart E. The Special 510(k) Program provides a least burdensome approach to the review of certain changes to a manufacturer's own legally marketed predicate device ("existing device") because a Special 510(k) provides an efficient pathway for manufacturers to provide the minimum required information necessary to establish substantial equivalence for a modified device. FDA intends to process Special 510(k)s within 30 days of receipt by the Document Control Center (DCC), rather than the 90 days for 510(k)s required by section 510(n)(1) of the FD&C Act.

2. Letters to File

One regulatory pathway for 510(k) holders to implement changes is by preparing internal documentation, that is, a "letter to file" for nonsignificant changes. While guidance for 510(k) changes addresses individual changes implemented at a single point in time, it does not address incremental, nonsignificant changes that could, in sum, be significant when evaluating the device holistically. Thus, letters to file document the sum of changes made to a device. Those letters can culminate in the submission of a so-termed catch-up 510(k) submission.

Risk analyses are particularly helpful in supporting the manufacturer's assessment of whether to submit a catch-up 510(k). During a retrospective review of letters to file for a cleared device, a 510(k) holder may determine one or more letters to file were erroneous or overreaching in determining the significance of a change(s). In this case, a 510(k) should have been submitted prior to implementing the change(s). In such circumstances, a 510(k) holder may choose to submit a "catch-up" 510(k) in an effort to mitigate the risk of a Form 483 or "Warning Letter" resulting from an FDA inspection.

510(k) holders should periodically review their device to determine whether the current device differs significantly from the cleared device. While each individual letter to file may be nonsignificant, the sum of changes may be. It is best practice to develop a procedure and steps to ensure that reviews of devices, to account for whether the sum of those changes are significant and should therefore culminate into a catch-up 510(k).

B. PMA Modifications

Consistent with how devices subject to a PMA experience more stringent premarket requirements than Class II devices, so too is the postmarket oversight of PMA devices. Virtually all device modifications must be submitted to FDA, yet some can forego agency approval prior to being incorporated. Simple changes related to the device documentation or manufacturing process documentation, such as rewording or expanding for clarification, translating from one language to another, correcting typographical errors, and moving component characteristics from an engineering drawing note to a different document (e.g., standard operating procedure), do not need to be reported in the annual report.

Whereas the standard between evaluating a new 510(k) and whether a modification requires a new 510(k) are distinct, the standard for PMA devices remains largely consistent in the premarket and postmarket setting—what is the nature of the data, if any, that is required to demonstrate the safety and effectiveness of the modified device.

The type of modification made to the device dictates whether it triggers a traditional PMA, panel track supplement, 180-day supplement, real-time supplement, Special PMA Supplement-Changes Being Effected, 30-day notice, manufacturing site change supplement, or periodic report.

1. When to Submit a Traditional PMA

In general, a traditional PMA (rather than a PMA supplement) is appropriate when the modifications to the approved PMA device result in a new device. A new device is one where a modification results in a device design so different from the original version that the preclinical ("analytical" for in vitro diagnostics (IVDs)) and clinical data previously submitted on the original device are not applicable (i.e., not supportive) for the specific change in demonstrating a reasonable assurance of the safety and effectiveness of the modified device.

In deciding whether to submit a supplement to your approved traditional PMA or to submit a new traditional PMA5 for a modified device, we recommend you first ascertain whether, and to what extent, you can rely on the preclinical testing and clinical data submitted in your traditional PMA to support the safety and effectiveness of your modified device. If you need to conduct both new preclinical testing and new clinical testing to demonstrate reasonable assurance of safety and effectiveness of the modified device, you should assume that this is a new device that will require a submission of a new traditional PMA.

2. Panel Track Supplement

A panel track supplement is appropriate when there is a new indication for use, but no change in design. The term "panel-track supplement" is defined in section 737(4)(B) of the act[5] as:

5. 21 U.S.C. § 379i(4)(B) (added by MDUFMA, as amended by the Medical Devices Technical Corrections Act (MDTCA) (Pub. L. No. 108-214 (2004)),

> a supplement to an approved premarket application or premarket report under section 515 that requests a significant change in design or performance of the device, or a new indication for use of the device, and for which substantial clinical data are necessary to provide a reasonable assurance of safety and effectiveness.

The agency considers panel-track supplements to be the most appropriate supplement type for changes in the indication for use requiring substantial clinical data (i.e., new clinical data), with or without limited new preclinical testing.[6] A change in the indication for use may incorporate a change to the intended patient population, disease state, or to other clinical aspects of the device use, such as duration of use, anatomical site, or surgical procedure. Changes in these clinical aspects would generally require significant labeling changes for which new clinical data are generally needed to support those changes. The FDA also considers a panel-track supplement to be the most appropriate supplement type for a change to, or removal of, a contraindication.

A panel-track supplement, therefore, should be submitted for a change in indication for use or a change to or removal of a contraindication of the device because substantial clinical data (i.e., new clinical data) is necessary to provide reasonable assurance of safety and effectiveness for that change. Additionally, a panel-track supplement should be submitted when indication or contraindication changes generally either do not require or require very limited new preclinical testing such that all or most of the preclinical data previously submitted and reviewed in the traditional PMA are still applicable for the change in indication. Examples of indication changes include different patient populations, different surgical procedure, different conditions of use, different sample type, and different physiological location, amongst others.

For panel-track supplements, a full PMA review will be required. This may include a review by an outside advisory panel.

3. 180-Day Supplement

A 180-day supplement is appropriate when the device undergoes a significant change requiring new preclinical test data. According to section 737(4)(C) of the act[7] "180-day supplement" is defined as:

---

6. 21 C.F.R. § 814.39(c).
7. 21 U.S.C. § 379i(4)(C).

> a supplement to an approved premarket application or premarket report under section 515 that is not a panel-track supplement and requests a significant change in components, materials, design, specification, software, color additives, or labeling.

Submission of a 180-day supplement is required for certain types of significant changes to the approved device that affect safety or effectiveness of the device, as listed earlier. In general, for a change to be submitted as a 180-day supplement, the clinical data provided in support of the traditional device approval should still be applicable in supporting the approval of the modified device. In most cases, for such modifications, only new preclinical testing is needed to demonstrate reasonable assurance of safety and effectiveness of the modified device.

In some instances, however, additional limited confirmatory clinical data may be necessary to provide a bridge between the clinical data set for the original device and the expected clinical performance of the modified device. Confirmatory clinical data typically involve a limited number of patients, shorter study duration, and/or a subset of endpoints as compared to the clinical data set for a traditional PMA. In these situations, FDA believes that a 180-day supplement, rather than a panel-track supplement, is appropriate because of the limited nature of the supplementary clinical data.

Certain significant changes requiring a 180-day supplement include the principle of operation, the control mechanism, the device design or performance, the labeling, and new testing requirements or acceptance criteria.

4. Real-Time Supplement

A real-time supplement is appropriate when a device undergoes minor changes supported by preclinical or animal testing, with no new clinical data. According to section 737(4)(D) of the act,[8] a "real-time supplement" is defined as:

> a supplement to an approved premarket application or premarket report under section 515 that requests a minor change to the device, such as a minor change to the design of the device, software, sterilization, or labeling, and for which the applicant has requested and the agency has granted a meeting or similar forum to jointly review and determine the status of the supplement.

8. 21 U.S.C. § 379i(4)(D) (added by MDUFMA, as amended by MDTCA).

In general, FDA believes a Real-Time PMA Supplement is appropriate for a minor change that can be expected within a product line, which includes changes to device design, software, instructions for use, warnings, or precautions or other labeling that does not affect the indications or contraindications, or sterilization and packaging methods. In addition, a minor change should be one that is expected for that device type, validated according to scientific principles we have relied on in previous reviews and accepted test methods or procedures for devices of that type, wherever applicable, such as an FDA-recognized standard or guidance document, adequately supported by preclinical or animal testing, with no new clinical data, and typically involves review within a single scientific discipline, rather than a multidisciplinary review.

FDA intends the review process for a Real-Time PMA Supplement to be interactive, although a face-to-face meeting may not always be part of the process. FDA will work with you to determine the type of interaction appropriate (e.g., face-to-face meeting, teleconference, written responses) based on the information in your request. If you and FDA agree a meeting is appropriate, FDA's response will also confirm a meeting date, which should be within 30 days of the proposed submission date of the supplement or the earliest date that both you and FDA personnel are available to meet.

A Real-Time PMA Supplement should identify all modifications planned for the device and labeling. FDA recommends including testing and results, along with a detailed risk assessment to support the continued safety and effectiveness of the modified device. The risk assessment should include a thorough review of all potential hazards associated with device use, considering the (incremental) modification proposed in your submission and the (cumulative) effects of any preceding modifications made since the approval of the original PMA. The risk assessment should also identify the steps taken to minimize any additional risks that may be created by incremental or cumulative modifications.

5. 30-Day Notice

Changes, which affect the safety or effectiveness of the device, that may qualify for submission as a 30-day notice, are changes to the manufacturing procedure or changes in method of manufacture. Section 515(d) of the act[9] permits a PMA applicant to submit written notification to the agency of a modification to the manufacturing procedure or method of

9. 21 U.S.C. § 360e, as amended by the Food and Drug Administration Modernization Act of 1997 (FDAMA) (Pub. L. No. 105-115).

manufacture affecting the safety and effectiveness of the device rather than submitting such change as a PMA supplement. The applicant may distribute the device 30 days after the date on which FDA receives the notice, unless FDA finds such information in the 30-day notice is not adequate, notifies the applicant that the submission has been converted to a 135-day supplement[10] and describes further information or action that is required for acceptance of the modification.

When changes also alter performance or design specifications or the designated physical or chemical specifications of the finished device, a 30-day notice is not appropriate. In these cases, a PMA holder should submit a 180-day PMA supplement or a real-time review PMA Supplement, as appropriate. Similarly, in these instances, a humanitarian device exemption (HDE) holder must submit a 75-day HDE supplement.

Changes should be submitted as 30-day notices only when the material was critical to the performance of the device, as determined by the manufacturer. If the material is not critical to the performance of the device, then any change should be submitted as part of the periodic report (often referred to as the annual report). Note, however, that if a manufacturing change involves adding a second supplier of a critical component, and the specifications of that component are different, a 30-day notice is not appropriate because the specifications have changed.[11] A PMA holder should submit a 180-day PMA supplement or a real-time review PMA Supplement, as appropriate. Similarly, in these instances, an HDE holder should submit a 75-day HDE supplement.[12]

Changes that qualify for a "Special PMA Supplement—Changes Being Effected" under 21 C.F.R. § 814.39(d)(2) for changes in quality controls or manufacturing process that add a new specification or test method, or otherwise provide additional assurance of purity, identity, strength, or reliability of the device can be submitted either as a "Special PMA Supplement—Changes Being Effected" or a 30-day notice. The manufacturing changes that may be reviewed as a Special PMA Supplement are generally those that add a step to the quality control or manufacturing process to enhance safety but do not impact effectiveness. If efficacy is also affected, those changes should be submitted as a 30-day notice.

Changes to the manufacturing procedure or method of manufacturing that do not affect the safety or effectiveness of the device must be

10. 21 C.F.R. § 814.39(f).
11. *Id.* § 814.39(a)(6).
12. *Id.* § 814.108.

submitted in the periodic report, that is usually referred to as an annual report.[13] Devices subject to premarket approval under section 515 of the act are also subject to periodic report requirements imposed by the PMA approval order. FDA typically specifies that a PMA holder submit a report one year from the date of approval of the original PMA and annually thereafter. Therefore, the periodic report is usually referred to as an annual report.

If a 30 day notice contains device design or labeling changes in addition to manufacturing changes, then the submission will automatically be converted to a 180-day PMA or 75-Day HDE supplement and reviewed accordingly.

If the change qualifies for a 30-day notice and the applicant has submitted complete information in the 30-day notice to FDA, the applicant may distribute the device 30 days after the date on which FDA received the notice, unless FDA provides notification within those 30 days that the notice is inadequate. However, if the information submitted is not adequate, FDA will inform the applicant within 30 days of receipt of the inadequate submission via e-mail or letter that a 135-day PMA supplement or for HDE holders, a 75-day HDE supplement is needed and shall describe additional information or action that is required for acceptance of that change. If no action occurs within 30 days of receipt of your 30-day notice and payment of the user fee, the device may be distributed without further action from FDA.

6. Manufacturing Site Change Supplement

As with a premarket approval application, a supplemental premarket approval application may be approved if it meets the applicable statutory and regulatory requirements. One such requirement is that the methods used in, or the facilities or controls used for, the manufacture, processing, packaging, storage or installation of a device conforms to the requirements of section 520(f) of the FD&C Act.[14] A preapproval inspection for a site change supplement may be necessary for FDA to find that the methods used in, or the facilities or controls used for, the manufacture, processing, packaging, storage, or installation of the device conform to the requirements of the QS regulation.[15]

---

13. 21 U.S.C. § 515.
14. *Id.* § 520(f).
15. 21 C.F.R. § 820. *See* 21 U.S.C. §§ 515(c)(1)(C), 515(d)(2)(C), 520(f); 21 U.S.C. §§ 360e(c)(1)(C), 360e(d)(2)(C), 360j(f).

FDA generally determines whether to conduct an inspection of a new site associated with a site change supplement based upon the following factors:

- the dates of the last inspections of the current site and the new site;
- the classifications of the last inspections of the current site and the new site;
- the relevance of the last QS regulation inspection to the moved manufacturing, processing, or packaging activities (e.g., whether similar products or processes were inspected);
- a review of relevant recalls and adverse events, associated with manufacturing processes for devices manufactured, processed or packaged at this site; and
- the risk to the safety or effectiveness of the device associated with the manufacturing activities performed at the new site.

Under section 515(d)(5) of the FD&C Act,[16] a supplemental application to an approved PMA (PMA supplement) must be submitted for review and approval by FDA before making a change that affects the device's safety or effectiveness, unless such change is a modification in a manufacturing procedure or method of manufacture, which would be eligible for a 30-day notice. The PMA regulations provide general criteria in 21 C.F.R. § 814.39 for determining when PMA holders (hereinafter referred to as "applicants") are required to submit a PMA supplement or are eligible to submit a 30-day notice. Under 21 C.F.R. § 814.39(a)(3), an applicant must submit a PMA supplement when it "use[s] a different facility or establishment to manufacture, process, or package the device," and the change affects the device's safety or effectiveness.

With respect to establishment inspections, section 510(h)[17] requires every registered establishment to be subject to inspections pursuant to section 704[18] and every such establishment engaged in the manufacture, propagation, compounding, or processing of a device or devices will be inspected in accordance with a risk-based schedule.

Manufacturing Site Change supplements have a relative complex history. In March 1996, CDRH sent a letter to the medical device industry that announced a one-year pilot to improve the processing of PMA supplements for changes in manufacturing sites. The letter discussed the

---

16. 21 U.S.C. § 360e(d)(5).
17. *Id.* § 360(h).
18. *Id.* § 374.

need to improve the speed and efficiency of CDRH review and approval of manufacturing site change supplements and stated that CDRH did not require a preapproval inspection for all manufacturing site changes. That letter described conditions under which a site generally would or would not be inspected. CDRH later developed the draft guidance entitled, "Likelihood of Facilities Inspections When Modifying Devices Subject to Premarket Approval," which was issued on August 5, 1999. This guidance was not finalized.

The PMA supplements described in the March 1996 letter and the 1999 draft guidance were called "site change supplements" or, if no preapproval inspection was required, they were termed "express supplements." FDA now identifies all such submissions as "site change supplements" and designates whether an inspection is needed before the change can be implemented. Based on feedback from the industry and the agency's experience over many years, FDA has made substantial revisions and updates to the 1999 draft guidance, which is being replaced by guidance entitled, "Manufacturing Site Change Supplements: Content and Submission."[19] The guidance is intended to help industry decide when a change in manufacturing site should be submitted in a PMA site change supplement.

The guidance is also intended to help the industry anticipate when a preapproval inspection in connection with a PMA supplement for a manufacturing site change will likely be needed to evaluate the firm's implementation of the Quality System (QS) regulation requirements.[20] As a result, the guidance should help firms manage the timeframes associated with implementing the changes in the manufacturing site and any processes, methods, procedures, qualifications, and validations. Regardless of whether an FDA preapproval inspection will be conducted, or whether a PMA supplement should be submitted, manufacturers of Class III finished devices must comply with the QS regulation requirements applicable to its operations found in 21 C.F.R. § 820. By developing and implementing QS processes, manufacturing-related problems can be minimized when using a different facility or establishment to manufacture, process, or package a device.

FDA's guidance intends to consider a different site for which a site change supplement should be submitted to include (1) where the site was not approved as part of the original PMA or a PMA supplement; or (2) where the site(s) was approved as part of the original PMA or PMA

19. 83 Fed. Reg. 64582.
20. 21 C.F.R. §§ 180 *et seq.*

supplement, but only for the performance of different manufacturing activities. Under these circumstances, the different site would have no experience with either the process or the technology, or a similar process or technology, for manufacturing the same or a similar device, and FDA would not have had the opportunity to evaluate the change because it would not have been evaluated in any way in the PMA application. In such instances, we would consider the change to constitute "the use of a different facility or establishment"[21] and the manufacturer should submit a 180-day PMA supplement if the change affects the device's safety or effectiveness.[22] While FDA recognizes that a manufacturing site change would rarely involve a completely new manufacturing technology for which the firm has no experience or the manufacture of a dissimilar device at the new site, for completeness of defining the underlying principle for what constitutes a different site FDA believes it is important to consider both the site's familiarity with the manufacturing technology and the similarity to the devices manufactured at the site.

An applicant should submit a 180-day PMA supplement for using a different site, as described earlier, that affects the device's safety or effectiveness, which is also referred to as a site change supplement that FDA reviews within 180 days of receipt.[23] Similarly, HDE holders are required to submit a 75-day supplement.[24] The site change supplement should clearly identify any manufacturing location changes and any associated changes to the manufacturing resulting from the site change (e.g., new facility requires changes to the water filtration for manufacturing). Manufacturing process changes that are not directly associated with the facility move should be submitted separately (e.g., 30-Day Notice or PMA Annual Report per existing regulations and guidance) and are not considered part of the manufacturing site change supplement. Approval of the 180-Day PMA Supplement is needed before any manufacturing site change and related changes can be implemented.

Certain changes in manufacturing sites may be submitted as 30-day notices if they are among the sites already approved in the PMA, and if they are for performance of the same or similar manufacturing activities and for the same or similar device as those at the PMA approved site. If the previously approved site and its personnel use and have experience with similar technology and processes for manufacturing a similar

21. *Id.* § 814.39(a)(3).
22. *Id.* § 515(d)(5)(A)(i).
23. *See id.* §§ 814.39(a)(3), 814.39(c), 814.40.
24. *Id.* §§ 814.108, 814.114.

device, then the new manufacturing site would not be considered "different" under 21 C.F.R. § 814.39(a)(3). Such a change would be considered a "modification" to an existing manufacturing procedure or method of manufacturing, under 21 C.F.R. § 814.39(f), and the applicant would be eligible to submit a 30-day notice if the manufacturing site change affects the device's safety or effectiveness.

FDA does not consider the use of a new facility or establishment for the manufacture, processing, or packaging of a component of a finished device to require a PMA supplement. Firms that manufacture components that do not also manufacture finished devices are not subject to the QS regulation requirements, under 21 C.F.R. § 820.1(a), but these manufacturers are encouraged to use appropriate provisions of 21 C.F.R. § 820 as guidance. The finished device manufacturer ensures compliance with QS requirements through the application of purchasing controls[25] and acceptance criteria[26] for all components purchased or otherwise received. Thus, an applicant should submit a 30-day notice, under 21 C.F.R. § 814.39(f), for use of a new supplier of those components that are critical to the finished device's function, operation, or specifications, because such modifications to the manufacturing procedures or methods affect the finished device's safety or effectiveness. Manufacturing changes to components that are not critical to the device's function, operation, or specifications do not require firms to submit a site change supplement or a 30-day notice; however, these changes must be reported in the Annual Report.

7. Supplement: Special Changes Being Effected

21 C.F.R. §§ 814.39(d)(1) and (d)(2) provide that certain labeling and manufacturing changes that enhance the safety of the device or the safety in the use of the device may be submitted as a supplement marked "Special PMA Supplement—Changes Being Effected." The Special PMA Supplement is a narrow exception to the general rule that prior FDA approval of changes to a PMA, including the labeling for a device, is a condition of lawful distribution and, therefore, may only be utilized when (1) the applicant has newly acquired safety-related information; (2) the information in question was not previously submitted to the FDA; and (3) the information involves labeling changes that add or strengthen a contraindication, warning, precaution, or information about an adverse reaction for which there is reasonable evidence of a causal association.

25. *Id.* § 820.50.
26. *Id.* § 820.80.

Prior to approving a PMA, the FDA undertakes a detailed review of the proposed labeling, allowing only those safety-related warnings for which there is reasonable evidence of a causal association. Allowing the applicant to add a safety-related warning using a Special PMA Supplement based on information that was known to the FDA during the rigorous PMA review process would undermine that important process. For the same reason, the applicant may not add a safety-related warning to avoid potential liability under state tort law if there is not reasonable evidence of a causal association for the new warning. Instead, the applicant may utilize the limited Special PMA Supplement *only* when it possesses new information that provides a scientifically legitimate foundation for modifying the FDA-approved labeling. For these types of changes, the applicant may place the change in effect prior to receipt of a written FDA order approving the supplement, provided that the following exist:

- the PMA supplement and its mailing cover are plainly marked "Special PMA Supplement—Changes Being Effected";
- the PMA supplement provides a full explanation of the basis for the changes;
- the applicant has received acknowledgement from FDA of receipt of the supplement; and
- the PMA supplement specifically identifies the date that such changes are being effected.

Although the applicant may place a change into effect prior to the receipt of a written FDA order approving the change, any such change should be considered temporary while FDA reviews the supplement, including the basis for how the change enhances the safety of the device or the safety in the use of the device. Design changes are not considered appropriate for a Special PMA Supplement. For example, if the applicant attempted to change the design of an implantable cardiac device so that it can be more securely held in place inside the patient's chest cavity, such a change would be inappropriate for a Special PMA Supplement.

Although the regulation allows both labeling and manufacturing changes that enhance the safety of the device or the safety in the use of the device to be submitted as a Special PMA Supplement, FDA believes that labeling changes (as described in 21 C.F.R. § 814.39(d)(2)) are most appropriate for a Special PMA Supplement. However, changes to the quality control or manufacturing process may fall under the scope of this provision. The manufacturing changes that may be reviewed as a Special PMA Supplement are generally those that add a step to the quality control or manufacturing processes to enhance safety but not to impact effectiveness.

If the quality control or manufacturing process modification enhances safety *and* impacts effectiveness, then that change is not appropriate for a Special PMA Supplement and, instead, a 30-day notice is more appropriate. However, a PMA supplement (e.g., real-time supplement, 180-day supplement) may be more appropriate if the quality control or manufacturing process change impacts the device specifications and/or performance of the device.

III. Reporting

Each year, the FDA receives several hundred thousand medical device reports of suspected device-associated deaths, serious injuries, and malfunctions. Medical Device Reporting (MDR) is one of the postmarket surveillance tools the FDA uses to monitor device performance, detect potential device-related safety issues, and contribute to benefit-risk assessments of these products.

Mandatory reporters (that is, manufacturers, device user facilities, and importers) are required to submit certain types of reports for adverse events and product problems to the FDA about medical devices. In addition, the FDA also encourages health care professionals, patients, caregivers and consumers to submit voluntary reports about serious adverse events that may be associated with a medical device, as well as use errors, product quality issues, and therapeutic failures. These reports, along with data from other sources, can provide critical information that helps improve patient safety.

Devices subject to premarket approval under section 515 of the FD&C Act are subject to periodic reporting requirements set forth in the PMA approval order.[27]

A. Annual Reporting

Section 130(a) of Title I of the Food and Drug Administration Section 130(a) of Title I of the Food and Drug Administration Modernization Act of 1997 ("the Modernization Act") became law on November 21, 1997, and added section 506B (Reports of Postmarketing Studies) to the Federal Food, Drug, and Cosmetic Act ("the act") (21 U.S.C. § 356b). This provision requires applicants to report to FDA annually on the progress of postmarketing requirements/commitments and for FDA to make certain information available to the public.

---

27. *Id.* §§ 814.82(a), 814.84(b).

1. PMA Annual Report

FDA may require as a condition of approval submission to FDA at intervals specified in the approval order of periodic reports containing the information required by 21 CFR § 814.84(b).[28] In most cases, after the PMA is approved, the PMA applicant is required to submit reports to FDA annually unless a different time frame is specified in the approval order. Accordingly, periodic reports are typically referred to by FDA and the industry as "annual reports."

Annual reports contain a variety of information, including information about manufacturing changes, design changes, and labeling changes that were made during the preceding year for the PMA product. FDA guidance recommends that information be analyzed and presented in annual reports in a way that will be most useful to both the applicant and FDA. For example, FDA's guidance recommends that the applicant describe in detail the rationale for changes made to the device, including, for example, whether the changes were the result of device improvement/enhancement, product complaints, or adverse events. This explanation will give FDA a more complete picture of the postmarket safety profile of the device. FDA guidance also recommends that the applicant include a summary of all changes that were made to the device during the reporting period, including listing all supplements submitted during the reporting period and, if approved, their approval date. Having the information submitted in this way will help ensure that limited agency resources are devoted to assessing meaningful information rather than requiring FDA to sift through vast amounts of data that have not been systematically reviewed by the firm. Annual reports that contain clear descriptions and meaningful information are an important tool for the agency and the industry to assure postmarket safety and protect the public. When applicants prepare and provide to FDA in annual reports the type of analysis this guidance describes, industry and FDA are better positioned to recognize and address possible safety issues.

Unless FDA specifies otherwise, a periodic report must:

- Identify changes described in 21 C.F.R. § 814.39(a) and changes required to be reported to FDA under 21 C.F.R. § 814.39(b); and
- Contain a summary and bibliography of the following information not previously submitted as part of the PMA:
  - Unpublished reports of data from any clinical investigations or nonclinical laboratory studies involving the device or

28. *Id.* § 814.82(a)(7),

related devices and known to or that reasonably should be known to the applicant.

- Reports in the scientific literature concerning the device and known to or that reasonably should be known to the applicant.

For changes that do not require the submission of a traditional PMA or a PMA supplement, applicants should provide this information as part of the annual report.

The applicant is primarily responsible for determining whether changes to the device design, labeling, or manufacturing processes impact safety or effectiveness and, thus, require a PMA Supplement or 30-Day Notice. This guidance is not intended to define when a PMA applicant should submit a new original PMA or any type of PMA Supplement. For that type of guidance, please refer to the FDA guidance, "Modifications to Devices Subject to Premarket Approval (PMA)—The PMA Supplement Decision-Making Process."

PMA applicants are also subject to other reporting requirements. In accordance with 21 CFR § 814.84(a), the applicant must comply with Medical Device Reporting (MDR) requirements, 21 C.F.R. § 803, and any applicable requirements in other regulations or by order approving the device, including Post-Approval Study Reports if FDA has imposed continuing evaluation (post-approval study) requirements on the device in the PMA approval order.[29]

FDA's review of annual reports allows the agency to assess several important issues related to postmarket safety and effectiveness of approved devices. These issues include the nature and adequacy of reported modifications and the adequacy of report documentation. If, after reviewing the annual report, FDA needs additional information, or if it is believed the device modifications that the applicant has reported require a PMA Supplement or a 30-Day Notice, FDA will notify the applicant via letter or e-mail. FDA reviews most annual reports within 90 days of receipt.

B. Device Reporting

The MDR regulation[30] contains mandatory requirements for manufacturers, importers, and device user facilities to report certain device-related adverse events and product problems to the FDA.

---

29. *Id.* § 814.82(a)(2).
30. *Id.* § 803.

1. Reports of Corrections or Removals (806 Reporting)

Manufacturers and importers are required to make a report to FDA of any correction or removal of a medical device(s) if the correction or removal was initiated to reduce a risk to health posed by the device or to remedy a violation of the act caused by the device that may present a risk to health.[31] A report must be made even if the event was caused by use error. A report is not required if the information has already been provided to FDA under Medical Device Reporting,[32] or Repurchase, Repairs or Replacement of Electronic Products,[33] or if the corrective or removal action was initiated by an FDA order under Medical Device Recall Authority.[34]

Manufacturers and importers must keep records of corrections and removals that are not required to be reported to FDA. if a report is not required under 21 C.F.R. § 806, the firm may nevertheless voluntarily report under 21 C.F.R. § 7.

The definition of "risk to health" under 21 C.F.R. § 806 tracks the definitions of Class I and Class II recalls in 21 C.F.R. § 7.3(m). Therefore, reports of corrections and removals are required for Class I and Class II recalls. Under 21 C.F.R § 806, manufacturers and importers need not report events categorized as Class III recalls under 21 C.F.R. § 7; only recordkeeping requirements would apply.

The following actions are exempt from the reporting requirements:

- Actions taken by device manufacturers or importers to improve the performance or quality of a device but that do not reduce a risk to health posed by the device or remedy a violation of the act caused by the device,
- Market withdrawals,
- Routine servicing, and
- Stock recoveries.

Manufacturers and importers are required to report a correction or removal of a product if it involves a risk to health. Only the person that initiates the correction or removal is required to report. The report must be submitted to FDA within ten working days from the time the firm initiates the correction or removal. If there is not a "risk to health" involved, a report to FDA is not required, but the manufacturer or importer must keep a record of the correction or removal.

---

31. Under *id.* §§ 806 *et seq.*
32. 21 C.F.R. § 803.
33. *Id.* § 1004.
34. *Id.* § 810.

Per § 806.10, the report must include:

- Registration number, date the report is made, sequence number (001, 002, etc.), "C" for Correction or "R" for Removal.
- Name, address, phone number, and contact person of the firm responsible for conducting the correction or removal.
- Brand name and common name of the device and intended use.
- FDA marketing status, that is, 510(k), PMA, pre-amendment status and device listing number.
- Model/catalog number, lot/serial number
- Manufacturer's contact information (name, address, phone number, contact person) if different from item #2.
- Description of event(s) and the corrective and removal actions that have been and are expected to be taken.
- Any illness or injuries that have occurred with the use of the device. If applicable, include any MDR numbers submitted under 21 C.F.R. § 803.
- The number of devices subject to the Correction or Removal.
- Date of manufacture or distribution; expiration date or expected life.
- Name, address, and telephone number of all consignees (domestic and foreign) and the dates and number of devices distributed to each consignee.
- A copy of all communications regarding the correction or removal.
- A statement as to why any required information is not available and a date when it will be submitted.

There are two ways to report corrections and removals: FDA Electronic Submission Software (eSubmitter) or e-mail.

The FDA encourages submission of reports through eSubmitter. Once created, the report is sent to CDRH through the FDA Electronic Submission Gateway (ESG). The report can be submitted via e-mail to FDA's Office of Regulatory Affairs Division Recall Coordinator. Foreign manufacturers and importers must e-mail the report to the DRC where their US agent is located.

If, after submitting a report, a manufacturer or importer determines that the same correction or removal should be extended to additional lots or batches of the same device, the manufacturer or importer must amend the original report by submitting an amendment within ten working days of initiating the extension of the correction or removal.[35] The amendment

35. *Id.* § 806.10(d).

should cite the original report number assigned, all of the information required by 21 C.F.R. § 806.10(c)(2), and any information required by 21 C.F.R. § 806.10(c)(3) through (c)(12) that differs from the information submitted in the original report. The manufacturer or importer must also state what required information is not readily available and a date for when it will be submitted.

The device manufacturer or importer who initiates a correction or removal of a device that is not required to be reported to FDA must maintain records of the correction or removal for a period of two years beyond the expected life of the device, even if the manufacturer or importer has ceased to manufacture or import the device. If there is a change in ownership, records required to be maintained must be transferred to the new manufacturer or importer of the device and maintained for the required period.

Records must contain the following information:

- The brand name, common or usual name, classification, name and product code, if known, and the intended use of the device.
- The model, catalog, or code number of the device and the manufacturing lot or serial number of the device or other identification number.
- A description of the event(s) giving rise to the information reported and the corrective or removal action that has been and is expected to be taken.
- Justification for not reporting the correction or removal action to FDA, which shall contain conclusions and any follow-ups, and be reviewed and evaluated by a designated person.
- A copy of all communications regarding the correction or removal.
- The manufacturer or importer must retain all records for a period of two years beyond the expected life of the device, even if the manufacturer or importer has ceased to manufacture or import the device. Records required to be maintained must be transferred to the new manufacturer or importer of the device and maintained for the required period.

C. Recalls

A recall is a method of removing or correcting products that are in violation of laws administered by the FDA. Recall is normally a voluntary action that takes place because manufacturers and distributors carry out their responsibility to protect the public health and well-being from products that present a risk of injury or gross deception or are otherwise defective.

Defects or performance failures of marketed medical devices can pose serious risks to public health. The recall process serves both to correct device defects and to notify users of potential risks and steps to minimize the impact of device failure or malfunction. Medical device recalls include voluntary recalls[36] either initiated by a firm on its own initiative or in response to a formal request from FDA, and mandatory recalls ordered by FDA.[37]

Medical device recalls are usually conducted voluntarily by the manufacturer. In rare instances, where the manufacturer or importer fails to voluntarily recall a device that is a risk to health, FDA may issue a recall order to the manufacturer. In this context, risk to health means (1) a reasonable probability that use of, or exposure to, the product will cause serious adverse health consequences or death; or (2) that use of, or exposure to, the product may cause temporary or medically reversible adverse health consequences, or an outcome where the probability of serious adverse health consequences is remote. FDA defines a device recall by regulation as a firm's removal or correction of a marketed device that the agency considers to be in violation of the laws that it administers and against which the agency would initiate legal action, for example, seizure.[38] A recalling firm is responsible for promptly notifying each of its affected direct accounts about the recall. The format, content, and extent of a recall communication should be commensurate with the hazard of the product being recalled and the strategy developed for that recall. In general terms, the purpose of a recall communication is to convey:

Finally, recall will be terminated when FDA determines that all reasonable efforts have been made to remove or correct the product in accordance with the recall strategy, and when it is reasonable to assume that the product subject to the recall has been removed and proper disposition or correction has been made commensurate with the degree of hazard of the recalled product.

36. *See id.* § 7(C).
37. *Id.* § 810.
38. *Id.* § 7.3(g).

1. Recall versus Enhancement

The key factor in distinguishing a medical device recall from an enhancement is the existence of a violation of the FD&C Act[39] or associated regulations enforced by the agency.

Neither the FD&C Act nor FDA's regulations define device enhancement. However, FDA guidance describes device enhancement as (1) a change to improve the performance or quality of a device that is (2) not a change to remedy a violation of the FD&C Act or associated regulations enforced by the agency. Device enhancements include, but are not limited to, changes designed to better meet the needs of the user, changes to make the device easier to manufacture, changes to improve a non-violative device's safety or performance, and changes to the appearance of the device that do not affect its use.

Importantly, a device enhancement is not a medical device recall. Only changes to devices to remedy a violation of the laws administered by FDA and against which the agency would initiate legal action fall within the definition of a medical device recall. Changes to non-violative devices are considered device enhancements and not medical device recalls. FDA generally considers devices that fail to meet represented specifications or that fail to perform as represented to be of a quality below that which they purport or are represented to possess, rendering them adulterated under section 501(c) of the FD&C Act.[40] Changes intended to resolve a failure to meet specifications or failure of the device to perform as represented would generally constitute recalls. An increase in overall failure rate, increase in a single failure mode rate, or the identification of a new failure mode may suggest a failure of the device to perform as represented. A change to the marketed device to address a failure to perform as represented, including a failure to perform to represented specifications, would generally constitute a medical device recall.

A change to a marketed device to address false or misleading labeling or other labeling violations would generally constitute a medical device recall. However, the addition of a new warning or other changes to the labeling of a non-violative device would not meet the definition of a recall.

39. 21 U.S.C. § 360(h).
40. *Id.* § 351(c).

2. Recall versus Stock Recovery and Market Withdrawal

Again, recall means a firm's removal or correction of a marketed product that the FDA considers to be in violation of the laws it administers and against which the agency would initiate legal action, for example, seizure.

Market withdrawal, by contrast, is a the removal or correction of a distributed product that involves a minor violation that would not be subject to legal action by the FDA or that involves no violation, for example, normal stock rotation practices, routine equipment adjustments and repairs, and so on. A market withdrawal is not a recall.[41]

Finally, stock recovery is the correction or removal of a device that has not been marketed or that has not left the direct control of the manufacturer, that is, the device is located on the premises owned, or under the control of, the manufacturer, and no portion of the lot, model, code, or other relevant unit involved in the corrective or removal action has been released for sale or use. A stock recovery, which applies only to undistributed devices, is not a recall. Distributed devices require a recall when they manifest violations for which a stock recovery was initiated.[42]

Recall, then, does not include a market withdrawal or a stock recovery.

3. Mandatory

Medical device recalls are usually conducted voluntarily by the manufacturer under 21 C.F.R. § 7. In rare instances, where the manufacturer or importer fails to voluntarily recall a device that is a risk to health, FDA may issue a recall order to the manufacturer under 21 C.F.R. § 810, which describes the procedures FDA will follow in exercising its medical device recall authority.[43]

If, after providing the appropriate person with an opportunity to consult with the agency, FDA finds that there is a reasonable probability that a device intended for human use would cause serious, adverse health consequences or death, the FDA may issue a cease distribution and notification order requiring the person named in the order to immediately cease distribution of the device, notify health professionals and device user facilities of the order, and instruct these professionals and device user facilities to cease use of the device.

The person named in the order will have an opportunity for a regulatory hearing or to provide a written request to FDA asking that the order

41. 21 C.F.R. § 7.3(j).
42. *Id.* § 7.3(k).
43. 21 U.S.C. § 518(e).

be modified, vacated, or amended. FDA may later amend the order to require a recall of the device.

4. Classification and Health Hazard Evaluation

An evaluation of the health hazard presented by a product being recalled or considered for recall is conducted by FDA and accounts for a variety of different factors including but not limited to whether any disease or injuries have already occurred from the use of the product, assessment of the hazard to various segments of the population, for example, children, surgical patients, pets, livestock, and so on, who are expected to be exposed to the product being considered, with particular attention paid to the hazard to those individuals who may be at greatest risk, assessment of the likelihood of occurrence of the hazard, and assessment of the consequences (immediate or long range) of occurrence of the hazard, amongst many others.

Recalls are classified into a numerical designation (I, II, or III) by the FDA to indicate the relative degree of health hazard presented by the product being recalled. First, Class I recalls generally involve a situation in which there is a reasonable probability that the use of, or exposure to, a violative product will cause serious adverse health consequences or death. Class II recalls involve a situation in which use of, or exposure to, a violative product may cause temporary or medically reversible adverse health consequences or where the probability of serious adverse health consequences is remote. Finally, Class III recalls occur when use of, or exposure to, a violative product is not likely to cause adverse health consequences.

Firms should initiate a recall strategy that accounts for several factors as they apply to the individual circumstances of the recall. A recall strategy should include the following:

- Results of health hazard evaluation
- Ease in identifying the product
- Degree to which the product's deficiency is obvious to the consumer or user
- Degree to which the product remains unused in the marketplace
- Continued availability of essential products

The FDA will review the adequacy of a proposed recall strategy and recommend changes as appropriate. A recalling firm should conduct the recall in accordance with an approved recall strategy but need not delay initiation of a recall pending review of its recall strategy.

A recall strategy will address the depth of the recall, its public warning, and effectiveness checks. The depth of the recall depends on the product's degree of hazard and extent of distribution. As such, the recall strategy will specify the level in the distribution chain to which the recall is to extend. The purpose of a public warning is to alert the public that a product being recalled presents a serious hazard to health. This is reserved for urgent situations where other means for preventing use of the recalled product appear inadequate. The FDA in consultation with the recalling firm will ordinarily issue such publicity. When the recalling firm decides to issue its own public warning, it is requested to submit to FDA its proposed public warning and plan for distribution of the warning for review and comment. Finally, the purpose of effectiveness checks is to verify that all consignees (at the recall depth specified by the strategy) have received notification about the recall and have taken appropriate action. Consignees may be contacted by personal visits, telephone calls, letters, or a combination thereof. The recalling firm will ordinarily be responsible for conducting effectiveness checks, but FDA will assist in this task where necessary and appropriate.

A firm may choose to remove or correct a distributed product for any reason and under any circumstance. If a firm believes its product is violative, it is required to immediately notify the FDA. Such removal or correction will be considered a recall only if the FDA determines the product is violative. In such cases, the FDA will ask the firm to provide information such as the identity of the product involved; the reason for the removal or correction and the date and circumstances under which the product deficiency or possible deficiency was discovered; an evaluation of the risk associated with the deficiency or possible deficiency; the total amount of such products produced and/or the time span of the production; the total amount of such products estimated to be in distribution channels; distribution information, including the number of direct accounts and, where necessary, the identity of the direct accounts; a copy of the firm's recall communication if any has issued, or a proposed communication if none has issued; the proposed strategy for conducting the recall; and the name and telephone number of the firm official who should be contacted concerning the recall.

The FDA will review the information submitted, advise the firm of the assigned recall classification, recommend any appropriate changes in the firm's strategy for the recall, and advise the firm that its recall will be placed in the weekly FDA Enforcement Report. Pending this review, the firm need not delay initiation of its product removal or correction.

A recall communication can be accomplished by telegrams, mailgrams, or first-class letters conspicuously marked, preferably in bold red type, on the letter and the envelope: "medical device recall [or correction]."

The letter and the envelope should be also marked "urgent" for Class I and Class II recalls and, when appropriate, for Class III recalls. Telephone calls or other personal contacts should ordinarily be confirmed by one of the aforementioned methods and/or documented in an appropriate manner.

The recalling firm is requested to submit periodic recall status reports so that the agency may assess the progress of the recall. The frequency of such reports will be determined by the relative urgency of the recall and will be specified by the FDA in each recall case. Recall status reports are to be discontinued when the recall is terminated by FDA.

A recall will be terminated when FDA determines that all reasonable efforts have been made to remove or correct the product in accordance with the recall strategy, and when it is reasonable to assume that the product subject to the recall has been removed and proper disposition or correction has been made commensurate with the degree of hazard of the recalled product. A recalling firm may request termination of its recall by submitting a written request stating that the recall is effective in accordance with the criteria set forth, and by accompanying the request with the most current recall status report and a description of the disposition of the recalled product.

5. Recall Database and Enforcement Report

FDA publishes a weekly FDA Enforcement Report that contains all enforcement actions including recalls, field corrections, seizures, and injunctions. All recalls monitored by FDA are included in the Enforcement Report once they are classified and may be listed prior to classification when FDA determines the firm's removal or correction of a marketed product(s) meets the definition of a recall. Once FDA completes the hazard assessment, the Enforcement Report entry will be updated with the recall classification.

Recall data in the Enforcement Report can be accessed through the weekly report publication, the quick and advanced search functionalities, and an Application Programming Interface (API).

D. Medical Device Reports (803 Reporting)

The MDR regulation[44] contains mandatory requirements for manufacturers, importers, and device user facilities to report certain device-related adverse events and product problems to the FDA. The regulation specifies that reports be filed on the FDA's Medwatch Form 3500A or an

44. 21 C.F.R. § 803.

electronic equivalent. The FDA published a final rule on February 14, 2014, requiring manufacturers and importers to submit MDRs to the FDA in an electronic format that the FDA can process, review, and archive. This rule is effective as of August 14, 2015.

1. Manufacturer

Manufacturers are required to report to the FDA when they learn that any of their devices may have caused or contributed to a death or serious injury. Manufacturers must also report to the FDA when they become aware that their device has malfunctioned and would be likely to cause or contribute to a death or serious injury if the malfunction were to recur.

A "manufacturer" is any person who manufactures, prepares, propagates, compounds, assembles, or processes a device by chemical, physical, biological, or other procedure.[45] The term includes any person who repackages or otherwise changes the container, wrapper, or labeling of a device in furtherance of the distribution of the device from the original place of manufacture, initiates specifications for devices manufactured by a second party for subsequent distribution by the person initiating the specifications, or manufactures components or accessories that are medical devices and that are (1) ready to be used and are intended to be commercially distributed and intended to be used as is, or (2) processed by a licensed practitioner or other qualified person to meet the needs of a particular patient.

All manufacturers of legally marketed medical devices in the United States, including foreign manufacturers who export devices to the United States, are subject to the MDR regulation and must submit required reports. U.S. manufacturers of medical devices that are not cleared or approved in the United States, but are exported to foreign locations, are also subject to the MDR regulation. Failure to submit required reports is a prohibited act.[46] Any person who reprocesses a single use device for reuse in human beings becomes the manufacturer of the device and is subject to all the requirements applicable to the original manufacturer, including the requirements of the MDR regulation.[47]

Manufacturers are considered to have "become aware" of an event whenever any employees become aware of information that reasonably

45. *Id.* § 803.3.

46. 21 U.S.C. § 331(q) (however, see section 4.11.1 of this guidance for the circumstances under which FDA generally does not intend to enforce MDR reporting requirements for those devices exported under sections 801(e) or 802 of the FD&C Act).

47. 69 Fed. Reg. 7490.

suggests that an event is required to be reported in a 30-day report or in a five-day report. Additionally, a manufacturer is considered to have "become aware" or when any of its employees with management or supervisory responsibilities over persons with regulatory, scientific, or technical responsibilities (including consultants or contractors) or whose duties relate to the collection and reporting of adverse events, become aware that an MDR reportable event(s) necessitates remedial action to prevent an unreasonable risk of substantial harm to the public health. In this case, a report must be submitted no later than five business days after the day the manufacturer becomes aware.[48]

The report must contain all the information required by 21 C.F.R. § 803.52 that is known, or reasonably known. Information considered reasonably known includes any information that can be obtained by contacting a user facility, importer, or other initial reporter that is in the firm's possession; or that can be obtained by analysis, testing or other evaluation of the device.[49]

2. User Facility

A "device user facility" is a hospital, ambulatory surgical facility, nursing home, outpatient diagnostic facility, or outpatient treatment facility that is not a physician's office. User facilities must report a suspected medical device-related death to both the FDA and the manufacturer. User facilities must report a medical device-related serious injury to the manufacturer, or to the FDA if the medical device manufacturer is unknown.

A user facility is not required to report a device malfunction but can voluntarily advise the FDA of such product problems using the voluntary MedWatch Form FDA 3500 under the FDA's Safety Information and Adverse Event Reporting Program. Health care professionals within a user facility should familiarize themselves with their institution's procedures for reporting adverse events to the FDA.

3. Importer

Importers are required to report to the FDA and the manufacturer when they learn that one of their devices may have caused or contributed to a death or serious injury. The importer must report only to the manufacturer if their imported devices have malfunctioned and would be likely to cause or contribute to a death or serious injury if the malfunction were to recur.

48. 21 C.F.R. § 803.3.
49. *Id.* § 803.50(b).

4. Voluntary

The Voluntary Malfunction Summary Reporting (VMSR) program was established in 2018 and permits manufacturers to report certain device malfunction MDRs in summary form on a quarterly basis In the Federal Register of December 26, 2017,[50] the FDA issued a notification outlining the FDA's proposal to grant an alternative under 21 C.F.R. § 803.19 to permit reporting by a manufacturer of certain device malfunctions in summary form on a quarterly basis, subject to certain conditions, and requested comments from the public. On August 17, 2018,[51] the FDA issued a notification granting this alternative and describing the overarching principles for the VMSR program. Key among these principles is transparency of information to the FDA and to the public, regardless of whether the information is reported as an individual MDR or VMSR. Under the VMSR program, manufacturers submit separate summary reports for each unique combination of brand name, device model, and problem code(s). Each summary report identifies the total number of reportable malfunctions and are available to the public. Importantly, mandatory submission of individuals reports of death or serious injury events, continue to be required, under sections 803.50 and 803.52, or 803.53, as applicable.

IV. Postmarket Studies

FDA may order postmarket surveillance studies to be conducted as a condition of PMA approval. FDA can order postmarket surveillance at the time of approval or at any time thereafter for any approved device if the failure of the device would be reasonably likely to have serious adverse health consequences; or the device is intended to be implanted in the human body for more than one year; or the device is expected to have significant use in pediatric populations; or the device is intended to be a life sustaining or life supporting device used outside a device user facility.

Manufacturers must submit a plan for approval within 30 days of receiving an order to conduct a postmarket surveillance study from FDA. After receiving the manufacturer's proposed plan, FDA has 60 days to determine if the person designated to conduct the surveillance is qualified and experienced, and if the plan will collect useful data that can

50. 82 Fed. Reg. 60922.
51. 83 Fed. Reg. 40973.

reveal unforeseen adverse events or other information necessary to protect the public health.

A. Post-Approval Studies

Post-approval studies (PAS) are conditions of device approval. A sponsor's failure to comply with any post-approval requirement may be grounds for withdrawing approval. The FDA may require a post-approval study (or studies) at the time of approval of a PMA, HDE, or product development protocol (PDP) application to help assure continued safety and effectiveness (or continued probable benefit, in the case of an HDE) of the approved device.

Prior to PMA approval, post-approval study protocols and subsequent changes to the approved protocols are submitted and reviewed as amendments to the PMA. However, after PMA approval, post-approval study protocols and subsequent changes are submitted and reviewed as post-approval study supplements to the PMA.

Ideally, the final protocol for a post-approval study and the schedule for study completion are based on agreements reached between FDA and the sponsor during the PMA review process prior to approval of the PMA. Accordingly, FDA recommends submission of a proposed post-approval study protocol or, at minimum, post-approval study plans, in the original PMA submission. FDA also recommends that interactive development of a post-approval study occur concurrently with the review of the premarket data, with the goal of having final agreed-upon protocols by the time of PMA approval.

However, if a final protocol is not agreed upon prior to the PMA approval, the PMA approval order will state that you must submit the post-approval study protocol as a PMA supplement within 30 days of the PMA approval date. The PMA supplement should be clearly labeled as a Post-Approval Study Protocol. If there are multiple protocols being finalized after PMA approval, we recommend each protocol be submitted as a separate PMA supplement. FDA intends to complete the review of a PMA supplement and respond within 60 calendar days.

B. 522 Studies

The 522 Postmarket Surveillance Studies Program encompasses design, tracking, oversight, and review responsibilities for studies mandated under section 522 of the Federal Food, Drug and Cosmetic Act. The program helps ensure that well-designed 522 postmarket surveillance studies are conducted effectively and efficiently and in the least burdensome manner. Postmarket surveillance is not a substitute for obtaining the necessary premarket information to support 510(k) clearance, PMA, HDE, or PDP approval, or grant of de novo order.

C. Use of Real-World Data

Real-world data (RWD) is the data relating to patient health status and/or the delivery of health care routinely collected from a variety of sources. Real-world evidence (RWE) is the clinical evidence regarding the usage and potential benefits or risks of a medical product derived from analysis of RWD. RWE can be generated by different study designs or analyses, including but not limited to, randomized trials, including large simple trials, pragmatic trials, and observational studies (prospective and/or retrospective).

RWD and RWE are playing an increasing role in health care decisions. FDA uses RWD and RWE to monitor postmarket safety and adverse events and to make regulatory decisions. The health care community is using this data to support coverage decisions and to develop guidelines and decision support tools for use in clinical practice. Medical product developers are using RWD and RWE to support clinical trial designs (e.g., large simple trials, pragmatic clinical trials) and observational studies to generate innovative, new treatment approaches.

The use of computers, mobile devices, wearables, and other biosensors to gather and store huge amounts of health-related data has been rapidly accelerating. This data holds potential to allow for better design and conduct clinical trials and studies in the health care setting to answer questions previously though infeasible. In addition, with the development of sophisticated, new analytical capabilities.

Under the right conditions, RWE may be suitable to support the clearance or approval of a new device, or the expansion of the indications for use of devices that are already on the market. RWE may also be used to supplement the total evidence required for such clearances or approvals. Other applications of RWE in premarket decision making may also be possible, particularly as RWD systems and analysis methodology advance.

Additionally, aggregation of RWD (e.g., in medical device registries) may prove useful as a postmarket control suitable for providing ongoing device safety surveillance and additional evidence for effectiveness. FDA has long applied postmarket controls to reduce premarket data collection, while still ensuring that the statutory standard of reasonable assurance of safety and effectiveness is met. FDA believes that applying postmarket controls to reduce premarket data collection, when appropriate, can help improve patient access to safe and effective medical devices.

The primary factors FDA considers for assessing the reliability of RWD include how the data were collected (data accrual), and whether the people and processes in place during data collection and analysis provide adequate assurance that errors are minimized and that data quality and integrity are sufficient (data assurance).

V. Tracked Devices

Manufacturers are required to track certain devices from their manufacture through the distribution chain when they receive an order from the FDA to implement a tracking system for a certain type of device. The purpose of device tracking is to ensure that manufacturers of certain devices establish tracking systems that will enable them to promptly locate devices in commercial distribution. The tracking provision is intended to ensure that manufacturers can expeditiously remove potentially dangerous or defective devices from the market and/or notify patients of significant device problems. Tracking information may be used to facilitate notifications and recalls ordered by FDA in the case of serious risks to health presented by the devices.

Manufacturers must adopt a method of tracking devices whose failure would be reasonably likely to have serious, adverse health consequences; or which is intended to be implanted in the human body for more than one year; or are life-sustaining or life-supporting devices used outside of a device user facility.[52]

FDA may add or remove devices from the list of tracked devices and may consider the additional guidance factors in conjunction with the review of premarket applications, recall data, medical device reporting, inspections, petitions, postmarket surveillance, or other information coming to its attention. When FDA determines that a device should no longer be tracked, it will notify the manufacturer by direct communication.

Manufacturers of a tracked device must establish a written standard operating procedure (SOP) which includes a method for tracking the device throughout distribution and a quality assurance program including audit procedures. Final distributors of these devices will be required to provide manufacturers with patient information. If a registry collects information required by 21 C.F.R. § 821, a registry can manage a device firm's tracking program. Manufacturers, however, remain responsible for making sure that the program complies with the tracking requirements. FDA understands that manufacturers will have different tracking

52. 21 C.F.R. § 821.

methods and procedures. However, manufacturers must have written standard operating procedures that define a method of tracking that will produce the information required by regulation. Manufacturers must make sure that the tracking program works. Manufacturers must perform audits at six-month intervals for the first three years after receiving tracking orders, and then annually after three years. Audits should verify that the tracking method works, and that the information collected is accurate so that, in the event of a recall, the right persons are notified in a timely fashion.

VI. Unique Device Identification

The FDA established the unique device identification system ("UDI system") to adequately identify medical devices sold in the United States from manufacturing through distribution to patient use.[53] When fully implemented, the label of most devices will include a unique device identifier (UDI) in human- and machine-readable form, which will ultimately improve patient safety, modernize device postmarket surveillance, and facilitate medical device innovation. All devices, as defined by 21 U.S.C. § 321(h), are subject to the requirements of the UDI Rule, unless an exception or alternative has been granted.

The UDI system seeks to improve the identification of medical devices by making it possible to rapidly and definitively identify a device and certain key attributes that affect its safe and effective use. The FDA intends this to facilitate more accurate reporting of adverse events by making it easier to pinpoint the device at issue in the submitted report. FDA, health care providers, and those in the industry may then more rapidly and precisely extract useful information from adverse event reports and thereby gain a better understanding of the underlying problems and improve the ability to take appropriate and better-focused corrective action.

The labeler must submit product information concerning devices to FDA's Global Unique Device Identification Database (GUDID), unless subject to an exception or alternative. The system established by the UDI rule requires the label and device package of each medical device to include a UDI and requires that each UDI be provided in a plain-text version and in a form that uses automatic identification and data capture (AIDC) technology. The UDI will be required to be directly marked on the device itself if the device is intended to be used more than once and

53. 78 Fed. Reg. 58785.

intended to be reprocessed before each use. The UDI will function as the key that can be used to obtain critical information from the GUDID about the medical product. The GUDID will include only information that is important to the identification of devices and will not include any information that would identify a patient.

A UDI on a device label or package is composed of two parts: a Device Identifier (DI)—a mandatory, fixed portion of a UDI that identifies (1) the labeler and (2) the specific version or model of a device—and a Production Identifier(s) (PI)—a conditional, variable portion of a UDI. If any of the following is included in the label of a device, it must also be included in the PI.

The FDA's implemented the rule to serve several important public health objectives including the reduction of medical errors, the simplification of integration of device use information into data systems, more rapid identification of medical devices with adverse events, more rapid development of solutions to reported problems, more rapid and efficient resolution of device recalls, and better focused and more effective FDA safety communications, amongst other benefits.

A. Exceptions

Under 21 C.F.R. § 801.30, the UDI rule provides general exceptions from UDI labeling requirements to certain categories of devices. A device within one or more of these exceptions is not required to bear a UDI. A labeler of a device identified in § 801.30 is not required to request an exception from the FDA.

There are four UDI direct marking exceptions outlined in 21 C.F.R. § 801.45(d). The requirement of 21 C.F.R. § 801.45(a) does not apply to any device that meets any of the following criteria:

1. Any type of direct marking would interfere with the safety or effectiveness of the device;
2. The device cannot be directly marked because it is not technologically feasible;
3. The device is a single-use device and is subjected to additional processing and manufacturing for the purpose of an additional single use; or
4. The device has been previously marked under 21 C.F.R. § 801.45(a).

A "single-use device" means a device that is intended for one use, or on a single patient during a single procedure (section 201(ll) of the FD&C Act (21 U.S.C. 321(ll)). FDA interprets 21 C.F.R. 801.45(d)(3) to mean that the UDI direct marking requirements do not apply to a device that the original labeler (as defined in 21 C.F.R. § 801.3) intends for one use, or use on a single patient during a single procedure, even if, subsequent to its initial use, the device is subjected to additional processing and manufacturing for the purpose of an additional single use on another patient.

The UDI regulation at 21 C.F.R. § 801.55 outlines the process for requesting a specific alternative to any UDI requirement, including direct marking, by submitting a request to FDA. Under 21 C.F.R. § 801.55(c), FDA may grant an alternative to UDI direct marking or any other UDI labeling requirement, if we determine that (1) an alternative would provide for more accurate, precise, or rapid device identification; or (2) an alternative would better ensure the safety or effectiveness of the device.

VII. Regulatory Actions to Revise Applicable Requirements

A. Application of New Special Controls

Special controls are regulatory requirements for Class II devices. FDA classifies into Class II devices for which general controls alone are insufficient to provide reasonable assurance of the safety and effectiveness of the device, and for which there is enough information to establish special controls to provide such assurance. By contrast, general controls apply to all medical devices, unless exempted by regulations. If a device is exempted from one of the general controls, such exemption is stated in the classification regulation for that device.

Special controls are usually device-specific and include performance standards, postmarket surveillance, patient registries, special labeling requirements, premarket data requirements, and guidelines. Devices classified into Class II are devices for which special controls, combined with general controls, are necessary to provide reasonable assurance of safety and effectiveness. The FDA maintains a list of documents related to the application of special controls to Class II devices on its website. While these documents describe a means by which a device may comply with the requirement of special controls, the risks to health identified in these documents must be addressed. Thus, a manufacturer who intends to market a device within a generic type of device covered by these documents must:

- conform to the general controls in section 513(a)(1)(A) of the FD&C Act;
- address the specific risks (section 513(a)(1)(B) of the FD&C Act) to health identified, either by meeting the recommendations

in the guidance/guidelines or by some other means that provides equivalent assurances of safety and effectiveness; and

- for devices not exempt from premarket notification, obtain a substantial equivalence determination (sections 510(k) and 513(i) of the FD&C Act, and 21 C.F.R. § 807.100) from FDA prior to marketing the device.

B. Reclassification

The FDA generally classifies medical devices based on the risks associated with the device and by evaluating the amount of regulation that provides a reasonable assurance of the device's safety and effectiveness. As described earlier, devices are classified into one of three regulatory classes: Class I, Class II, or Class III. The regulatory class of a device type,[54] and its implementing regulation,[55] may be changed through the process of reclassification. The main purpose of reclassification is to apply the appropriate level of regulatory controls for a device type based on the most current information regarding its safety and effectiveness. Reclassification is applied to a device type and not an individual device.

To change the classification of the device, it is necessary that the proposed new class have sufficient regulatory controls to provide reasonable assurance of the safety and effectiveness of the device for its intended use. If the FDA receives a petition requesting a reclassification, it may ask a device classification panel to review the information and make a recommendation on the petition. After all information is considered, the FDA will issue an order approving or denying the petition. If the FDA approves the petition, the order will describe the reasons for reclassification and identify the risks to health (if any) presented by the device type.

Under section 513(e) of the FD&C Act, FDA may initiate, or respond to, an interested person's petition for reclassification of a device type that is already classified. Whether the reclassification is based on FDA's own initiative or in response to a petition from an interested person, the basis for reclassification is the availability of new information regarding the device. To reclassify a device under section 513(e) of the FD&C Act, the FDA must do the following before making the reclassification final:

---

54. As defined in section 513(a) of the Federal Food, Drug and Cosmetic Act (FD&C Act) (21 U.S.C. § 360c(a)).

55. 21 C.F.R. § 860.3.

- Publish a proposed order in the Federal Register which includes the proposed reclassification and a summary of the valid scientific evidence that supports the reclassification,
- Convene a device classification panel meeting, and
- Consider comments from the relevant public docket.

If the FDA proposes to reclassify the device from Class II to Class III, the available scientific evidence must show that general controls and special controls together are not sufficient to provide a reasonable assurance of safety and effectiveness of the device. If, on the other hand, the FDA proposes to reclassify the device from Class III to Class II, the available scientific evidence must show that general controls and special controls are sufficient to provide a reasonable assurance of safety and effectiveness of the device. Finally, if the FDA proposes to reclassify a device from either Class III or Class II to Class I, the available scientific evidence must show that general controls would provide a reasonable assurance of safety and effectiveness of the device.

Devices that were not available on the market before the enactment of the Medical Device Amendments to the FD&C Act, on May 28, 1976 (generally referred to as postamendments devices), are automatically classified into Class III under section 513(f)(1), without any FDA rulemaking process and regardless of the risks they pose.

FDAMA added the de novo classification option as an alternate pathway to classify novel medical devices that had automatically been placed in Class III after receiving a "not substantially equivalent" (NSE) determination in response to a premarket notification (510(k)) submission. Section 513(f)(2) of the FD&C Act was amended by section 607 of FDASIA, on July 9, 2012, to allow a sponsor to submit a de novo classification request to the FDA without first being required to submit a 510(k).

CHAPTER 7

Compliance and Enforcement

Paul Gadiock and Jamie Ravitz

Compliance refers to conformity with regulatory requirements, which are discussed in earlier chapters. General controls are basic provisions that apply to all medical devices, unless otherwise exempt. The May 28, 1976, Medical Device Amendments ("Amendments") to the Federal Food, Drug and Cosmetic Act (FD&C Act), 21 U.S.C. §§ 301 et seq., provide the authorities for ensuring the safety and effectiveness of medical devices, including enforcement powers, provisions on misbranding, adulteration, establishment registration and medical device listing, premarket notification, and Quality System Regulation (QSR), among others.

Due to limited FDA resources, FDA relies substantially on voluntary compliance of the FD&C Act and the QSR by companies. That said, FDA can conduct routine or scheduled inspections, for example, prior to PMA approval, or unannounced inspections to evaluate a company's regulatory compliance. FDA also issues various compliance policy guides and compliance program guidance manuals that inform companies how the FDA interprets and implements the laws and regulations. Although these guidance documents are not legally binding, they have a significant effect on enforcement decisions and the conduct of companies.

Enforcement, on the other hand, refers to administrative and judicial tools that the FDA can use to compel companies into compliance in response to a finding of noncompliance or when a company's conduct poses a significant risk to public health or safety. In general, FDA takes a risk-based approach when deciding to pursue enforcement actions, including the seriousness of the violation, number of people impacted, degree to which people are impacted, strength of the evidence relating to the violation, likelihood of success of the remedy sought, and the availability of resources to resolve the problem. FDA is not legally required to enforce the law against all violators and has discretion to not take enforcement action in certain situations. FDA provides prior notice of violation to companies and representatives before taking enforcement actions, although it is not legally required to give prior notice.

Through both compliance and enforcement measures, the FDA ensures that the medical devices distributed or marketed in the United States are safe and effective.

The FDA has significant discretion in which violations of the FD&C Act will be pursued as well as the type of enforcement action taken. FDA also has discretion to take informal administrative actions, including meeting with company representatives to encourage voluntary compliance or refer certain problems to state and local authorities to take enforcement actions under state laws. Formal administrative enforcement tools include inspections, Form 483s, Warning Letters, product recalls, delay, suspension or withdrawal of product clearances or approvals, exclusion from government contracts, or detention of imported products. Three main judicial enforcement tools include civil seizures, civil injunctions, and criminal prosecutions, as well as court order for assessing civil monetary penalties. FDA also works with the Department of Justice (DOJ) to bring enforcement litigation against companies or executive for violations under the FD&C Act, which helps to deter noncompliance, punish violative conduct by companies, and reinforce FDA's credibility and authority in the industry.

Based on available evidence and benefit-risk profiles of devices, the FDA also issues enforcement discretion policy guides, such as the 2019 guidance on General Wellness products and the 2014 draft guidance on regulatory oversight of laboratory developed testes (LDTs), that set forth specific criteria for certain products that are considered low risk and for which the FDA will not review as medical devices within the definition of the FD&C Act or for which the FDA does not intend to enforce the requirements under the FD&C Act. During the COVID-19 public health emergency, FDA has used its enforcement discretion to relax various QSR requirements to help facilitate the development and increase the accessibility of COVID-19 related countermeasures through the emergency use authorization pathway.

In 2019, the FDA's Center for Devices and Radiological Health's (CDRH) reorganized its infrastructure in order to better meet the needs of the medical device industry, including reorganizing its premarket and postmarket programs along product lines and taking a more team-based approach to facilitate FDA's decision-making process across the entire life cycle of products. This reorganization provides a more holistic approach that consolidates and integrates premarket and postmarket functions and expertise, spanning from product review to quality, surveillance, and enforcement. Companies should take a similar holistic approach to ensure regulatory compliance across premarket and postmarket operations.

Similarly, to improve FDA's response to public health needs and to changes in scientific innovation, FDA's Office of Regulatory Affairs (ORA) has also shifted from a geographic-based management structure to a program-based structure along product lines regulated by the FDA. This alignment between the ORA and the CDRH allows agency experts to better leverage their product-specific expertise across different functions.

I. Misbranding

21 U.S.C. § 331 prohibits, in part, introducing into interstate commerce any medical device that is misbranded. At a high level, a device's labeling misbrands the product if its labeling is false or misleading. Section 502 of the FD&C Act sets forth a number of conditions that would deem a device to be misbranded, including:[1]

- False or misleading labeling or advertising, including failure to reveal material facts regarding consequences resulting from the use of the device under the conditions of use prescribed in the labeling or advertising thereof or under such conditions of use as are customary or usual;
- Not prominently displaying or clearly stating any required wording;
- Lack of adequate directions for use, including warnings and precautions where the use of the device may be dangerous or pose risks to users;
- Failure to meet the device labeling requirements;
- Failure to comply with the establishment registration and product listing requirements;
- Failure to obtain the applicable premarket notification or marketing authorization for the device;

1. FDA, *Labeling Requirements—Misbranding*, https://www.fda.gov/medical-devices/general-device-labeling-requirements/labeling-requirements-misbranding.

- Lack of labeling regarding compliance with the performance standard applicable to the device;
- Failure or refusal to comply with any notification requirements or other remedies prescribed under Section 518 of the FD&C Act, failure to furnish any materials or information pursuant to Section 519 of the FD&C Act, or failure to furnish materials or information relating to reports and records as required by Section 522 of the FD&C Act; or
- Any representation that creates an impression of official approval.

II. Adulteration

A device is held to be adulterated if it includes any filthy, putrid, or decomposed substance, or if it is prepared, packed, or held under unsanitary conditions. The adulteration provisions are set forth under section 501 of the FD&C Act, including:[2]

- Containing any filthy, putrid, or decomposed substance, or being prepared, packed, or held under insanitary conditions whereby the device may be contaminated with filth, or whereby it may have been rendered injurious to health;
- Lack of compliance with performance standard under Section 514;
- Failure of a Class III medical device to conform to the requirements for an approved premarket approval application or a notice of completion of a product development protocol;
- Is a banned device;
- Failure to comply with the good manufacturing practice requirements or the Quality System Regulation at 21 CFR 820; or
- Failure to comply with an Investigational Device Exemption (IDE).

III. FDA Inspections

The FDA conducts periodic inspections of regulated facilities to determine a firm's compliance with the FD&C Act and implementing regulations, including the Quality System Regulation. An inspection typically involves an investigator visiting a firm's location. In general, FDA uses

2. FDA, *General Controls for Medical Devices*, https://www.fda.gov/medical-devices/regulatory-controls/general-controls-medical-devices#adulteration.

a risk-based approach for inspecting device establishments, prioritizing inspections of firms with high-risk devices, such as implantable devices or life sustaining devices, over low-risk devices. Firms with recently marketed devices are also given higher priority as well as firms with prior violations and complaints.[3]

There are four types of inspections—pre-approval inspections, routine inspections, compliance follow-up inspections, and "for cause" inspections:

Pre-Approval Inspections – conducted after a firm submits an application to FDA to market a new device; these inspections focus on verifying data included in the application and confirming that the facility is capable of manufacturing the device; the inspector will determine if FDA approval is recommend based on the outcome of the pre-approval inspection. Findings of noncompliance during pre-approval inspection, depending on the seriousness of the violation, may delay PMA approval or result in a denial of PMA approval.

For Class III medical devices, FDA conducts a Bioresearch Monitoring (BIMO) audit before PMA approval, which is an audit of clinical study data. In some cases, FDA has issued Warning Letters to investigators for conducting clinical studies under objectionable conditions or in a manner that violates the FD&C Act, such as failure to ensure proper monitoring and institutional review board (IRB) review and approval of the clinical study, failure to submit complete and accurate progress reports to FDA, or failure to maintain accurate, complete, and current records of shipment, receipt, use or disposition of the investigational device. FDA also conducts a manufacturing inspection for all original PMAs and may conduct inspections of PMA supplements regarding approval of alternative or additional manufacturing or sterilization facilities, during which FDA will assess the facility's compliance with the QSR requirements.

A finding of noncompliance during a pre-approval inspection may result in a "not approvable" letter or a denial of approval. If an applicant receives a "not approvable" letter, the applicant may amend the PMA as requested by FDA, request administrative

3. FDA, *General Wellness: Policy for Low Risk Devices*, https://www.fda.gov/regulatory-information/search-fda-guidance-documents/general-wellness-policy-low-risk-devices.

review by filing a petition for reconsideration, or withdraw the PMA.

FDA may deny approval of a PMA for any of the following reasons:

- False statement of material fact in the PMA;
- Failure of the proposed labeling to comply with the labeling requirements in 21 CFR Parts 801 or 809;
- Not permitting an authorized FDA employee to inspect the facilities and controls in which the device will be manufactured or to have access to and to copy and verify all records pertinent to the PMA;
- Failure of an essential nonclinical laboratory study described in the PMA to comply with the good laboratory practice (GLP) regulations, or where noncompliance does not support the validity of the study; or
- Failure to comply with IRB regulations or informed consent regulations, or lack of compliance with regulations that protect human subject rights or safety.

When issuing an order denying PMA approval, the order will describe the deficiencies identified in the PMA and notice of an opportunity to request review under Section 515(d)(3) of the FD&C Act. An order denying approval is published in the *Federal Register* on a quarterly basis. When a notice of PMA denial is made publicly available, a detailed summary of the information submitted to FDA with respect to the safety and effectiveness of the device and the basis for the order will also become publicly available.

Routine Inspections – mandated inspections every 2 years for class II and class III device manufacturers, which follow the Quality System Inspection Technique (QSIT); a serious public health risk identified during a routine inspection can become a "for cause" inspection.

Compliance Follow-Up Inspections –reviews actions taken by a firm/manufacturer in response to a previous inspection that resulted in significant 483 observations or a Warning Letter; conducted to verify the adequacy of corrective action taken to address previous violations, to document continuing violations, or to support future regulatory action.

"For Cause" Inspections – used to investigate a specific problem reported to FDA; will focus on the reported issue but can also cover unrelated elements of the firm's operations; inspections typically are more in-depth than routine inspections and may not follow a QSIT approach.

A majority of the inspections conducted by FDA each year are routine inspections, which prioritize establishments based on the following risk factors.

- Class III > II > I
- Premarket and postmarket (PMA)
- Initial inspections of Class III
- Compliance follow-up
- For cause inspections
- Consumer complaint
- Manufacturers of higher-risk devices

For domestic inspections, the pre-announcement is typically provided for pre-approval and routine inspections no less than five calendar days in advance of an inspection.[4] The pre-announcement for foreign inspections is generally more than five calendar days. For both domestic and foreign inspections, the notification includes information about the type and nature of the inspection. FDA retains the authority to conduct unannounced for-cause inspections under section 704(h)(1) of the FD&C Act.

Quality System Inspection Technique (QSIT) is a validated method for FDA investigators to conduct medical device inspections, which uses a "top down" approach to investigate procedures, ask questions, and review records. There are two types of QSIT inspections: Level I Abbreviated and Level 2 Baseline.[5] A Level 2 Baseline QSIT inspection is a comprehensive inspection covering all four major subsystems of the Quality System, which are management controls, corrective and preventive actions (CAPA), design controls, and production and process controls. A Level 2 Baseline QSIT inspection is conducted when a firm has never had a Level 2 inspection, and then every six years. A Level 1 Abbreviated QSIT inspection is conducted after a firm has had a Level 2 inspection, and the Quality System was found to be in compliance with all requirements. Level 1 inspections always include the CAPA subsystem and one other

4. FDA, *FDA Medical Device Inspections*, https://www.fda.gov/media/94076/download.

5. FDA, *Guide to Inspections of Quality Systems*, https://www.fda.gov/media/76038/download.

major subsystem. A different subsystem is chosen for each subsequent Level 1 inspection.

For compliance following-up inspections, or Level 3 inspections, FDA will verify whether adequate remediation has been implemented to address deficiencies identified in a Form 483 and, if not implemented or if all the observations were not effectively addressed, verify that the deficiencies continue to exist and document adequate evidence to support a possible regulatory action.

"For Cause" inspections are carried out in response to specific information that raises questions, concerns, or problems associated with an FDA-regulated firm or product, including but not limited to observations made during prior inspections, recall or market withdrawal, consumer or employee complaint, adverse reaction report, or suspicion of fraud. "For Cause" inspections are generally more in-depth in areas associated with the reported or suspected issue, which can include tracing the underlying cause. Serious public health issue encountered during a QSIT inspection can give rise to a "For Cause" inspection.

IV. Inspection Process

Typical inspections range from three to six continuous business days, depending on the complexity of a firm's operations, availability of knowledgeable staff, and the nature of observed deficiencies, among other factors. When time and circumstances permit, investigators will make reasonable effort to discuss their observations with the firm personnel in charge to minimize errors and for clarification. These discussions may address observations not documented on the FDA Form 483, which may be recorded by either FDA or the firm if there is advance notice and mutual consent by the other party. Routine inspections generally focus on compliance with the following regulations: 21 CFR Parts 806 (Corrections and Removals), 807 (Registration and Listing), 820 (QS), 803 (MDR), and 821 (Tracking). For applicable devices, compliance with the Electronic Product Radiation Control requirements are also inspected.

An inspection generally begins by identifying the management official in charge of regulatory compliance. An FDA inspector will present his/her credentials, issue an FDA 482, a Notice of Inspection, and conduct an opening meeting before performing a walk-through of the establishment.

During the inspection, the inspector will conduct multiple walk-throughs of the facility, point out 483 observations, provide daily updates, and interview relevant firm personnel in charge of various firm operations.

Major and minor observations are documented on an FDA Form 483 Form. Corrective actions taken in response to 483s are reviewed during the next inspection. Discussion items between the inspector and the firm are not documents in the 483s, but are typically documented in the final report, or the Established Inspection Report (EIR).

At the end of an inspection, the inspector conducts a close-out meeting, issues an FDA Form 483 and discusses the observations cited and any discussion items. Firms usually have 15 business days to respond to the FDA district office regarding the observations listed in the FDA Form 483.

After the inspection, the investigator prepares an EIR, which is endorsed by the Investigations Branch and classified by the Compliance Branch. An Investigation Branch schedules next inspection and a copy of the EIR is sent to firm.

Depending on the observations, an inspection can be one of three Inspection Classifications, as follows:[6]

- No Action Indicated (NAI)—means no objectionable conditions or practices were found during the inspection (or the objectionable conditions found do not justify further regulatory action);
- Voluntary Action Indicated (VAI)—means objectionable conditions or practices were found but FDA is not prepared to take or recommend any administrative or regulatory action, or
- Official Action Indicated (OAI)—means regulatory and/or administrative actions will be recommended.

VAI can include a Form 483 identifying observations that should be addressed for the next inspection. OAI includes a Form 483 in addition to a warning letter, seizure, injunction, civil money penalties, or prosecution.

V. Medical Device Single Audit Program (MDSAP)

Recognizing the importance of auditing and monitoring manufacturing of medical devices on an international scale, the Medical Device Single Audit Program (MDSAP) allows a MDSAP-recognized auditing organization to conduct a single regulatory audit of a medical device manufacturer

6. FDA, *Inspections Database Frequently Asked Questions*, https://www.fda.gov/inspections-compliance-enforcement-and-criminal-investigations/inspection-references/inspections-database-frequently-asked-questions.

that satisfies the relevant requirements of all regulatory authorities participating in the program as MDSAP members, which include Therapeutic Goods Administration of Australia; Brazil's Agência Nacional de Vigilância Sanitária; Health Canada; Japan's Ministry of Health, Labour and Welfare and the Japanese Pharmaceuticals and Medical Devices Agency; and U.S. Food and Drug Administration.[7] The MDSAP official observers are the World Health Organization (WHO) Prequalification of In Vitro Diagnostics (IVDs) Programme and the European Union (EU). MDSAP affiliate members are Argentina's National Administration of Drugs, Foods and Medical Devices (ANMAT) and Republic of Korea's Ministry of Food and Drug Safety. Under the MDSAP, FDA will continue to accept MDSAP audit reports as a substitute for routine FDA inspections, except Electronic Product Radiation Control (EPRC) provisions of the act, which require FDA inspection.

VI. Form 483

One outcome of an inspection is FDA Form 483, which is an inspectional observation form used by investigators that lists major and minor observations identified during inspection.[8] Observations are listed in the order of significance, from major observations to minor observations, which, in the investigator's judgment, represent potential violations of the FD&C Act. The FDA Form 483 is not a comprehensive list of all deficiencies and does not include observations of questionable or unknown significance at the time of the inspection. Firms are responsible to take corrective action to address the listed objectionable conditions and any related objectionable conditions, whether listed in the Form 483 or not. Form 483 is not a final determination by the agency as to whether any condition is in violation of the FD&C Act or implementing regulations. The FDA Form 483, the Establishment Inspection Report, and any responses made by the firm provide evidence for any further action that the agency may take to protect public health.

For each fiscal year, FDA publishes a spreadsheet summarizing the common inspection observations and regulations cited in Form 483s.

7. FDA, *Medical Device Single Audit Program (MDSAP)*, https://www.fda.gov/medical-devices/cdrh-international-programs/medical-device-single-audit-program-mdsap.

8. FDA, *FDA Form 483 Frequently Asked Questions*, https://www.fda.gov/inspections-compliance-enforcement-and-criminal-investigations/inspection-references/fda-form-483-frequently-asked-questions.

According to the published data for FY 2020, some of the commonly cited inspection observations for medical devices include:

- Noncompliance with the unique device identifier (UDI) requirements
- Lack of adequate document control procedures
- Inadequate records with respect to suppliers, contractors, and consultants
- Inadequate design validation, verification, and risk analysis
- Lack of or inadequate complaint procedures
- Inadequate design history records
- Lack of or inadequate procedures for control and distribution of finished products
- Lack of or inadequate procedures for storage areas and stock rooms
- Lack of signed investigator agreements
- Lack of written procedures for monitoring investigational device studies
- Lack of or inadequate documentation of justification for not reporting a correction or removal action to FDA

VII. FDA Enforcement Actions

A. Letters to Industry

FDA may publish a variety of letters or notices to industry, including warning letters, untitled letters, "It Has Come to Our Attention" (IHC-TOA) letters, and other letters used to communicate broadly with industry.[9] Warning letters and certain untitled letters are published on FDA website, which can negatively impact a company's business. IHCTOA letters are not considered enforcement actions, which communication letters regarding specific devices or a class of devices are generally provided to the industry for informational purposes.

Warning letters are typically issued for significant regulatory violations, including violations that may lead to enforcement action if not promptly and adequately corrected, and are intended to elicit voluntary corrective action by firms. Warning letters are used to compel voluntary compliance and to establish prior notice of further enforcement action by the FDA. Companies are expected to promptly address any violations

9. FDA, *Letters to Industry*, https://www.fda.gov/medical-devices/industry-medical-devices/letters-industry.

identified in a warning letter, which typically requires a written response within 15 days, which can be shortened depending on the seriousness of the violation. One context where FDA may issue a warning letter is where a company repeatedly does not address deficiencies identified in a Form 483 or take corrective actions that the company promised to do in response to a Form 483.

Since the start of the COVID-19 public health emergency, FDA has issued a number of warning letters to companies for marketing or distributing unapproved or unauthorized, adulterated, and misbranded COVID-19 related products, including various COVID-19 testing products. Earlier in 2020, FDA has also issued warning letters to foreign companies following import alerts. Examples of warning letter citations track the commonly cited violations in Form 483s discussed earlier, including failure to establish adequate design controls, failure to establish and maintain procedures for validating device design and risk analysis, and failure to establish and maintain procedures related to product controls and product conformity.

Untitled letters advise companies of violations that do not meet the threshold for a warning letter and do not warn firms that failure to promptly correct the violation may result in enforcement action. FDA can choose to publish untitled letters on the center's website based on one or more of the following factors: (1) FDA has received or anticipates receiving three or more requests for the letter under the Freedom of Information Act (FOIA); (2) FDA believes that publishing the Untitled Letter would inform the public about violations that may pose a risk to public health; (3) FDA believes that publishing the untitled letter would deter future violations, inform similar companies of activities and practices FDA considers violative, and increase voluntary compliance.

IHCTOA letters are used when CDRH becomes aware that companies may be promoting a medical device that potentially violates the FD&C Act and seeks to obtain additional information as an early communication. While certain IHCTOA Letters have been published by the FDA in the past, FDA has currently taken the position that these letters will not be published going forward because they are not intended to communicate that FDA is considering enforcement action. These letters, however, are subject to disclosure through a FOIA request.

B. Recalls

Most recalls are permissive or voluntary. In general, a recall is a firm's removal or correction of a marketed product that the FDA considers to be in violation of the FD&C Act and implementing regulations and against which FDA would initiate a legal action, such as seizure.[10] A correction typically addresses a problem with a medical device in the place where it is used or sold, whereas removal addresses a problem with a medical device by removing it from where it is used or sold. The types of actions considered for recall include inspecting the device for problems, repairing the device, adjusting settings on the device, re-labeling the device, destroying the device, and notifying and monitoring patients for health issues. A recall does not include market withdrawal, which refers to a firm's removal or correction of a distributed product that involves a no violation or a minor violation that would not be subject to a legal action by the FDA, including withdrawals for normal stock rotation practices or routine equipment adjustments and repairs.

FDA posts correction and removal actions in the Medical Device Recall Database, which is updated after FDA classifies the recall and after termination of a recall. FDA may also publish notices or press releases about recalls, market withdrawals, and safety alerts. In particular, FDA publishes a weekly *FDA Enforcement Report* that discloses all enforcement actions taken by the FDA, including recalls, field corrections, seizures, and injunctions, which can impact a firm's business and reputation.

A voluntary recall occurs when manufacturers and distributors voluntarily recall distributed products that present a risk of injury or gross deception or are otherwise defective, providing an alternative to an FDA-initiated court action for removing or correcting such distributed products. 21 C.F.R. § 7 sets forth the procedures and requirements for recalls. Although most recalls are initiated voluntarily by manufacturers, FDA can also issue a recall order to the manufacturer under 21 C.F.R. § 810 under its recall authority under section 518(e) of the FD&C Act. Manufacturers and importers are also required to report to FDA of any correction or removal of medical devices initiated to reduce a risk to public health under 21 C.F.R. § 806.

FDA will also conduct a health hazard evaluation for a product being recalled or considered for recall, which takes into account, among other factors, whether any disease or injuries have occurred from the use of the product and assessment of hazard to various segments of the population, the severity of the health hazard to those at risk of exposure, the likelihood of the hazard, and the consequences (immediate or long-range) of

10. FDA, *Recalls, Corrections and Removals (Devices)*, https://www.fda.gov/medical-devices/postmarket-requirements-devices/recalls-corrections-and-removals-devices; FDA, *What Is a Medical Device Recall?*, https://www.fda.gov/medical-devices/medical-device-recalls/what-medical-device-recall.

such hazard. Based on the health hazard evaluation, FDA will assign the recall classification, that is, Class I (reasonable probability of serious adverse health consequence or death), Class II (remote probability), or Class III (not likely to cause adverse health consequences), to indicate the relative degree of health hazard of the product being recalled or considered for recall.

The recalling firm should develop a recall strategy that takes into account the depth of recall, such as consumer or user level or retail level, public warning, and effectiveness checks to verify that notification of the recall and appropriate action have been taken, among other factors. Such recall strategy is reviewed by FDA. The recalling firm will also need to submit periodic recall status reports to FDA until the recall is terminated. A recall is terminated when FDA determines that all reasonable efforts have been made to remove or correct the distributed product in accordance with the recall strategy, and when it is reasonable to assume that the recalled product has been removed and appropriately disposed of.

In rare instances, where FDA finds there is a reasonable probability that a device intended for human use would cause serious, adverse health consequences or death, FDA may issue order to cease distribution and notification, or order a mandatory recall under the procedures set forth at 21 C.F.R. § 810 and section 518(e) of FD&C Act.

C. Detention and Hearing

Products in shipments that are deemed violative or appear to violate FDA regulatory requirement may be designated as "detained" by FDA.[11] Products subject to detention include adulterated or misbranded products; products manufactured, processed, or packed under unsanitary conditions; or products that are banned or restricted products. Such FDA notice of detention and of violation of FDA laws and regulations is done by issuing a Notice of Detention and Hearing. The Notice of Detention and Hearing will provide a "respond by" date for the responsible party to provide FDA with evidence, or testimony, to overcome the appearance of a violation. Besides submitting evidence, the firm can also submit a request to recondition the product to correct the violation. If the firm is not able to overcome the appearance of a violation, the detained product will be refused admission into the U.S., and the firm should work with the U.S. Customs and Border Protection (CBP) and FDA to destroy the product or to export it from the United States within 90 days of the refusal.

11. FDA, *Detention & Hearing*, https://www.fda.gov/industry/actions-enforcement/detention-hearing.

The firm responsible for the detained product may appeal the detention and request a hearing, which provides an opportunity for the firm to present evidence, or testimony, to overcome the appearance of a violation and to demonstrate that the product is in compliance with FDA regulatory requirements. The hearing can vary from a series of e-mail or telephone conversations to more formal meetings.

D. Import Alerts and Refusals

FDA may also issue import alerts to inform the agency's field staff and the public that there is sufficient evidence to allow for Detention Without Physical Examination (DWPE) of products that appear to be in violation of FDA's regulatory requirements.[12] DWPE allows the agency to detain products without physically examining the products at the time of entry.

1. Import Refusals

An import refusal is FDA's final decision that a detained shipment violates FDA laws and regulations, which must be either be destroyed or exported under the supervision of CBP and FDA within 90 days of the date of the Refusal Notice.[13] Products that may be refused by FDA include those where the responsible party did not respond to the FDA Notice of Detention and Hearing within the specified deadline or where the evidence provided by the firm did not overcome the appearance of a violation. When FDA issues a refusal, CBP is notified and will request the responsible party to redeliver the product to a CBP approved location at a port of entry within 90 days. If the firm fails to return the refused products, CBP may assess liquidated damages against the bond. FDA publishes an Import Refusals Report (IRR) that lists refusals by country/area and by product based on the industry code.

E. Medical Device Bans

Section 516 of the FD&C Act authorizes FDA to ban devices that present substantial deception or unreasonable and substantial risk of illness or injury, and imposes total prohibition on the current and future sales,

12. FDA, *Import Alerts*, https://www.fda.gov/industry/actions-enforcement/import-alerts.

13. FDA, *Import Refusals*, https://www.fda.gov/industry/actions-enforcement/import-refusals.

distribution, and manufacturing of the banned device.[14] FDA rarely acts on this authority and has only banned three devices since 1983.

If the reason for the ban can be corrected by a change in the labeling, FDA must notify the responsible person regarding the required change in labeling and set the time period for making the change. If the labeling is not changed in the specified time and manner, or if the deception or risk cannot be addressed by a change in labeling, then FDA may publish the proposed ban in the Federal Register and allow interested parties an opportunity for an informal hearing on the proposal. Once the proposal is finalized, FDA will publish a final regulation banning the device. Except under an approved investigational device exemption, a banned device cannot be legally marketed on and after the date of publication of the final regulation.

F. Civil Enforcement Litigation

Civil enforcement litigation can be used to seek seizures, injunctions, or civil monetary penalties. These cases are initiated by a local U.S. attorney or the DOJ by filing a complaint in the federal court.

G. Seizure

Seizure is an enforcement action brought against an FDA-regulated product that is deemed adulterated and/or misbranded and allows FDA to quickly remove the violative goods from commerce. FDA's seizure authority comes from section 304 of the FD&C Act. There are three different types of seizures, including lot-specific seizures directed to a specific lot or batch, mass seizures directed to all products of a particular establishment or facility, or open-ended seizures directed to all units of a violative product regardless of the lot or batch number. A seizure action is a judicial action, which entails coordinating with the U.S. Attorney's Office to request an Assistant United States Attorney (AUSA) to file a seizure request and Complaint for Forfeiture in the U.S. District Court where the product is located. The complaint requests a warrant for arrest of the product, specifies the location of the product for seizure, and a directive for the U.S. Marshals Service to execute the seizure. Upon seizure by the Marshals, the seized products will remain in the control and custody of the Marshals. An interested party may challenge the seizure in court by timely filing a claim for the products and an answer to the complaint. The claiming party may enter into a consent decree with the government regarding disposition of the products. If a

---

14. FDA, *Medical Device Bans*, https://www.fda.gov/medical-devices/medical-device-safety/medical-device-bans.

company fails to claim the products, the government may move to dispose of the products under a default decree, including destruction, conversion, or sale of the products.

H. Injunctions

Injunction is an order by a court that requires an individual or a firm to do or refrain from doing a specific act. FDA may seek injunctions against individuals and/or companies to prevent them from violating or causing violations under the FD&C Act. Proposed injunctions are generally recommended after a series of inspections that suggest serious violations of the FD&C Act. An injunction recommendation is generally prepared by the District Compliance Officer, which includes a memorandum, draft complaint, and other necessary pleadings, which are reviewed by the center before being forwarded to the Office of the Chief Counsel (OCC). If there is sufficient evidence to support the charges, the OCC refers the matter to the DOJ and prepares a draft consent decree. The DOJ will send a "sign-or-sue" letter to the proposed defendants, who may accept the consent decree or seek changes to the consent decree. Where the parties cannot come to an agreement, the Justice Department will to file an action seeking injunctive relief. Once the injunction action is filed, litigation of the case is handled by an AUSA with attorneys from the FDA, and/or the Office of Consumer Litigation (OCL).

For example, in the landmark 1999 decision in *United States v. Universal Management Services Inc.*,[15] FDA obtained a consent decree of injunction with Abbott Laboratories and equitable monetary relief under the doctrine of disgorgement to settle good manufacturing practice violations. This case has been cited in other cases where FDA sought injunction and equitable disgorgement for violations under the FD&C Act.

I. Civil Money Penalties

For civil actions, FDA may pursue civil monetary penalties for violations under the FD&C Act, such as submitting false or misleading information, failing to submit required certifications, and knowingly submitting false certifications. The FD&C Act sets a maximum penalty of $10,000 for all violations adjudicated within a single proceeding, or, $10,000 per day of continuing noncompliance if a defendant fails to remedy its noncompliance within the notice period. These amounts are adjusted for inflation under 45 C.F.R. § 102.3. For 2020, the inflation-adjusted amounts were $12,316.

15. United States v. Universal Mgmt. Services Inc., 191 F.3d 750 (6th Cir. 1999).

J. Criminal Prosecution and Criminal Fines

FDA is also authorized to pursue criminal prosecution for violations of section 301 (Prohibited Acts) of FD&C Act, including imprisonment, fines, and penalties for companies and individuals. Violations under the FD&C Act may be misdemeanors or felonies, depending on whether the defendant has knowledge or intent to defraud or to mislead. FDA's Office of Criminal Investigations (OCI) is FDA's criminal law enforcement arm and works with the U.S. Attorney's Office, Department of Justice, and Federal Bureau of Investigation (FBI) on criminal matters, including investigations and criminal prosecution.

Under the Park Doctrine, based on the 1975 Supreme Court decision in *United States v. Park*, a "responsible corporate official" can be held liable for a first-time misdemeanor and potentially subsequent felony for violations under the FD&C Act without having to prove that the official participated in or was aware of the violations. The Park Doctrine essentially provides strict liability for crimes of corporate officials who are in a position of authority to prevent or to correct an alleged violation. A conviction of a misdemeanor under the Park Doctrine can serve as the basis for debarment by FDA, which can exclude the responsible corporate official from participation in any federal health care program for as many as 12 years. In applying the Park Doctrine in an indictment, FDA will consider whether the violation was obvious, pattern of illegal behavior or failure to heed warnings, the extent of the violation, and actual or potential harm to the public, among other factors.

The Criminal Fine Enforcement Act of 1994 (Public Law 98-596) provides criminal fines for violations of Federal law. Misdemeanor convictions, which do not require proof of intent, can result in fines and/or imprisonment up to one year, as follows:

- Up to $100,000 for a misdemeanor by an individual that does not result in death.
- Up to $200,000 for a misdemeanor by a corporation that does not result in death.
- Up to $250,000 for a misdemeanor by an individual that results in death, or a felony.
- Up to $500,000 for a misdemeanor by a corporation that results in death, or a felony.

Felony convictions, which apply in a second violation or intent to defraud or mislead, can result in fines and/or imprisonment up to three years.

Criminal enforcement cases typically involve allegations of falsifying data submitted to the FDA, mail and wire fraud, smuggling counterfeit, misbranded or adulterated products, and conspiracy. Examples of criminal enforcement actions in the medical device space include:[16]

- Candy Color Lenses: The owner and operator of the Candy Color Lenses website was sentenced to 46 months in prison and forfeited $1.2 million in proceeds in connection with an international scheme to import counterfeit and misbranded contact lenses, including some that were contaminated with bacteria, from Asia, which he distributed to U.S. customers without a prescription.
- Apollo Endosurgery: A salesperson and his cohort were sentenced to federal prison for wire fraud for selling expired LAP-BAND adjustable gastric banding systems to physicians by changing the serial numbers and expiration dates and using false labels on these misbranded and adulterated devices.
- Westmoreland: A Maryland woman was sentenced to two years in federal prison for injecting nonmedical grade silicone into customers' buttocks and other parts of the body to enhance their appearance.

16. FDA, *Criminal Investigations Case Activity*, https://www.fda.gov/inspections-compliance-enforcement-and-criminal-investigations/criminal-investigations/criminal-investigations-case-activity#devices.

CHAPTER 8

Import/Exports

Allison Fulton

I. Introduction

A. Statutory Framework; FDCA Chapter VIII: Imports and Exports

Chapter VIII of the Food, Drug, and Cosmetic Act (FDCA) provides the statutory framework for importing and exporting products regulated by the U.S. Food and Drug Administration (FDA).[1]

Section 801 of Chapter VIII authorizes FDA to inspect and refuse medical devices that are offered for import into the United States. Section 801 also provides rules for exporting products, including products are legally marketed in the United States, and those that are not (for example, a device that does not have the appropriate premarket clearance in the U.S.).

Section 802 provides for the exportation of unapproved medical devices and those intended for investigation. The export requirements vary depending on the device's marketing authorization status in certain recognized countries.

B. Overview of the Chapter

This chapter will first explore the import program, beginning with an examination of the relevant statutory framework and corresponding requirements, followed by discussion of the process to import a medical device into the United States and actions that can prevent or delay import into the United States. In brief, all FDA-regulated products that are imported into the United States must meet both FDA and U.S. Customs and Border Protection (CPB, or Customs) requirements. If it

1. *See* 21 U.S.C. §§ 381–384; FDCA §§ 801–804.

appears, from the examination of samples or otherwise, that an imported medical device may be noncompliant with FDA law (i.e., the product is adulterated or misbranded), FDA may detain the product upon its arrival in the United States. FDA ultimately may release the detained product, or refuse its admission.

This chapter will then describe the laws for exporting medical devices under sections 801 and 802. The requirements for export vary based on the marketing status of the device in the United States and in certain recognized countries. For example, devices that are legally marketed in the United States have fewer requirements for export than those that are not approved in the United States. Also, unapproved devices that have valid marketing authorization in Australia, Canada, the EU, and other "listed countries" must meet fewer requirements than unapproved devices that are not authorized in the listed vountries. These rules, and other requirements, are explored in this chapter.

Lastly, the chapter will provide a look at recent enforcement by FDA.

II. Importing Devices into the United States

A. Statutory and Regulatory Requirements

1. Ex-U.S. Manufacturers and Imported Devices Must Meet All Requirements Applicable to Devices Manufactured in the United States

FDA has jurisdiction over imported products at the time of entry into the United States, and after the products have entered into U.S. commerce. Medical devices that are imported into the United States must comply with all U.S. laws and regulations that are applicable to devices manufactured in the Unites States. FDA does not recognize foreign approval of medical devices. Therefore, manufacturers and medical devices imported in the United States must:

- Have the appropriate premarket clearance (510K notification) or premarket approval, as applicable;[2]
- Meet facility registration and product listing requirements;[3]
- Be manufactured in accordance with the Quality System regulation (i.e., cGMP);[4]

2. *See* 21 C.F.R. pt. 807 (registration and listing requirements); *see also* 21 C.F.R. pt. 814 (premarket approval).

3. *See* 21 U.S.C. § 360(i); FDCA § 510(i) (registration of foreign establishments); *see* 21 U.S.C. § 360(j); FDCA § 510(j) (listing of devices).

4. *See* 21 C.F.R. pt. 820 (GMP requirements of the Quality System regulation).

- Meet product labeling requirements;[5]
- Meet reporting and notification requirements (e.g., corrections or removals);[6] and
- Reporting of adverse events/medical device reports (MDRs).[7]

A device that is imported as an investigational device must likewise meet the U.S. requirements for investigational devices.[8]

A foreign establishment involved in the manufacturing, preparation, propagation, or processing of a medical device must register its facility with FDA. Otherwise, its devices may be refused admission.[9] Registrants must provide the establishment's name and place of business, the name of the establishment's U.S. agent, and the name of each importer of the device.[10] Similar to U.S. manufacturing facilities, foreign facilities must register with FDA annually between October 1 and December 31.[11] At the time of registration, a list of devices manufactured, prepared, propagated, or compounded at the establishment must be provided, along with certain statements and accompanying disclosures.[12] A device or article that is refused entry into the United States for failing to include a statement of registration will be held at the port of entry, or removed to a secure facility, until such statement is provided.[13]

The GMP requirements of the Quality System Regulation (QSR) apply to any finished device that is intended for human use and is imported or offered for import into the United States.[14] If the foreign manufacturer refuses to allow FDA to inspect its facility for the purposes of determining compliance with the QSR, FDA may deem the device to be adulterated under the FDCA and can refuse admission of the article.[15]

---

5. *See* 21 U.S.C. § 352; FDCA § 502 (labeling must not be false or misleading).

6. *See* 21 U.S.C. § 360(k); FDCA § 510; *see also* 21 C.F.R. pt. 806 (reports of correction or removal); *see also* 21 C.F.R. 895.22 (submitting data to FDA regarding whether the device presents a deception, unreasonable and substantial risk of illness or injury, or unreasonable, direct, and substantial danger to the health of individuals).

7. *See* 21 C.F.R. pt. 803 (requirements for MDRs).

8. *See id.* pt. 812 (investigational device exemptions).

9. *See* 21 U.S.C. § 360(i); FDCA § 510(i) (registration requirements for foreign facilities); 21 U.S.C. § 381(o); FDCA § 801(o) (registration must be provided at the time of import).

10. *See* 21 U.S.C. § 360(i)(1)(A); FDCA § 510(i)(1)(A).

11. *Id.*

12. *Id.*; *see also* listing requirements under 21 U.S.C. § 360(j); FDCA § 510(j).

13. *See* 21 U.S.C. § 381(o); FDCA § 801(o).

14. *See* 21 C.F.R. § 820.1(a)(2).

15. *Id.* § 820.1(d).

Medical device tracking requirements also apply to imported devices.[16] Importers must keep all information required of manufacturers, such as the name, address, and telephone number of the device distributor or the location of the device, if it has not been distributed to a patient.[17]

2. Designation of U.S. Agent

A foreign establishment must designate a U.S. agent to be the entity's official correspondent with FDA.[18] The agent's responsibilities include (1) helping with communication between the foreign establishment and FDA; (2) responding to inquiries related to the devices that are being offered for import into the U.S.; (3) aiding FDA in scheduling inspections of the foreign establishment; and (4) receiving documentation or information on behalf of the foreign establishment if FDA is not able to directly or expeditiously reach out to the establishment.

The U.S. agent, and the importer, must be identified in FDA's electronic device registration and listing system (known as FURLS, FDA Unified Registration and Listing System).[19] The U.S. agent must either reside in the United States or maintain a place of business in the United States.

B. The Import Process

1. Role of FDA and CBP

All products offered for entry into the United States must be declared to U.S. Customs and Border Protection (CBP). CBP has initial authority over all imported products, including medical devices.

When CBP receives an article for import that is regulated by FDA, CBP forwards the product information to FDA for review. FDA determines whether the products are admissible into U.S. commerce. The products are held by CBP until the FDA has determined their admissibility.

FDA may refuse entry to any product that violates or appears to violate any provisions of the FDCA. For example, FDA may refuse products that are (or appear to be):

16. *Id.* § 821.4.
17. *Id.* § 821.25.
18. *Id.* § 807.40.
19. *Id.* § 807.41.

- adulterated, meaning the product is contaminated, is not safe, is unapproved, or does not otherwise meet applicable standards;
- misbranded, meaning the labels contain false or misleading information, or the product is not registered and listed, if required; or
- banned or restricted for sale.

FDA may detain imported product for sampling and evaluation before it determines the product's admissibility. If the device is released, it may be introduced into U.S. commerce. If the device is refused, it must be either exported or destroyed (typically within 90 days).

2. The Importer of Record

An "importer of record" is the individual who files entry information for article offered for importation. The importer of record is responsible for making sure all imported goods comply with U.S. requirements and is responsible for the product's entry into the United States.

Companies often contract the services of a customs broker to be the importer of record. Customs brokers are trained and licensed to facilitate the importation of goods into the U.S. under applicable U.S. laws for importers. They prepare and file the necessary customs entries, arrange for the payment of duties, take steps to arrange the release of the goods in CBP custody, and otherwise represent their principals in customs matters.

3. The Entry Process

The CBP requires persons importing products to complete an electronic filing process for each imported product. CBP currently uses the Automated Commercial Environment (ACE) for entry of FDA regulated articles into the United States.[20]

The ACE filer, typically the importer of record or customs broker, must submit product identifying information and contact information (telephone, email address) of the importer.[21] Product information includes information such as: (1) the country where the article was last manufactured or processed; (2) the FDA product code, which must be consistent with the invoice description of the product; (3) the device's intended use; (4) establishment registration and product listing information; and (5) premarket clearance numbers (i.e., 510(k) or PMA number),

20. *See* 81 Fed. Reg. 85854 (Nov. 29, 2016).
21. *See* 21 C.F.R. § 1.72.

if applicable.[22,23] There are additional requirements for investigational devices, articles that are only components of a medical device,[24] products with lead wires/patient cables, impact resistant lenses, and convenience kits.[25] Filers importing radiation emitting electronic products also must submit certain declarations at the time of filing.[26]

FDA uses multiple electronic review systems to review the documentation for an product offered for import. An importer may upload entry documentation into FDA's import tracking system, called Import Trade Auxiliary Communication System (ITACS).[27] ITACS allows an importer to track the progress of the entry and upload additional documentation requested by FDA. FDA also uses a risk-based analytics tool called PREDICT to electronically screen regulated shipments offered for importing into the United States.[28] PREDICT uses automated data mining, pattern discovery, and automated queries to determine the risk profile of a particular shipment.

C. Detentions and Refusals of Admission

FDA may refuse and detain a device that appears not to be in compliance with U.S. laws. Devices not in compliance with U.S. laws includes those that are misbranded or adulterated, including those that do not have the appropriate premarket clearance, are labeled incorrectly, or do not comply with GMP.[29]

If FDA decides to detain a product, it will issue a Notice of Detention and Hearing. The notice contains information regarding the laws the product has allegedly violated, the product's holding location, and a "respond by" date.[30] The response date is typically ten business days. Responding party's may provide evidence to FDA demonstrating the product meets U.S. laws by e-mail, telephone, or in person in a formal meeting.[31] While decision is pending, FDA may authorize the delivery

22. *Id.*
23. *Id.* § 1.76(a).
24. *Id.* § 1.76(b)–(d).
25. *Id.* § 1.76(e)–(g).
26. *Id.* § 1.77.
27. *See* FDA ITACS webpage.
28. PREDICT is an anagram for Predictive Risk-based Evaluation for Dynamic Import Compliance Targeting. For more information regarding PREDICT please see FDA's webpage, Entry Screening Systems and Tools.
29. *See* 21 U.S.C. § 381; FDCA § 801.
30. *See* 21 C.F.R. § 800.55; *see also* FDA Detention and Hearing webpage.
31. *Id.*

of the detained articles to the owner or consignee upon the execution of a sufficient bond that provides for the payment of liquidated damages in the event of default.[32]

The owner or consignee may submit an application to bring the article into compliance by relabeling or reconditioning the device, or by other action.[33] The application must contain (1) a detailed proposal for bringing the article into compliance with the FDCA and (2) the time and place where such operations will be carried out and the approximate time for their completion.[34] If FDA grants permission to recondition the product to fix the violation, FDA will specify the requirements for reconditioning, the timing, and other such conditions necessary to maintain adequate supervision and control over the article.[35] The owner or consignee must pay for the costs of supervising the relabeling (or other action).[36]

If the product is ultimately refused admission, FDA will issue a Notice of Refusal of Admission. Refusals are final, and unless there was a clerical error, may not be rescinded.[37] The Notice is sent to the importer of record. After the product has been refused, it must be either exported from the United States or destroyed within 90 days of the notice.[38] The exportation or must be conducted under the supervision of FDA and CBP.

D. Product Sampling and Examination

The FDA has the authority to conduct examinations and/or sample collections to determine if a product offered for import is in compliance with the FDA regulations and laws. As part of the entry review process, an FDA entry reviewer will designate the entry for examination. An examination may consist of any combination of a field examination, label examination, or sample collection.

FDA may conduct a physical examination or collect a sample based on the product risk, the product or manufacturer history of past violations, or as part of routine surveillance. When the FDA decides to examine or collect a sample, it will Notice of FDA Action to the filer, importer, owner or consignee. Upon receipt of the notice, the owner or consignee

32. *See* 21 U.S.C. § 381(b); FDCA 801(b).
33. *See* 21 C.F.R. § 1.95.
34. *Id.*
35. *See* 21 C.F.R. § 1.96.
36. *Id.* § 1.99.
37. *See* FDA Import Refusals webpage.
38. *See* 21 U.S.C. § 381(a); FDCA § 801(a).

must hold the product, and not distribute it until further notice.[39] FDA import personnel will visit the location where the product is located to perform the examination and/or sample collection.

If the physical examination or analytical results indicate that the product appears to be in violation, FDA will issue a Notice of Detention and Hearing. The product will remain on hold pending additional follow-up that will result in either the products being refused or released. For products where the FDA does not find any apparent violations, FDA will issue a Notice of FDA Action indicating the release of those products. The current status will also be sent electronically to the entry filer.

E. Import Alerts, Detention without Physical Examination (DWPE)

Import alerts are FDA notifications that a product is subject to Detention Without Physical Examination (DWPE) due to alleged violations of FDA laws and regulations. DWPE allows the agency to detain a product without physically examining it at the time of entry.

FDA may issue an alert that covers a specific manufacturer or shipper, products from a particular country or geographic area, or product from all countries outside the United States. For example, FDA could issue an import alert for "Detention Without Physical Examination of Puffer Fish," which would prevent import of puffer fish from any country, or "Detention without Physical Examination of Imported Soft Cheese and Soft Ripened Cheese from France," which would exclude soft cheese from France only. In the context of medical devices, FDA has issued an import alert for devices manufactured in facilities that do not meet GMP requirements. For example, the import alert titled "Detention Without Physical Examination of Devices from Firms that Have not met Device Quality System Requirements," prevents importation of devices from all ex-U.S. countries that have been manufactured in noncompliant facilities. The import alert titled "Detention Without Physical Examination of Devices without Approved PMA's or IDE's and Other Devices Not Substantially Equivalent or Without a 510(k)" has a similar scope. Each import alert will describe the conditions that cause a firm, product, or region to be placed on the alert.

A firm may petition FDA to be removed or exempted from an import alert by submitting a petition to FDA's Division of Import Operations (DIO).

---

39. *See* 21 C.F.R. § 1.90.

F. Import for Export

FDA's "import for export" (IFE) rules allow for the importation of products that are unapproved, or otherwise do not comply with FDA laws and regulations, if the products are imported for further processing and ultimately exported out of the United States.[40] Products imported under the IFE provision may not be distributed or sold in the U.S.

FDA has noted IFE can cover a wide range of activities, including packaging or labeling of finished products and specialized processing (such as sterilization) of a product.[41] Merely storing a product in the U.S. before export, however, does not qualify for IFE.

In order to qualify for the "IFE" exemption, individuals must provide FDA with information regarding your intention to further process the product.[42] If FDA determines that there is credible evidence or information indicating that such article is not intended to be further processed, it may can be refused for admission into the US.[43]

G. Popular Topics

1. Importation of Goods for Personal Use

In most circumstances, it is illegal for individuals to import drugs or devices into the U.S. for personal use because the products have not been cleared or approved by the FDA for sale in the U.S. For example, a device approved for use in another country but not approved by the FDA would be considered an unapproved device in the U.S. and, therefore, illegal to import.

FDA has developed a "Personal Importation Policy," setting forth FDA's enforcement priorities related to the personal importation of drugs that are not FDA approved and, therefore, are in violation of the FDCA. A similar policy has not been developed for devices, but the same principles may apply.[44] The PIP is not intended to permit personal importation of cheaper versions of FDA approved drugs from Canada or other foreign countries.

Commercial and promotional shipments are not subject to the personal importation policy. Whether or not a shipment is commercial or promotional may be determined by a number of factors including, the

40. *See* 21 U.S.C. § 381(d)(3)(A); FDCA § 801(d)(3)(A).
41. *See* FDA Import for Export Overview webpage.
42. *Id.*
43. *See* 21 U.S.C. § 381(d)(3)(B); FDCA § 801(d)(3)(B).
44. *See* FDA Guidance, Personal Importation Policy (PIP) Frequently Asked Questions (FAQs).

type of product, the destination of the shipment, and whether the quantity shipped suggests commercial distribution. Commercial shipments generally include shipments other than those products that are personally carried, shipped by a personal noncommercial representative, or shipped from a foreign medical facility where a person has undergone treatment.

2. Foreign Trade Zones

Foreign Trade Zones (FTZ) are secure areas under U.S. Customs and Border Protection (CBP) supervision that are generally considered to be outside the Customs territory of the U.S. FTZs are located in or near CBP ports of entry, they are the United States' version of what are known internationally as free-trade zones. FTZs may be used for many purposes, including the deferral of duty payment until the goods are offered for Customs entry out of the FTZ. Other uses for FTZs include manufacturing, warehousing, packaging, labeling, and inspection.

The FDA considers FTZs to be within "interstate commerce," however under section 801 of the FDCA goods admitted into FTZs are not considered imported or offered for import. FDA therefore does not apply the requirements under section 801 until the goods are offered for Customs entry.

3. Importing through U.S. Mail

When products are sent from abroad into the U.S., they initially arrive at a United States Postal Service (USPS) sorting facility, known as an international mail facility (IMF). There are currently nine IMF locations across the U.S., with locations in Florida, Hawaii, Illinois, New Jersey, New York, Puerto Rico, U.S. Virgin Islands, respectively, and two locations in California.[45]

Upon initial screening at arrival, USPS sends packages to CPB for examination. CBP provides the initial analysis of these packages and then refers FDA regulated products to FDA for further review. Packages that appear to potentially violate the FDCA go through the FDA's sample and evaluation process described in Section II.D. If FDA determines that a package is suspected of containing a controlled substance during its review, then the package is referred back to CBP for an admissibility determination.

45. *See* FDA International Mail Facilities webpage.

III. Exporting Devices from the U.S.

A. Statutory and Regulatory Requirements

Sections 801 and 802 of Chapter VIII of the FDCA identify rules governing the export of medical devices, including the export of products that are legally marketed in the U.S. and products that do not have premarket clearance or approval in the U.S.

FDA requires U.S. manufacturers that manufacture devices for export only to register their facility and list the devices the manufacture, even if the devices are not distributed in the U.S.[46]

B. Export of Devices Legally Marketed in the U.S.

An medical device that is legally in commercial distribution in the U.S. may be exported anywhere in the world without prior notice or approval from FDA. For a device to be legally in commercial distribution in the U.S., the following requirements must be met:

- The manufacturing facility must be registered with the FDA;
- The device must be listed with the FDA;
- The device must have a cleared Premarket Notification (510(k)) or Premarket Approval (PMA), unless exempted
- The device must meet the labeling requirements of 21 C.F.R. Part 801 and 21 C.F.R. 809, if applicable; and
- The device must be manufactured in accordance with the Quality System (QS) Regulation of 21 C.F.R. Part 820 (also known as GMP), unless exempted by regulation.

In addition, the U.S. exporter must comply with the laws of each importing country.

1. Certificate to Foreign Government

While FDA does not restrict the export of legally marketed devices, certain importing countries may require written certification that a firm, or its devices, is in compliance with U.S. law. For these countries, U.S. companies can request from FDA a Certificate to Foreign Government (CFG). FDA will review and issue a CFG to the requesting company. The CFG form is a self-certification form. By completing the required form, a firm certifies that it is registered and listed, that its product is legally marketed in the U.S. and is not the subject of an open recall, that all facilities involved in the manufacturing of the device comply with

46. *See* 21 C.F.R. § 807.20(a)(2).

FDA's regulations, and that the product is being exported from the U.S. Certificates are typically issued within a week or so.

C. Export of Unapproved Class I and Certain Class II Devices under FDCA 801(e)(1)

Medical devices that are not FDA cleared or approved for marketing in the U.S. may be exported under section 801(e)(1) of the FDCA, if they are intended for export only and are Class I or Class II devices that are not required to meet performance standards under section 514 of the FDCA.

Under section 801(e)(1), medical devices may be exported legally and without prior notice or approval from FDA, provided they are Class I or Class II devices (that are not required to meet performance standards) and are:

1. In accordance with the specifications of the foreign purchaser;
2. Not in conflict with the laws of the country to which they are intended for export;
3. Labeled on the outside of the shipping package that they are intended for export; and
4. Not sold or offered for sale in the U.S.

An exporter is required to keep records that demonstrate compliance with each of these requirements and these records must be available to FDA during an inspection.[47]

The following types of devices may not be exported under section 801(e)(1):

- Devices that require (and do not have) premarket approval (i.e., a PMA);
- Devices that do not meet FDA performance standards;
- Devices for investigational use; and
- Banned devices.[48]

The aforementioned devices may qualify for export under section 802 or under section 801(e)(2). Export under section 801(e)(2) is more onerous than under section 802 because it requires a determination by FDA that the export of the device is not contrary to public health and safety (in the form of an Export Approval Letter) and the approval of the receiving country.

---

47. *See* 21 C.F.R. § 1.101(b); *see* FDA Guidance for Industry: Exports Under the FDA Export Reform and Enhancement Act of 1996 (July 23, 2007).

48. *See* 21 U.S.C. § 381(e)(2); FDCA § 801(e)(2).

1. Certificate of Exportability

The importing country may require documentation from the FDA confirming that the imported device meets the above criteria. Companies may request an export Certificate of Exportability (COE) from FDA under section 801(e)(1). In order to demonstrate that the device is in accordance with the specifications of the foreign purchaser, the exporter must maintain records that contain sufficient information to match the foreign purchaser's specifications to a particular export.[49] These documents must be made available during an FDA inspection.

In order to demonstrate that a device is not in conflict with the laws of the foreign country an exporter can either (1) provide a letter from an appropriate foreign authorized body stating that the product has marketing approval from the foreign government or does not conflict with that country's laws, or (2) provide a notarized certification by a responsible company official in the U.S. that the product does not conflict with the laws of the importing country.[50]

2. "For Export Only" Labeling

Devices that are for export only must be labeled "For Export Only" (or similar wording) on the shipping packages or, if the exported product does not have a shipping package or container, on its labeling, shipping invoices or other documents accompanying the exported product.[51] In order to demonstrate that an export is not sold or offered in domestic commerce, an exporter must retain production and shipping records for the exported product and promotional materials.[52]

D. Exporting Devices While Waiting for FDA Clearance

By policy, FDA allows the export of a device without 510(k) marketing clearance under section 801(e)(1) if the device meets two conditions:

- The device meets the requirements of section 801(e)(1), and
- There is reasonable expectation that the device could obtain 510(k) marketing clearance in the U.S. if reviewed by the FDA because it is similar in design, construction, and intended use to an already-approved or cleared device.

49. *See* 21 C.F.R. § 1.101(b)(1).
50. *Id.* § 1.101(b)(2).
51. *Id.* § 1.101(b)(3).
52. *Id.* § 1.101(b)(4).

Class III devices are not included in this policy, nor are devices that are found not to be substantially equivalent to an existing 510(k) device (including devices that require a de novo application).

E. Exporting Unapproved Class III and Certain Class II Devices under Section 802

Class III devices that do not have an approved Premarket Approval (PMA) and Class II devices that are required to meet performance standards under Section 514 of the FDCA[53] may be exported under Section 802 of the FDCA if certain criteria are met. Devices that may be exported under Section 802 include investigational devices, banned devices,[54] and unapproved Class III devices.

1. Device Must Have Valid Marketing Authorization in a "Listed Country"

Devices exported under Section 802, with two exceptions, must have valid marketing authorization in a "Listed Country" (also called a "Tier 1" country).[55] The two exceptions are for (1) devices that are intended for further processing in anticipation of market authorization in a Listed Country (see Section H) and (2) devices intended for the diagnosis, treatment, or prevention of a tropical disease or other rare disease (see Section I).

The Listed Tier 1 Countries are identified by statute, and currently include: Australia, Canada, Israel, Japan, New Zealand, Switzerland, South Africa, and member of the European Union or the European Economic Area, if the device is marketed in the member country or is authorized for general marketing in the European Economic Area.[56] The Secretary of the Department of Health and Human Services has authority to expand the list of listed countries.[57]

The device being exported must be approved for commercial distribution in a listed Tier 1 Country, and not merely approved for investigational or other restricted use. Additionally, the receiving country must accept the marketing authorization by the listed country. If the appropriate authorities of a non-Tier 1 country will not accept the marketing

53. Currently, electrode wires and patient cables are the only devices subject to an FDA performance standard under section 514 of the FDCA. *Id.* § 898.

54. Banned devices currently include synthetic hair fibers intended for implant and powdered surgeon's gloves, powdered patient examination gloves, and absorbable powder for lubricating a surgeon's gloves.

55. *See* 21 U.S.C. § 382(b)(1)(A); FDCA § 802(b)(1)(A) (list of countries).

56. *See* 21 U.S.C. § 382(b)(1)(A); FDCA § 802(b)(1) (list of countries).

57. *See* 21 U.S.C. §§ 382(b)(1) & (b)(2); FDCA §§ 802(b)(1) & (b)(2).

authorization of a Tier 1 country, then the exporter can obtain a permit under section 801(e)(2).

2. Device Must Meet Requirements in 801(e)(1) and 802(f)

In order to qualify for export under section 802, the devices must meet the four requirements under section 801(e)(1) (see Section C). The devices also must meet the "basic requirements" under section 802(f):

- The device must be manufactured, processed, packaged, and held in "substantial conformity" with cGMP;
- Must not be adulterated (other than by lack of U.S. marketing approval);
- The product must have the quality that it purports or is represented to possess;
- The product may not be the subject of a notice by the Department of Health and Human Services that re-importation of the exported product would present an imminent hazard to the public health and safety of the United States, or to the receiving country;
- The product must be labeled in accordance with the requirements and conditions of use in the country which it received valid marketing authorization and the country to which it will be exported, and must be labeled in the language and units of measurement of the country of export; and
- The device must be promoted in accordance with its labeling requirements.

If the requirements of either section 801(e)(1) or 802(f) are not met, then the device may not be exported under section 802. However, the device may qualify for exportation under FDCA section 801(e)(2) (see Section F). Exporters are responsible for determining whether export is permitted under the FDCA, and whether their exports meet the requirements in section 802(f).

3. Firm Must Notify FDA When Export Begins

Exporting under section 802 does not require prior approval from the FDA. The exporter must notify FDA when the firm begins export.[58] The notification is called a "simple notification" to FDA. The notification must identify (1) the product's trade name; (2) type of device; (3) model

58. *See* 21 U.S.C. § 382(f); FDCA § 802(f).

number; and (4) country of export if it is not a Tier 1 country.[59] The notification may, but is not required to, identify the Listed Tier 1 Countries (or may state that the export is intended for a Listed Tier 1 Country, without identifying the Listed Country). Notification may be sent to FDA electronically or via standard mail.[60]

4. Firms Must Maintain Records of Export

Firms also must keep records of the devices exported and the countries to which they were exported.[61] These records must include (1) the product's trade name, (2) the type of device, (3) the product's model number, (4) the consignee's name and address, and (5) the date on which the product was exported and the quantity of product exported.[62] Export records must be maintained for the same period of time that required under the QSR.[63] Export records must be available to FDA upon request.[64]

5. Certificate of Exportability

Even though FDA does not require a firm to obtain written permission prior to export under section 802, a foreign purchaser may request proof of compliance with U.S. law prior to export. Upon request, FDA will provide a Certificate of Exportability (COE) to the exporter to facilitate export of a medical device.

F. Exporting Unapproved Class III and Certain Class II Devices under Section 801(e)(2)

Unapproved Class III devices, Class II devices that do not meet performance standards, investigational devices intended for a non-listed country, banned devices, and other devices that do not meet the criteria in section 802 may qualify for export under section 801(e)(2). Devices exported under section 801(e)(2) must obtain a receive an Export Permit Letter from the FDA.

Devices exported under section 801(e)(2):

- Must meet the four requirements under section 801(e)(1) of the FDCA (see Section C);

59. *Id.*; *see also* FDA Submitting Simple Notification webpage.
60. *Id.*
61. *See* 21 U.S.C. § 382(f); FDCA § 802(g).
62. *See* 21 C.F.R. § 1.101(e).
63. *Id.*
64. *Id.*

- Be subject to review by FDA and determination that the exportation of the device is not contrary to public health and safety; and
- Have approval of the country to which it is intended for export.

1. Export Permit Letter

FDA must conduct a review to determine that the exportation of the device is not contrary to public health and safety. If FDA determines export is not contrary to public health, it will issue an export permit letter.

Firms requesting an export permit letter must provide:

(i) a complete description of the device intended for export;

(ii) the status of the device in the U.S. (e.g., investigational, banned, unapproved);

(iii) a statement indicating that the requestor conducted a search of the Medical Literature Analysis and Retrieval System database and a summary of the search results, as well as a summary of safety data to demonstrate that export of the device will not endanger the public health and safety (or documentation of exemption from this requirement); and

(iv) a letter from the appropriate foreign liaison stating that the device is not in conflict with the laws of the export country, the foreign government has full knowledge of the status of the device in the U.S., and importing the device is permitted (or not objected to).[65]

A firm may be exempted from providing safety data when (1) the device has an FDA-approved Investigational Device Exemption and is intended for clinical trials in the importing country for the same intended use, or (2) the manufacturer has been informed by two Institutional Review Boards in the U.S. that the device is a nonsignificant risk device, and the device is intended for clinical trials in the importing country for the same intended use.

G. Exporting Unapproved Devices for Investigational Use

A manufacturer wanting to export an unapproved device for investigational use (e.g., for use in a clinical trial) may export the device under section 802(c) or 801(e)(2) of the FDCA, depending on the country of export.

---

65. *See* 21 U.S.C. §§ 381(e) & 382(f); FDCA § 801(e) & 802(f); *see also* FDA How to Request Export Certificates/Permits and Submitting Simple Notification webpage.

Under section 802(c), an investigational device may be exported to any of the Listed Tier 1 Countries (currently Australia, Canada, Israel, Japan, New Zealand, Switzerland, South Africa, or member countries of the European Economic Area (EEA)) without FDA authorization if the unapproved device is exported in accordance with the laws of the importing country. Devices exported under section 802(c) are not required to meet the requirements of the Investigational Device Exemption (IDE) regulation under 21 C.F.R. Part 812. The firm and the device also must meet the requirements of 801(e)(1) (see Section C) and section 802(f) (see Section E.2).

Export of an investigational device to any country *other* than a Listed Tier 1 Country requires authorization by FDA in the form of an Export Permit Letter. The device also must meet the criteria under section 801(e)(2) (see Section F).

H. Exporting Devices for Further Processing under Section 802(d)

Section 802(d) allows export of a device that is intended for packaging, labeling, or further processing in anticipation of market authorization in any Listed Tier 1 Country.[66] FDA has stated that "in anticipation of market authorization" requires the firm exporting the device to have filed an application or submission for marketing authorization in the Tier 1 Country.[67] The device may be exported, so long as the device is in accordance with the laws of the receiving country. FDA has indicated that activities that qualify as "further processing" are broad, but would not include mere storage of a device.[68]

The device and manufacturer also must comply with the "basic requirements" under section 802(f) (see Section E.2) and keep export records 802(g) (i.e., records of the devices exported and the countries to which they were exported).

I. Exporting Devices for Tropical and Other Diseases Not of Significant Prevalence under Section 802(e)

A device used in the diagnosis, prevention, or treatment of a tropical disease or another disease not of significant prevalence in the United States, and which does not otherwise qualify for export under section 802 of the FDCA, may be exported upon approval of an application. FDA may grant

66. *See* 21 U.S.C. § 382(d); FDCA § 802(d).

67. *Id.*

68. *See* Guidance for Industry: Exports Under the FDA Export Reform and Enhancement Act of 1996.

approval if it finds that the device will not expose patients in the receiving country to an unreasonable risk of illness or injury, and the probable benefit to health from the use of the device (under conditions of use prescribed, recommended, or suggested in the labeling or proposed labeling of the device) outweighs the risk of injury or illness from its use.[69]

Firms obtaining approval must comply with adverse event reporting requirements under section 802(e)(2).[70] The device and manufacturer must also comply with the basic requirements under section 802(f) (see Section E.2) and the recordkeeping requirements under section 802(g) (see Section E.4).

IV. Actions and Enforcement

A. Import Alerts for GMP Violations, Inspection Refusals

FDA conducts establishment inspections of foreign manufacturers that produce FDA-regulated articles intended for sale in the U.S. FDA inspects facilities for compliance with the GMP requirements in the Quality System regulation (QSR). FDA has taken enforcement action against companies that manufacture medical devices and do not comply with the QSR in the form of FDA Form 483s and warning letters. Violations of the QSR can form the basis for FDA issuing an import alert. An import alert can be for specific products or for specific facilities. FDA also may inspect multiple facilities of the same manufacturer and issue an import alert that covers more than one inspected facility.

In the drug context, FDA also has issued warning letters, and import alerts, for significant violations of data integrity principles. FDA has not been as active in issuing Warning Letters to medical device companies for violations of data integrity standards, but medical device companies should consider adding compliance with data integrity standards to their GMP/QSR compliance programs to avoid a potential import alert.

FDA also can issue an import alert for firms that refuse an inspection by FDA. A firm's refusal to permit inspection, or provide reasonable access to FDA inspectional personnel during an inspection can provide an appearance that the firm's products are manufactured, processed, or packed under insanitary conditions. Such products are deemed to be adulterated under the FDCA.

69. *See* 21 U.S.C. § 382(e); FDCA § 802(e)
70. *Id.*

CHAPTER 9

Fraud and Abuse Laws

Charlene Cho and Jennifer Michael

I. Introduction

In January 2020, ResMed Corporation, a manufacturer of durable medical equipment (DME), agreed to pay more than $37 million to resolve allegations that it had paid kickbacks in various forms, such as free patient outreach services and free or below cost diagnostic devices, to DME suppliers, sleep labs, and health care providers to induce the purchase of ResMed's products.[1]

In March 2019, Covidien,[2] a manufacturer of vein ablation devices, agreed to pay almost $18 million to settle allegations that it had unlawfully remunerated physicians by providing, among other things, free or discounted customized marketing plans and practice development support to induce the purchase of its ablation catheter, which was billed to Medicare and the California and Florida Medicaid programs.[3]

And in March 2018, Alere Inc., a manufacturer of devices used in the diagnosis of acute coronary syndrome and other serious conditions, agreed to pay over $33 million to resolve allegations that it had caused the

1. See https://www.justice.gov/opa/pr/resmed-corp-pay-united-states-375-million-allegedly-causing-false-claims-related-sale.

2. Covidien p.l.c. was acquired by Medtronic, Inc. in 2015 for $42.9 billion in cash and stock. See https://newsroom.medtronic.com/news-releases/news-release-details/medtronic-acquire-covidien-429-billion-cash-and-stock-0. See also https://investorrelations.medtronic.com/medtronic-covidien-transaction-information.

3. https://www.justice.gov/opa/pr/covidien-pay-over-17-million-united-states-allegedly-providing-illegal-remuneration-form.

submission of false claims to Medicare, Medicaid, and other federal health care programs by knowingly selling unreliable point-of-care products.[4]

These are but a few examples of how the federal government uses the Anti-Kickback Statute (AKS) and the False Claims Act (FCA) to prosecute medical device manufacturers for health care fraud and abuse.[5] Such efforts typically involve the Department of Justice (DOJ), the Department of Health and Human Services Office of the Inspector General (OIG), the Centers for Medicaid & Medicare (CMS) and U.S. Attorney's Offices, as well as state and local law enforcement partners. In certain instances, other federal agencies, such as the Federal Bureau of Investigation (FBI), the Internal Revenue Service (IRS), and the Department of Defense (DOD), also may provide investigative assistance.[6] Since 1986, the federal government has recovered more than $62 billion from False Claims Act settlements and judgements. And matters involving the health care industry constitute a significant proportion of these recoveries.[7]

In this chapter, we describe the legal framework for health care fraud and abuse. We also describe certain safe harbors that are particularly relevant to medical device manufacturers. We conclude by describing guidance that has been issued by the federal government about how a corporate compliance program may be weighed in the decision to prosecute a business organization and some steps that medical device manufacturers can take to reduce risks of engaging in health care fraud and abuse.

II. The False Claims Act

A. Brief History

The history of the False Claims Act (FCA)[8] dates back to the Civil War. Suppliers of goods to the Union Army were defrauding the federal

4. https://www.justice.gov/opa/pr/alere-pay-us-332-million-settle-false-claims-act-allegations-relating-unreliable-diagnostic.

5. The AKS and FCA are not the only statutes under which medical device manufacturers may be held liable for health care fraud and abuse. For example, the Food, Drug, and Cosmetic Act (FDCA) and the Physician Payments Sunshine Act (PPSA), also known as the Open Payments Program, have been used by federal regulators to prosecute medical device manufacturers.

6. See https://www.justice.gov/criminal-fraud/health-care-fraud-unit.

7. See https://www.justice.gov/civil/fraud-section.

8. The FCA is codified at 31 U.S.C. §§ 3729–3733 and at 18 U.S.C. § 287. The former covers the civil FCA, and the latter covers the criminal FCA. The focus of this chapter is on the civil FCA. In general, criminal liability requires the same elements as civil liability but unlike civil liability, criminal liability requires a showing

government in various ways, including by shipping sawdust instead of gunpowder, misrepresenting ships with rotting hulls as "new," and duplicating sales of the same cavalry mules.[9] Outraged that money intended to aid the war effort was being misappropriated, Congress sought to enact legislation to punish and prevent fraud against the government. The result was the FCA, also known as "Lincoln's Law," named eponymously after the president who signed it into law on March 2, 1863. Since then, the FCA has undergone a number of revisions and amendments.

B. Violative Conduct

Liability under FCA may attach for a variety of acts. All of the acts involve a claim for money or property made directly to the government or indirectly through an intermediary, such as a contractor, grantee or other recipient of federal funds.[10] The two most common scenarios are those involving the submission of a false claim[11] and the creation of false records or statements in support of a false claim.[12] A party also may be liable for failing to pay the government or improperly retaining the government's overpayment,[13] as well as withholding money or property from the government.[14] Making or delivering a false receipt of property used (or to be used) by the government[15] or buying property from a government officer or employee of the government who is not authorized to sell it[16] can also result in liability. Conspiring to commit a violation of any of the foregoing constitutes a violation of the FCA as well.[17]

---

of specific intent to defraud. *See* United States v. Maher, 582 F.2d 842, 847 (4th Cir. 1978), *cert. denied*, 439 U.S. 1115 (1979) ("Under § 287, the government must prove beyond a reasonable doubt that the defendant performed forbidden acts with a criminal intent. The prohibition of the statute is absolute in that the defendant's liberty is at stake. . . . The nature of the proceedings, the standards of proof, and the defendant's interests at stake are wholly different under these two statutes.").

9. https://scholarship.law.uc.edu/cgi/viewcontent.cgi?article=1153&context=uclr.
10. 31 U.S.C. § 3729(a).
11. *Id.* § 3729(a)(1)(A).
12. *Id.* § 3729(a)(1)(B).
13. *Id.* § 3729(a)(1)(G).
14. *Id.* § 3729(a)(1)(D).
15. *Id.* § 3729(a)(1)(E).
16. *Id.* § 3729(a)(1)(F).
17. *Id.* § 3729(a)(1)(C).

C. Elements of a FCA Violation

For liability to attach under the FCA, four elements must be satisfied. The first element is presentation of the claim. The FCA defines "claim" broadly. In general, it includes any action with the purpose or effect of inducing the government to pay money not lawfully due or to be deprived of money lawfully owed.[18] This broad definition of "claim" is consistent with the legislative history of the FCA, which makes clear that Congress intended for liability to attach even if the government does not pay the claim or otherwise suffer a loss.[19]

The second element is falsity of the claim. The FCA does not define falsity, but a definition has developed through case law. In general, a false or fraudulent claim is one that is "aimed at extracting money the government otherwise would not have paid."[20] Courts have examined falsity in two respects: factual and legal.[21] Factual falsity is observed, for example, when a party makes a reimbursement claim to the government with "an incorrect description of goods or services provided" or a description for "goods or services never provided."[22] By contrast, legal falsity occurs when a party misrepresents that it is "in compliance with a federal statute or regulation or prescribed contractual term."[23]

This misrepresentation can take two forms: express false certification and implied false certification. Each has been recognized as a valid theory of liability under the FCA.[24] For example, under the express false certification theory, a party that submits to the government a signed invoice misrepresenting that it has complied with some contractual, regulatory or statutory requirement explicitly stated on the face of the invoice

---

18. Under 31 U.S.C. § 3729(d), tax claims are specifically excluded from the FCA.

19. S. Rep. No. 345, 99th Cong., 2d Sess. 22 (July 28, 1986), reprinted in 1986 U.S.C.C.A.N. 5266, 5273.

20. *See* United States ex rel. Kester v. Novartis Pharm. Corp., 41 F. Supp. 3d 323, 328–29 (S.D.N.Y. 2014) (quoting Mikes v. Straus, 274 F.3d 687 (2d. Cir. 2001)).

21. *See* United States ex rel. Wilkins v. United Health Grp., Inc., 659 F.3d 295, 305 (3d. Cir. 2011) ("There are two categories of false claims under the FCA: a factually false claim and a legally false claim.").

22. *See* United States ex rel. Forcier v. Computer Scis. Corp., 2017 WL 3616665, at *7 (S.D.N.Y. Aug. 10, 2017).

23. *See* Mikes v. Straus, 274 F.3d 687, 696 (2d. Cir. 2001).

24. *See* United States ex rel. Connor v. Salina Reg'l Health Ctr., Inc., 543 F.3d 1211, 1217 (10th Cir. 2008) ("... legally false certification claims can rest [on] one of two theories—express false certification, and implied false certification.").

would be liable under the FCA.[25] Under the implied false certification theory, however, a party's statement, signature or other express act is not the basis of liability. Instead, it is "the underlying contracts, statutes or regulations themselves" that determine whether "compliance is a prerequisite to the government's payment."[26]

In June 2016, the Supreme Court addressed the split among circuit courts about whether the implied false certification could give rise to liability under the FCA and held "that the implied certification theory can be a basis for liability, *at least where two conditions are satisfied:* first, the claim does not merely request payment, but also makes *specific representations* about the goods or services provided; and second, the defendant's failure to disclose noncompliance with material statutory, regulatory, or contractual requirements makes those representations misleading half-truths."[27]

The third element is knowledge of the falsity. For liability to attach under the FCA, a party must act "knowingly."[28] This scienter requirement is satisfied when the party either (1) has actual knowledge of the [falsity]; (2) acts in deliberate ignorance of the truth or falsity of the information; or (3) acts in reckless disregard of the truth or falsity of the information.[29] No specific intent to defraud is required.[30] But the lack of a specific intent requirement is not to be construed as a means for FCA liability to attach to "innocent mistakes or simple negligence."[31] Instead, the scienter requirement for civil FCA liability is "designed to address the problem of

---

25. See United States ex rel. Hobbs v. MedQuest Assocs., Inc., 711 F.3d 707, 714 (6th Cir. 2013) ("In an express false certification, the defendant is alleged to have signed or otherwise certified to compliance with some law or regulation on the face of the claim submitted.").

26. See United States ex rel. Siewick v. Jamieson Sci. & Eng'g., Inc., 214 F.3d 1372, 1376 (D.C. Cir. 2000). *See also* Mikes v. Straus, 274 F.3d 687, 699 (2d. Cir. 2001) (An implied certification claim is "based on the notion that *the act of submitting a claim for reimbursement itself implies compliance* with governing federal rules that are a precondition to payment.") (emphasis added).

27. *See Universal Health Services v. United States ex rel. Escobar,* 136 S. Ct. 1989, 2001 (2016).

28. 31 U.S.C. § 3729(b)(1).

29. *Id.* § 3729(b)(1)(A)(i)–(iii).

30. *Id.* § 3729(b)(1)(B). By contrast, specific intent to defraud is required for criminal liability to attach under the criminal FCA, which is codified at 18 U.S.C. § 287.

31. *See* United States ex rel. Phalp v. Lincare Holdings, Inc., 857 F.3d 1148, 1155 (11th Cir. 2017).

the 'ostrich-like' refusal to learn of information which an individual, in the exercise of prudent judgment, had reason to know."[32]

And the fourth element is materiality. For liability to attach under the FCA, the false record or statement must be material. The FCA defines material as "having a natural tendency to influence, or be capable of influencing, the payment or receipt of money or property."[33]

Materiality is a complex issue, and circuits have grappled with whether it is a question of fact or question of law.[34] In 2016, the Supreme Court explained that whether or not something is material for purposes of triggering liability under the FCA is a fact-specific inquiry, and to the extent that a particular statutory, regulatory, or contractual requirement is labeled by the government as a condition of payment, it is "relevant but not automatically dispositive." In support, the Court noted that the materiality inquiry would include (but not be limited to) proof that ". . . the Government consistently refuses to pay claims in the mine run of cases based on noncompliance with the particular statutory, regulatory, or contractual requirement."[35]

Conversely, if the government pays a particular claim in full despite actual knowledge that certain requirements were not met, that "is very strong evidence that those requirements are not material."[36] Accordingly, the Court rejected the contention that "any statutory, regulatory, or contractual violation is material so long as the defendant knows that the Government would be entitled to refuse payment were it aware of the violation."[37] In short, the Court held that that "[t]he materiality standard is demanding,"[38] and "looks to the effect on the likely or actual behavior of the recipient of the alleged misrepresentation."[39]

---

32. *See* Horn & Assoc., Inc., v. United States, 123 Fed. Cl. 728, 763 (2015). *See also* United States ex rel. Harper v. Muskingum Watershed Conservancy Dist., 842 F.3d 430, 437 (6th Cir. 2016) ("unless the circumstances of a case show that a defendant knows of, or 'acts in deliberate ignorance' or 'reckless disregard' of, the fact that he is involved in conduct that violates [the FCA], the defendant cannot be held liable").

33. 31 U.S.C. § 3729(b)(4).

34. The 10th Circuit has noted that materiality is a "mixed question of law and fact." *See* United States v. Williams, 865 F.3d 1302, 1310 (10th Cir. 2017) (citing United States v. Schulte, 741 F.3d 1141, 1154 (10th Cir. 2014)).

35. *Id.*

36. *See Universal Health Services v. United States ex rel. Escobar,* 136 S. Ct. 1989, 2003–04 (2016).

37. *See id. at* 2003–04.

38. *See id.* at 2003.

39. *See id. at* 2002.

D. Damages and Penalties

In 1863, when the FCA was first signed into law, a guilty party was liable for double the damages sustained by the government, as well as $2,000 per false claim, forfeiture, and up to five years' imprisonment.[40] Since then, various amendments to the FCA have been passed, and the current provisions provide for mandatory treble damages[41] and, for each false claim, a mandatory minimum of $11,665 and a mandatory maximum of $23,331.[42] A guilty party also is liable for the government's costs of bringing a civil action to recover penalties and damages.[43]

E. The Whistleblower Provision

The whistleblower provision, formally known as the *qui tam* provision,[44] allows any person to bring an action to recover damages on behalf of the United States.[45] Such persons are known as relators and typically are employees or contractors of the defendant. To file suit, a relator need not have suffered an injury from the conduct in question. However, the relator must be represented by counsel.[46] As articulated by the *Bowens* Court, "[A] private party seeking to litigate FCA claims is not entitled to proceed *pro se* because that party is not litigating his or her own interest, but rather, the interest of the government."[47]

---

40. Section 3, Act of Mar 2, 1863, 12 Stat. 696 at 898.

41. 31 U.S.C. § 3729(a)(2). The mandatory treble damages may be reduced to mandatory double damages if the liable party self-discloses the fraudulent activity. At the time of self-disclosure, the liable party must not be the subject of an administrative action, civil action, or criminal prosecution relating to the FCA violation and be able to show that it did not have actual knowledge of the government's investigation of the FCA violation. Additionally, the liable party must fully cooperate with the government's investigation, including, within 30 days of learning about the FCA violation, providing the government with all pertinent information.

42. 31 U.S.C. § 3729(a)(1); 28 C.F.R. § 85.5. *See* Civil Monetary Penalties Inflation Adjustment, 85 Fed. Reg. 37004 (June 19, 2020).

43. 31 U.S.C. § 3729(a)(3).

44. The term *qui tam* derives from a longer Latin phrase that essentially means "he who prosecutes for himself as well as for the King." The concept was recognized under English common law, and a *qui tam* provision was provided under the original FCA enacted in 1863. See page 1 at https://fas.org/sgp/crs/misc/R40785.pdf.

45. Section 4, Act of Mar 2, 1863, 12 Stat. 696 at 898.

46. *Tavares v. Rhode Island Super. Ct.*, 2019 WL 2269225, at *2 (D.R.I. May 28, 2019); *McGhee v. Light*, 2019 WL 2122893, at *2 (S.D. Ohio May 15, 2019); *Bowens v. Correctional Assn. of New York*, 2019 WL 1586857, at *5 (E.D.N.Y. Apr. 12, 2019).

47. *Bowens*, 2019 WL 1586857 at *5, citing *United States ex rel. Mergent Services v. Flaherty*, 540 F.3d 89, 93 (2d Cir. 2008).

A relator must file his complaint under seal[48] and provide the government with a copy of the complaint, as well as substantially all material evidence and information related to the complaint.[49] The complaint remains under seal for at least 60 days and within that time period, the government must investigate the relator's complaint.[50] It is not uncommon for the government to seek an extension of the 60 days, which the court may grant for good cause shown.[51]

One of the most powerful tools that the government has at its disposal for an investigation is the civil investigative demand (CID), which is explicitly provided for under the FCA.[52] CIDs permit the government to issue interrogatories, conduct depositions and request documents and require neither unsealing of the relator's complaint or formal service of the complaint on the defendant.[53]

Following its investigation, the government must decide whether or not to intervene in one or more counts of the pending *qui tam* action.[54] If the government chooses to intervene, it will assume primary responsibility for litigating the case.[55] Alternatively, if the government declines to intervene, the relator may choose to litigate the case on behalf of the government, but the government will not be a party to the proceedings apart from receiving pleadings and its right to any recovery. A third option is that the government may move to dismiss the relator's complaint, either due to a lack of factual support for a FCA violation or because the case conflicts with significant statutory interests or government policies.[56] This third option, however, requires that the relator be provided an opportunity for a hearing on the government's motion to dismiss.[57]

Relators have a strong incentive to file *qui tam* actions. If they prevail, relators may collect a significant percentage of any judgment or settlement. For example, if the government elects to intervene, the relator may collect between 15 percent and 25 percent, depending on to the

48. The defendant is not served or otherwise formally notified of the complaint while the complaint is under seal.

49. 31 U.S.C. § 3730(b)(2).

50. *Id.*

51. *Id.* § 3730(b)(3).

52. *Id.* § 3733.

53. *Id.* § 3733(a)(1).

54. *Id.* § 3730(b)(2).

55. The relator remains a party to the case, but the relator's participation in the case is at the government's discretion.

56. See https://www.justice.gov/sites/default/files/usao-edpa/legacy/2012/06/13/InternetWhistleblower%20update.pdf.

57. 31 U.S.C. § 3730(c)(2)(a).

extent to which the relator and his or her counsel contributed to the prosecution of the *qui tam* action.[58] If the government declines to intervene, a relator may collect between 25 percent and 30 percent, subject to what the court deems reasonable.[59] Moreover, regardless of whether the government intervenes, a relator who prevails also is entitled to reasonable expenses, attorneys' fees and costs.[60]

In certain instances, the court may reduce the relator's recovery. For example, if the relator planned or initiated the violative conduct at issue, the court may reduce the relator's percentage of the judgment or settlement.[61] In addition, if the relator's conduct in planning or initiating the FCA violation resulted in a criminal conviction, the relator would not be entitled to any proceeds and his or her *qui tam* action would be dismissed.[62]

Other circumstances may give rise to dismissal of a *qui tam* action or preclude the filing altogether. For example, if another relator has already filed a *qui tam* action based on the same underlying facts, a duplicate *qui tam* may not be filed, or if filed, may be dismissed.[63] Similarly, if the government is a party to a civil suit or an administrative civil money penalty (CMP) proceeding based on the same underlying facts, a relator's *qui tam* action may preclude filing or be dismissed.[64]

Interestingly, in January 2018, Michael Granston, the Director of the Fraud Section in DOJ's Commercial Litigation Branch issued a memorandum (the "Granston Memo") describing the non-exhaustive factors that prosecutors should consider in deciding whether to move for dismissal of a declined *qui tam* action. These factors include (1) "curbing meritless cases"; (2) "preventing parasitic or opportunistic" cases providing "duplicative information already known to the government"; (3) "preventing interference with agency policies and programs"; (4) controlling litigation to "avoid the risk of unfavorable precedent"; (5) "safeguarding classified information and national security interests"; (6) "preserving government resources" "when the government's expected costs are likely

58. *Id.* § 3730(d)(1).
59. *Id.* § 3730(d)(2).
60. *Id.* § 3730(d)(1)–(2).
61. *Id.* § 3730(d)(3).
62. *Id.* § 3730(d)(3).
63. *Id.* § 3730(b)(5).
64. *Id.* § 3730(e)(3).

to exceed any expected gains"; and (7) addressing "egregious procedural errors" by relators.[65]

III. The Anti-Kickback Statute

A. Legislative History

In 1935, Congress enacted the Social Security Act (SSA) to provide a federal safety net for the elderly, disabled, and unemployed.[66] Thirty years later, Congress established the Medicare and Medicaid programs under the 1965 amendments to the SSA to assist the elderly and low-income families access health care.[67] Not long thereafter, it became clear that due to their reimbursement structure (e.g., fee-for-service model), Medicare and Medicaid created incentives for overutilization.[68] Seeking to contain costs as well as address the potential for fraud and abuse,[69] Congress passed the Anti-Kickback Statute (AKS) as part of the 1972 amendments to the SSA.[70]

Under the 1972 provisions, the AKS made it a misdemeanor to solicit, offer, or accept kickbacks, bribes, or rebates in exchange for patient referrals under the Medicaid or Medicare programs. No specific intent was required (i.e., violators were strictly liable), and a conviction could result in a fine of up to $10,000, not more than one year of imprisonment, or both.[71]

To be clear, prior to 1972, prosecutors could avail themselves of a penalty provision in the SSA to take action against those committing fraud and abuse. But it related to the making of false statements or misrepresentations of material fact and imposed a fine of no greater than $1,000, up to one year of imprisonment, or both.[72] But the limited and narrow

65. https://www.insidethefca.com/wp-content/uploads/sites/300/2018/12/Granston-Memo.pdf.

66. https://www.ssa.gov/history/35act.html.

67. https://www.ourdocuments.gov/doc.php?flash=false&doc=99#.

68. *See* Tamsen D. Love, *Toward a Fair and Practical Definition of "Willfully" in the Medicare/Medicaid Anti-Kickback Statute*, 50 Vand. L. Rev. 1029, 1034 (2019).

69. *See* H.R. Rep. No. 231, 92d Cong., 2d Sess., reprinted in 1972 U.S.C.C.A.N. 4989, 5093. The legislative history shows that Congress was concerned about "certain practices which have long been regarded by professional organizations as unethical, as well as unlawful in some jurisdictions, and which contribute appreciably to the cost of the Medicare and Medicaid programs."

70. Social Security Amendments of 1972, Pub. L. No. 92-603, 86 Stat. 1329, 1419, codified as amended at 42 U.S.C. §§ 1720a–1776.

71. 42 U.S.C. § 1307(a) (1982).

72. *Id.* § 1307(a). The 1972 language is equivalent to the current language.

nature of the SSA's penalty was ineffective at encouraging compliance and generally impeded efforts to prosecute those committing fraud and abuse in the Medicare and Medicaid programs.[73]

Recognizing that the punitive power of the 1972 AKS was wanting and aware of increasing fraud in the Medicare and Medicaid programs,[74] Congress sought to amend the AKS with the goal of empowering the government to prosecute and punish perpetrators.[75] In 1977, Congress broadened the scope of the AKS to include "any remuneration," directly or indirectly, overtly or covertly, in cash or in kind. The penalty for non-compliance also was elevated to a felony, with a fine of up to $25,000, up to five years imprisonment, or both. Additionally, Congress mandated the exclusion of guilty parties from participating in Medicare and Medicaid.[76]

In 1980, Congress again amended[77] the AKS in response to concerns that, in the absence of a mens rea element, the statute could be used to unfairly impose criminal penalties on parties who had inadvertently engaged in improper conduct.[78] In response, Congress required that prosecutors show that violative conduct was committed "knowingly and willfully."[79]

In 1981, Congress passed legislation[80] to address cases that the DOJ had declined to pursue but which nevertheless involved fraudulent practices in the Medicare and Medicaid programs.[81] The Department of Health and Human Services (HHS) was now authorized to administratively

73. Even with the possibility of invoking federal statutes prohibiting mail fraud (18 U.S.C. § 1341) and conspiracies to defraud the government (18 U.S.C. § 371), the government had to overcome the burden of proving, beyond a reasonable doubt, that the perpetrators committed fraud "knowingly" and/or "willingly."

74. See H.R. Rep. No. 393, 95th Cong., 1st Sess., reprinted in 1977 U.S.C.C.A.N. 3039, 3047, 3055.

75. Medicare and Medicaid Anti-Fraud and Abuse Amendments of 1977, Pub. L. No. 95-142 § 4, 91 Stat. 1175 (1977).

76. 42 U.S.C. § 1320(a)-7b(b).

77. Omnibus Reconciliation Act of 1980, Pub. L. No. 96-499, 94 Stat. 2599 (1980).

78. See H.R. Rep. No. 1167, 96th Cong., 2d Sess., reprinted in 1980 U.S.C.C.A.N. 5526, 5572.

79. Sec. 917, *supra* note 20.

80. Omnibus Reconciliation Act of 1981, Pub. L. No. 97-35, 95 Stat. 357 (1981).

81. *See* Richard P. Kusserow, *Civil Money Penalty Law of 1981: A New Effort to Confront Fraud and Abuse in Federal Health Care Programs*, 58 Notre Dame L. Rev. 985, 989 (1983).

impose civil monetary penalties (CMPs),[82] assessments,[83] and exclusions against those who submitted improper claims to Medicare or Medicaid for payment.[84]

In 1987, in light of concerns about persistent fraudulent activity in the Medicare and Medicaid programs[85] and complaints from health care providers that the AKS was so broad that it subjected to criminal prosecution "many innocuous, or even beneficial, commercial arrangements" used to deliver health care,[86] Congress amended the AKS once again.[87] Among the provisions was one that mandated that HHS promulgate regulations, also known as "safe harbors," designating certain payment practices and business arrangements as exempt from criminal prosecution.[88]

In 1996, the AKS was further amended through passage of the Health Insurance Portability and Accountability Act (HIPAA).[89] In recognition of the need for transparency between the OIG and the public, Congress included provisions[90] about soliciting proposals from the public about new safe harbors, issuing fraud alerts about improper conduct, and establishing a procedure for Advisory Opinions.[91]

---

82. Sec. 2105, *supra* note 23. For each claim, item, or service that the person knew (or had reason to know) was false or otherwise improper, HHS could impose a penalty of $2,000.

83. *Id.* HHS was authorized to assess up to twice the amount claimed against any person who presented (or caused to be presented) an improper claim for reimbursement against Medicare or Medicaid.

84. The term "improper claims" included claims (1) for an item or service that was not provided as claimed; (2) from an excluded individual or entity for items or services furnished during a period of exclusion; (3) that exceeded statutory standards; or (4) for payment that violated the permissible charges in either a Medicare assignment or an agreement with a state's Medicaid agency. Kusserow, *supra* note 79.

85. "[T]his bill will fight fraud and abuse in Medicare, Medicaid, Maternal and Child Health, and Social Service programs under the Social Security Act." The Medicare and Medicaid Patient Protection Act of 1987. 133 Cong. Rec. S20,923 (daily ed. July 23, 1987) (statement of Sen. Packwood).

86. Medicare and State Health Care Programs; Fraud and Abuse; OIG Anti-Kickback Provisions, 56 Fed. Reg. 35,952 (July 29, 1991).

87. Medicare and Medicaid Patient and Program Protection Act of 1987, Pub. L. No. 100-93, 101 Stat. 680 (1987).

88. Medicare and Medicaid Patient and Program Protection Act of 1987, Pub. L. No. 100-93, § 14(a), 101 Stat. 680, 697 (1987).

89. Health Insurance Portability and Accountability Act of 1996, Pub. L. No. 104-191, 110 Stat. 1999 (1996).

90. Health Insurance Portability and Accountability Act of 1996, Pub. L. No. 104-191, 110 Stat. 1999, §§ 205, 216, (1996).

91. Advisory Opinions (AOs) are legal opinions from OIG about the applicability of certain fraud and abuse laws to an existing or proposed commercial arrangement.

In 1997, Congress passed legislation[92] that vested HHS with the authority to impose CMPs specifically for violations of the AKS, a criminal statute. For any violations committed after August 5, 1997, and upon a showing of a mere preponderance of the evidence,[93] HHS could impose a civil fine of $50,000 for each act prohibited under the AKS and damages of up to three times the amount paid or received, irrespective of whether any portion of the payment was for a legitimate reason.[94]

In 2010, with passage of the Patient Protection and Affordable Care Act (PPACA),[95] Congress explicitly acknowledged that a violation of the AKS could constitute a *per se* violation of the FCA. Relying on the provision that "a claim that includes items or services resulting from a violation of [the AKS] constitutes a false or fraudulent claim for purposes of [the FCA],"[96] cases were filed to capitalize on the assumption that an AKS violation is a FCA violation. But courts have rejected that assumption as flawed. For example, the Third Circuit recently held that to prevail in an AKS-predicated FCA case, the government (or relator) must show that an AKS violation (e.g., a patient referral induced by a kickback) directly resulted in a violation of the FCA (e.g., submission of a false reimbursement claim for that patient). Absent such a causal link, the government (or relator) could not prevail.[97]

In 2018, partly in response to claims that "providers that engage in health care fraud may consider the civil penalties and criminal fines a cost of doing business,"[98] Congress amended the AKS once again by increasing the criminal fine from $25,000 to $100,000 and the maximum prison sentence from five years to ten years for a felony conviction. In

---

General guidance from OIG about AOs may be found here: https://oig.hhs.gov/compliance/advisory-opinions/index.asp.

92. Balanced Budget Act of 1997, Pub. L. No. 105-33, 111 Stat. 383 (1997).

93. By contrast, the standard of proof for conviction under a criminal statute is "beyond a reasonable doubt." John Kaplan, Robert Weisberg & Guyora Binder, Criminal Law: Cases and Materials § 2 (5th ed. 2004).

94. Balanced Budget Act of 1997, Pub. L. No. 105-33, 111 Stat. 383, §4304(b) (1997); 42 U.S.C. § 1320a-7a(b).

95. Patient Protection and Affordable Care Act of 2010, Pub. L. No. 111-148, 124 Stat. 119 (2010).

96. 42 U.S.C. § 1320a-7b(g).

97. *See* United States ex rel. Greenfield v. Medco Health Solutions, Inc., 880 F.3d 89 (3d Cir. 2018).

98. See H.R. Rep. No. 115-448, Part 1, at 2 (1997).

addition, the maximum CMP amounts that OIG could assess for violating the AKS doubled from $50,000 to $100,000.[99]

B. Violative Conduct

Liability under the AKS attaches to any party that knowingly and willfully offers, pays, seeks or accepts remuneration to induce or reward referrals of items or services reimbursable by a federal health care program.[100] The AKS is a broad statute, and its prohibitions apply to both the party that makes the payment and the party that receives it. The premise of the AKS is relatively simple: The government is concerned that kickbacks may result in the corruption of medical judgment, overutilization of products and services, increased costs to the federal health care programs and beneficiaries, and unfair competition.[101] Violations need not be egregious to run afoul of the AKS, and even common industry practices can constitute AKS violations. For example, medical device companies often find it necessary or advisable to enter into medical directorships with physicians. Many such compensation arrangements are legitimate and represent fair market value compensation for bona fide services the physicians actually provide. However, OIG has warned that such compensation arrangements may violate the AKS if even one purpose of the arrangement is to compensate a physician for his or her past or future referrals of federally reimbursable business.[102]

C. Elements of an AKS Violation

For liability to attach under the AKS, four elements must be satisfied. First, a person must have offered, paid, solicited or received remuneration. Remuneration is broadly defined, and includes not only kickbacks, bribes and rebates, but also "free rent, expensive hotel stays and meals, and excessive compensation for medical directorships or consultancies."[103] The idea that "remuneration" should be interpreted to cover "anything of value in any form or manner whatsoever"[104] is supported by the legis-

99. Bipartisan Budget Act of 2018, Pub. L. No. 115-123, 132 Stat. 220, § 50412 (2018).

100. 42 U.S.C. § 1320a-7b.

101. *See, e.g.*, OIG Special Fraud Alert: Laboratory Payments to Referring Physicians (June 25, 2014).

102. See *OIG Fraud Alert: Physician Compensation Arrangements May Result in Significant Liability* (June 9, 2015), *available at* https://oig.hhs.gov/compliance/alerts/guidance/Fraud_Alert_Physician_Compensation_06092015.pdf.

103. *See* https://oig.hhs.gov/compliance/physician-education/01laws.asp.

104. 56 Fed. Reg. 35952, 35958 (July 29, 1991).

lative history of and rulemaking under the AKS.[105] Examples of allegedly unlawful remuneration provided by medical device manufacturers include free telephone call center services and other free patient outreach services and interest-free loans provided to DME suppliers, sleep labs, and other health care providers, as described in the ResMed settlement, and free or discounted practice development and market development support provided to physicians, as alleged in the Covidien settlement.

As noted previously, because the AKS applies to offers, payments, solicitations, and receipt of remuneration, both the party seeking or accepting the remuneration,[106] and the party offering or paying the remuneration are subject to liability under the AKS.[107] The conduct of either party need not be obvious, as the language of the AKS explicitly states that the act of soliciting, offering, paying, or receiving remuneration may occur "directly or indirectly" or "overtly or covertly."[108]

Second, the remuneration must be paid to induce or reward patient referrals or the generation of business. The AKS has been interpreted to apply to any arrangement if one purpose of the remuneration was to persuade a party to recommend, purchase, or order (or arrange for the purchasing or ordering of) a federally reimbursable good or service.[109]

Defendants in AKS cases have argued that, if a portion of the remuneration is for a legitimate purpose (e.g., the compensation is for a medically necessary service or good), then the remuneration is not prohibited under the AKS. This "cleansing effect" contention has been rejected by a number of courts.[110] For example, in *United States v. Borrasi*,[111] the Seventh Circuit declined to adopt the position that "only the primary motivation of remuneration is to be considered," noting instead that, "'the statute [is] violated, even if the payments were also intended to compensate for professional services.'"[112]

---

105. "[T]he substance rather than simply the form of a transaction should be controlling" (123 Cong. Rec. 30,280 (1977), Statement of Chairman of the House Committee on Ways and Means and principal author of H.R. 3, Representative Rostenkowski). *Also see* H.R. Rep. No. 393, 95th Cong., 1st Sess., reprinted in 1977 U.S.C.C.A.N. 3058.

106. 42 U.S.C. § 1320a-7b(b)(1).

107. *Id.* § 1320a-7b(b)(2).

108. *Id.* § 1320a-7b(b)(1) and (2).

109. United States v. Greber, 760 F.2d 68 (3d Cir. 1985).

110. *See* United States v. Davis, 132 F.3d 1092, 1094 (5th Cir. 1998); United States v. Kats, 871 F.2d 105, 108 (9th Cir. 1989); and United States v. McClatchey, 217 F.3d 823, 835 (10th Cir. 2000).

111. 639 F.3d 774 (7th Cir. 2011).

112. *Id.* at 783.

Third, the business generated must involve items or services that are payable, in whole or in part, by a federal health care program. In general, any good, service, facility or item that is covered, in whole or in part, by a federal health care program, including but not limited to Medicaid, Medicare, and TRICARE (formerly CHAMPUS), is subject to the AKS. Although the AKS applies only to federally reimbursable items or services, arrangements that attempt to "carve-out" federal health care business may nonetheless implicate the AKS if the remuneration exchanged for the commercial business is intended to induce or reward the referral of federally reimbursable business.[113]

Finally, the conduct must be knowing and willful, which speaks to the scienter, or intent, of the party (or parties) that may be liable. Historically, courts took different approaches to interpreting the AKS's "knowingly and willfully" standard. For example, the court in *Hanlester Network v. Shalala*[114] held that, for conduct to be knowing and willful under the AKS, the prosecution must show that the party (or parties) had knowledge that the AKS prohibits offering or paying remuneration to induce referrals and that the parties acted with the specific intent to violate the law. However, in *United States v. Starks*, the court held that the AKS's "knowingly and willfully" standard requires only that the defendant knew that they were acting unlawfully.[115] In 2010, with the passage of the PPACA, Congress clarified that a person need not have actual knowledge of the AKS or the specific intent to violate the AKS to commit a violation of the AKS.[116]

D. Safe Harbors

Because the AKS is so broad in nature, it may have implications for conduct that is beneficial for patients and presents a low risk of fraud and abuse. In recognition of the reach of the AKS, OIG has exempted certain

---

113. *See, e.g.,* OIG Advisory Opinion No. 06-02 (Mar. 21, 2006) (stating, "[t]he 'carve out' of Federal business is not dispositive, however, on the question of whether the proposed program potentially violates the anti-kickback statute. The OIG has a long-standing concern about arrangements pursuant to which parties 'carve out' referrals of Federal health care beneficiaries or business generated by Federal health care programs from otherwise questionable financial arrangements. Such arrangements may violate the anti-kickback statute by disguising remuneration for Federal referrals through the payment of amounts purportedly related to non-Federal business.").

114. 51 F.3d 1390, 1400 (9th Cir. 1995).

115. 157 F.3d 833 (11th Cir. 1998).

116. 42 U.S.C. § 1320a-7b(h) ("[a] person need not have actual knowledge of [the AKS] or specific intent to commit a violation of [the AKS]").

types of arrangements from liability under the AKS.[117] Known as "safe harbors," these exemptions are codified in regulations and describe practices that are not subject to prosecution under the AKS because they are unlikely to result in fraud or abuse. An important caveat, however, is that safe harbor protection is available only to those arrangements that satisfy *all* of the conditions set forth in the safe harbor. Safe harbors are affirmative defenses; persons or entities that satisfy all of the safe harbor's conditions will not be prosecuted or sanctioned for the arrangement that qualifies for safe harbor protection.[118] Some of the most relevant AKS safe harbors[119] to medical device manufacturers are the following:

- Equipment Rental[120]
- Personal Services and Management Contracts[121]
- Warranties[122]
- Employees[123]
- Group Purchasing Organizations (GPOs)[124]
- Ambulatory Surgical Centers[125]

An arrangement that does not squarely satisfy all of a safe harbor's requirements is not necessarily unlawful under the AKS. As explained by OIG in the preamble to the 1991 Final Rule promulgating the original safe harbor provisions:

> This (safe harbor) regulation does not expand the scope of activities that the statute prohibits. The statute itself describes the scope of illegal activities. The legality of a particular business arrangement must be determined by comparing the particular facts to the proscriptions of the statute.
>
> The failure to comply with a safe harbor can mean one of three things. First * * * it may mean that the arrangement does not fall within the ambit of the statute. In other words, the arrangement is not intended to induce the referral of business

117. Medicare and Medicaid Patient and Program Protection Act of 1987, Pub. L. No. 100-93, § 14(a), 101 Stat. 680, 697 (1987).
118. 42 U.S.C. § 1320a-7b(b)(3); 42 C.F.R. § 1001.952.
119. https://oig.hhs.gov/compliance/provider-compliance-training/files/listofakssafeharbors508.pdf.
120. 42 C.F.R. § 1001.952(c).
121. *Id.* § 1001.952(d).
122. *Id.* § 1001.952(g).
123. *Id.* § 1001.952(i).
124. *Id.* § 1001.952(j).
125. *Id.* § 1001.952(r).

> reimbursable under (a Federal health care program); so there is no reason to comply with the safe harbor standards, and no risk of prosecution.
>
> Second, at the other end of the spectrum, the arrangement could be a clear statutory violation and also not qualify for safe harbor protection. In that case, assuming the arrangement is obviously abusive, prosecution would be very likely.
>
> Third, the arrangement may violate the statute in a less serious manner, although not be in compliance with a safe harbor provision. Here there is no way to predict the degree of risk. Rather, the degree of risk depends on an evaluation of the many factors which are part of the decision-making process regarding case selection for investigation and prosecution. Certainly, in many (but not necessarily all) instances, prosecutorial discretion would be exercised not to pursue cases where the participants appear to have acted in a genuine good-faith attempt to comply with the terms of a safe harbor, but for reasons beyond their control are not in compliance with the terms of the safe harbor. In other instances, there may not even be an applicable safe harbor, but the arrangement may appear innocuous. But in other instances, we will want to take appropriate action. . . .[126]

In cases where an arrangement implicates the AKS but does not satisfy a safe harbor's requirements, the government reviews the arrangement's facts and circumstances to determine the level of risk it poses to the federal health care programs and program beneficiaries. As evidenced by the numerous favorable Advisory Opinions OIG has issued over the years,[127] the government may find that an arrangement that does not satisfy all of a safe harbor's requirements nonetheless poses a low risk of fraud and abuse.

126. 56 Fed. Reg. 35952, 35954 (July 29, 1991).

127. An Advisory Opinion is a legal opinion issued by OIG to a particular party about the application of OIG's fraud and abuse authorities to an existing or proposed arrangement. Advisory Opinions are legally binding only on OIG and the requesting parties and may not be relied upon by others. However, Advisory Opinions provide valuable insights into OIG's interpretation to the AKS. Examples of favorable Advisory Opinions include Advisory Opinion No. 15-10 (regarding a hospital system's proposed employee lease and management service); Advisory Opinion No. 16-10 (regarding a public agency's proposed transportation program); and Advisory Opinion No. 18-10 (regarding a surgical device and wound care manufacturer's proposed warranty program).

In December 2020, OIG published a Final Rule establishing new and modifying existing safe harbors under the AKS to protect certain value-based arrangements (VBAs) and outcomes-based payment arrangements.[128] These new and modified safe harbors are designed to encourage innovative arrangements that parties reasonably anticipate will improve quality and health outcomes and produce health system efficiencies. However, OIG precluded significant segments of the health care and life sciences industry, including medical device manufacturers, from receiving protection under the VBA and outcomes-based payment arrangements safe harbors, with one exception. That exception provides a pathway for protection for certain "digital health technology" arrangements involving "limited technology participants" that are otherwise ineligible to use the value-based safe harbors.

OIG recognized that medical device manufacturers can play an important role in some VBAs, and that digital health technologies such as remote patient monitoring hold great promise for improving the coordination and management of patient care.[129] The new safe harbor for "care coordination arrangements to improve quality, health outcomes, and efficiency"[130] protects digital health technology that a medical device manufacturer provides to another person or entity if the arrangement satisfies all of the safe harbor's conditions. Those conditions include that the digital health technology must be used predominately to engage in specific "value-based activities" that are directly connected to the coordination and management of care of a defined target patient population, and that the parties to the arrangement monitor the arrangement's outcomes. A second new safe harbor for "arrangements for patient engagement and support to improve quality, health outcomes, and efficiency"[131] protects digital health technology that a medical device manufacturer furnishes directly to a patient when the patient's health care professional recommends the device for the patient and all of the other safe harbor's conditions are satisfied. This safe harbor limits the aggregate retail value of remuneration an entity may provide to a patient to $500.

In addition to promulgating new safe harbors in its Final Rule, OIG modified the existing safe harbor for warranties[132] to protect warranties

128. *See* OIG, "Medicare and State Health Care Programs: Fraud and Abuse; Revisions to Safe Harbors Under the Anti-Kickback Statute, and Civil Monetary Penalty Rules Regarding Beneficiary Inducements," 85 Fed. Reg. 77684 (Dec. 2, 2020).

129. *Id.* at 77711-12.

130. 42 C.F.R. § 1001.952(ee).

131. *Id.* § 1001.952(gg).

132. *Id.* § 1001.952(g).

for bundles of items, as well as warranties for one or more items and related services. To be protected, the items and services that are the subject of the warranty must be reimbursed by the same federal health care program and in the same federal health care program payment.[133] OIG acknowledged that this requirement would preclude safe harbor protection for "population-based warranties" that relate to the performance of items and services across a patient population and stated that it is considering protection for such arrangements in a future rulemaking.[134]

The warranties safe harbor protects only remuneration that is provided as a warranty remedy. Any free items or services that a seller offers in connection with a warranty arrangement are not protected by the warranties safe harbor. The safe harbor caps the amount of remuneration that may be offered pursuant to a warranty to the cost of the items and services subject to the warranty, and prohibits a seller from conditioning any warranty on a buyer's exclusive use, or minimum purchase, of any of the seller's items or services.

E. Special Fraud Alerts

Special Fraud Alerts are intended to "inform[] the public of practices which the Inspector General considers to be suspect or of particular concern under the Medicare program."[135] OIG has issued two Special Fraud Alerts addressing the fraud and abuse risks associated with arrangements involving medical devices or medical device manufacturers.

Most recently, in November 2020, OIG issued a Special Fraud Alert highlighting the fraud and abuse risks associated with pharmaceutical and device manufacturers' payment of remuneration in connection with speaker programs.[136] OIG noted that drug and device companies had reported paying nearly $2 billion to health care professionals in 2017–2019 for making speeches or presentations at company-sponsored events. OIG expressed skepticism about the educational value of such programs, noting that health care professionals often receive generous compensation to speak at programs that "are not conducive to learning," and said that such circumstances "strongly suggest" that at least one purpose of the payment to is to induce or reward referrals.

OIG warned that both the device companies that pay speaking fees and the health care professionals who receive them may be subject to

133. *Id.* § 1001.952(g)(5).
134. 85 Fed. Reg. at 77853.
135. 42 U.S.C. § 1320a-7d(c).
136. OIG Special Fraud Alert: Speaker Programs (Nov. 16, 2020).

increased scrutiny and identified certain characteristics it considered suspect, including:

- Little or no substantive content is presented at the program;
- The company sponsors a large number of substantially similar programs;
- Attendees include individuals who have no legitimate business reason to attend, such as friends and family members;
- The company's sales or marketing department influences the selection of the speakers; and
- The company pays health care professionals more than fair market value, or compensation that takes into account the health care professionals' referrals, for speaking.

In March 2013, OIG issued a Special Fraud Alert on physician-owned distributorships, or "PODs," which are physician-owned entities that sell implantable medical devices that the PODs' physician-owners use in surgeries that they perform on their own patients. OIG characterized PODs as "inherently suspect" under the AKS, because the financial incentives PODs provide to their physician-owners may induce the physicians both to perform more procedures (and more extensive procedures) than are medically necessary, and to choose the PODs' devices over other, potentially more clinically appropriate, devices. OIG identified certain POD characteristics that caused them particular concern, including:

- The investment opportunity offered to each physician varies with the anticipated use of the PODs' devices;
- POD physician-owners implicitly or directly condition their referrals to hospitals on the hospitals' purchase of the PODs' devices;
- The POD is a shell entity or does not maintain continuous oversight of all distribution functions; and
- When a hospital requires physicians to disclose conflicts of interest, the PODs' physician-owners either do not inform the hospital of, or actively conceal, their ownership interest in the POD.

F. Penalties and Damages

As noted previously, Congress amended the AKS in 2018 by increasing the criminal fine from $25,000 to $100,000 and the maximum prison sentence from five years to ten years for a felony conviction. In addition, Congress doubled the maximum CMP amounts that OIG could impose for each instance of violating the AKS from $50,000 to $100,000.[137]

---

137. Bipartisan Budget Act of 2018, Pub. L. No. 115-123, 132 Stat. 220, § 50412 (2018).

For health care providers and health care entities, the prospect of being subject to CMPs, as well as assessments of up to three times the total remuneration and exclusion from federal health care programs can be daunting and stressful. In 1998, OIG announced that it had created a self-disclosure protocol (SDP) for health care providers and health care entities who may be facing CMP liability.[138] According to OIG, the "principal purpose" of the SDP was not to "make firm commitments as to how a particular disclosure will be resolved" but "to provide guidance to health care providers that decide voluntarily to disclose irregularities in their dealings with the Federal health care programs."[139]

In the 1998 SDP, OIG provided guidance about (1) parties eligible for the SDP; (2) the substantive content required in an SDP disclosure; and (3) the factors weighed in resolving matters under the SDP.[140] In 2006, 2008, and 2009, OIG issued open letters to explain how it intended to apply and implement the SDP.[141] For example, in the 2009 open letter, OIG indicated that disclosure of potential Stark Law violations would not be appropriate under the SDP "in the absence of a colorable anti-kickback statute violation" and that kickback-related submissions would require a minimum $50,000 settlement amount to resolve the matter.[142]

In 2013, OIG updated the SDP to provide clearer guidance about the mechanics of the SDP.[143] For example, for disclosures relating to Stark Law violations involving a potential AKS violation, OIG required (1) an explicit acknowledgement that the conduct or arrangement may "constitute potential violations of the [AKS], and, if applicable, the Stark Law"; (2) a narrative statement describing in detail the arrangement or conduct at issue; and (3) an analysis of why the arrangement or conduct could constitute a violation.[144]

The 2013 update to the SDP also provided entirely new guidance about disclosures relating to parties who appear on OIG's List of Excluded

---

138. 63 Fed. Reg. 58,399 (Oct. 30, 1998).

139. 63 Fed. Reg. 58,399, 54,000 (Oct. 30, 1998).

140. 63 Fed. Reg. 58,399 (Oct. 30, 1998).

141. See https://oig.hhs.gov/compliance/self-disclosure-info/index.asp.

142. See 2009 Open Letter at https://oig.hhs.gov/compliance/self-disclosure-info/index.asp.

143. See 2013 Updated SDP at https://oig.hhs.gov/compliance/self-disclosure-info/index.asp [hereinafter SDP].

144. SDP at 11.

Individuals and Entities (LEIE).[145] For example, in such disclosures, the submission must include the following information:

1. The identity of the excluded individual and any provider identification number.
2. The job duties performed by that individual.
3. The dates of the individual's employment or contract.
4. A description of any background checks the disclosing party completed before and/or during the individual employment or contract.
5. A description of the disclosing party's screening process and any flaw or breakdown in the process that led to the hiring or contracting with the excluded individual.
6. A description of how the conduct was discovered.
7. A description of any corrective action (including copies of revised policies or procedures) implemented to prevent future hiring of excluded individuals.

Importantly, before submitting a disclosure relating to excluded parties, the disclosing party must screen all current employees and contractors against OIG's LEIE.[146]

Arguably, the most significant sections of the 2013 update to the SDP are those relating to the settlement amounts, the calculation of damages, and the deadline for completing internal investigations. For disclosures unrelated to the AKS, the minimum settlement amount is $10,000. And for those related to AKS, the minimum settlement amount is $50,000.[147] The calculation of damages for disclosures involving false billing may be based on the actual claims affected or a statistically valid, random sample of the actual claims. In cases where a disclosing party elects to use a statistically valid, random sample of claims, OIG requires that the disclosing party observe certain specific parameters.[148]

One benefit of using OIG's SDP is that the disclosing party may be subject to reduced damages as compared to the damages that could be assessed in connection with a government investigation. For example, OIG stated that its general practice for calculating damages in connection with SDP settlements is to use a multiplier of 1.5 times single damages.[149]

145. The LEIE is available here: Search the Exclusions Database | Office of Inspector General (hhs.gov).

146. SDP at 9.

147. SDP at 14.

148. SDP at 7–9.

149. SDP at 14.

By contrast, a damages calculation based on a government investigation may result in treble damages.

The 2013 update to the SDP also abbreviated the timeframe for submitting to OIG documented findings based on the internal investigation and self-assessment that all disclosing parties must conduct. Under the 1998 SDP, the written report was due within 90 days of acceptance into the SDP. Under the 2013 update to the SDP, the written report is due within 90 days of the initial submission to OIG.[150]

IV. Other Fraud and Abuse Considerations

A. The Physician Payments Sunshine Act

The Physician Payments Sunshine Act (PPSA),[151] also known as the "Sunshine Act" or "Open Payments Program," requires manufacturers of drugs, medical devices, biologics, or medical supplies covered by Medicare, Medicaid, or the Children's Health Insurance Program (CHIP)[152] to report payments and transfers of value to certain recipients[153]

150. SDP at 3.

151. The Sunshine Act was enacted in 2010 as section 6002 of the Patient Protection and Affordable Care Act (PPACA), Pub. L. No. 111-148, 124 Stat. 689 (2010); 42 U.S.C. § 1320a-7g. Since then, certain provisions of the Sunshine Act have been amended by the Health Care and Education Reconciliation Act of 2010, Pub. L. No. 111-152 and the SUPPORT for Patients and Communities Act of 2018, Pub. L. No. 115-271.

152. 42 C.F.R. § 403.902. Manufacturers means entities that operate in the United States and either (1) are engaged in the production, preparation, propagation, compounding, or conversion of a covered drug, device, biological, or medical supply, but not if such covered drug, device, biological, or medical supply is solely for use by or within the entity itself or by the entity's own patients; or (2) are under common ownership with an entity described in part (1) of this definition, which provides assistance or support to such entities with respect to the production, preparation, propagation, compounding, conversion, marketing, promotion, sale, or distribution of a covered drug, device, biological, or medical supply.

153. 42 C.F.R. § 403.902. Recipients includes doctors of medicine, doctors of osteopathy, dentists, podiatrists, optometrists, chiropractors, physician assistants, nurse practitioners, clinical nurse specialists, certified registered nurse anesthetists, and certified nurse midwives who are not bona fide employees of the manufacturer who is reporting the payment. Residents are excluded.

and teaching hospitals.[154] PODs and Group Purchasing Organizations (GPOs)[155] also are subject to the reporting requirements under the Open Payments Program.[156]

The purpose of the Open Payments Program is to provide patients with visibility of the activities and financial relationships between health care providers and manufacturers that could create a conflict of interest and potentially affect a health care provider's professional judgment. To promote transparency, Congress directed that manufacturers, GPOs, and PODs track and report information pertaining to those activities and financial relationships to CMS, which could serve as a neutral custodian of the information and make it available on a publicly accessible website.[157] To be clear, the Open Payments Program neither prohibits payments or transfers of value nor restricts interactions or collaborations between covered entities and health care providers.[158]

The Open Payments Program covers three reporting categories. The first category is payments and transfers of value and includes meals, lodging, travel, entertainment, consulting fees, grants, gifts, royalties, and licenses.[159] For the 2021 calendar year, manufacturers and GPOs must report a payment or transfer of value (e.g., meal) worth $11.04 or more. If the item is worth less than $11.04, a report to CMS is still required if the sum total of all items provided to the recipient exceeds $110.40 during the 2021 calendar year.[160]

The second category is ownership and investment interests held by physicians or their immediate family members in manufacturers, PODs,

---

154. 42 C.F.R. § 403.902. Teaching hospitals are hospitals that received payment for Medicare direct graduate medical education (GME), inpatient prospective payment system (IPPS), indirect medical education (IME), or psychiatric hospital IME programs during the last calendar year for which such information is available.

155. 42 C.F.R. § 403.902. A Group Purchasing Organization (GPO) is an entity that purchases, arranges for or negotiates the purchase of drugs, devices, biologicals, or medical supplies covered by Medicare, Medicaid, or CHIP for a group of individuals or entities, but not solely for use by the entity itself.

156. CMS has created a table to help parties determine whether they may be subject to the reporting requirements under the Open Payments Rule. See https://www.cms.gov/OpenPayments/Program-Participants/Applicable-Manufacturers-and-GPOs/Applicable-Manufacturers-and-GPOs and https://www.cms.gov/OpenPayments/Program-Participants/Reporting-Entities/Changes-for-Reporting-Entities.

157. https://openpaymentsdata.cms.gov/.

158. https://www.advamed.org/sites/default/files/resource/advamed_sunshine_brochure_for_physicians_v18_webview.pdf.

159. 42 C.F.R. § 403.904(e)(2).

160. https://www.cms.gov/OpenPayments/Program-Participants/Applicable-Manufacturers-and-GPOs/Data-Collection.

and GPOs. With limited exceptions, financial instruments such as stocks, stock options, partnership shares, limited liability memberships, loans, bonds, and certain types of financial instruments are all included within "ownership and investment interests."[161]

The third category is research payments, which includes payments to certain health care providers and teaching hospitals for basic research, applied research (e.g., clinical trials, pre-clinical research, etc.), and product development activities. Under the regulations, research is defined as a systematic investigation designed to develop or contribute to generalizable knowledge relating broadly to public health, including behavioral and social-sciences research.[162] To qualify as a research payment under the Open Payments Program, the research payment or transfer of value (e.g., study equipment, implantable devices, surgical instruments, etc.) must be the subject of a written agreement or a research protocol.[163]

Parties that fail to comply with the reporting requirements under the Open Payments Program are subject to stiff penalties. For each payment, transfer of value or ownership or investment interest that is not reported in a timely, accurate or complete manner, a CMP of at least $1,176 but not more than $11,766[164] may be imposed by CMS,[165] up to an annual maximum of $176,495.[166] The penalties are more severe when the party knowingly fails to report. CMS may impose a CMP of at least $11,766 but not more than $117,664 for each payment, transfer of value or ownership, or investment interest that is not reported in a timely, accurate, or complete manner.[167] The annual maximum, however, is $1,176,638.[168]

A recent settlement announced by DOJ illustrates how serious the consequences can be for medical device companies that conceal payments that should be reported under the Open Payments Program. In October 2020, Medtronic agreed to pay over $9.2 million to settle allegations that it violated the AKS and the reporting requirements under the Open Payments Program. More than $1.1 million of the $9.2 million that Medtronic paid was to resolve allegations that it violated the Open Payments Program by failing to accurately report to CMS payments it made

---

161. 42 C.F.R. § 403.902.
162. *Id.*
163. *Id.* §403.904(f).
164. *Id.* § 403.912(a) and (c). All figures cited are adjusted for FY2020.
165. https://www.cms.gov/OpenPayments/Program-Participants/Applicable-Manufacturers-and-GPOs/Audits-and-Penalties.
166. 85 Fed. Reg. 2869, 2878 (Jan. 17, 2020).
167. 42 C.F.R. 403.912(b)–(c). All figures cited are adjusted for FY2020.
168. 85 Fed. Reg. 2869, 2879 (Jan. 17, 2020).

to or for the benefit of Wilson Asfora, a South Dakota neurosurgeon whom Medtronic had identified as a "targeted physician" in the context of increasing sales of its SynchroMed II Intrathecal Infusion Pumps.[169]

Specifically, Asfora had requested that Medtronic host "educational events" at Carnaval Brazilian Grill, a local restaurant that Medtronic knew was owned by Dr. Asfora and his wife. Despite Medtronic's written compliance policies, Asfora's request was approved. As a result, from August 8, 2013, to July 9, 2019, Medtronic paid for 74 events at Carnaval, which included consumption of expensive meals and alcohol by not only physicians but also "social acquaintances, business partners, favored colleagues, and potential and existing referral sources" and "spouses and significant others."

However, instead of reporting the full value of the payments made to Carnaval, Medtronic reported only the value of the food and drink personally consumed by each physician based on information provided by the Medtronic sales force. As a result of under-reporting the payments to Asfora, Medtronic was liable under the Physician Payments Sunshine Act.[170]

B. The Physician Self-Referral Law

The Physician Self-Referral Law,[171] commonly known as the "Stark Law," prohibits physicians from referring Medicare patients for "designated health services" (DHS) to an entity with which the physician (or the physician's immediate family member) has a financial relationship, unless an exception applies. It also prohibits an entity from presenting or causing to be presented a claim or bill for DHS based on a prohibited referral. In short, the Stark Law's purpose is to prevent physicians from making medical decisions for their patients based on financial incentives.

The Stark Law is a strict liability statute, meaning that specific intent to violate the law is not required for a violation to occur. In other words, if an arrangement implicates the Stark Law and does not satisfy an exception, the arrangement violates the Stark Law and the individual or entity is subject to enforcement. Individuals or entities that present (or cause to be presented) a claim that they know (or should have known) violated the Stark Law may be subject to CMPs and exclusion from participation in

169. https://www.justice.gov/opa/pr/medtronic-pay-over-92-million-settle-allegations-improper-payments-south-dakota-neurosurgeon#:~:text=Medtronic%20also%20agreed%20to%20pay,%26%20Medicaid%20Services%20(CMS).

170. https://www.justice.gov/opa/press-release/file/1332261/download.

171. 42 U.S.C. § 1395nn.

the federal health care programs. In addition, claims that are prohibited under the Stark Law are false claims for purposes of the FCA.

Medical devices are not DHS. Consequently, medical device manufacturers generally will not be subject to enforcement under the Stark Law.[172]

V. Reducing the Risk of Health Care Fraud and Abuse

A. DOJ Policy Regarding Investigations of Corporate Wrongdoing

In September 2015, Sally Yates, the DOJ's Deputy Attorney General at the time, issued a memorandum (the "Yates Memo") outlining the Department's policy regarding civil and criminal investigations of corporate wrongdoing. Among the issues addressed was whether officers and employees of companies could be held accountable for company misconduct, even if they lacked visibility of the day-to-day activities that established the basis of misconduct. Citing the need to "redress misconduct and deter future wrongdoing," the Yates Memo stated that the DOJ "will not release culpable individuals from civil or criminal liability when resolving a matter with a corporation."[173] For many, the Yates Memo represented an explicitly articulated policy about how DOJ would pursue its civil and criminal investigations of corporate wrongdoing.

The concept of holding officers and employees of companies for corporate misdeeds was not new in 2015. In 1943, the Supreme Court held in *United States v. Dotterweich* that individuals who have a "responsible share in the furtherance of the transaction which the [FDCA] outlaws"

172. CMS has noted that, "[i]n some problematic circumstances, an unbroken chain of financial relationships will connect the physician owner of a [physician-owned implant and medical device company, or 'POC'] to a DHS entity to which the physician makes referrals." CMS noted that such problematic arrangements would violate the Stark Law if the Stark Law's other required elements were present and solicited public comments regarding whether the agency should address POCs in the Stark Law regulations. 73 Fed. Reg. 23528, 23697 (Apr. 30, 2008). However, CMS declined to adopt the position that physician-owned implant or other medical device companies "perform the DHS" and therefore are an "entity" for purposes of the Stark Law. 73 Fed. Reg. 48434, 48726-27.

173. See Memorandum from Deputy Attorney General Sally Q. Yates to Department of Justice Attorneys Regarding Individual Accountability for Corporate Wrongdoing, September 9, 2015. Available at https://www.justice.gov/archives/dag/file/769036/download.

may be held criminally liable,[174] even absent proof of knowledge of the event or intent that the violative conduct be performed.[175]

Three decades later, the "Responsible Corporate Officer" doctrine was affirmed by the Supreme Court in 1975 in *United States v. Park*, which held that criminal liability under FDCA may attach to an individual at a corporation who has "responsibility or authority either to prevent in the first instance, or promptly to correct, the violation complained of, and that he failed to do so."[176]

There is no indication that the Supreme Court intends to overturn or revise the "Responsible Corporate Officer" or "Park" doctrine.[177] And prosecutors continue to use it as a statutory basis to charge company officers and employees with liability for corporate acts that violate the FDCA, which also may implicate FCA or AKS (or both). For example, William Facteau, the former CEO of Acclarent, Inc. and Patrick Fabian, the former Vice President of Sales for Acclarent, Inc. were convicted by a jury of ten counts of introducing adulterated and misbranded devices into interstate commerce, which is prohibited under the FDCA.[178] At the same time, Acclarent, Inc. agreed to pay $18 million to resolve allegations that it had violated the FCA by causing health care providers to submit false claims for a medical device to Medicare and other federal health care programs.[179]

B. DOJ Criminal Division Guidance: Evaluation of Corporate Compliance Programs

In conducting an investigation of a corporation, bringing charges and negotiating plea or other agreements, the Criminal Division of DOJ

174. *See* United States v. Dotterweich, 320 U.S. 277, 284 (1943).

175. *Id.* at 281. Although the Court recognized that application of the strict liability standard for criminal prosecution under the FDCA was inconsistent "with the conventional requirement . . . of awareness of some wrongdoing," the Court reasoned that the strict liability standard was necessary because it was "[i]n the interest of the larger good [that the FDCA placed] the burden of acting at hazard upon a person otherwise innocent but standing in responsible relation to a public danger."

176. *See* United States v. Park, 421 U.S. 658, 672–74 (1975).

177. In 2017, the Supreme Court denied a petition to review a case that resulted in prison time and monetary fines for two corporate executives under the "Responsible Corporate Officer" or "Park" doctrine. *See* United States v. DeCoster, 828 F.3d 626, 629 (8th Cir. 2016), *cert. denied*, 137 S. Ct. 2160, 198 L. Ed. 2d 232 (2017).

178. See https://www.justice.gov/usao-ma/pr/former-acclarent-inc-executives-convicted-crimes-related-sale-medical-devices.

179. See https://www.justice.gov/usao-ma/pr/medical-device-manufacturer-acclarent-inc-pay-18-million-settle-false-claims-act.

weighs a number of factors, including "the adequacy and effectiveness of the corporation's compliance program at the time of the offense, as well as at the time of a charging decision" and the corporation's remedial efforts "to implement an adequate and effective corporate compliance program or to improve an existing one."[180]

The existence and effectiveness of a corporate compliance program is a factor in other prosecutorial contexts as well. For example, the United States Sentencing Guidelines (U.S.S.G.) advise that prosecutors consider whether the corporation had an effective compliance program at the time of misconduct when calculating the appropriate organizational criminal fine.[181] Additionally, in weighing whether to appoint a monitor in cases of a deferred prosecution agreement (DPA), a non-prosecutorial agreement (NPA) or a plea agreement with a corporation, DOJ's policy is to take into account "whether the corporation has made significant investments in, and improvements to, its corporate compliance program and internal control systems."[182]

In June 2020, DOJ updated its guidance for prosecutors evaluating corporate compliance programs in the context of criminal investigations.[183] Noting that while "the Criminal Division does not use any rigid formula to assess the effectiveness of corporate compliance programs" because a company's risk profile will depend on a variety of factors (e.g., company size, industry, regulatory landscape, etc.), prosecutors should consider three fundamental questions in their evaluation:

1. Is the corporation's compliance program well designed?
2. Is the corporation's compliance program being applied earnestly and in good faith?
3. Does the corporation's compliance program work in practice?

---

180. Title 9 of Justice Manual, Section 28.300, "Factors to be Considered." See https://www.justice.gov/jm/jm-9-28000-principles-federal-prosecution-business-organizations#9-28.300.

181. United States Sentencing Commission, *Guidelines Manual*, §§ 8B2.1, 8C2.5(f) and 8C2.8(11) (Nov 2018). See https://www.ussc.gov/guidelines/2018-guidelines-manual-annotated.

182. See Memorandum from Assistant Attorney General Brian A. Benczkowsi to All Criminal Division Personnel Regarding Selection of Monitors in Criminal Division Matters, October 11, 2018. Available at https://www.justice.gov/opa/speech/file/1100531/download.

183. U.S. Dep't of Justice, Criminal Division, "Evaluation of Corporate Compliance Programs" (Jun 1, 2020), https://www.justice.gov/criminal-fraud/page/file/937501/download.

In the eyes of DOJ, a corporate compliance program that is well designed should include (1) regular risk assessments; (2) easily accessible policies and procedures that promote a culture of compliance; (3) periodic training and communications about corporate policies and procedures, including those relating to misconduct; (4) a confidential reporting structure and investigation process that is known to company employees as well as third parties; (5) managing any potential "risks posed third-party partners, including the third party partners' reputations and relationship, if any, with foreign officials"; and (6) conducting comprehensive due diligence of any acquisition targets to reduce the risk that any misconduct at the target company will continue pre- or post-acquisition.[184]

A corporate compliance program that is "being applied earnestly and in good faith" is one that is adequately resourced and empowered to function effectively. In other words, the corporation must be able to show that (1) members of management and corporate leadership "have clearly articulated the company's ethical standards, conveyed and disseminated them in clear and unambiguous terms, and demonstrated rigorous adherence by example";[185] (2) company personnel responsible for compliance have "sufficient seniority" (i.e., to exercise authority within the organization), "sufficient resources" (i.e., to undertake auditing, documentation and analysis of compliance matters), and "sufficient autonomy from management" (i.e., to have direct access to the Board of Directors);[186] and (3) "the company has clear disciplinary procedures in place . . . enforces them consistently . . . and ensures that the procedures are commensurate with the violations."[187]

184. *Id.* at 2–9, https://www.justice.gov/criminal-fraud/page/file/937501/download.

185. The Guidance suggests that instances of managers "tolerating greater compliance risks in pursuit of new business or greater revenues" or "encourage[ing] employees to act unethically to achieve a business objective, or imped[ing] compliance personnel from effectively implementing their duties" would undermine a claim of adherence to ethical standards and compliance requirements. See U.S. Dep't of Justice, Criminal Division, "Evaluation of Corporate Compliance Programs" (June 1, 2020), at 10, https://www.justice.gov/criminal-fraud/page/file/937501/download.

186. *See id.* at 11–12.

187. As an example of how a company could provide incentives for compliance and dis-incentives for noncompliance, the Guidance states the following: "By way of example, some companies have found that publicizing disciplinary actions internally, where appropriate and possible, can have valuable deterrent effects. At the same time, some companies have also found that providing positive incentives—personnel promotions, rewards, and bonuses for improving and developing a compliance program or demonstrating ethical leadership—have driven compliance. Some companies

A corporate compliance program that works in practice is defined by a number of features.[188] For example, it should be characterized by (1) continuous improvement, periodic testing, and review; (2) mechanisms for timely and thorough investigations of actual or suspected misconduct; and (3) analysis and remediation of any underlying misconduct. With respect to analysis and remediation, the Guidance notes that certain considerations may be helpful. For example, conducting a root cause analysis may identify what controls, if any, failed and led to the misconduct. Also, if a vendor was involved in the misconduct, it may be illuminating to review the process for vendor selection and how it was applied to the vendor. Importantly, remediation of the issue may require specific changes to protocols or policies to reduce the risk that the same (or similar) event will occur again. Lastly, holding managers accountable for misconduct that occurred under their supervision may be warranted, which, depending on the circumstances, may result in termination.

C. OIG Guidance: Oversight of Compliance Program by Board of Directors

OIG has issued a number of educational resources intended to explain its thinking about corporate responsibility for compliance matters.[189] The most recent is a document entitled, "Practical Guidance for Health Care Governing Boards on Compliance Oversight," which

---

have even made compliance a significant metric for management bonuses and/or have made working on compliance a means of career advancement." *See id.* at 13.

188. The Guidance notes that the mere fact that misconduct occurred does not "mean that a compliance program did not work or was ineffective at the time of the offense. *See* U.S.S.G. § 882.1(a) ("[t]he failure to prevent or detect the instant offense does not mean that the program is not generally effective in preventing and deterring misconduct."). Indeed, "[t]he Department recognizes that no compliance program can ever prevent all criminal activity by a corporation's employees." JM 9-28.800. "Of course, if a compliance program did effectively identify misconduct, including allowing for timely remediation and self-reporting, a prosecutor should view the occurrence as a strong indicator that the compliance program was working effectively." *Id.* at 14.

189. OIG and AHLA, *Corporate Responsibility and Corporate Compliance: A Resource for Health Care Boards of Directors* (2003); OIG and AHLA, *An Integrated Approach to Corporate Compliance: A Resource for Health Care Organization Boards of Directors* (2004); OIG and AHLA, *Corporate Responsibility and Health Care Quality: A Resource for Health Care Organization Boards of Directors* (2007). OIG and AHLA, *The Health Care Director's Compliance Duties: A Continued Focus of Attention and Enforcement* (20010, 2011). See https://oig.hhs.gov/compliance/compliance-guidance/compliance-resource-material.asp.

addresses issues relating to a Board's oversight and review of compliance program functions, including the: (1) roles of, and relationships between, the organization's audit, compliance, and legal departments; (2) mechanism and process for issue-reporting within an organization; (3) approach to identifying regulatory risk; and (4) methods of encouraging enterprise-wide accountability for achievement of compliance goals and objectives.[190]

Undergirding OIG's expectations that a board should exercise oversight over its organization's compliance program is the director's fiduciary duty of care, which requires a director to act in good faith to ensure that (1) a corporate information and reporting system exists; and (2) the reporting system brings appropriate, compliance-related information to the attention of the board in a timely manner and as a matter of course. Failure to do so could "render a director liable for losses caused by non-compliance with applicable legal standards."[191]

The scope and adequacy of a compliance program should be evaluated in the context of the size and complexity of the organization for which it is designed. To facilitate that analysis, OIG has provided a series of questions that directors can ask themselves. The questions fall into one of two general categories: "structural" and "operational." Both types of questions are aimed at exploring the board's understanding of the organization's compliance program, but the former is more focused on the scope of the program, while the latter is focused on challenges with achieving the compliance program's goals.[192]

In the view of OIG, a compliance program would be insufficient if it relied solely on an organization's compliance personnel. Instead, the structure of a robust compliance program should promote "cooperation and collaboration" between compliance officers and legal advisors, internal auditors, human resources, and quality assurance. OIG has acknowledged that the availability of sufficient resources at an organization may limit supporting such a structure, but it is of paramount importance that the independence of each function be protected. Accordingly, OIG has

---

190. OIG, AHIA, AHLA, and HCCA, *Practical Guidance for Health Care Governing Boards on Compliance Oversight* (2015). See https://oig.hhs.gov/compliance/compliance-guidance/docs/Practical-Guidance-for-Health-Care-Boards-on-Compliance-Oversight.pdf.

191. *In re* Caremark Int'l, Inc. Derivative Litig., 698 A.2d 959 (Del. Ch. 1996).

192. OIG and AHLA, *Corporate Responsibility and Corporate Compliance: A Resource for Health Care Boards of Directors* (2003). See https://oig.hhs.gov/fraud/docs/complianceguidance/040203CorpRespRsceGuide.pdf.

stated that it "believes that there is some risk to establishing an independent compliance function if that function is subordina[te] to the [organization]'s [G]eneral [C]ounsel."[193] In more pointed terms, OIG later stated that it "believes an organization's Compliance Officer should neither be counsel for the provider, not be subordinate in function or position to counsel or the legal department, in any manner."[194] OIG has developed a series of questions that directors can ask themselves to (1) understand the roles of the General Counsel and Chief Compliance Officer in supporting the organization's compliance program; and (2) identify what processes exist to communicate information about compliance matters in a timely manner to the board.[195]

OIG also recommends that the board receive regular reports about the organization's risk mitigation and compliance efforts from audit, compliance, human resources, legal, quality, and information technology, as well as "set and enforce expectations for receiving particular types of compliance-related information from various members of management." OIG believes that by adopting such an approach, the board can identify who among the leadership team and others deeper within the organization can provide "relevant information about operations and operational risks."[196]

The board also should employ processes for identifying risk areas. In health care, certain activities are extremely vulnerable to fraud and abuse. For example, referral arrangements, quality assurance and billing problems (e.g., upcoding, submitting false claims, etc.) are but a few that medical device manufacturers face regularly. As a result, the board should ensure that it has visibility to management's reviews of existing risk areas, as well as identification of emerging risk areas. The board also should have visibility of any corrective action that management develops and the results obtained from implementation of the corrective action.[197]

---

193. OIG and AHLA, *An Integrated Approach to Corporate Compliance: A Resource for Health Care Organization Boards of Directors* (2004). See https://oig.hhs.gov/fraud/docs/complianceguidance/Tab%204E%20Appendx-Final.pdf.

194. OIG, AHIA, AHLA, and HCCA, *Practical Guidance for Health Care Governing Boards on Compliance Oversight* (2015). See https://oig.hhs.gov/compliance/compliance-guidance/docs/Practical-Guidance-for-Health-Care-Boards-on-Compliance-Oversight.pdf.

195. OIG and AHLA, *An Integrated Approach to Corporate Compliance: A Resource for Health Care Organization Boards of Directors* (2004). See https://oig.hhs.gov/fraud/docs/complianceguidance/Tab%204E%20Appendx-Final.pdf.

196. *Id.*

197. OIG, AHIA, AHLA and HCCA, *Practical Guidance for Health Care Governing Boards on Compliance Oversight* (2015). See https://oig.hhs.gov/compliance

OIG has stated that "organizations can effectively communicate the message that everyone is ultimately responsible for compliance" by implementing "a system of defined compliance goals and objectives against which performance can be measure and incentivized." For example, an organization could assess the performance of an individual, department or facility based partly on compliance and quality outcomes, including steps taken to promote compliance and quality assurance. These assessments can then be used to enhance or diminish performance incentives.[198]

D. AdvaMed Code of Ethics

Founded in 1974, the Advanced Medical Technology Association (AdvaMed) is a U.S.-based trade association for companies that develop, produce, manufacture, and market medical technologies.[199] Its membership consists of over 400 companies, including both small technology innovators and large multinational companies,[200] and its mission is to advocate globally for the highest ethical standards, timely patient access to safe and effective products, and economic policies that reward innovation.[201]

The AdvaMed Code of Ethics (the "AdvaMed Code" or the "Code") provides medical technology companies with guidance on ethical interactions and relationships with health care professionals.[202] A company that adopts the Code[203] is required to communicate the Code's provisions to

---

/compliance-guidance/docs/Practical-Guidance-for-Health-Care-Boards-on-Compliance-Oversight.pdf.

198. *Id.*

199. https://www.advamed.org/sites/default/files/resource/advamed-code-of-ethics_2020_july20.pdf.

200. https://www.advamed.org/join/members.

201. https://www.advamed.org/about-advamed.

202. The AdvaMed Code of Ethics defines the term "health care professional" as any person or entity (a) authorized or licensed in the United States to provide health care services or items to patients or (b) who is involved in the decision to purchase, prescribe, order, or recommend a Medical Technology in the United States. This term includes individual clinicians (for example, physicians, nurses, and pharmacists, among others), provider entities (for example, hospitals and ambulatory surgical centers), and administrative personnel at provider entities (for example, hospital purchasing agents). This term does not include health care professionals who are bona fide employees of a company, while acting in that capacity. See https://www.advamed.org/issues/code-ethics/code-ethics.

203. A company can affirm that it has adopted the AdvaMed Code is through certification, which requires a company's Chief Executive Officer (CEO) and Chief Compliance Officer (CCO), or other senior individuals with equivalent responsibilities, to sign and affirm that their company has agreed to abide by the AdvaMed Code

its employees, agents, dealers, and distributors, with the expectation that they will adhere to the Code.[204] In addition to requiring certifying companies to comply with all applicable laws and regulations, the AdvaMed Code encourages companies to adopt an effective ethics and compliance program aimed at (1) promoting an organizational culture that encourages ethical practices and a commitment to comply with the law; and (2) preventing and detecting inappropriate conduct.[205]

AdvaMed has developed a number of training materials and other resources that can be used to facilitate company efforts to establish an effective ethics and compliance program, which are available to members and non-member companies. For example, AdvaMed has published a slide deck that can be used to introduce company employees to the AdvaMed Code.[206] In addition, AdvaMed also has published thirteen decision trees that may assist employees in ethical and compliant decision making.[207]

---

and that they have implemented policies and procedures to implement the AdvaMed Code as part of an effective compliance program. Once certified, a company may display the AdvaMed Code of Ethics Logo to represent their commitment to effective compliance programming and ethical interactions with health care providers. See https://www.advamed.org/issues/code-ethics/certify-now.

204. AdvaMed Code of Ethics (2018), Effective January 1, 2020 (p. 4). See https://www.advamed.org/sites/default/files/resource/advamed-code-of-ethics_2020_july20.pdf.

205. *Id.*

206. https://www.advamed.org/resource-center/advamed-code-training-slides-2020.

207. https://www.advamed.org/sites/default/files/resource/395_AdvaMedCode_Illustrative_Best_Practices_Tools_EntireLibrary_2015_03_09_v3.pdf.

CHAPTER 10

Coverage, Coding, and Reimbursement for Medical Devices

Beth Halpern, with Mahmud Brifkani, Boyd Jackson, Soraya Keskey, and Maria Malas

I. Introduction

What is the market for a medical device? Who will use it, who will buy it, and who will pay for its use? The answers to these questions are found in understanding the coverage and reimbursement policies that apply to the device. Coverage and reimbursement, along with the coding that facilitates claims payment, are crucial to the marketing success of medical devices.

Coverage, coding, and reimbursement are interrelated concepts. Coverage refers to the ability and willingness of health plans to pay for a device or for a procedure using a device. To be covered, an item or service must be included in the payers' benefits, either by contract, as in the case of commercial payers, or by statute or regulation, as in the case of Medicare and other government programs. Coding refers to the use of standard code sets, recognized under the Health Insurance Portability and Accountability Act (HIPAA)[1] for use in claims processing. The relevant code set for a device will depend on the payment system under which it is reimbursed. Reimbursement refers to the amount and method of payment for an item or service. When the item or service is covered, the payer's reimbursement policies will determine how payment is made for it and which codes are needed to identify the item or service on claims. If a device is covered, but reimbursement is inadequate, then providers may

1. 42 U.S.C. § 1320d-2; 45 C.F.R. § 162.1002.

be discouraged from using it or from making an effort to list the code for it on a claim, which could affect future payment rates. This chapter discusses each of these concepts in depth.

The U.S. health care system is a patchwork quilt of hundreds of payers. In 2018, 49 percent of Americans had employer-sponsored coverage, 20 percent were enrolled in Medicaid or were dually eligible for Medicaid and Medicare, 14 percent were enrolled in Medicare, 6 percent had nongroup coverage, 1 percent had military coverage, and 9 percent were uninsured.[2] This chapter will focus on the Medicare program, the government health care program for people age 65 and older, the disabled, and people with end-stage renal disease (ESRD), because it is the single largest payer for health care services in the United States. It also is the most transparent of all of the payers, with all of its coverage, coding, and reimbursement policies available to the public regardless of participation in the program, and its decisions often set precedents for other payers.

II. Coverage: Will Medicare Pay for a Device?

Medicare will cover an item or service if it is included in a statutory Medicare benefit category, is not statutory excluded from coverage, and is "reasonable and necessary for the diagnosis or treatment of illness or disease or to improve the functioning of a malformed body member."[3] These requirements apply to traditional Medicare as well as Medicare Advantage (MA) plans, but MA plans may cover additional services and might not cover exactly the same services as traditional Medicare. An MA plan must cover services that covered by Medicare's national coverage determinations (NCDs) and general coverage guidelines, as well as services covered by local coverage determinations (LCDs) for the MA plan's service areas.[4] MA plans that serve patients in across Medicare contracting jurisdictions have a choice of LCDs to follow, however.[5] When there is no written coverage policy from the Centers for Medicare & Medicaid Services (CMS, the agency that administers the Medicare program) or the relevant Medicare Administrative Contractor (MAC, an entity that processes claims for a specific region), an MA plan is permitted to establish

2. Kaiser Family Foundation, Health Insurance Coverage of the Total Population 2018, https://www.kff.org/other/state-indicator/total-population/?currentTimeframe=0&sortModel=%7B%22colId%22:%22Location%22,%22sort%22:%22asc%22%7D.

3. Social Security Act (SSA) § 1862(a).

4. *See* 42 C.F.R. § 422.101(b).

5. 42 C.F.R. § 422.101(b)(4) and (5).

different policies for items and services that are covered by MACs on a claim-by-claim basis.

A. Benefit Categories

Medicare's statutory benefit categories include physicians' services, services and supplies furnished as an incident to a physician's professional service, inpatient hospital services, outpatient hospital services, ambulatory surgical center (ASC) services, durable medical equipment (DME), and renal dialysis services.[6] All of these benefit categories include either coverage for a device itself or for procedures using devices, or both. For example, many physician procedures involve the use of a device. Coverage of those procedures is essential to ensuring patients' access to the device. The services and supplies furnished incident to a physician's service also include devices and services related to devices. To be payable as "incident to a physician's service" in a noninstitutional setting, an item or service, including a medical device, must be:

- An integral, although incidental, part of the physician's professional service;
- Commonly rendered without charge or included in the physician's bill;
- Of a type that are commonly furnished in physician's offices or clinics; and
- Furnished by the physician or by auxiliary personnel employed by or under the physician's direct supervision.[7]

Similarly, the hospital, ASC, and renal dialysis benefit categories include coverage for devices or use of devices in those settings of care.

The DME benefit category provides coverage for certain devices without an associated professional service. A medical device is eligible for coverage under the DME benefit if it:

- Can withstand repeated use;
- Effective with respect to items classified as DME after January 1, 2012, has an expected life of at least three years;
- Is primarily and customarily used to serve a medical purpose;

6. SSA §§ 1811(a)(1); 1832(a)(2)(B) and (F); 1861(b), (s)(1), (s)(2)(A), (s)(2)(B), (s)(2)(F), (s)(6).

7. 42 C.F.R. § 410.26(b); Medicare Benefit Policy Manual, ch. 15, § 60(A).

- Generally is not useful to an individual in the absence of an illness or injury; and
- Is appropriate for use in the home[8]

In general, Medicare may cover devices approved by the Food and Drug Administration (FDA) through the premarket approval (PMA) process, devices cleared by the FDA through the 510(k) process; FDA-approved Investigational Device Exemption (IDE) Category B devices, and hospital IRB-approved nonsignificant risk devices.[9]

A device may fit into multiple benefit categories and be subject to different coverage rules based on the category. For example, use of an infusion pump could be covered as incident to a physician's service when used in a physician's office, as part of a hospital service on either an inpatient or outpatient basis, and as an item of DME, depending on the setting of care. In addition, as discussed later, the reimbursement and coding requirements will vary based on the benefit category.

B. Statutory Exclusions

If an item or service is statutory excluded from coverage, Medicare will not cover it. Statutory exclusions include expenses for physical checkups, hearing aids, and eyeglasses (except for a single pair following cataract surgery with insertion of an intraocular lens), cosmetic surgery, and routine foot care.[10]

C. Reasonable and Necessary

The Medicare statute prohibits payments for items and services that "are not reasonable and necessary for the diagnosis or treatment of illness or injury or to improve the functioning of a malformed body member" or are not specific types of covered preventive services.[11] An item or service is "reasonable and necessary" if it is:

- Safe and effective;
- Not experimental or investigational (exception: routine costs of qualifying clinical trial services with dates of service on or after September 19, 2000, which meet the requirements of the Clinical Trials NCD are considered reasonable and necessary); and
- Appropriate, including the duration and frequency that is considered appropriate for the item or service, in terms of whether it is:

8. 42 C.F.R. § 410.202.
9. Medicare Benefit Policy Manual, ch. 14, § 10.
10. 42 U.S.C. § 1395y(a)(7), (10), (13)(C).
11. *Id.* § 1395y(a)(1)(A).

- Furnished in accordance with accepted standards of medical practice for the diagnosis or treatment of the patient's condition or to improve the function of a malformed body member;
- Furnished in a setting appropriate to the patient's medical needs and condition;
- Ordered and furnished by qualified personnel;
- One that meets, but does not exceed, the patient's medical need; and
- At least as beneficial as an existing and available medically appropriate alternative.[12]

"Reasonable and necessary" is not synonymous with the FDA's determination that a product is safe and effective. While CMS requires an FDA-regulated product to have "received FDA approval or clearance (unless exempt from the FDA premarket review process) for at least one indication to be eligible for consideration of Medicare coverage (except in specific circumstances)," CMS notes, "FDA approval or clearance alone does not entitle that technology to Medicare coverage."[13] CMS generally looks at whether there is strong clinical evidence that an item or service improves health outcomes for Medicare beneficiaries.[14]

In a regulation promulgated in January, 2021, CMS created a new coverage pathway for devices with Breakthrough designation from the FDA. The "Medicare Coverage of Innovative Technology" pathway is intended to provide immediate coverage of these devices and allow time to collect clinical evidence to support long-term coverage.[15] Under the MCIT pathway, Medicare will cover these devices, related care and services, and any reasonable and necessary procedures, items, and services to implant or maintain the device and to treat complications arising from use of the device.[16] Eligible devices must have received FDA authorization within the two years prior to the effective date of the regulation, be

12. Medicare Program Integrity Manual, ch. 13, § 13.5.4; effective March 15, 2021, this definition also will be codified at 42 C.F.R. § 405.201(b).

13. 78 Fed. Reg. 48164, 48165 (Aug. 7, 2013).

14. *See, e.g.,* CMS, Decision Memo for Vagus Nerve Stimulation (VNS) for Treatment Resistant Depression (TRD) (CAG-00313R2), Appendix A, Feb. 15, 2019; CMS, Decision Memo for Ambulatory Blood Pressure Monitoring (ABPM) (CAG-00067R2), Appendix A, July 2, 2019.

15. Medicare Program; Medicare Coverage of Innovative Technology (MCIT) and Definition of "Reasonable and Necessary," 86 Fed. Reg. 2987, 2990 (Jan. 14, 2021).

16. 42 C.F.R. § 405.605.

used according to their FDA-approved or cleared indication for use, be within a Medicare benefit category, not be the subject of an NCD, and not be excluded from coverage through law or regulation.[17] The coverage period for these devices would extend for four years from the date the manufacturer notifies CMS that it is opting into the pathway.[18] After that period expires, the device would be subject to Medicare's usual process for making coverage decisions. In May 2021, CMS delayed the effective date of this rule until December 15, 2021, to allow the agency more time to address concerns raised by stakeholders about implementation of the rule.[19]

D. Process for Making Coverage Decisions

Medicare coverage policies can be established through NCDs, LCDs, or on a claim-by-claim basis. An NCD is a determination by CMS with respect to whether or not a particular item or service is covered nationally under Medicare statute,[20] while an LCD is determination by a MAC regarding whether or not a particular item or service is covered on a contractor-wide basis" in accordance with the "reasonable and necessary provision of the Social Security Act.[21] NCDs are issued by CMS, while LCDs are issued by the MACs that process claims in various regions across the county. Medicare's coverage determinations for most items and services are made by the MACs on a claim-by-claim basis without a written NCD or LCD.

NCDs are developed through a process that is governed by statutory deadlines and requirements for notice and comment. By statute, a proposed decision must be released within six months of the date CMS starts its review, or within nine months if CMS commissions a technology assessment or convenes a meeting of the Medicare Evidence Development and Coverage Advisory Committee (MedCAC) to discuss the technology.[22] CMS must provide a 30-day comment period on the proposed decision, and it must issue a final decision within 60 days of the end of the comment period.[23] LCDs are also subject to statutory and sub-regulatory

17. *Id.* § 405.603.
18. *Id.* § 405.607.
19. 86 Fed. Reg. 26849 (May 18, 2021).
20. 42 U.S.C. § 1395y(l)(6).
21. *Id.* § 1395ff(f)(2)(B).
22. *Id.* § 1395y(l)(2).
23. *Id.* § 1395y(l)(3).

requirements for notice and comment.[24] LCDs may not conflict with an NCD and are binding on providers in a MAC's jurisdiction.

CMS develops NCDs, and the MACs develop LCD, upon request by beneficiaries or other members of the public or on their own initiative. CMS has identified the following circumstances that could cause it to consider developing an NCD:

- Practitioners, patients, or other members of the public have raised significant questions about the health outcomes attributable to the use of the items or services for the Medicare beneficiary population.
- New evidence or reasonable reinterpretation of previously available evidence indicates that a national coverage review may be warranted.
- Local coverage policies on a particular item or service may vary in language or implementation.
- The health technology represents a substantial clinical advance and is likely to result in a significant improvement in patient health outcomes or positive impact on the Medicare program.
- When rapid diffusion of an item or service is anticipated the evidence may inadequately address questions regarding impact on the Medicare population, target subgroup populations, practitioner or facility qualifications, etc., or on beneficiary health outcomes.[25]

Cost is not a factor CMS uses in deciding whether to cover an item or service, but the "impact on the Medicare population" could include changes in utilization of services and costs to beneficiaries or on the Medicare program as a whole.

CMS evaluates only six to eight therapies per year for NCDs.[26] As a result, statistically speaking, the likelihood of CMS creating an NCD for any new therapy is low.

E. Clinical Trials

Medicare covers devices and related services when used in clinical trials under several types of policies. Medicare devices subject to IDE Studies

---

24. *Id.* § 1395y(l)(5)(D); Medicare Benefit Policy Manual, ch. 13, § 2.
25. 78 Fed. Reg. 48164, 48167 (Aug. 7, 2013).
26. CMS, National Coverage Annual Report (data for 2015 to 2019), https://www.cms.gov/Medicare-Coverage-Database/reports/national-coverage-annual-report.aspx?year=2019&DocType=NCA&bc=AIAAAIAAAAAA&#ResultsAnchor.

and related services may be eligible for coverage under Medicare's IDE policies. Items and services in certain other types of clinical trials may be eligible for coverage under Medicare's NCD on clinical trials. Finally, CMS has also developed a special approach to coverage for items and services for which the evidence that the service is reasonable and necessary is promising, but not sufficient to support coverage under CMS's usual standards. This is known as Coverage with Evidence Development (CED).

Except as provided in Medicare's IDE and clinical trial policies, Medicare does not cover "experimental and investigational" devices.[27] Medicare also does not cover services related to use of noncovered devices, including "services furnished in preparation for the use" of the device, "services furnished contemporaneously with and necessary to the use" of a noncovered device, and "services furnished as necessary aftercare that are incident to recovery from the use of the device."[28] However, Medicare does cover services "to treat a condition or complication that arises due to the use of a noncovered device or a noncovered device-related service."[29]

1. Medicare Coverage of IDE Devices and Related Services

The key pathway for Medicare coverage for a device study is through the policy on IDE devices. Medicare covers "routine care and services" related to IDE Category A (Experimental) and Category B (Nonexperimental/investigational) devices furnished in conjunction with FDA-approved clinical services that meet the requirements specified in Medicare's regulations.[30] A Category A (Experimental) device is "a device for which 'absolute risk' of the device type has not been established (that is, initial questions of safety and effectiveness have not been resolved) and the FDA is unsure whether the device type can be safe and effective."[31] A Category B (Nonexperimental/investigational) device is "a device for which the incremental risk is the primary risk in question (that is, initial questions of safety and effectiveness of that device type have been resolved), or it is known that the device type can be safe and

27. 42 C.F.R. § 411.15(o).

28. *Id.* § 405.207(a); *see also* Medicare Benefit Policy Manual, ch. 14, § 40, ch. 16, § 180.

29. 42 C.F.R. § 405.207(b)(1).

30. 42 U.S.C. 1395y(m); 42 C.F.R. § 405.207(b)(2) and (3).

31. 42 C.F.R. § 405.201(b).

effective because, for example, other manufacturers have obtained FDA premarket approval or clearance for that device type."[32]

Coverage for devices with a Category A IDE designation is somewhat limited, as it extends only to routine care items and services furnished in the study but does not include coverage for the Category A device itself. In contrast, coverage for devices with Category B IDE designation is broader, including routine care items and services furnished in the study and the Category B device itself.[33] "Routine care and services" is defined as "items and services that are otherwise generally available to Medicare beneficiaries (that is, a benefit category exists, it is not statutorily excluded, and there is no national noncoverage decision) that are furnished during a clinical study and that would be otherwise furnished even if the beneficiary were not enrolled in a clinical study."[34]

In addition to routine care and services, Medicare may cover Category B devices and hospital Institutional Review Board (IRB)-approved nonsignificant risk (NSR) devices.[35] Category B devices and IRB-approved NSR devices may be covered if "there are no regulations, national coverage policies, or manual instructions that would otherwise prohibit Medicare coverage."[36]

In order for there to be coverage for items or services in a Category A or Category B IDE study, the study must be approved by CMS through a centralized review process. The study sponsor makes a request to CMS that includes certain information. First, the sponsor must show that the Category B device or the routine care associated with a Category A or Category B device to be covered in an IDE study meets the following criteria:

1. The principal purpose of the study is to test whether the device improves health outcomes of appropriately selected patients.
2. The rationale for the study is well supported by available scientific and medical information, or it is intended to clarify or establish the health outcomes of interventions already in common clinical use.
3. The study results are not anticipated to unjustifiably duplicate existing knowledge.

32. *Id.*
33. Medicare Benefit Policy Manual, ch. 14, § 20.1.
34. 42 C.F.R. § 405.201(b); Medicare Benefit Policy Manual, ch. 14, § 20.
35. Medicare Benefit Policy Manual, ch. 14, § 10.
36. *Id.*

4. The study design is methodologically appropriate and the anticipated number of enrolled subjects is adequate to confidently answer the research question(s) being asked in the study.
5. The study is sponsored by an organization or individual capable of successfully completing the study.
6. The study is in compliance with all applicable Federal regulations concerning the protection of human subjects found at 21 C.F.R. Parts 50, 56, and 812 and 45 C.F.R. Part 46.
7. Where appropriate, the study is not designed to exclusively test toxicity or disease pathophysiology in healthy individuals. Studies of all medical technologies measuring therapeutic outcomes as one of the objectives may be exempt from this criterion only if the disease or condition being studied is life threatening and the patient has no other viable treatment options.
8. The study is registered with the National Institutes of Health's (NIH's) National Library of Medicine's ClinicalTrials.gov.
9. The study protocol describes the method and timing of release of results on all prespecified outcomes, including release of negative outcomes and that the release should be hastened if the study is terminated early.
10. The study protocol must describe how Medicare beneficiaries may be affected by the device under investigation, and how the study results are or are not expected to be generalizable to the Medicare beneficiary population. Generalizability to populations eligible for Medicare due to age, disability, or other eligibility status must be explicitly described.[37]

The MACs also apply these criteria to determine whether to cover studies of NSR devices approved by a hospital IRB.[38] In addition, the sponsor must provide the following information to CMS: a complete FDA approval letter of the Category A or Category B IDE; the IDE study protocol; the IRB approval letter; the National Clinical Trial (NCT) number; and other supporting materials, as appropriate.[39]

37. 42 C.F.R. § 405.212(a).

38. Medicare Benefit Policy Manual, ch. 14, § 30.

39. 42 C.F.R. § 405.211(c); CMS, Medicare Coverage Related to Investigational Device Exemption (IDE) Studies, (last updated Mar. 27, 2020), https://www.cms.gov/Medicare/Coverage/IDE/index.html.

2. Medicare's NCD on Routine Costs in Clinical Trials

Medicare's NCD on Routine Costs in Clinical Trials allows coverage of "qualifying clinical trials."[40] Although this policy technically applies to devices as well, the ability for device trial to be considered a "qualifying clinical trial" is limited. The device trial must be funded by one of the listed government entities or supported by a center or cooperative group funded by one of those government entities, which is not common.

Under the NCD policy, "routine costs" is defined to include "all items and services that are otherwise generally available to Medicare beneficiaries (i.e., there exists a benefit category, it is not statutorily excluded, and there is not a national non-coverage decision) that are provided in either the experimental or the control arms of a clinical trial," such as:

- Items or services that are typically provided absent a clinical trial (e.g., conventional care);
- Items or services required solely for the provision of the investigational item or service (e.g., administration of a noncovered chemotherapeutic agent), the clinically appropriate monitoring of the effects of the item or service, or the prevention of complications; and
- Items or services needed for reasonable and necessary care arising from the provision of an investigational item or service in particular, for the diagnosis or treatment of complications.[41]

"Routine costs" exclude:

- The investigational item or service, itself unless otherwise covered outside of the clinical trial;
- Items and services provided solely to satisfy data collection and analysis needs and that are not used in the direct clinical management of the patient (e.g., monthly CT scans for a condition usually requiring only a single scan); and
- Items and services customarily provided by the research sponsors free-of-charge for any enrollee in the trial.[42]

Under this policy, the investigational item or service is covered only if it would otherwise be covered by Medicare outside of the clinical trial. Because devices that lack FDA approval or clearance for any indication

40. National Coverage Determination Manual, § 310.1.
41. *Id.*
42. *Id.*

are not covered by Medicare, as described above, these devices cannot gain coverage under this NCD.

Any trial whose routine costs are covered under this policy must meet the following three requirements:

- The subject or purpose of the trial must be the evaluation of an item or service that falls within a Medicare benefit category (e.g., physicians' service, DME, diagnostic test) and is not statutorily excluded from coverage (e.g., cosmetic surgery, hearing aids).
- The trial must not be designed exclusively to test toxicity or disease pathophysiology. It must have therapeutic intent.
- Trials of therapeutic interventions must enroll patients with diagnosed disease rather than healthy volunteers. Trials of diagnostic interventions may enroll healthy patients in order to have a proper control group.[43]

In addition to these three requirements, CMS identifies seven "desirable characteristics" for covered trials:

1. The principal purpose of the trial is to test whether the intervention potentially improves the participants' health outcomes;
2. The trial is well-supported by available scientific and medical information or it is intended to clarify or establish the health outcomes of interventions already in common clinical use;
3. The trial does not unjustifiably duplicate existing studies;
4. The trial design is appropriate to answer the research question being asked in the trial;
5. The trial is sponsored by a credible organization or individual capable of executing the proposed trial successfully;
6. The trial is in compliance with federal regulations relating to the protection of human subjects; and
7. All aspects of the trial are conducted according to the appropriate standards of scientific integrity.[44]

The following types of trials are presumed to meet these characteristics and are automatically deemed to be "Qualifying clinical trials:"

1. Trials funded by NIH, the Centers for Disease Control and Prevention (CDC), Agency for Healthcare Research and Quality (AHRQ), CMS, Department of Defense (DOD), and Department of Veterans Affairs (VA);

43. *Id.*
44. *Id.*

2. Trials supported by centers or cooperative groups that are funded by the NIH, CDC, AHRQ, CMS, DOD, and VA;
3. Trials conducted under an investigational new drug application (IND) reviewed by the FDA; and
4. Drug trials that are exempt from having an IND under 21 C.F.R. § 312.2(b)(1) will be deemed automatically qualified until the qualifying criteria are developed and the certification process is in place. At that time the principal investigators of these trials must certify that the trials meet the qualifying criteria in order to maintain Medicare coverage of routine costs. This certification process will only affect the future status of the trial and will not be used to retroactively change the earlier deemed status.[45]

Other trials that meet the seven "desirable characteristics" may be covered if the "treatments are considered reasonable and necessary by the local contractor."[46]

3. Coverage with Evidence Development

CMS developed CED for items and services for which the evidence that the service is reasonable and necessary is promising, but not sufficient. CED allows coverage for items and services pending collection of additional data through clinical trials or registries. When making CED coverage determinations, CMS conducts a "review of the medical literature to cover an item or service only in the context of an approved clinical study or when additional clinical data are collected to assess the appropriateness of an item or service for use with a particular beneficiary."[47] The CED coverage process requires continued data collection, such as through a registry or a clinical trial meeting certain design specifications established by CMS, in order for the item or service to be covered.[48] The approach has been used to establish coverage policies for several devices, including transcatheter aortic valve replacement (TAVR) devices.[49] In some cases, the approach has been used at the request of manufactur-

---

45. *Id.*

46. CMS, Final Decision for Clinical Trial Policy Q's and A's, https://www.cms.gov/Medicare/Coverage/DeterminationProcess/downloads/id210qa.pdf.

47. CMS, Guidance for the Public, Industry, and CMS Staff Coverage with Evidence Development (Nov. 20, 2014), https://www.cms.gov/medicare-coverage-database/details/medicare-coverage-document-details.aspx?MCDId=27.

48. *Id.*

49. CMS, Decision Memo for Transcatheter Aortic Valve Replacement (TAVR) (CAG-00430R), https://www.cms.gov/medicare-coverage-database/details/nca-decision-memo.aspx?NCAId=293.

ers and other stakeholders who were prepared to collect data; in others, CMS has implemented CED on its own initiative, without prior plans by manufacturers or stakeholders to implement a registry or a clinical trial.

III. Coding: How Is a Device Identified on Claims?

Codes help payers identify items and services on claims for payment. The type of code needed depends on the setting of care and payment system. In some cases, a code may be needed to identify a specific device, and in others, a code may be needed to identify the procedure using the device. Bear in mind that if an item or service is not covered, or if there is no separate payment for the device or the associated procedure, there might not be a need for a code.

There are three main systems of codes used to facilitate payment of medical devices: Current Procedural Terminology (CPT)® codes,[50] Healthcare Common Procedure Coding System (HCPCS) codes, and the International Classification of Diseases, 10th Revision (ICD-10) codes. These systems are the standard, national medical code sets.[51] The following table represents which codes are used in different settings of care:

Setting of Care	Applicable Code
Hospital inpatient	ICD-10
Hospital outpatient	HCPCS/CPT
ASC	HCPCS/CPT
Physician's office	HCPCS/CPT
Home (DME)	HCPCS
Dialysis clinic	HCPCS

A. Current Procedural Terminology Codes

The American Medical Association's (AMA) CPT Editorial Panel is responsible for maintaining the CPT code set, which are Level I HCPCS codes. CPT codes provide a systematic language to describe physician and certain non-physician practitioner services. CPT codes do not describe devices directly; they describe procedures using devices or other technologies. If a new device requires physicians to perform a procedure not currently described by a CPT code, a new or revised code might be needed to allow physicians to bill for that procedure.

50. CPT® is a registered trademark of the American Medical Association.

51. *See* 45 C.F.R. § 162.1002.

There are three categories of CPT codes: Category I, Category II, and Category III, all of which are five digits and can be either numeric or alphanumeric. Category I codes are numerical, permanent codes that describe most of the health care procedures and services in the CPT. Category II codes are alphanumeric codes that are considered supplemental, and are not required for correct coding. Category III codes are alphanumeric, temporary codes that describe new and emerging technologies, and that allow for data collection on clinical efficacy, utilization, and outcomes of these technologies. The CPT also includes "unlisted" or "miscellaneous" codes (Category I codes that end in "99") that can be used when no code exists that describes a specific procedure.[52] The AMA generally requires that a requested Category I or III CPT code to be, among other things:

- Unique, well-defined, and describe a procedure or service that is clearly identified and distinguished from existing procedures and services;
- Consistent with current editorial panel standards for code set maintenance;
- Neither a fragmentation of an existing procedure or service nor currently reportable as a complete service by one or more existing codes (with the exclusion of unlisted codes);
- An accurate reflection of the procedure or service as typically performed; and
- Not proposed as a means to report extraordinary circumstances related to a procedure or service already described in the CPT code set.[53]

Additionally, there are specific criteria for Category I and Category III codes. Services described by Category I codes must also be:

- Approved by the FDA as required for performance of the procedure or service;
- Performed by many physicians or other qualified health care professionals across the U.S.;
- Performed with frequency consistent with the intended clinical use (i.e., a service for a common condition should have high

52. AMA, CPT Overview and Code Approval, *available at* https://www.ama-assn.org/practice-management/cpt/cpt-overview-and-code-approval.

53. AMA, CPT Overview and Code Approval, *available at* https://www.ama-assn.org/practice-management/cpt/cpt-overview-and-code-approval.

volume, whereas a service commonly performed for a rare condition may have low volume); and
- Consistent with current medical practice.[54]

Category III codes may be assigned to services that do not meet all of the requirements for a Category I code. For example, a service may receive a Category III code even if it is not widely performed, has not received FDA approval or FDA approval is not imminent, or the clinical efficacy of the service has not been proven. These differences may make it easier to obtain a Category III code sooner than a Category I code. To be eligible for a Category III code, a procedure or service must be currently or recently performed in humans and must meet at least one of the following additional criteria:

- Have an application supported by at least one relevant AMA advisor representing practitioners who would use the procedure or service; or
- The actual or potential clinical efficacy of the specific procedure or service is supported by peer-reviewed literature available to the CPT Editorial Panel; or
- There is
    - At least one IRB-approved study of the procedure or service being performed; or
    - A description of a current and ongoing U.S. trial outlining the efficacy of the procedure or service; or
    - Other evidence of evolving clinical utilization.[55]

Further, the clinical efficacy of the procedure or service must be documented in literature that meets the requirements set forth in a CPT code change application.[56] Changes to the CPT code set, such as the addition, modification or deletion of a code, must be submitted through the CPT code change application process, which is reviewed and decided on by the CPT Editorial Panel.[57] Each of the Panel members reviews the literature provided, and independently evaluates whether the quality and

54. *Id.*

55. *Id.*

56. AMA, CPT Code Change Applications, *available at* https://www.ama-assn.org/practice-management/cpt/cpt-code-change-applications; *see also* AMA, Coding Change Application, *available at* https://www.ama-assn.org/system/files/2019-11/cpt-code-change-request.pdf (last updated Feb. 11, 2019).

57. AMA, Code Change Instructions, *available at* https://www.ama-assn.org/practice-management/cpt/code-change-instructions.

quantity of the literature sufficiently meets the necessary criteria for a code change.

The number of required articles and the specific level of evidence required to support a code change varies depending on the service or procedure. For example, for new technologies with typical levels of utilization, a Category I code application requires at least one peer-reviewed publication with a majority U.S. patient population and at least two publications with no overlapping patient populations, with at least one of these articles meeting evidence level IIa. For services that use existing or noncontributory technologies, the same number of studies is required, but the minimum level for at least one article is level IIIa or IIIb.[58]

In addition to fulfilling the minimum requirements for the application, device manufacturers need to solicit support for their application from the relevant medical specialty societies, especially those represented on the CPT Advisory Committee, while complying with the AMA's prohibition on "lobbying."[59] This policy permits applicants to seek "input or assistance" from a medical society, but not to make unsolicited communications "for the purpose of attempting to improperly influence either: CPT/HCPAC Advisors' or their societies' evaluation of or comments on" an application or "voting by members of the Editorial Panel" on an application.[60] Applicants may not request assistance from medical specialty societies after the application has been submitted to the AMA.

Once the AMA receives a request for a coding change, AMA staff reviews the application to confirm that all necessary information has been submitted and that the request has not previously been addressed by the CPT Editorial Panel. If the request is deemed complete, it is then forwarded to the CPT Advisory Committee for detailed, substantive review. If the Advisory Committee approves the request, the request is then forwarded to the CPT Editorial Panel for a final decision. The CPT Editorial Panel meets three times a year, and the Panel requires applications to be submitted at least three months prior to the meeting at which the CPT Editorial Panel is requested. A new Category I code would become effective on January 1 of the following year. New Category III codes are released twice each year, on January 1 and July 1, and become effective six months later.[61]

---

58. *See* AMA, Coding Change Application.

59. AMA, CPT Statement on Lobbying, https://www.ama-assn.org/practice-management/cpt/statement-lobbying.

60. *Id.*

61. AMA, The CPT Code Process, https://www.ama-assn.org/about/cpt-editorial-panel/cpt-code-process.

There are three potential outcomes to the submission of a Category I CPT Code application:

1. The CPT Editorial Panel creates a new Category I CPT code that would become effective January 1 of the applicable calendar year;
2. If the CPT Editorial Panel does not grant a new Category I code, either because sufficient clinical evidence to support a Category I application was unavailable or sufficient support from the relevant specialty society was not forthcoming, the CPT Editorial Panel could simply deny the application for a Category I CPT code; or
3. The CPT Editorial Panel could deny the application for a Category I CPT code and instead create a Category III CPT code to collect additional data.

B. HCPCS

While the AMA maintains the CPT code set, CMS is responsible for maintaining the HCPCS Level II coding system to describe and identify health care services and supplies that do not fall within the CPT code set jurisdiction. The HCPCS code sets are divided into two subsets, the first being Level I, which as previously described, is the CPT coding system. Level II codes are alphanumeric codes consisting of a single alphabetical letter and four numeric digits.[62]

Level II codes are typically the most important type of codes for manufacturers of DME and certain devices used in hospital outpatient settings and ASCs. If no existing HCPCS code appropriately describes a new device, an application for a new HCPCS code can be submitted. Decisions regarding the addition, deletion, or revision of HCPCS codes are separate from the process for making determinations regarding coverage and payment. CMS has adopted policies for applying and implementing new HCPCS codes. There are three kinds of revisions to HCPCS coding that can be requested:

- The addition of a new code, including splitting an existing code category;
- That the language used to describe a code that already exists be changed; and
- That an existing code be deleted or discontinued.[63]

---

62. CMS, HCPCS Level II Coding Procedures, *available at* https://www.cms.gov/Medicare/Coding/MedHCPCSGenInfo/Downloads/2018-11-30-HCPCS-Level2-Coding-Procedure.pdf.

63. *Id.*

CMS has created an HCPCS Decision Tree to evaluate external requests to add or revise codes.[64] The application review involves a first and second tier review. The first tier review factors include:

- Whether the application was complete and submitted in a timely fashion;
- Whether HCPCS Level II is the appropriate code jurisdiction (i.e., not capital equipment, not used exclusively in an inpatient setting, not appropriate for a different code set);
- If the product or item is primarily medical in nature, in that it is used by providers for diagnostic and therapeutic purposes;
- If there is FDA approval for the product or item, if required; and
- If there is a national program operating need for Medicare, Medicaid, and/or private payors.

If these factors are met, then CMS engages in a second tier review that includes:

- Whether the item performs a significantly different function that items currently categorized in HCPCS;
- If there is not a significantly different function, then CMS evaluates whether the item operates differently, and if there is a significant therapeutic distinction compared to the existing coded treatment or product;
- CMS then evaluates whether the item meets certain marketing criteria, which must be evidenced by three months of marketing activity for non-drug products.

The application to revise an HCPCS Level II code requires certain information to support the requested change. If there is a significant therapeutic distinction, detail on the clinical theory behind the claim, how the product results in a significantly improved medical or clinical outcome, and copies of all results from a systematic analysis of the available literature must be provided. Articles that are unfavorable must also be provided with any appropriate rebuttal or explanation. The application must also include information regarding FDA clearance (or an explanation on why a product is exempt from FDA review). If FDA clearance was required, the application must include a copy of the cover sheet submitted to the FDA requesting clearance, as well as a copy of the final,

64. CMS, HCPCS Decision Tree, *available at* https://www.cms.gov/Medicare/Coding/MedHCPCSGenInfo/Downloads/HCPCS_Decision_Tree_and_Definitions.pdf.

unredacted FDA approval letter. The application also requires information on the target patient population, durability of the item, warranty, billing, prescribing, medical use, setting of care, and marketing practices.[65]

As of 2020, CMS accepts and considers applications for DMEPOS and other non-drug and non-biological coding cycles bi-annually. If approved, a new code takes effect nine months after the January or June application deadline. CMS announces preliminary decisions approximately four months after the application deadline, shortly before a public meeting. The bi-annual public meetings allow interested parties to make presentations and submit comments in response to the publication of preliminary decisions for new DMEPOS and other non-drug and non-biological coding applications. This gives manufacturers an opportunity to speak in support of a submitted application and respond to the initial decision made by CMS regarding the application.

C. ICD-10 Codes

The ICD-10 is the standard code set for medical diagnosis coding under HIPAA.[66] The ICD-10 has two components, a diagnosis coding system and a procedure coding system. The ICD-10 code sets are a standard language, like the other coding sets already described, that provide unique codes for substantially different health conditions. In addition, new procedures and diagnosis can easily be incorporated into the coding set as new codes for existing and future clinical protocols.[67]

Device manufacturers can apply for ICD-10 codes for procedures using their devices through a bi-annual application process. The ICD-10 Coordination and Maintenance Committee (C&M), a federal interdepartmental committee that consists of representatives from CMS and the CDC National Center for Health (NCHS), is responsible for approving coding changes, and developing errata, addenda and other modifications to the ICD code set.[68] The committee meets twice a year (spring and fall) for two days at CMS headquarters in Baltimore, Maryland, to review requests for coding changes. These meetings are open to the public and registration opens approximately one month prior to the meeting. The

---

65. CMS, HCPCS Level II Code Modification Application Instructions for the 2020 Coding Cycle, *available at* https://www.cms.gov/Medicare/Coding/MedHCPCSGenInfo/Downloads/2020-HCPCS-Application-and-Instructions.pdf.

66. 74 Fed. Reg. 3328 (Jan. 16, 2009).

67. *Id.* at 3330.

68. CMS, ICD-10 Coordination and Maintenance Committee Meetings, https://www.cms.gov/Medicare/Coding/ICD10/ICD-10-Coordination-and-Maintenance-Committee-Meetings.

first day of the meeting is devoted to procedure code issues and is led by CMS. The second day is devoted to diagnosis code issues and is led by CDC.

A proposal for a new or revised ICD-10 Procedure Coding System (ICD-10-PCS) code must be submitted to CMS in advance of the published deadline for the bi-annual meetings, which is generally two months prior to the scheduled meeting. Proposals must include the following information:

- Description of the code(s)/change(s) being requested;
- Rationale for why the new code/change is needed (including clinical relevancy); and
- Supporting clinical references and literature should also be submitted.[69]

Requests should include a background paper that describes the procedure and why the current ICD-10-PCS code does not sufficiently cover or address the procedure. This background paper should include information describing the procedure and the steps involved, as well as detail on outcomes, complications and any other information that may be relevant. If the procedure is a variation on a procedure already contemplated in ICD-10-PCS, then the difference between how the procedures are performed should be clearly delineated. In addition, the background paper should include descriptive detail on the target patient population, care setting, and the diagnosis/diagnoses the procedure is indicated to address.

CMS staff reviews requests for procedure code changes and then informs requestors whether their proposal has been approved for presentation at the C&M Committee meeting for further evaluation. For approved proposals, requestors then make a presentation at the C&M Committee meeting to describe the clinical issues and the procedure or technology. The participants at the meeting may ask questions concerning clinical and coding issues and may offer recommendations in a discussion led by CMS staff. Recommendations concerning proposed code revisions may be made both in person at the C&M Committee meeting and in writing before the end of the comment period. Final decisions on code revisions are made through a clearance process within HHS and no final decisions are made at the meeting.[70]

69. National Center for Health Statistics, ICD-10 Coordination and Maintenance Committee, https://www.cdc.gov/nchs/icd/icd10_maintenance.htm.

70. CMS, Process for Requesting New/Revised ICD-10-PCS Procedure Codes, https://www.cms.gov/Medicare/Coding/ICD10/newrevisedcodes.

IV. Reimbursement: How Medicare Pay for the Device?

Medicare has separate payment systems for each setting of care, such as the Physician Fee Schedule (PFS), Hospital Inpatient Prospective Payment System (IPPS), Hospital Outpatient Prospective Payment System (OPPS), ASC Payment System, ESRD PPS, and DME, Prosthetics, Orthotics, and Supplies (DMEPOS) Fee Schedule. Under many of these payment systems, devices typically are not separately reimbursed, but are reimbursed as part of the payment for the related procedure or other services. Some of these systems have mechanisms to make additional payments for new technologies.

A. Physician Fee Schedule

Medicare reimburses for physician services, including the costs of devices used to perform those services, under the Medicare PFS. The fee schedule establishes payment rates for thousands of physician services, including office visits, surgical procedures, and a broad range of other diagnostic and therapeutic services.

The fee schedule is based on a resource-based relative value scale that compares the work and resources associated with a procedure to other procedures. Each procedure, as identified with a CPT or HCPCS code, has a set of relative value units (RVUs) assigned to it. The RVUs account for the relative resources used to provide physician services:

1. Physician work (based on physicians' assessments of the relative levels of time, effort and skill associated with each service);
2. Practice expenses (PE) (based on the expenses physicians incur when they rent office space, buy supplies, buy or rent equipment, and hire non-physician clinical and administrative staff); and
3. Malpractice expenses (expenses for professional liability insurance based on premiums physicians pay).[71]

Each of these three RVUs is adjusted to reflect variations based on the local geographic market in which the services are rendered using the geographic practice cost indexes (GPCIs).[72] Payments also may be adjusted to reflect other factors. To determine the payment rate, geographically adjusted RVUs are added together and then multiplied by a uniform conversion factor.[73]

---

71. *See* 84 Fed. Reg. 62568, 62571 (Nov. 15, 2019).
72. *See*, e.g., *id.* at 62571.
73. *See*, e.g., *id.*

Payments for use of medical devices would fall under the PE RVU. For many services that can be performed in the physician office setting or in a hospital or ASC, the fee schedule lists different PE RVUs for non-facility (physician office) and facility (hospital or ASC). This difference reflects who bears the overhead cost of providing a service—the physician or the hospital/ASC.[74] As a result, Medicare PFS payment rates for services performed in the physician office are typically greater than payment rates for services performed in the hospital/ASC setting because this payment rate includes the overhead of performing the procedure, such as the costs of the equipment, supplies, and non-physician labor needed to perform the service. For services performed in the hospital or ASC setting, the facility fee to the hospital under the OPPS accounts for these costs.

The PE RVU includes two categories of direct expenses under which devices may be classified: equipment and supplies. The equipment cost in the PE RVU is calculated on a per-minute basis using a detailed formula put forth by CMS in federal regulations. The calculation uses standardized interest rates, depreciation rates, lifetime of the equipment, maintenance, and usage rates.[75] This method is used because the equipment is used over the course of years, and the reimbursement is intended to spread the cost of using the machine across the many uses based on how many minutes the equipment is used. Medical supplies, by contrast, are calculated on a per-unit basis because they tend to be single-use products.

CMS updates the PFS through an annual rulemaking cycle that starts with release of a proposed rule for public comment in the summer, release of a final rule by November 1, and rates set under that rule taking effect on January 1 of the following year. Through this rulemaking process, CMS periodically updates the cost inputs that are used to calculate RVUs based on recommendations from the AMA Relative (Value Scale) Update Committee (RUC). This subcommittee reviews information gather from surveys of special society members about the costs associated with performing particular services. CMS reviews these recommendations and can adopt or revise them, and can use other information about the time and cost associated with providing services, including invoice prices for devices, to determine the RVUs for services.[76]

Ultimately, the Medicare PFS does not directly pay specifically for medical devices. Rather, the costs associated with using the device are

74. *See*, e.g., *id.* at 62573.
75. *Id.* at 62581.
76. Social Security Act § 1848(c)(2)(M).

one factor of the overall amount reimbursed to the physician. The PFS accounts for the resources involved in delivering a service, and medical devices are captured in the PE portion of that calculation as either the amount of time a device is used or the number of units of disposable medical supplies. The calculation, though, is based on the typical patient, rather than the specific inputs for a given patient. That is, when performing a procedure, the physician inputs the code, and the reimbursement for that code takes into account the resources for a typical patient. It is not based on the number of minutes the device is used for the particular patient, but on the typical time the device is used for that coded procedure.

B. Hospital Outpatient Prospective Payment System

Medicare pays for services provided to hospital outpatients under the OPPS. The OPPS groups services, as identified using CPT or HCPCS codes, into ambulatory payment classifications (APCs) grouped based on clinical and cost similarity. The payment rate for services in an APC is calculated using the geometric mean cost of services assigned to that APC, and these rates typically include payment for the devices used, unless the device is granted pass-through status, as discussed later.

Payment rates for APCs are set based on the most recent claims data available and a formula that derives costs from hospital charges. If a patient receives multiple services, the hospital may receive reimbursement through multiple APCs. Medicare does not make payment for services that are "integral, ancillary, supportive, dependent, or adjunctive," however.[77] Payment for those procedures, including many procedures whose codes identify them as add-ons to other procedures, is included in payment for the related primary procedure. Inclusion of payment for one item or service in the payment for another item or service is called "packaging."

CMS updates the OPPS each year through a rulemaking process that includes release of a proposed rule in the summer and release of a final rule around November 1. Changes take effect on January 1 of the following year, and the payment system can be updated quarterly as new technologies are granted pass-through status or procedures are assigned to New Technology APCs, as discussed below. OPPS payment rates are adjusted for local variations in labor costs and for hospital's participation in a quality reporting program.

In general, payment for devices under the OPPS is made through payment for the related procedure. If a new device is considered to be a

77. *See* 84 Fed. Reg. 61142, 61174, Nov. 12, 2019.

tool for performing an existing procedure, rather than a new procedure by itself, then its use would be included in the reimbursement for the codes of the original procedure. If the use of a new device is viewed as a distinct procedure, then an "unlisted" code would be reported for that procedure until a new code could be created and assigned to an APC. Any new code created would be assigned initially to an APC based on the anticipated cost of the procedure. APC assignments and payment rates can change over time as CMS collects data about the cost of the procedure through claims for procedures using the device.

The OPPS has two mechanisms to ensure that new medical technologies are appropriately reimbursed: transitional pass-through payments for categories of medical devices and New Technology APCs.

1. Pass-Through Payments

Pass-through payments help ensure beneficiaries' access to technologies that are too new to be adequately represented in the data CMS uses to establish traditional OPPS payment rates. CMS bases payment for pass-through devices on each hospital's costs, determined by charges adjusted to costs using a cost-to-charge ratio.[78] The transitional pass-through rates are in effect for at least two years, but not more than three years, from the date of the first pass-through payment made under the OPPS for any medical device in the category. CMS assigns HCPCS codes to devices that are granted pass-through status to facilitate claims processing.

To be eligible for a transitional pass-through payment, a device must (1) if required by the FDA, have received approval or clearance; (2) be an integral part of the service furnished, be used for one patient only, come in contact with human tissue, and be surgically implanted, inserted, or applied in or on a wound or skin lesion; and (3) *not* be equipment, instrument, apparatus, implement, or item for which depreciation and financing expenses are recovered as depreciable assets or a material or supply furnished incident to a service.[79]

To qualify for pass-through status, a device must be new, meet the "not insignificant cost" threshold, and be a substantial clinical improvement.[80] To be considered new, it must not be appropriately described by an existing or previously established category for pass-through payments. A "not insignificant" average cost is determined by demonstrating (1) the estimated average reasonable cost of devices in the category exceeds

78. 42 C.F.R. § 419.66(h).
79. 84 Fed. Reg. 61273.
80. *Id.*

25 percent of the applicable APC payment amount for the service related to the category of devices; (2) the estimated average reasonable cost of the devices in the category exceeds the cost of the device-related portion of the APC payment amount for the related service by at least 25 percent; and (3) the difference between the estimated average reasonable cost of the devices in the category and the portion of the APC payment amount for the device exceeds 10 percent of the APC payment amount for the related service.[81] A substantial clinical improvement requires that the device substantially improve the diagnosis or treatment of an illness or injury or improve the functioning of a malformed body part compared to the benefits of a device or devices in a previously established category or other available treatment.[82]

Additionally, as of 2020, CMS established an alternative pathway to the substantial clinical improvement criterion. Devices approved under the FDA's Breakthrough Devices Program and that have received FDA marketing authorization will not be evaluated for substantial clinical improvement for the purposes of determining device pass-through payment status.[83] Breakthrough medical devices must still meet the other requirements, but they are considered to have met the substantial clinical improvement requirement by virtue of the Breakthrough designation.

Manufacturers can apply for pass-through status through a quarterly application process.

2. New Technology APCs

Procedures and services that are not eligible for transitional pass-through payments may qualify for assignment to a New Technology APC. New Technology APCs are classified by cost, not by a procedure's clinical qualities. CMS can assign a procedure to a New Technology APC to allow the agency to gather sufficient claims data to assign the procedure to a permanent APC. In general, these assignments last from two to three years.

To qualify for a New Technology APC, a procedure must, among other things:

- Be truly new and significant enough to warrant having its own code under the HCPCS coding system;

81. *Id.*
82. *Id.*
83. *Id.* at 61296.

- Not be appropriately billed under an existing HCPCS code or APC;
- Not be adequately represented in the claims data being used for the most current annual OPPS payment update;
- Not reasonably be placed in an existing APC group that is appropriate in terms to clinical characteristics and resource costs;
- Be a distinct procedure, with a beginning, middle, and end;
- Not qualify for a transitional pass-through payment; and
- Fall with the scope of Medicare benefits and be determined to be reasonable and necessary for the diagnosis or treatment of illness or injury or to improve the functioning of a malformed body part.[84]

In addition, any devices used in the procedure must have received FDA approval or clearance, if required by the FDA.

CMS uses a quarterly application process to consider requests for new technology APCs.

C. Ambulatory Surgical Center Payment System

Medicare's payment rates for services performed in ASCs are based on the rates calculated for procedures under the OPPS and an adjustment that produces payment rates about 50 percent less than under the OPPS. Not all procedures that are payable under the OPPS are payable in ASCs, however. Medicare pays for procedures in ASCs if the agency "determines [the procedures] do not pose a significant safety risk and are not expected to require an overnight stay following the surgical procedure."[85] Procedures identified with unlisted codes are not reimbursed in ASCs because CMS cannot evaluate those procedures' safety risks. The packaging policies that apply under the OPPS also apply under the ASC Payment System, so that procedures that are not separately payable under the OPPS also are not separately reimbursed under the ASC Payment System. ASC payment rates are adjusted for local variations in labor costs and for an ASC's participation in a quality reporting program.

Devices with pass-through status under the OPPS are separately reimbursed under the ASC Payment System, as well.

---

84. Process and Information Required to Apply for Assignment to a New Technology APC Group Under the OPPS, *available at* https://www.cms.gov/Medicare/Medicare-Fee-for-Service-Payment/HospitalOutpatientPPS/downloads/newtechapc.pdf; *see also* 66 Fed. Reg. 59855, 59897 (Nov. 30, 2001).

85. 73 Fed. Reg. 68502, 68802 (Nov. 18, 2008).

CMS also uses a modified method to calculate payment for procedures that have significant device costs. CMS divides payment for these "device intensive" procedures into a device portion (including the cost of the device itself) and a non-device portion. CMS pays the ASC the same amount it would pay under the OPPS for the device portion of the service but pays the standard ASC rate for the non-device portion of the service.[86] The non-device portion is adjusted for geographic differences while the device portion would be the same across geographic regions.

To be considered to be device intensive, a procedure must (1) involve implantable device(s) assigned a HCPCS code; (2) the required device(s) (including single use devices) must be surgically inserted or implanted; and (3) the device offset amount must be significant, which is defined as exceeding 30 percent of the procedure's mean cost.[87] Additionally, for purposes of satisfying the device-intensive criteria, a device-intensive procedure must involve a device that: (1) has received FDA marketing authorization, has received an FDA IDE and has been classified as a Category B device by FDA or meets another appropriate FDA exemption from premarket review; (2) is an integral part of the service furnished; (3) is used for one patient only; (4) comes in contact with human tissue and is surgically implanted or inserted (either permanently or temporarily); and (5) is not either of the following—(i) equipment, an instrument, apparatus, implement, or item of this type for which depreciation and financing expenses are covered as depreciable assets; or (ii) a material or supply furnished incident to a service (for example, a suture, customized surgical kit, scalpel, or clip, other than a radiological site marker).[88]

For new HCPCS codes describing procedures requiring the implantation of medical devices that do not yet have associated claims data, CMS applies device-intensive status with a default device offset set at 31 percent until claims data are available to establish the HCPCS code-level device offset for the procedures.[89] The purpose of applying the 31 percent default device offset to new codes that describe procedures that implant or insert medical devices is to ensure ASC access for new procedures until claims data become available. In certain rare cases (e.g., in the case of a very costly implantable device), CMS will temporarily assign a

86. MedPAC, Payment Basics: Ambulatory Surgical Center Services Payment System, 2019.

87. 84 Fed. Reg. at 61298.

88. *Id.*

89. *Id.*

higher offset percentage to the new procedure if warranted by additional information such as pricing data form a device manufacturer.[90]

D. Inpatient Prospective Payment System

Under the IPPS, Medicare makes a single payment for all items and services provided to a patient during a hospital inpatient admission. Each admission is assigned to a payment group, called a Medicare Severity-Diagnosis Related Group (MS-DRG) based on the patient's ICD-10 diagnosis and procedure codes. Payment rates are adjusted for geographic variations in cost, disproportionate share hospital status, and teaching hospital status, and participation in quality reporting programs, among other factors.

Admissions that use medical devices may qualify for new technology add-on payments (NTAP). To be eligible, manufacturers of new technologies must submit an application to CMS demonstrating that the technology meets stringent criteria.

The NTAP policy provides additional payments for two to three years for cases with high costs involving eligible new technologies. For technologies that meet the eligibility criteria and are granted NTAP by CMS, the determination of the NTAP amount is based on the cost to hospitals for the new technology. In practice, the NTAP amount is calculated distinctly for each eligible discharge that includes the technology, and NTAP only may be made when the estimated cost of the case exceeds the payment that otherwise would be made to the hospital. The payment mechanism is based on the cost to hospitals for the new technology and is the lesser of 65 percent of the amount by which the total covered costs of the case exceed the MS-DRG payment, or 65 percent of the costs of the new technology.[91]

CMS releases its NTAP application annually.[92] NTAP applications are due to CMS approximately one year in advance of the potential effective date of the NTAP. For example, the deadline to submit an application for FY 2021 NTAP, which would take effect on October 1, 2020, was October 11, 2019.

The NTAP application requires that the applicant demonstrate to CMS that the candidate technology meets the following three established criteria:

---

90. *Id.*

91. 84 Fed. Reg. 42044 (Aug. 16, 2019).

92. *See* CMS, FY 2022 New Technology Application Packet, *available at* https://www.cms.gov/files/zip/fy-2022-new-technology-application-packet.zip.

1. The technology must be "new";[93]
2. The technology must be an advance in medical technology that represents a substantial clinical improvement relative to technologies previously available;[94] and
3. The technology would be inadequately paid under the MS-DRG system.

"New" means within two or three years after the point at which data begin to become available reflecting the ICD–10 code assigned to the new service or technology (depending on when a new code is assigned and data on the new service or technology become available for MS-DRG recalibration). CMS also has identified three criteria for assessing whether the technology meets the newness criteria: (1) whether the product uses the same or similar mechanism of action to achieve a therapeutic outcome, (2) whether the product is assigned to the same or different MS-DRG, and (3) whether the new use of the technology involved the treatment of the same or similar type of disease and the same or similar patient population. If a technology meets all three of these criteria, then it would be considered substantially similar to an existing technology and would not be considered "new" for purposes of NTAP.[95]

A "substantial clinical improvement" means that the new technology significantly improves clinical outcomes for a patient population compared to those treatments currently available. For example, CMS may consider factors such as decreased rate of subsequent diagnostic or therapeutic interventions, decreased future hospitalizations or physician visits, and reduced recovery time. Evidence that may be sufficient to establish the conclusion of substantial clinical improvement includes "[c]linical trials, peer reviewed journal articles; study results; meta-analyses; consensus statements; white papers; patient surveys; case studies; reports; systematic literature reviews; letters from major healthcare associations; editorials and letters to the editor; and public comments. Other appropriate information sources may be considered."[96]

CMS uses a complicated algorithm to assess whether a technology would be inadequately paid under the IPPS. Specifically, the average charges for cases using the technology must exceed the MS-DRG specific cost threshold established by CMS. To qualify, the average costs must exceed a threshold set at the lesser of 75 percent of the standardized

93. 45 C.F.R. § 412.87(b)(2).
94. 66 Fed. Reg. 46902, 46912 (Sept. 7, 2001).
95. 74 Fed. Reg. 43813-43814 (Aug. 27, 2009).
96. *Id.* at 42611–12.

amount increased to reflect the difference between costs and charges (based on the national case weighted cost-to-charge ratio) or 75 percent of one standard deviation (based on the logarithmic values of the charges and transformed back to charges) beyond the geometric mean standardized charge for all cases in the DRGs to which the new technology is assigned (or the case weighted average of all relevant MS-DRGs, if the new technology is used in cases assigned to many different MS-DRGs).[97]

CMS has established an alternative pathway for NTAP eligibility for "transformative new devices" that are part of the FDA's Breakthrough Devices Program and have received FDA marketing authorization. Devices approved through the alternative pathway do not need to meet the newness or substantial improvement criterion under the existing NTAP pathway but must continue to meet the cost criterion. Under the Breakthrough Devices Program, eligible devices must meet one of the following criteria: (1) they must "represent breakthrough technologies"; (2) there must be "no approved or clear alternatives"; (3) they must "offer significant advantages over existing approved or cleared alternatives"; or (4) their availability must be "in the best interest of patients."[98]

After receipt of NTAP applications, CMS organizes a town hall meeting at which "organizations representing hospitals, physicians, manufacturers and any other interested party may present comments, recommendations, and data to the clinical staff of CMS concerning whether the service or technology represents a substantial clinical improvement."[99] The purpose of this meeting is to allow for a discussion of the substantial clinical improvement criteria for each of the NTAP applicants. Individuals may submit written comments after the Town Hall. NTAP applicants may make a formal presentation at the meeting and/or submit written comments to CMS after the Town Hall Meeting.

CMS publishes a discussion of each new NTAP applicant in the IPPS proposed rule for the forthcoming fiscal year (FY) that usually is published each April. CMS accepts comments from the manufacturer and the public on whether an applicant satisfies the criteria for NTAP and whether NTAP should be granted for an applicant. During this time, we recommend that manufacturers work with trade associations, patient groups, and others to gather support for NTAP for the drug. CMS publishes its

---

97. New Medical Services and New Technologies, *available at* http://www.cms.gov/Medicare/Medicare-Fee-for-Service-Payment/AcuteInpatientPPS/newtech.html.

98. Federal Food, Drug, and Cosmetic Act § 515B(b); 21 U.S.C. § 360e-3(b).

99. 81 Fed. Reg. 78814 (Nov. 9, 2016).

final decisions with respect to NTAP in the IPPS final rule that usually is published each August.

E. End-Stage Renal Disease Prospective Payment System

Medicare pays for outpatient dialysis services for beneficiaries with ESRD under the ESRD PPS. This payment system provides a single payment to dialysis facilities for each session of dialysis, subject to adjustments for differences in labor costs and certain patient characteristics.

Beginning with 2021, the ESRD PPS includes the Transitional Add-on Payment Adjustment for New and Innovative Equipment and Supplies (TPNIES) to support ESRD facilities in the uptake of new and innovative equipment and supplies under the ESRD PPS.[100] CMS accepts applications annually, and qualifying technologies receive TPNIES for two calendar years.

To be eligible for TPNIES, renal dialysis equipment and supplies must (1) have been designated by CMS as a renal dialysis service; (2) be "new," meaning granted marketing authorization by FDA on or after January 1, 2020; (3) be commercially available by January 1 of the particular calendar year, meaning the year in which the payment adjustment would take effect; (4) have a HCPCS application submitted in accordance with the official Level II HCPCS coding procedures by September 1 of the particular calendar year; (5) be "innovative," meaning they meet the IPPS substantial clinical improvement criteria and related guidance; and (6) except for home dialysis machines used by a single patient, not be capital-related assets.[101]

The TPNIES amount is based on 65 percent of the price established by the MACs, using invoice information and other relevant sources of information.[102]

F. Durable Medical Equipment Reimbursement

Medicare uses two methods to pay for durable medical equipment, prosthetics, orthotics, and supplies (DMEPOS): a fee schedule and competitive bidding.

---

100. Medicare Program; End-Stage Renal Disease Prospective Payment System, 84 Fed. Reg. 60648, 60684–60692 (Nov. 8, 2019).

101. *Id.* at 60961.

102. *Id.* at 60967.

1. DMEPOS Fee Schedule

If an item meets the definition of DME then it will be categorized into one of the following payment classes: (1) inexpensive or other routinely purchased DME; (2) items requiring frequent and substantial servicing; (3) certain customized items; (4) other prosthetic and orthotic devices; (5) other DME (capped rental items); (6) oxygen and oxygen equipment; or (7) transcutaneous electrical nerve stimulators (TENS).[103] To determine how a device will be reimbursed under the DME fee schedule, one must determine first if the device is described by a HCPCS code that is reimbursed under the fee schedule. Devices that are described by existing codes are reimbursed at the rates established for those codes, which are based on historic charge data and list prices. If the device is not described by such a code, the manufacture can apply for a new code and a new payment rate will be established for it.

In 2019, CMS revised its policy for establishing payments for new codes under the DME fee schedule. Under this policy, CMS establishes fee schedule pricing for new codes based on the following sources of pricing information, in order of preference: (1) fee schedule pricing history for codes that have previously been used to pay for the item described the new code ("continuity of pricing"); (2) gap-filling with fee schedule pricing history for "comparable items"; and (3) gap-filling with supplier or commercial prices. If the historic pricing data is established via gap-filling, the gap-filled prices are deflated to the historic base period and updated based on statutory factors to determine the fee schedule amount for the new code. The first priority is to determine whether the item described by the new code "has a fee schedule pricing history," i.e., whether the item was classified and paid for previously under a different code. If the item is determined to have a pricing history, the previous fee schedule amounts for the old code(s) are mapped to the new code(s) in a specified manner depending on the type of coding change, in order to ensure continuity of pricing.[104] Under the "continuity of pricing" mechanism, how the payment for the new code is determined is based on the particular coding change (e.g., dividing or combining of codes).[105]

If the DME item does not have a fee schedule pricing history (i.e., not classified and paid for previously under a different code), CMS will seek to establish the fee schedule amount for the new code by using

103. 42 C.F.R. § 414.210; Medicare Claims Processing Manual, ch. 20, § 30.
104. 42 C.F.R. § 414.236(a).
105. *See id.* § 414.236(b).

"comparable" items with existing fee schedule amounts.[106] Comparability determinations are based on, but not limited to, CMS's evaluation of five component categories and related attributes:[107]

- Physical: Aesthetics, Design, Customized vs. Standard, Material, Portable, Size, Temperature Range/Tolerance, Weight
- Mechanical: Automated vs. Manual, Brittleness, Ductility, Durability, Elasticity, Fatigue, Flexibility, Hardness, Load Capacity, Flow-Control, Permeability, Strength
- Electrical: Capacitance, Conductivity, Dielectric Constant, Frequency, Generator, Impedance, Piezo-electric, Power, Power Source, Resistance
- Function and Intended Use: Function, Intended Use
- Additional Attributes and Features: "Smart", Alarms, Constraints, Device Limitations, Disposable, Parts, Features, Invasive vs. Non-Invasive

The comparability analysis gives the agency flexibility regarding the basis for determining an item is "comparable" to another item. For instance, the comparison can be based on the items as a whole, subcomponents, or a combination of items. Further, a new product need not be comparable within each category, and there is no prioritization of the categories. As these categories and attributes were only identified in the recently completed rulemaking, there is no clear history on how CMS performs the "comparability" assessment with respect to specific items.

Only if there is no fee schedule pricing history and CMS is unable to identify comparable items with existing DME fee schedule amounts, will CMS establish the fee schedule amount for the new code using supplier price lists, including catalogs and other retail price lists (such as internet retail prices) that provide commercial pricing information.[108] Appropriate sources of commercial pricing information may include payments made by Medicare Advantage plans and verifiable information from supplier invoices and non-Medicare payer data. In addition, CMS makes clear that is will no longer use manufacturer suggested retail prices (MSRPs).[109] Based on recent changes, it is increasingly possible that CMS would use prices to any customer, including to self-pay patients, when establishing a fee schedule amount determined using supplier or commercial price lists

106. *Id.* § 414.238(b).
107. *See* 84 Fed. Reg. at 60734.
108. 42 C.F.R. § 414.238(c)(1).
109. 84 Fed. Reg. at 60730.

(instead of using the above discussed continuity of pricing or comparability mechanisms). Further, we note that if CMS sets the rate using supplier or commercial pricing information, if the price for a new item decreases within five years, CMS may reassess and adjust the payment rate. This one-time adjustment applies only if (1) the supplier or commercial price used to establish the fee schedule amount decreases by any amount below 15 percent with 5 years; and (2) if the new fee schedule amount would be no more than 15 percent lower as a result of the adjustment.[110]

2. Competitive Bidding

CMS is authorized to conduct competitive bidding to establish reimbursement rates for DME. Under the DMEPOS Competitive Bidding Program (CBP) Medicare pays for selected DMEPOS items in certain areas of the country using a single payment amount (SPA), rather than paying the current Medicare DMEPOS fee schedule payment amounts.[111] The SPA is based on bids submitted by DMEPOS suppliers competing to become Medicare contract suppliers to furnish certain items within a product category in competitive bidding areas (CBAs). DMEPOS items that are subject to payment under the CBP are specified by statute and include off-the-shelf orthotics, enteral nutrients, equipment and supplies, and certain DME and medical supplies which are covered items.[112]

The DMEPOS CBP was first implemented on January 1, 2011, and has undergone two rounds of contracts through competitive bidding—the Round 1 2017 contracts (effective January 1, 2017) and the Round 2 Recompete and National Mail-Order Recompete contracts (effective July 1, 2016).[113] These contracts applied to enteral nutrients, equipment, and supplies; general home equipment and related supplies and accessories (including hospital beds, pressure reducing support surfaces, commode chairs, patient lifts, and seat lifts); nebulizers and related supplies; negative pressure wound therapy (npwt) pumps and related supplies and accessories; respiratory equipment and related supplies and accessories (including oxygen and oxygen equipment, continuous positive pressure airway devices, and respiratory assist devices); standard mobility equipment and related accessories (including walkers, standard manual wheelchairs,

110. *See* 42 C.F.R. § 414.238(c)(2); 84 Fed. Reg. at 60736.

111. *See* 42 U.S.C. § 1395w-3(b)(5)(A).

112. *See id.* § 1395w-3(a)(1).

113. CMS, Durable Medical Equipment, Prosthetics, Orthotics, and Supplies Competitive Bidding Program Health Status Monitoring Summary of Findings thru the Fourth Quarter of 2019, https://www.cms.gov/Medicare/Medicare-Fee-for-Service-Payment/DMEPOSCompetitiveBid/Monitoring (last visited June 25, 2020).

and standard power wheelchairs); and transcutaneous electrical nerve stimulation (TENS) devices and supplies.[114] After these DMEPOS CBP contracts expired on December 31, 2018, a temporary gap in the entire DMEPOS CBP was in effect from January 1, 2019 until December 31, 2020. During this time, Medicare beneficiaries were permitted to receive DMEPOS items from any Medicare enrolled DMEPOS supplier.

A new round of competitive bidding, Round 2021, became effective January 1, 2021, and will extend through December 31, 2023.[115] In this round, CMS will implement the lead item pricing methodology for all items included in the product categories established in the final rule published on November 14, 2018.[116] Rather than submitting individual bids for each item within a product category, bidders will only submit one bid for the lead item in the product category. The supplier's bid for the lead item represents the supplier's bid for furnishing the lead item and all other items (the non-lead items) in the product category. Bids for the lead item in the product category will be used to calculate the SPAs for all of the items within that product category. The SPA for the lead item will be the maximum bid submitted for that item by bidders whose bids for the item are in the winning range in that CBA and product category combination. The SPAs for the non-lead items within the product category are determined by multiplying the lead item SPA by a relative ratio. The ratios are based on the historic differences in the fee schedule amounts for the lead item and non-lead items.

CBP rates also affect payment rates outside CBAs. Fee schedule amounts in rural and non-contiguous areas where competitive bidding has yet to be implemented are set using a 50/50 blend of competitive bidding pricing and historic ("unadjusted") fee schedule amounts.[117] The fee schedule amounts for other areas where competitive bidding has yet to be implemented are adjusted using competitive bidding pricing only.[118] Fee schedule amounts also are adjusted for former competitive bidding areas using competitive bidding pricing when there is a gap in the DMEPOS CBP.[119]

---

114. 83 Fed. Reg. 56922, 57017 (Nov. 14, 2018).

115. *See* CMS, DMEPOS Competitive Bidding Program Round 2021 Announcement (Mar. 7, 2019), https://dmecompetitivebid.com/cbic/cbic2021.nsf/DocsCat/News~CHWUC00H4E?open&navmenu=|| (last visited June 25, 2020).

116. 83 Fed. Reg. 56922 (Nov. 14, 2018).

117. *Id.* at 57039.

118. *Id.*

119. *Id.*

V. Conclusion

Coverage, coding, and reimbursement pathways for medical devices vary significantly based on the type of device and the setting in which it is used. Manufacturers need to analyze the unique characteristics of their devices, and how and where they are used, to determine how they will be covered and reimbursed and whether new codes are needed for them. In addition, manufacturers may use Medicare's policies as a benchmark, but should recognize that coverage, coding, and payment may vary across payers.

CHAPTER 11

AI—Products Liability

Terrence Dee

I. Traditional Theories of Product Liability

Developers, manufacturers, and users of medical AI tools must consider product liability and other litigation risks associated with the impacts of product failure or malfunction on a patient. An AI tool that engages in clinical decision making in combination with or in lieu of a clinician may be considered a dangerous or high-risk product under common law theories of liability and various state consumer protection laws. The developer, manufacturer, or health care provider could be held responsible for deficiencies or other problems associated with the use of the AI tool or the monitoring or interpretation of data produced by AI.[1]

There are three general theories of product liability that may apply to AI tools: strict liability, breach of warranty, and negligence.

A. Strict Liability

Manufacturers or developers may be held to a strict liability standard when a product is sold or used on a patient that: (1) contains a defect that is unreasonably dangerous; (2) the defect causes harm to the consumer; and (3) the harm results in actionable injury.[2] For strict liability claims, the plaintiff does not need to prove the defendant acted carelessly. Rather, the plaintiff only needs to show a product defect at the time of sale that caused the plaintiff's harm, regardless of fault.[3] Manufacturers of prescription drugs and medical devices that may be legally sold or otherwise

1. *See* 1 AHLA Digital Health Practice Guide § 3.2.4.2 (2018).
2. David G. Owen, Products Liability Law (3d ed. 2014).
3. Restatement (Third) of Torts: Products Liability § 2 (1998).

distributed pursuant to a health care provider's prescription are liable when defects cause harm to patients.[4]

The defect can be in the design, manufacture, or labeling of the product.[5] A *design defect* may be found where a product is in a "defective condition unreasonably dangerous to [a] user or consumer" or if the "foreseeable risks of harm could have been reduced by the adoption of a reasonable alternative design."[6] A medical drug or device is defectively designed if the foreseeable risks of harm posed by the drug or device are sufficiently great in relation to its foreseeable therapeutic benefits such that reasonable providers would not prescribe it to any class of patients.[7] A *manufacturing defect* occurs when the manufactured product does not conform to the manufacturer's own specifications or requirements and causes harm.[8] For example, a defibrillator with defective wire insulation that could trigger electric shocks in a patient may constitute such a defect. Additionally, a *labeling defect* can lead to a failure to warn claim, based on the "manufacturer's failure to provide adequate warnings to the consumer of dangers inherent to the product or to provide instructions for the safe use of the product."[9] In the health care context, because the law accepts that prescription medical products have inherent and unavoidable risks and require physician approval prior to use, warnings, or instructions are inadequate where they fail to reasonably disclose risks to prescribing and other health care providers who are in a position to reduce risks of harm.[10]

B. Breach of Warranty

Plaintiffs can also bring products liability claims under breach of warranty theories, which provide in independent basis of liability under

---

4. Hannah R. Sullivan & Scott J. Schweikart, *Are Current Tort Liability Doctrines Adequate for Addressing Injury Caused by AI?*, 21 AMA J. ETHICS 160, 162 (2019), https://journalofethics.ama-assn.org/article/are-current-tort-liability-doctrines-adequate-addressing-injury-caused-ai/2019-02.

5. *See* RESTATEMENT (THIRD) OF TORTS: PRODUCTS LIABILITY (1998).

6. RESTATEMENT (SECOND) OF TORTS § 402(A) (1965); *see also* Jason Chung & Amanda Zink, *Hey Watson—Can I Sue You for Malpractice—Examining the Liability of Artificial Intelligence in Medicine*, 11 ASIA PACIFIC J. HEALTH L. & ETHICS 51, 68 (2018) (citing David C. Vladeck, *Machines without Principals: Liability Rules and Artificial Intelligence*, 89 WASH. L. REV. 117, 135 (2014)).

7. Sullivan & Schweikart, *supra* note 4.

8. RESTATEMENT (THIRD) OF TORTS: PRODUCTS LIABILITY § 2(*a*) (1998); Chung & Zink, *supra* note 6 (citing Vladeck, at 139).

9. Chung & Zink, *supra* note 6 (internal citations omitted).

10. Sullivan & Schweikart, *supra* note 4.

the Uniform Commercial Code (UCC).[11] The elements for breach of warranty are similar to strict liability and plaintiffs can assert them in jurisdictions that do not recognize strict products liability as a cause of action.[12] Breach of *express warranty* claims arise when the seller makes "express" guarantees that the product will perform in a particular way. Such an express warranty is usually set forth in a sales contract, but the seller can also convey express warranties through oral representations about the product.

The UCC also recognizes two *implied warranties*: (1) the *implied warranty of merchantability* and (2) the *implied warranty of fitness for a particular purpose*. Manufacturers may be held liable for breach of warranty of merchantability when the manufacturer sells a product to a consumer that is not reasonably fit for the purposes or intended use for which that product or similar products are sold. Similar to a manufacturing defect claim, an implied warranty of merchantability claim arises when the manufacturer sells a product that departs from the manufacturer's specifications, regardless of fault.[13]

Claims for breach of the implied warranty of fitness for a particular purpose arise when a seller knows a consumer is buying a product for a specific purpose, the seller knows the consumer relies on the seller's skill and expertise in choosing the right product for that intended purpose, and the product is not appropriate for that purpose.[14] For this type of claim, the product does not need to be defective for a seller to violate the implied warranty of fitness.

C. Negligence

A showing of negligence requires a plaintiff (e.g., patient) to show that a defendant (e.g., the physician and/or manufacturer): (1) had a *duty* of care to the consumer; (2) breached the duty by subjecting the consumer to *unreasonable risk of harm*; (3) *caused* the consumer harm; and (4) the harm resulted in an *actionable injury*.[15] A plaintiff must generally prove the defendant acted unreasonably considering foreseeable risks, and the standard is based on what an objective and hypothetical "reasonable"

---

11. Restatement (Third) of Torts: Products Liability § 9 (1998).
12. 1 AHLA Digital Health Practice Guide § 3.2.4.2 (2018).
13. *See* Restatement (Third) of Torts: Products Liability § 2 (1998).
14. Marc A. Primack, *Representations, Warranties and Covenants: Back to the Basics in Contracts*, Nat'l L. Rev. (Dec. 1, 2009), https://www.natlawreview.com/article/representations-warranties-and-covenants-back-to-basics-contracts.
15. Restatement (Second) of Torts § 281 (1965).

person would have done under the circumstances.[16] Negligence therefore rests on a showing of fault leading to product defect.[17] For a claim of negligence to succeed in the context of medical AI, the plaintiff would likely focus on the manufacturer's development, validation, or manufacturing processes; appropriateness of clinician training; effectiveness of the instructions for use, warnings, or other disclaimers; or postmarket adverse event and response (e.g., consumer warning, recall) processes.[18]

D. Common Defenses

1. Learned Intermediary

Despite the existence of these and other product liability pathways, several courts have adopted the learned intermediary doctrine as a defense to the rule that manufacturers have a duty to warn patients directly about the risk of certain products.[19] The doctrine protects manufacturers of prescription drugs and restricted (e.g., prescription) medical devices from product liability arising under failure to warn theories if the manufacturer provided adequate warning to the prescribing physician about the product's risks. If the defense is successful, the patient's remedy is limited to a medical malpractice or negligence claim against the physician.

The strength of the learned intermediary defense has eroded in recent years.[20] Several courts have refused to apply the learned intermediary doctrine in personal injury actions involving prescription drugs and devices that were aggressively marketed to the public through direct-to-consumer advertisements, Internet, and other forms of media.[21] Courts have found that where the manufacturer's market efforts "drown-out" warnings and limitations on use, the learned intermediary doctrine may not insulate manufacturers from liability.

2. Preemption

The Federal Food, Drug, and Cosmetic Act's (FDCA) medical device preemption provision has been used in some product liability actions to limit negligence or failure to warn theories arising under state laws.[22]

---

16. *See* Ryan Abott, *The Reasonable Computer: Disrupting the Paradigm of Tort Liability*, 86 G. Wash. L. Rev. 1, 12–13 (2018).

17. Restatement (Third) of Torts: Products Liability § 2 (1998).

18. 1 AHLA Digital Health Practice Guide § 3.2.4.2 (2018).

19. Restatement (Third) of Torts: Products Liability § 6 cmt. d (1998).

20. 1 AHLA Digital Health Practice Guide § 3.2.4.2 (2018).

21. *See, e.g.*, Centocor, Inc. v. Hamilton, 372 S.W.3d 140 (Tex. 2012).

22. 21 U.S.C. § 360k(a).

In *Riegel v. Medtronic, Inc.*,[23] the Supreme Court held that 21 U.S.C. § 360k(a) bars common law claims against a manufacturer that challenge the safety or effectiveness of a Class III medical device if the device received premarket approval from the FDA.[24] For example, in the context of prescription drugs, the FDA requires the manufacturer to put specific warning language on the label. If the manufacturer uses that language, the FDCA preempts a plaintiff's claim for failure to warn of a dangerous condition or side effect.[25] Several judicial decisions have limited the scope and applicability of medical device preemption to high risk devices that have undergone PMA approval.[26] There are also exceptions to preemption, such as if the drug manufacturer knew of adverse effects and did not disclose those effects to the FDA.

The Biomaterials Access Assurance Act (BAAA) also preempts state and federal claims against biomaterials suppliers who provide component parts to manufacturers of implant medical devices.[27] The BAAA defines an implant as

> (A) a medical device that is intended by the manufacturer of the device . . . (i) to be placed into a surgically or naturally formed or existing cavity of the body for a period of at least 30 days; or (ii) to remain in contact with bodily fluids or internal human tissue

23. 552 U.S. 316 (2008).

24. *See* Dana Koerner, *Doctor Roboto: The No-Man Operation*, 51 U. Tol. L. Rev. 125, 135 (2019).

25. Richard L. Jr. Cupp, *Preemption's Rise (and Bit of a Fall) as Product Liability Reform—*Wyeth, Riegel, Altria, *and the* Restatement (Third)*'s Prescription Product Design Defect Standard*, 74 Brook L. Rev. 727, 737 (2009).

26. 1 AHLA Digital Health Practice Guide § 3.2.4.2 (2018). Circuits continue to define the limits of preemption—creating a circuit split in the treatment of state claims against manufacturers. *See* Stengel v. Medtronic Inc., 704 F.3d 1224, 1228 (9th Cir. 2013) (holding that 21 U.S.C. § 360k(a) does not preempt common law claims against a manufacturer that "parallel" federal requirements).

27. *See* 21 U.S.C. §§ 1601–1606. Sadler v. Advanced Bionics, LLC, 2013 WL 1636374, at *2 (W.D. Ky. Apr. 16, 2013) ("Congress enacted the BAAA to protect companies that manufacture component parts for implant devices from suit, because suppliers of materials do not design, test or produce medical devices, so they are not responsible, at common law or by statute, for ensuring the safety of medical devices. Nonetheless, when a medical device is alleged to have caused harm, biomaterials suppliers are often named along with manufacturers as defendants in lawsuits alleging inadequate design and testing or inadequate warning related to the use of the device.").

through a surgically produced opening for a period of less than 30 days; and (B) suture materials used in implant procedures.[28]

The act defines a component as "a manufactured piece of an implant" and includes "a manufactured pieces of an implant" that "(i) has significant non-implant applications; and (ii) alone, alone, has no implant value or purpose, but when combined with other component parts and materials, constitutes an implant."[29]

II. Application of Product Liability Theories to Health Care AI

A. Product versus Software

A threshold question in determining whether traditional theories of product liability apply to medical AI is whether the AI system is considered a "product" and thus subject to strict liability and/or breach of warranty. If the AI system is considered merely a service tool that assists health care providers in making treatment decisions, then liability would likely require analysis under a negligence theory of liability.[30] The Restatement (Third) of Torts: Product Liability, defines "product" as "tangible personal property distributed commercially for use or consumption" or any other item whose "context of . . . distribution and use is sufficiently analogous to [that] of tangible personal property."[31] Relying on this definition, the Third Circuit held that the New Jersey Products Liability Act does not apply to an AI algorithm used by the state to evaluate prisoner candidates for its pretrial release program because an "algorithm" or "formula" does not constitute "tangible personal property" nor is it remotely "analogous to it" and therefore is not a "product" under the NJPLA.[32]

Although courts have traditionally been reluctant to apply product liability theories to software developers, that view may change as AI software becomes more integrated into certain medical AI devices.[33] As more algorithms are designed to automate the performance of clinical diagnostic tasks, the FDA could categorize these technologies as medi-

28. 21 U.S.C. § 1602(5).

29. *Id.* § 1602(3).

30. Alicia Bromfield & Kristin McMahon, *Artificial Intelligence in Healthcare: Preparing for a new legal liability landscape*, IRONSHORE (2019), http://www.ironshore.com/pdfs/general/LM-IS_Artificial_Intelligence_Healthcare.pdf.

31. RESTATEMENT (THIRD) OF TORTS: PRODUCTS LIABILITY § 19(a) (1998).

32. Rodgers v. Christie, 795 Fed. Appx. 878, 880 (3d Cir. 2020).

33. *See* W. Nicholson Price, *Artificial Intelligence in Health Care: Applications and Legal Implications*, 14 THE SCITECH LAWYER 10, 11 (2017), https://repository.law.umich.edu/articles/1932/.

cal devices, either because the algorithms are embodied in traditional medical devices, or classified under the FDA's Software as a Medical Device guidance.[34] In the context of other technologies, courts have started to examine whether the software was integrated with a physical object, whether the object was mass-produced, or whether it had dangerous potential.[35] For example, two crashes of the Boeing 737 MAX that left no survivors illustrate software design issues that contributed to serious harms.[36] Although the software at issue did not involve AI systems, Boeing may be liable under strict liability and warranty theories because the software was so integrated into the aircraft.[37] Similarly, in the context of autonomous vehicles, courts have determined that AI software embodied in a machine capable of causing great harm is a product.[38] Courts could make that same determination for AI machine vision software used for medical imaging where that AI software is integrated into a tangible machine with cameras and sensors.[39]

Courts may also treat different types of AI systems differently for products liability purposes. Some medical professionals and researchers suggest a classification system based on the AI device's level of autonomy or system capabilities.[40] Consider AI devices performing simple tasks like automating the patient check-in process at health clinics versus an AI-enabled system used to identify abnormalities in MRI images. The latter system continues to evolve and modify its decision-making process for a more accurate response through self-learning.[41] Should the

---

34. Zach Harned, Matthew P. Lungren & Pranav Rajpurkar, *Machine Vision, Medical AI, and Malpractice*, HARV. J.L. & TECH. DIG., 4 (2019), https://jolt.law.harvard.edu/digest/machine-vision-medical-ai-and-malpractice; *see generally Software as a Medical Device (SAMD): Clinical Evaluation—Guidance for Industry and Food and Drug Administration Staff*, FDA (Dec. 8, 2017), https://www.fda.gov/downloads/medicaldevices/deviceregulationandguidance/guidancedocuments/ucm524904.pdf.

35. Karni A. Chagal_Feferkorn, *Am I an Algorithm or a Product: When Products Liability Should Apply to Algorithmic Decision-Makers*, 30 STAN. L. & POL'Y REV. 61, 83–84 (2019).

36. John Villasenor, *Products Liability Law as a Way to Address AI Harms*, BROOKINGS (Oct. 31, 2019), https://www.brookings.edu/research/products-liability-law-as-a-way-to-address-ai-harms/.

37. *See* Tom Hals et al., *Ethiopia Crash May Test Boeing's Success in Defeating U.S. Lawsuits: Legal Experts*, REUTERS (Mar. 14, 2019), reuters.com/article/us-ethiopia-airplane-lawsuit/ethiopia-crash-may-test-boeings-success-in-defeating-u-s-lawsuits-legal-experts-idUSKCN1QW05T.

38. Harned, Lungren & Rajpurkar, *supra* note 34, at 8.

39. *Id.*

40. Koerner, *supra* note 24; Chagal_Feferkorn, *supra* note 35, at 69.

41. Sullivan & Schweikart, *supra* note 4, at 160–61.

same theories of liability apply? As AI technology and its applications in medicine continue to develop, practitioners should follow carefully whether courts apply product liability concepts differently to those different classifications.

B. Test to Determine Whether Health Care AI Is Defective

In the event a particular health care AI is considered a product, the question is then how courts will determine whether it is defective. Strict liability claims involving AI software as a medical device are more likely to be brought under theories of design defect or failure to warn.[42]

Design defects are generally established through one of two tests depending on whether the jurisdiction follows the Restatement (Second) of Torts or the Restatement (Third) of Torts, with minor state-by-state variation: the consumer expectations test from the Restatement (Second) of Torts or the risk-utility test from the Restatement (Third) of Torts.[43] Under the consumer-expectations test, a product is defective in design if the product is in a "defective condition unreasonably dangerous to [a] user or consumer.[44] An "unreasonably dangerous defect" is one that makes a product fail to perform as safely as an ordinary consumer would expect when used in an intended or reasonably foreseeable way.[45] However, the consumer expectations test only applies where the everyday experience of the user permits the conclusion that the product's design violated minimum safety assumptions.[46] While the California Supreme Court articulated a model of the consumer expectations test for complex products, which specifies that for complex products the consumer's everyday experience permits a conclusion that the products design violated minimum safety assumptions regardless of expert opinions about the merits of the design, that California model is a minority view.[47] The majority of jurisdictions hold that a product is defective if it is dangerous beyond the extent anticipated by an ordinary user without expressly

42. Joe Fornadel & Wes Moran, *Predicting Liability Risks Based on the Existing Regulatory and Legal Framework*, For The Defense 48, 51 (Sept. 2020).

43. David C. Vladeck, *Machines without Principals: Liability Rules and Artificial Intelligence*, 89 Wash. L. Rev. 117, 132–39 (2014); Greg Swanson, *Non-Autonomous Artificial Intelligence Programs and Products Liability: How New AI Products Challenge Existing Liability Models and Pose New Financial Burdens*, Comment, 42 Seattle U. L. Rev. 1201, 1213–19 (2019).

44. Restatement (Second) of Torts § 402A(1) (1965).

45. Vladeck, *supra* note 43, at 135.

46. Fornadel & Moran, *supra* note 42, at 51.

47. Swanson, *supra* note 43, at 1214.

accounting for the product's complexity.[48] Because medical AI consists of specialized medical devices that incorporate AI-based algorithms, it is therefore unlikely for the consumer expectations to apply.[49] Instead, the risk-utility test is more likely to apply to medical AI.[50]

Under the risk-utility test, a plaintiff must show "the foreseeable risks of harm posed by the product could have been reduced by the adoption of a reasonable alternative design."[51] The word "reasonable" imports a quantitative cost-benefit analysis into the risk-utility test such that a product is defective in design if the inherent risks in the design outweigh the benefits.[52]

AI tools can be extremely beneficial—particularly in the health care context—as they can speed analysis, expand the knowledge base of the provider, and speed the review of vast amounts of data.[53] Medical AI has enormous potential in prognostics, diagnostics, image analysis, resource allocation, and treatment recommendations.[54] Some health diagnostic tools that employ advanced AI systems in development appear capable of performing as well as their human counterparts, and sometimes better.[55] In the future, technological performance is expected to continue to improve, and the number and scope of activities subject to this kind of automation will likely increase.[56]

The benefit of health care AI is evident amid the global Coronavirus pandemic, as software developers, scientists from top universities, and companies are teaming up to research whether AI can curb the spread of the disease and help fight against future global health crises.[57] AI software can help predict potential coronavirus outbreaks by learning to flag

48. *Id.* at 1214–15.

49. Fornadel & Moran, *supra* note 42, at 51.

50. *Id.*

51. Restatement (Third) of Torts: Products Liability § 2(b) (1998).

52. Vladeck, *supra* note 43, at 135; Fornadel & Moran, *supra* note 42, at 51.

53. 1 AHLA Digital Health Practice Guide § 3.2.4.3 (2018).

54. Price, *supra* note 33, at 10.

55. Taylor Kubota, *Deep Learning Algorithm Does as well as Dermatologists in Identifying Skin Cancer*, Stanford News (Jan. 25, 2017), http://news.stanford.edu/2017/01/25/artificial-intelligence-used-identify-skin-cancer/ (last visited Apr. 4, 2017).

56. Evan Sweeney, *Study: Artificial Intelligence Can Diagnose Skin Cancer as Well as Doctors Do*, FierceHealthcare (Jan. 26, 2017). http://www.fiercehealthcare.com/it/study-artificial-intelligence-can-diagnose-skin-cancer-as-well-as-doctors (last visited Apr. 4, 2017).

57. William J. Broad, *A.I. Versus the Coronavirus*, N.Y. Times (Mar. 26, 2020), https://www.nytimes.com/2020/03/26/science/ai-versus-the-coronavirus.html.

disease risk and outbreak threats based on personal data, such as medical history, real-time body-temperature readings, current symptom reports, and demographics.[58] Researchers are hopeful AI will help find ways to slow the spread of disease through contact tracing, speed the development of medical treatments, design and repurpose drugs, plan clinical trials, predict the disease's evolution, judge the value of interventions, improve public health strategies, and find better ways to fight future infections outbreaks.[59]

Design defects under the risk-utility test are typically established through expert testimony, especially in cases involving advanced technology such as AI-based algorithms.[60] In a design defect case involving AI software as a medical device, the plaintiff's expert would need to establish that the risks of using the AI-based software to diagnose or treat a patient outweighed the benefits.[61] In response, a manufacturer would likely hire an expert to claim that the design pushed the limits of technological feasibility and that the costs of any alternative designed far outweighed any minimal safety improvement.[62] Important considerations include the magnitude of the harm posed by the design (how a patient could be harmed if a diagnosis is missed or an incorrect treatment is recommended); the likelihood that such a harm would occur (the algorithm's error rate); the feasibility of a safer alternative design; and the financial cost of the safer alternative design.[63] The risk-utility test may ultimately hinge on whether the medical AI performed at least as safely as its human counterparts.[64] Even if there were no safer alternative design, the manufacturer would have to demonstrate that it adequately warned of the risks.[65]

---

58. In early April, outreach nurses from an Oklahoma-based health care provider began calling individuals to advise them on proper hygiene and social-distancing requirements after AI software flagged 255 people from a group of 4,800 based on a combination of lifestyle, hospitalization, emergency-room use, and mortality and outcomes data, along with social determinants of health. *See* Daniela Hernandez, *Coronavirus Trackers Try Out AI Tools as Eyes Turn to Reopening*, WALL ST. J. (Apr. 19, 2020), https://www.wsj.com/articles/coronavirus-trackers-try-out-ai-tools-as-eyes-turn-to-reopening-11587294000.

59. Broad, *supra* note 57.

60. Fornadel & Moran, *supra* note 42, at 51.

61. *Id.*

62. Vladeck, *supra* note 43, at 138–39.

63. Fornadel & Moran, *supra* note 42, at 51–52.

64. Swanson, *supra* note 43, at 1213–16.

65. Fornadel & Moran, *supra* note 42, at 52

In applying either test to medical AI, there will be significant hurdles in applying concepts of foreseeable consumer uses and anticipated harms.[66] The complexity underlying AI systems make demonstrating the availability of alternative programming designs extremely difficult. Additionally, because the AI systems are designed to interact and evolve with the user over time, it will be difficult to import traditional product liability understandings of foreseeability.[67] Under both theories of design defects, testing, simulations, and field performance data for foreseeable uses and misuses would help demonstrate reasonable safety and the benefits for both the consumer expectations and risk-utility tests.[68]

C. Potential Sources of Liability

In the context of harms resulting from health care AI, adding to the complexity of whether it qualifies as a "product" and what "defect" test applies, there is the issue of who is responsible. There could be several companies involved in the algorithmic design of the product, multiple entities included in the chain of distribution, and different types of AI technologies that complicate traditional applications of product liability.[69] Take, for example, a medical device that utilizes AI software for identifying abnormalities in MRI images. The AI-enabled device is marketed to health care providers as a tool for increasing efficiency in interpreting MRIs.[70] The AI algorithm is developed by coders working for a software company. Trainers test and refine the algorithm's accuracy in detecting abnormalities using millions of pieces of data.[71] A hardware manufacturer then integrates the software into a physical device with scanners and sensors. A radiology clinic implements the device in its practice and a radiologist then uses the device to interpret the MRI of Patient X. There are various potential sources of defects if Patient X is misdiagnosed.

---

66. Swanson, *supra* note 43, at 1214–15.

67. *Id.* at 1215–19.

68. *See* Fornadel & Moran, *supra* note 42, at 51–53.

69. *See* Lora Spencer, *The Inevitable Collision of AI Healthcare Technologies and Product Liability*, LIFE SCIENCE LEADER (Feb. 28, 2020), https://www.lifescienceleader.com/doc/the-inevitable-collision-of-ai-healthcare-technologies-and-product-liability-0001.

70. *See* Villasenor, *supra* note 36; *see also* Talya Van Embden, *Paging Dr. Robot: Applying an Outdated, Regulated Scheme to Robotic Medicine*, 43 NOVA L. REV. 387, 401 (2019), https://nsuworks.nova.edu/cgi/viewcontent.cgi?article=2390&context=nlr.

71. *See* Shailin Thomas, *Artificial Intelligence and Medical Liability (Part II)*, HARVARD BILL OF HEALTH BLOG (Feb. 2, 2017), https://blog.petrieflom.law.harvard.edu/2017/02/10/artificial-intelligence-and-medical-liability-part-ii/.

Those involved in developing and training the algorithms could be the source of the defect. If the algorithm developer wrote code that causes the system to misinterpret a type of abnormality, the coder or software company could be liable for negligence or a design defect. If the AI system is trained in a way that makes it better at identifying certain abnormalities but worse at identifying others, the trainers could be subject to claims of design defect for developing a system that evolved in ways that allowed for performance trade-offs.[72]

The product manufacturers are another potential source of harm. If a device is manufactured with a faulty sensor, there could be a claim based on a manufacturing defect. If the system is designed to read images meeting a certain resolution threshold and the product does not contain a warning that lower-resolution images could lead to misdiagnosis, there could be liability based on both negligence and failure to warn.[73] If marketing campaigns alleged the device detects abnormalities more accurately than radiologists and that turns out not to be the case, there could be claims based on breach of warranty theories of liability.

Moreover, the health care providers utilizing the product could be the source of liability. If an updated standard of care reflects the use of AI (as discussed later), health care facilities and professionals using such devices might have a duty to evaluate algorithms and validate results before implementing the devices into patient care.[74] If the radiologists at the clinic are not properly trained on how to use the device, the clinic could be subject to liability for misdiagnosis. If the radiologist disagrees with the AI-system's interpretation but follows it anyway, there could be a claim for negligence. With respect to AI devices within a clinical setting—and particularly those that are subject to training—some form of the learned intermediary doctrine may become more relevant.

D. Negligence: Standard of Care

Liability for medical errors is based on a different standard of care than that of the "reasonable person," and is instead based on the "reasonable physician."[75] Any professional is held to a standard of care that, at its most fundamental level, recognizes that the professional will exercise his or her judgment in the performance of the profession.[76] That judgment

72. *See* Villasenor, *supra* note 36.
73. *See id.*
74. Sullivan & Schweikart, *supra* note 4, at 164.
75. *Id.* at 161.
76. 1 AHLA Digital Health Practice Guide § 3.2.4.3 (2018).

is exercised in the context of past and ongoing learning, training, experience, and the utilization of existing tools that assist the professional in exercising that judgment.[77] The professional takes the facts and circumstances and weighs various options regarding a course of action. For physicians, the usual standard of care is the reasonable degree of skill, knowledge, and care ordinarily possessed and exercised by members of the medical profession under similar circumstances.[78]

AI systems could affect the basic standard of care for health care providers in two ways.[79] First, as with any new technology, the general availability of the AI system may impact the practical application of the standard. If these types of AI systems are available, and they have demonstrated their ability to improve performance, then utilization of the tool may, at some point, constitute the standard of care. On its face, this is no different from any other technology; but as AI systems continue to improve, the imperative for their utilization may increase, and given the general lack of need for close geographic proximity for some tools, the importance of geographic factors will diminish.[80] Second, as an AI system continues to improve, not only may the imperative to use the tool increase, but an imperative for the individual practitioner to defer to the AI system in circumstances normally reserved for human judgment may be created.[81] While this may seem to be just the other side of the coin, this dynamic can create some complexity and may require legal and regulatory evolution.

Additionally, privacy concerns underlie the development of medical AI devices. Medical AI devices use data from a variety of sources: electronic health records; medical literature; clinical trials; insurance claims data; pharmacy records; and information entered by individuals on smartphones and fitness trackers.[82] Privacy is essential in gathering large amounts of health care data in both developing algorithms and in sharing that data to oversee the algorithms.[83] This technology comes with added risk to patient privacy and confidentiality.[84] As developing and training

77. *Id.*

78. Avivi v. Centro Medico Urgente Med. Ctr. (2008) 159 Cal. App. 4th 463, 470–71.

79. 1 AHLA Digital Health Practice Guide § 3.2.4.3 (2018).

80. *Id.*

81. *Id.*

82. Price, *supra* note 33, at 10.

83. *Id.* at 12–13.

84. Michael J. Rigby, *Ethical Dimensions of Using Artificial Intelligence in Health Care*, 21 AMA J. Ethics 121, 121–22 (2019).

machine learning algorithms requires data from multiple sources, that data may then be shared with other health care entities for the purpose of evaluation and validation. HIPAA's Privacy Rule requirements related to the disclosure and use of protected health information by covered entities is a major concern.[85] While the Privacy Rule does not govern de-identified information or data collected by non-covered entitles like Google or Apple, the potential for data aggregation and re-identification remains.[86] As more data is shared across a variety of organizations, policies and procedures related to de-identifying and sharing data need to be developed to protect patient privacy.[87] Ensuring that systems are secure against hackers and other non-authorized entries is also a necessity in preventing confidentiality breaches of personal health information.[88]

E. Other Considerations

1. Black Box AI

One complication when considering potential sources of defect or causation for liability purposes is how these theories of liability hold up against different types of AI. Can the same theories of causation apply to an algorithm using open source code and to a "black box" algorithm where the reasons behind its conclusions are unknown or undiscoverable? For an open source or transparent algorithm, experts should be able to determine whether a flaw in the code was the source of a defect. Indeed, in a transparent AI program, one would imagine experts and the court could determine the precise cause of the defect. Where an AI enabled medical device functions in a way that can be traced back to the human programming, design, and knowledge inputs, existing products liability doctrines will be adequate to assign fault and allocate responsibility.[89]

On the other hand, determining cause in the black box AI context, the algorithm cannot demonstrate the path to its conclusion, so the mechanisms behind its recommendations are unknown.[90] The opacity of black box AI stems from deep neural networks modeled after the human brain. The system can take an MRI image and use a neural network trained on

85. Price, *supra* note 33, at 12–13.

86. *Id.*

87. Ken Abrams et al., *The Future of Artificial Intelligence in Health Care: How AI Will Impact Patients, Clinicians, and the Pharmaceutical Industry*, DELOITTE (2019), https://www2.deloitte.com/us/en/pages/life-sciences-and-health-care/articles/future-of-artificial-intelligence-in-health-care.html.

88. *Id.*

89. Vladeck, *supra* note 43, at 120.

90. Sullivan & Schweikart, *supra* note 4, at 160.

a large data set to produce a classification of the abnormality, but the reasoning that led to its conclusion is undiscoverable.[91] Furthermore, in the same way the human brain learns and modifies its decision-making process, self-teaching algorithms can learn and evolve to improve accuracy in ways that are not explainable, even by those that developed and trained the algorithm. This self-learning capability leads to increased autonomy, and the algorithms become less intelligible to developers, trainers, and users with each improvement.[92] The application of existing product liability law becomes more challenging.

For example, the "black box" nature of some AI devices presents particular challenges in the preemption defense.[93] Some argue that although AI medical devices are capable of learning and making improvements over time, which could lead to significant changes from what the FDA initially approved, the *Riegel* preemption framework still applies.[94] If the FDA approves an algorithm that is constantly changing and self-learning, the FDA is approving the algorithm, not the outcome. If the changes are within the scope of what the FDA approved, the AI device should still be preempted. Others take the position that there can never be preemption of black box AI medical devices.[95]

In addition, the self-learning algorithms present challenges to the concept of foreseeability—how can theories of liability based on foreseeability apply to these technologies when they make decisions that humans cannot comprehend? For instance, with deep learning, which is a category of machine learning processes based on unsupervised learning from data, it may be impossible to understand and foresee an algorithm's decision-making process.[96] Similarly, AI programs with reinforcement learning capabilities are able to identify, categorize, and incorporate or

---

91. *Id.*

92. Sullivan & Schweikart, *supra* note 4, at 160–61.

93. Edward Maggio, *AI Medical Device Makers Still Protected by Preemption—But For How Long?*, THE EXPERT INSTITUTE (July 18, 2019), https://www.theexpertinstitute.com/ai-medical-device-makers-still-protected-by-preemption-but-for-how-long/; Fink Densford, *AI-Based Med Devices Could Leave Makers Liable for 'Learned' Changes*, MASS DEVICE (May 15, 2019), *available at* https://www.massdevice.com/report-ai-based-med-devices-could-leave-makers-liable-for-learned-changes/.

94. *See* Maggio, *supra* note 93; Bexis, *Artificial Intelligence Is No Threat to PMA Preemption*, DRUG & DEVICE LAW BLOG (May 27, 2019), https://www.druganddevicelawblog.com/2019/05/artificial-intelligence-is-no-threat-to-pma-preemption.html.

95. *See* Maggio, *supra* note 93.

96. Karni Chagal-Feferkorn, *The Reasonable Algorithm*, 2018 U. ILL. J.L. TECH. & POL'Y 111, 133–35 (2018).

exclude new data derived from aftermarket data inputs from consumers.[97] Future incorporation of consumer data could lead to unforeseeable risks or injuries outside the control of the original programmers or manufacturers.

Coupled with this challenge in applying traditional products liability theories to medical AI is that with increased autonomous learning capabilities, fewer parties (such as clinicians, health care organizations, and AI designers) have agency or control over AI devices. With non-autonomous technologies, human involvement and control over the algorithms lead to clear paths to liability for the individuals and entities that utilize such technologies. For example, in litigation over the safety of surgical robots, the non-autonomous robots are agents or instruments of entities that have legal capacity as individuals, such as surgeons and hospitals, and liability attaches based on some form of agency theory.[98] In contrast, as more autonomous devices become available that can act independently of human instruction and continue to self-learn and evolve, attributing legal liability to individuals and entities for the actions or decisions of autonomous devices becomes more tenuous.[99] And with self-learning AI devices, how does this tenuous connection impact the learned intermediary doctrine? Different gradations of AI could lead to different applications of products liability theories, and defenses, based on a sliding scale of the complexity of the underlying AI systems, autonomy, and self-learning abilities.

Thus, the black box nature of AI systems may pose a challenge for the basic standard.[100] How can we tell if there is such a defect? Should the "trainers" of the AI system be evaluated; and if so, against which standard? Does this standard have a role in evaluating and holding these types of AI systems accountable?[101] On the other hand, the social call for some strict liability standard may be heightened with direct to consumer AI products.[102] If the products purport to provide actionable health-related

---

97. Swanson, *supra* note 43, at 1207.

98. Vladeck, *supra* note 43, at 121.

99. Sullivan & Schweikart, *supra* note 4, at 163. While some commentators suggest the possibility of conferring legal personhood on AI systems, treating AI systems like corporations is an impractical solution. *See* Iria Giuffrida, *Liability for AI Decision-Making: Some Legal and Ethical Considerations*, 88 FORDHAM L. REV. 439, 444 (2019).

100. 1 AHLA DIGITAL HEALTH PRACTICE GUIDE § 3.2.4.3 (2018).

101. *Id.*

102. *Id.*

information or advice—particularly outside of a clinical setting—then, the risk of injury may increase.[103]

2. Patient Informed Consent

As the use of AI systems becomes increasingly common in diagnosing and evaluating patient conditions and treatment recommendations, "informed consent" may become an important feature of the patient-physician relationship.[104] Effective informed consent requires that a patient fully understand the health care treatment that he or she is agreeing to undergo.[105] While the requirement of informed consent emanates from the goal of a patient consenting to whatever is done with his or her body, we can easily see its expansion to circumstances in which a physician turns over the professional conclusion and advice to a machine, particularly when the technology remains new and, perhaps, unproven or untrustworthy in the eyes of the general public.[106] Just as a patient may refuse prescribed treatment, should the patient not also be able to refuse diagnosis by a machine?[107] If a patient has a preference to not turn over significant conclusions to an AI system, then what sort of informed consent may be appropriate? Further, if an AI system can quantify its confidence, should the informed consent process be different?[108] If a patient is able to avoid AI diagnosis, should this impact the applicable standard of care and the potential liability of the physician?[109]

3. Medical Malpractice

The U.S. medical malpractice regime holds physicians to accepted reasonable standards of care and assigns liability when the care provided by physicians constitutes negligence or recklessness.[110] In general, courts apply a national standard (for specialties) or a state-specific standard and evaluate whether a physician's actions are consistent with the degree of skill, care, and learning that is possessed and exercised by members of

---

103. *Id.*

104. *Id.* § 3.2.4.3.1.

105. The Joint Comm'n, *Informed Consent: More than Getting a Signature*, 21 Quick Safety 1, 1 (Feb. 2016), available at https://www.jointcommission.org/assets/1/23/Quick_Safety_Issue_Twenty-One_February_2016.pdf.

106. 1 AHLA Digital Health Practice Guide § 3.2.4.3.1 (2018).

107. *Id.*

108. *Id.*

109. *Id.*

110. Restatement (Third) of Torts: Phys. & Emot. Harm. § 6 (2010).

the medical profession in good standing.[111] In medical malpractice cases, expert witnesses testify as to what the appropriate standard of care should be.[112]

Although very few cases address directly the issue of malpractice risk associated with the use of AI systems specifically, and case law has not yet established distinct principles for evaluating the medical malpractice standard of care in the context of AI systems, courts generally have applied a standard of care for physicians that is neither static nor rigid.[113] Rather, courts will take into consideration the totality of the circumstances, including the physician's specialty, resources available to the physician, and the advances of the medical profession at the time of the physician's alleged negligent act.[114] Courts have recognized that medical standards of care typically evolve over time in response to empirical research, scientific progress, and the development of new technology.[115]

4. Data Privacy

As AI evolves and accelerates analysis of personal information, it magnifies the risk of invasions of privacy interests.[116] For instance, the emergence of advanced facial recognition software has prompted cities to ban certain uses of the technology.[117] As Congress works to pass privacy legislation that protects individuals against adverse effects of the use of personal information in AI, much of the debate has centered on algorithmic bias and the potential for algorithms to produce discriminatory results.[118] The current data privacy legislation and Federal Trade Commission enforcement is based on "notice-and-choice" models of consent where consumers have the burden of protecting individual privacy

---

111. 1 Steven E Pegals, American Law of Medical Malpractice § 3:3 (3d ed. 2016).

112. 1 AHLA Digital Health Practice Guide § 3.2.4.3.2 (2018).

113. *Id.*

114. Pegals, *supra* note 111.

115. *Id.*

116. Cameron F. Kerry, *Protecting Privacy in an AI-Driven World*, Brookings (Feb. 10, 2020), https://www.brookings.edu/research/protecting-privacy-in-an-ai-driven-world/.

117. Sara Merken, *Berkeley Bans Government Face Recognition Use, Joining Other Cities*, Bloomberg Law, (Oct. 16, 2019); Nikolas DeCosta-Klipa, *Brookline Becomes 2nd Massachusetts Community to Ban Facial Recognition*, Boston.com, (Dec. 12, 2019). Tori Bedford, *Cambridge Votes To Ban Face Surveillance Technology*, WGBH, (Jan. 13, 2020).

118. Kerry, *supra* note 116.

through notifications linked to lengthy privacy policies and terms and conditions.[119] With the use of AI systems, legislators and privacy stakeholders have expressed desire to shift the burden of protecting individual privacy from consumers to the businesses that collect the personal data, which could lead to liability under products liability theories.[120]

With the increasing prevalence of networks of connected devices, referred to as the Internet of Things (IoT), cyberattacks at the hands of hackers threaten data privacy.[121] Products liability doctrine may be a way to hold manufacturers liable for insecure devices, as manufacturers are in a better position to mitigate the damage of cyberattacks.[122] For instance, a software company could be liable for a design defect where default security settings can be easily accessed by hackers.[123] Consumers could also bring manufacturing or design defect claims for certain coding errors and oversights.[124] If a system was produced with vulnerabilities making it susceptible to a cyberattack, a consumer could allege the manufacturer failed to warn of that danger.[125] Questions on how traditional product liability law will apply to data privacy mirror those in the medical AI context: How do you allocate responsibility for damages? If there is a software failure versus an actual defect in the product, can and should the maker of a product be held liable for the software failure? How will liability be judged at trial if there are no standard safety requirements?[126] While plaintiffs have filed suit involving IoT devices alleging products liability claims, the litigation thus far has focused on standing issues (related to the lack of actual harm posed by vulnerability to future hackers) instead of the product liability issues.[127] While courts have not yet addressed how products liability theories will apply to data privacy concerns, it will likely be up to regulators and legislators to give initial guidance on these issues.

---

119. *Id.*

120. *Id.*

121. *See* Alan Butler, *Products Liability and the Internet of (Insecure) Things: Should Manufacturers Be Liable for Damage Caused by Hacked Devices?*, 50 U. Mich. J. L. Reform 913 (2017).

122. *Id.* at 918.

123. *Id.* at 926.

124. *Id.*

125. Leta Gorman, *The Era of the Internet of Things: Can Product Liability Laws Keep Up?*, Defense Counsel Journal (Feb. 7, 2020), https://www.iadclaw.org/defensecounseljournal/the-era-of-the-internet-of-things-can-product-liability-laws-keep-up/.

126. *Id.*

127. *Id.*

F. Allocation of Responsibility

Given the black box nature of AI systems and the unique ways they are developed to perform their functions, determining liability will become complicated. As noted earlier, different actors performing different functions (including the AI system, its trainers, and those tasked with maintaining it) may be implicated, and the role and function of the health care practitioner may begin to change given the nature of some of these AI systems.[128] The practitioner may take on responsibility for AI system training or testing. Further, the practitioner may be working with data and diagnostic information from tools chosen by the patient and not the physician. Patients may be more empowered to take more control of their health care and utilize physicians in different ways.[129] The allocation of responsibility is a difficult question, and one that will likely evolve over time.

1. Contracting Responsibility

One way to allocate responsibility for AI-caused harm is through contract. Contractual warranties, indemnities, and limitations among entities involved in the design, manufacturing, and implementation of AI systems and devices can reduce uncertainty by explicitly allocating liability.[130] Contractual liability can also solve questions about which law governs and which theories of liability might apply to any future disputes.[131]

2. Joint and Several/Enterprise Liability

Joint and several or enterprise liability theory is another potential solution for allocating responsibility for AI-caused harm. Under an enterprise theory of liability, where a common enterprise exists, such as developing and manufacturing an AI medical device, each entity within the enterprise may be held jointly and severally liable for the actions of any entity apart of the group.[132] If an AI system causes injury, instead of assigning fault to a specific person or entity, all groups involved in the use and implementation of the AI system should jointly bear some responsibility.[133] In the context of an AI-enabled medical device, the several enti-

---

128. 1 AHLA Digital Health Practice Guide § 3.2.4.3.2 (2018).
129. *Id.*
130. *See* Giuffrida, *supra* note 99, at 442–45.
131. *See id.* at 445.
132. Vladeck, *supra* note 43, at 149 (internal citations omitted).
133. Sullivan &. Schweikart, *supra* note 4, at 164; *see also* Vladeck, *supra* note 43, at 149–50.

ties responsible for the development and training of the AI software and the hardware device manufacturers could all share liability. Because an inference of liability would be shared among all relevant parties and no finding of fault is required, this solution avoids some of the challenges posed by black-box AI.[134]

3. Legislative Regulation

Since the case law surrounding AI in medicine is underdeveloped, legislatures may be in a better position to allocate responsibility and establish public policy through lawmaking.[135] As AI technology and its potential applications in medicine continue to evolve, so too will the existing legislative framework for tort and product liability.[136]

With the advancement of medical AI systems, the allocation of responsibility among actors will need to account for these higher functioning systems – and as noted earlier, existing structures may not provide satisfactory frameworks.[137] Physicians, in particular, can play a vital role in ensuring that the evolving legal and regulatory structures guarantee patient safety and ensure that AI systems and human health care providers are put to their "highest and best" use.[138] Regulators and the health care delivery and payment infrastructure must recognize and meaningfully—not necessary strictly—regulate these aspects of industry that play a part in arming consumers with ever stronger and effective health care tools.[139] We must also all recognize that the full potential of AI systems in health care delivery may require the evolution of our traditional health care infrastructure and the roles of individual actors within it.[140]

G. Case Law from Other Industries

Because the case law on AI medical technology is underdeveloped and questions related to the application of traditional theories of products liability remain unanswered, life science leaders can turn to other industries.[141] For example, autonomous vehicles in the transportation industry may offer potential insights on what to expect when health care AI and product liability law collide. Various lawsuits have been filed against

---

134. Sullivan & Schweikart, *supra* note 4, at 164.
135. *See* Abott, *supra* note 16, at 34–35.
136. *See id.*
137. 1 AHLA Digital Health Practice Guide § 3.2.4.3.3 (2018).
138. *Id.*
139. *Id.*
140. *Id.*
141. *See* Spencer, *supra* note 69.

autonomous vehicle manufacturers alleging products liability claims.[142] The first autonomous vehicle lawsuit in California, *Nilsson v. General Motors LLC*,[143] arose from an accident where a motorcycle collided with a vehicle in self-driving mode 2017.[144] In *Huang v. Tesla Inc.*, a Tesla owner died after the vehicle collided with the concrete median the vehicle failed to detect. The lawsuit alleged product liability theories of design defect, failure to warn, intentional and negligent misrepresentation, and false advertising.[145]

Despite predictions that autonomous vehicles will change car accident litigation by shifting liability from vehicle owners and drivers to manufacturers under product liability law, that change has been slow.[146] Manufacturer defendants in recent lawsuits claimed that human error contributed to the accidents involving semi-autonomous systems, which suggests that fault by human parties is still a feature of the existing autonomous vehicle litigation.[147] Because these suits have settled or are still pending, the application of product liability theories remains to be seen.

Another feature of autonomous vehicle litigation is identifying the relevant manufacturer. Similar to medical AI devices, autonomous vehicle systems are comprised of components like processors, sensors, mapping systems, and software that companies like Tesla outsource to third-party manufacturers and developers. While recent plaintiffs have

---

142. *See* Complaint for Damages, Nilsson v. Gen. Motors LLC, No. 3:18-cv-00471-KAW (N.D. Cal. Jan. 22, 2018); Complaint, Hudson v. Tesla Inc., 2018-CA-011812-O (Fla. Cir. Ct. Oct. 30, 2018); Complaint, Lommatzsch v. Tesla Inc., 2:18-cv-00775 (Utah D. Ct. Sept. 4, 2018); Complaint for Damages, Huang v. Tesla Inc., No. 19-cv-346663 (Super. Ct. Santa Clara Cnty. Apr. 26, 2019). *See* Geoffrey Wyatt, *Manufacturers Won't Bear All Liability for Driverless Vehicles*, LAW360 (Aug. 26, 2019), available at https://www.law360.com/articles/1191712/manufacturers-won-t-bear-all-liability-for-driverless-vehicles.

143. No. 3:18-cv-00471-KAW (N.D. Cal. Jan. 22, 2018).

144. Tiffany Y. Gruenberg, *Self-Driving Cars Will Likely Increase Product Liability Litigation*, NAT'L L. REV. (Jan. 22, 2019), https://www.natlawreview.com/article/self-driving-cars-will-likely-increase-product-liability-litigation. The motorcyclist alleged that the self-driving car negligently veered into his lane, causing the accident and resulting injuries. GM agreed to settle the lawsuit in 2018. R.J. Vogt, *GM Settles First-Known Suit Over Self-Driving Car Crash*, LAW360 (June 1, 2018), https://www.law360.com/articles/1049776/.

145. Alan Ohnsman, *Tesla Sued By Family of Silicon Valley Driver Killed In Model X Autopilot Crash*, FORBES (May 1, 2019), https://www.forbes.com/sites/alanohnsman/2019/05/01/tesla-sued-by-family-of-silicon-valley-driver-killed-in-model-x-autopilot-crash/#906d94f1c3f6.

146. Wyatt, *supra* note 142.

147. *Id.*

named several co-defendants in autonomous vehicle litigation, this adds complexity to determining the source of the defect and causation.[148] A further complication is that autonomous vehicle manufacturers have claimed that data associated with the crash is proprietary. In a lawsuit related to a 2019 accident involving Tesla's autopilot system, the driver has been unable to obtain data from the car's black box where that data was not recorded, but instead sent over the airwaves to Tesla's remote cloud computer repository.[149]

While the case law on autonomous vehicles is still underdeveloped, parallel considerations in the regulatory and legislative context are informative for the health care sphere. The U.S. Department of Transportation (DOT) through the National Highway Traffic Safety Administration (NHTSA) partners with state and local governments to regulate vehicles and set safety standards. In 2016, the NHTSA published the first policy guidance on automated vehicles to offer uniform safety regulations and discuss relevant regulatory tools.[150] Industry experts have been able to weigh in on the effort to regulate autonomous vehicles. For example, the Society of Automotive Engineers created a six-level scale that the NHTSA adopted. The scale classifies autonomy from zero to five, with zero being entirely human-controlled and five requiring no human input.[151] The degree of vehicle autonomy will be a relevant factor in future regulation, and will likely be an important consideration in the health care context.

Federal oversight related to autonomous vehicles has been of considerable interest to Congress.[152] While there are currently no specific regulations at the federal level, since 2012, at least 41 states have considered legislation related to autonomous vehicles and 29 states have enacted

148. *Id.*

149. Russ Mitchell, *Your Tesla Could Explain Why It Crashed. But Good Luck Getting Its Autopilot Data*, LA Times (Feb. 24, 2020), https://www.latimes.com/business/story/2020-02-24/autopilot-data-secrecy.

150. U.S. Dep't. of Trans., *Federal Automated Vehicles Policy*, Sept. 2016, available at https://www.transportation.gov/AV/federal-automated-vehicles-policy-september-2016.

151. Wyatt, *supra* note 142.

152. In the 115th Congress, autonomous vehicle legislation passed the House as H.R. 3388, the SELF DRIVE Act, and a separate bill, S. 1885, the AV START Act, was reported from a Senate committee. Neither bill was enacted. In the 116th Congress, interest in autonomous vehicles remains strong, but similar comprehensive legislative proposals have not been introduced. Congressional Research Service, *Issues in Autonomous Vehicle Testing and Deployment*, Feb. 11, 2020, available at https://fas.org/sgp/crs/misc/R45985.pdf.

legislation.[153] Various jurisdictions have considered different approaches in assigning liability to autonomous vehicles.[154] One solution is the creation of a compulsory no-fault quasi-insurance system in which the victim of a self-driving car accident receives a payment without the need to prove why the vehicle caused the harm.[155] Such a system would be funded by a surtax on autonomous vehicles.[156] The autonomous vehicle industry therefore suggests that regulation related to health care AI will likely be addressed at the state level following guidance from federal regulatory agencies.

III. Conclusion

As AI systems continue to develop, improve, and become more ubiquitous, driven perhaps by consumer demand or utilization of even more sophisticated tools, the relationships between physicians, technology and consumers needs to evolve as well. The allocation of responsibility within, and the way we regulate, this evolving continuum of health care is not clear given the profound capabilities of AI systems that are realistically imaginable and, in some instances, just around the corner.[157] While health care AI raises some unique risk and allocation issues, there is no reason to believe current products liability doctrine cannot adapt to allow courts, industry, and consumers to resolve and manage disputes in this evolving area.

---

153. National Conference of State Legislatures, *Autonomous Vehicles | Self-Driving Vehicles Enacted Legislation*, NCSL (Feb. 18, 2020), available at https://www.ncsl.org/research/transportation/autonomous-vehicles-self-driving-vehicles-enacted-legislation.aspx.

154. Giuffrida, *supra* note 99, at 448.

155. *Id.* at 448–49.

156. *Id.* at 449.

157. 1 AHLA DIGITAL HEALTH PRACTICE GUIDE § 3.2.4.3.3 (2018).

Index

E

G

S

V